THE CHALLENGES OF ADMINISTRATIVE POLITICAL AND DEVELOPMENTAL RENEWAL IN AFRICA: ESSAYS ON RETHINKING GOVERNMENT AND REORGANIZATION

AFRICAN POLITICAL, ECONOMIC, AND SECURITY ISSUES SERIES

Focus on Zimbabwe
Alfred J. Cartage (Editor)
2009. 978-1-60692-186-9

State Building and Democracy in Africa:
A Comparative and Developmental Approach
John W. Forje
2009. 978-1-60741-371-4

The Land and Maritime Boundary Disputes of Africa
Rongxing Guo
2009. ISBN: 978-1-60741-637-1

The Challenges of Administrative Political and Developmental Renewal in Africa:
Emerging Issues
John W. Forje
2009. ISBN: 978-1-60741-265-6

The Challenges of Administrative Political and Developmental Renewal in Africa:
Essays on Rethinking Government and Reorganization
John W. Forje
2009. ISBN: 978-1-60741-266-3 (hardcover)
2011. ISBN: 978-1-61209-027-6 (softcover)

AFRICAN POLITICAL, ECONOMIC, AND SECURITY ISSUES SERIES

THE CHALLENGES OF ADMINISTRATIVE POLITICAL AND DEVELOPMENTAL RENEWAL IN AFRICA: ESSAYS ON RETHINKING GOVERNMENT AND REORGANIZATION

JOHN W. FORJE

Nova Science Publishers, Inc.
New York

LIBRARY OF CONGRESS CATALOGING-IN-PUBLICATION DATA

Forje, John W.
 The challenges of administrative political and developmental renewal in Africa : essays on rethinking government and reorganization / John W. Forje.
    p. cm.
 Includes bibliographical references and index.
  ISBN 978-1-61209-027-6 (softcover)
  1. Africa--Politics and government--21st century. 2. Administrative agencies--Africa--Management. 3. Administrative agencies--Africa--Reorganization. 4. Civil service reform--Africa. I. Title.
 JQ1875.F68 2009
 351.6--dc22
                                    2009012388

Published by Nova Science Publishers, Inc. ✦ *New York*

CONTENTS

FOREWORD

When humanity is in total perplexity and panic, struck by the global crises and challenges affecting the four corners of the globe, across all spheres and strata of life, there are as well individuals who have taken upon themselves to be of relevance to rescuing and addressing issues of paramount concern, regarding the present and impending disquiets of our societies, nations, with much consideration paid to the African continent with precision to propositions of lasting values for an effective leadership and change in Africa.

Running through the pages of this book are thought provoking, paradigm shifting and mind boggling concepts postulated by Dr John W. Forje, which must be adhered to and strictly followed for there to be a renewal in the Administrative, Political as well as the Developmental sectors in the continent.

Dr John Forje has taken time with very infelisitima'l detail addressing the geopolitical situation, poor governance, the sluggish administrative bureaucratic procedure, technological issues, as well as the limited infrastructural facilities, the imbalance in socio-economic strata, the inability to make a clear-cut difference of politics and party in African leadership, just to name but a few in the list of pending issues of the continent with a view to embarking on change that is necessary at this point in time in the life of the African continent.

Looking at the different factors that must be juxtaposition in the renewal process of change, the African Association for Public Administration and Management [AAPAM], New Partnership for African Development [NEPAD] African Union [AU], etc. as well as the social actors and civil societies in addition to considering the public and private interference in new phase of partnership amongst others, have a part to play in dismantling the mountain of dependency, destitution, poverty and bad governance in the continent. However, if effectiveness will be achieved, concerns must also be on issues of value, morality and ethics, visionary leadership, a living conscience and the political will which adds impetus to this process of change.

"The Challenges in Administrative, Political and Developmental Renewal in Africa', does cut across the very beginning overview of issues as it stands. Looking at governance and the role of political parties and politics played, plus the interest groups in address the issues, not forgetting the function of scientific and technological advancement that is needed for the socio-economic transformation, and the right timely intervention of the international community amongst other social actors of change.

Dr Forje causes us to rethink the way of functioning our government and political systems in a bid to bring change in Africa, faced with challenges as well as opportunities that is brought to our table.

If we also have to consider enhancing sustainable development and governance in the societies of Africa, not oblivious of the fact that human capital investments and quantity and quality management of resources are of primordial importance, this piece of art, the apposite delicacy of the century is what is served us at the table of choice. Hence, I strongly recommend this book to the very African elite, to our governments and the average of us as social actors of change, for a review of our paradigm, in view of bringing a change that will not only affect the African continent but transcend to the boarders to be emulated by others, contributing to a responsible and responsive leadership.

E. Paul Mbuagbor
Founder and President
Global Development Network Organisation [GLODNAS]
and
GLODNAS Leadership Institute
Life-style Consultant,
Author, Coach, Lecturer and Educator
Yaoundé, Cameroon

August 15, 2009

PREFACE

This book, "Administrative, Political and Developmental Renewal in Africa" is the third in CARAD's publication series on Strategic Policy Studies on State, Democracy Governance and Management. The second series is on "State-Building and Democracy in Africa: A Comparative and Development Approach". These series seek to contribute to the ongoing debate on Democratisation, Governance and Development since the collapse of the Communist System and Africa's Lost Decades of the 1980s. The subject of a 'developmental state and the challenges of governance' remains topical, and is hoped the views expressed here puts the various issues firmly at the centre of the debate, calling for transparency, social justice, the rule of law and accountability agenda that sows the seeds of a genuine renewal of state and society's role in embodying and shaping democracy on the African continent. There is need for building capacities for sustainable development to bring Africa in line with global development.

Chapter 1 - In recent years most governments have increasingly engaged in what they refer to as partnership with the private sector and civil society in order to hasten the achievement of national development goals and those imposed by the international community – for example, United Nations Millennium Development Goals (MDG). This idea underpins both a national and global contract to improve the social environment and quality of livelihood of the people. The crux of the matter is that centralisation over the years has failed to produce a balance social construct in society; rather it spreads wide manifestation of disillusionment, exclusion and foster greater divide between the centre and periphery. There is an urgent need to narrow the divide – between central administration and local communities, between male and female gender, between the urban and rural areas or hamlets, and between the "haves" and have-nots" to ensure sustainable development for present and future generations.

The magnitude of development problems facing transitional polities like Cameroon cannot be over-stated. Much of the blame for these outcomes, however, is attributed to the centralisation of administrative machinery. Poor governance, crony capitalism and ethnic hegemonic forces in various ways combine to accelerate the divide in social and economic inequality in the society. The paper argues that centralisation is an impediment to development when not properly controlled – and decentralisation accelerates the development process: "power to the people and equal opportunities for all" constitute a level playing ground for all to be participants and partners in the development process. It is imperative for the state with its centralised administration to relinquish some of its inherent powers to the people, local communities and private sectors in order to enhance and accelerate quality service delivery to better improve the living standards of the population.

To achieve these goals, the paper argues, that human resources development and institutional capacity building are necessary implements to promote democratic governance. There is need for modifying government by changing structures, including the relationship between the public and private sectors as well as bringing on board civil society. Thus a multiplicity of suppliers providing a range of choices or consumers, public-private partnership (PPPs) and a maximum of local autonomy are advocated to achieve improvements, for example, schools and hospitals that serving their communities.

The paper rejects the "top-down" approach: advocates the ideological approach of "bottom-up" strategy, and creating an enabling or people-focused rather than a "bureaucratic" approach backed with promoting technological innovation, building competitive enterprises and the use of market forces with a human face to achieve public ends. With this approach value is added to the rich natural resources of the country. The conclusion centres within the simple and essential elements of empowerment of civil society and community institutions as well as giving the private sector a larger role in public life. Inputs and outputs of activities should operate on the basis of partnership, participation, accountability, responsibility and equitable benefit sharing for the common good.

Chapter 2 - Five decades after attaining independence, Africa is still equated with underdevelopment, failed states, mismanagement, corruption, conflicts and wars. Whatever indicators applied (per capita income, economic growth, debt statistics, debts etc.), the conclusion is inescapable. Africa finds itself within the plethora of a chronic crisis, political instability with the politics of exclusion over-riding that of inclusion. We need to understand why Africa is in such a mess? What are the remedies? However diverse the thinking has been, there is an emerging consensus that conventional theories of development have been callously implemented with the net effect that the quality of livelihood of the vast majority of the population is far worse today than four-five decades ago. One begins to question the structural nature of independence handed the people: second the kind of development theory forced down the throat of the new colonies: and third, to seriously questioning leadership role in the process - the extent to which their political skills helped marginalized or bleed their respective countries to death.

It could be argued that social science (political science, sociology and anthropology) failed to give the right signals in reconstructing Africa, with the contextual slogan "seek yeh the political kingdom". This failure helped in derailing the first wave of democratization process that mainly focused on attaining independence at all cost. The concept of seeking the political kingdom gave a wrong view of democracy: it failed bringing on board the idea of economic empowerment, participation, and public-private sectors–civil society interface. The absence of a functional public sector embedded with credence of quality services delivery enhancing and improving the livelihood quality of the people added to the woes of the people.

Political empowerment did not lead to economic empowerment, efficient public service sector, hence the status of failed, collapsed, and banana republics glittering the continent. The root causes could be traced to the failure of development from above and imposed from outside. The practice and discipline of public administration ignored its enriching past becoming prisoners in accelerating the process of a knowledge-based economy of the 21st century. A new holistic, valuable alternative for African public administration paradigm shift is necessary for proper functioning within the global political and economic space.

Chapter 3 - After half-a-century of independence, and many decades of limited successes in eliminating abject poverty, new ideas about sustainable growth and development are emerging which transitional societies should adopt in addressing their predicaments for the nation to move forward. Eliminating the poverty cankerworm, which is gradually, destabilising and even disintegrating the society calls for vigilant, concerted and comprehensive policy strategies encompassing the state, civil society, the private sector and the international community?

The paper adopts the conceptual approach of the quality of livelihood as the new development strategy for the continent. It argues that the politics of exclusion and the absence of good governance and quality service delivery are major contributing factors to

The increasing state of abject poverty and misery in the midst of plenty. Development has to be more human focused and oriented, targeting the poor by placing the poor first, and the affluent or rich last in the development continuum. It takes a crosscutting edge approach to multiple deprivation and social exclusion.

The conceptual approach further builds on issues of exclusion, marginalisation, ethnic hegemony, misuse or abuse of power, inequitable resources distribution or wealth sharing and responsibilities. It advances proactive strategic policy measures for providing and sustaining quality livelihood for the vast majority of the poor and excluded population. Though the focus is on Cameroon lessons and experiences from other regions are incorporated as we mover deeper and deeper into the realities of the unstoppable forces of a global village of the 21st century and beyond.

Based on the conceptual framework of the quality of livelihood, the conclusion is that in designing poverty-related activities or programmes, it is more prudent to respect the vision of poverty articulated and aggregated by the poor themselves. In doing so, priority should be reducing variability of income, as well as strengthen women's participation and autonomy politics of inclusion should replace the existing one of exclusion. Above all, the poor and vulnerable should be placed on the plus, and not minus side of the development continuum in improving and creating conducive environment for the participation of the poor in the development process. Fundamentally important is to build on the politics of partnership, participation, responsibility, and of course, equitable wealth sharing.

Chapter 4 - Politics and governance cannot be completely value free. No government can function efficiently and effectively without a set of directives that will steer it in the direction which society expects it to move. Although governments have different cultural, political, and administrative environments, they often confront similar democratic, ethical challenges and responses in their ethics management show common characteristics. How are democratic governance and quality management in South Africa explained and what can be conjectured about the challenges as future prospects?

This paper looks at the salient features of the political economy of the rainbow Nation viz the intense internal constraints in light of the growing fragmentation that plagues the continent: poor leadership, poor performance in economic development, political instability, corruption, genocides and the growing politics of divide and rule between ethnic communities, and social classes.

What is it that has brought South Africa to it current status? What must be done to consolidate its democratisation and quality management prospects? What factors internal and external that impact in slowing or accelerating the process of consolidating democratic governance form a decade after the collapse of the apartheid system? Is South Africa setting a course for the rest of Africa to follow? What are the challenges and future prospects?

The paper argues for a dedicated effort in consolidating the democratic process through the realm of expanding the 'politics of inclusion, partnership, responsibility and equitable sharing of the wealth of the nation" among the key actors. To sustain and improve on its newly won democratic freedom, the politics of "exclusion" must be avoided, rejected and buried. It is only through reconciliation, consensus and ensuring the reign of and values of human dignity and solidarity that the country can best consolidate the pursuit of social justice and quality livelihood for all.

Chapter 5 - The focus of the paper is on the interface between the State, Civil Society and the Private Sector should play in advancing the process of African integration in light of the challenges of globalisation and the new political dispensation that emerged almost two decades ago. It focuses on and addresses common characteristics emerging in three different but inter-related trends, namely, the relationship between leadership, democratisation and civil society. The paper departs from the premises that the return to liberal democracy in Africa is witnessing a new jump-start riddled with much cynicism: how civil society organisations (CSO) are able to fit into the new political dispensation: and what is or are the response{s} from the State towards the new forces challenging its established hegemony partly born out of the monolithic State system that existed during the greater part of these former colonies. It questions the nature of African civil society and whether it exists at all. The paper addresses issues of empowering civil society through community development, and making it an instrument for socio-economic transformation and integration: while in the processes, the underlying issues of participation, partnership and responsibility sharing among other stakeholders are discussed.

The theoretical framework builds on concepts of democratic governance and civil society advanced by Ake (2000), Diamond (1998, 1997), Bratton and Walle (1997), Bujura (2003), Guy Peters (2000) among others. Without a deepening knowledge and understanding of the democratisation and governance process, state, civil society and the private sector cannot inject the necessary inputs so required for national, regional and continental integration necessary to uplift the quality living standards of the population currently lavishing in squalor and abject poverty.

Proactive strategic policy measures are advanced as the way forward for Africa in reconstructing governance and integration in the age of a knowledge based global society.

Chapter 6 - The paper exams ways and means of putting war torn Liberia back on the path of sustainable development. Following years of conflict, Liberia now needs both domestic and external support for its recovery, reconstruction and development process on the basis of a platform that harnesses the resources of both domestic and international partners. The country is entering a new era and beginning which calls for total solidarity from different quarters in assisting the people build quality livelihood for themselves and future generations.

What measures are needed to improve international assistance as well as mobilising domestic resources to kick-start the long road to recovery and development? Obviously, the state must be reconstituted. For without a democratic governance environment it would be difficult to build trust and confidence as well as mobilise the requisite financial resources needed for the socio-economic transformation of the society from a war to a peace situation

The report ends by advancing recommendations for Liberia to engage in a new beginning from state failure to state building. This can only be possible when the people develop a new mindset of reconciliation and consensus building of give and take and healing the wounds of many years of conflict and wanton destruction that has taken away so many lives and destroyed property and caused untold human suffering.

Chapter 7 - The Wind of Change – A Journey Through Africa's Political Landscape – is a simplistic and descriptive travel through memory lane, concerning Africa's transition from colonialism to the global knowledge-based age of the 21st century. The sub-theme of the paper "In Search of An Alternative' draws inspiration from Prof Archie Mafeje's book titled "In Search of An Alternative – A Collection of Essays on Revolutionary Theory and Politics" published by SAPES in 1992. The paper address issues concerning "The National Question and African Unity", Gender Empowerment", and the "Politics of Exclusion and Inclusion" among others. Many questions are raised, for example, why is Africa poor in the midst of plenty? Why has chaos prevailed over coherence? Why ethnic hegemony over national unity?

It departs from the premises of the 'politics' of the trinity of technology and the baobab tree' and how the technology of human destruction can be converted into the "technology for human development". The trinity of technology encompasses three inter-related factors, namely, the "technology of violence, the technology of mobility and the technology of knowledge", which contributes to South Africa's triple heritage, for political and socio-economic transformation. It calls for a new vision with the politics and techniques of the "baobab tree", forming the cornerstone for African integration, African Renaissance and African Transformation before the continent can claim the 21st century.

Africa needs genuine structural transformation by breaking out of its existing colonial mentality, to innovate itself out of the scourge of poverty and marginalisation, by making the best use of its human and natural resources. It is time for intellectual, economic, political and natural resources of the continent are put at the disposal of the marginalised majority and excluded poor of the continent.

Chapter 8 - When in Africa we speak and dream of and work for, a rebirth of that continent as a full participant in the affairs of the world in the next century, we are deeply conscious of how dependent that is on the mobilisation and strengthening of the continent's resources of learning". *[Nelson Mandela 1998]*

"The promotion of an NSI as framework for social and economic policy maximises the possibilities for all parts of the system to interact with each other to the benefit of stakeholders and the advancement of national goals. The close co-operation between government, industry and research institutions is a pre-requisite for projects designed to produce growth and development in accordance with national goals". *[DACST. 1996:5]*

Chapter 9 - The issue of leadership is a world wide problem, but more acute in transitional polities, Cameroon in particular and Africa in general. The absence of a democratic developmental state can be attributed to the kind of leadership practiced in country. Thus where quality leadership exist, political leadership looms highest in the minds of many for a number of very important reasons, namely that of shaping the national vision and overseeing priority strategic policies for change and development for the common good.

Referring to Cameroon, one can demonstrate, however, that a country can undergo fundamental transformation process within a relatively short period of time if quality and visionary leadership exists, and especially when such political leadership is strong, dedicated and backed by high professional and performing managerial and bureaucratic structure capable of independently and apolitical articulating and aggregating effective quality service delivery to the people. Cameroon has been success story within the central African Sub-region. What lies behind this? What factors impede further success? It is believed that "leadership is cause: everything else is effect". How does this relate to the Cameroon situation? What lessons can other nations draw from the Cameroon experience?

The paper further penetrates into issues of democratic governance being fundamental as this advertently or inadvertently promotes or undermines effective and complementary roles of the political and managerial leadership. The paper identifies a number of leadership secrets and how the principles of leadership can be applied to ensure sustainable change and development. The conclusion builds on the fact that the kind of leadership to propel Cameroon or most African countries from the state of underdevelopment to a developed polity must be qualitatively different from what currently exist. Proactive strategic policy measures are recommendations are advanced.

Chapter 10 - Reforming the public sector constitutes a long-standing issue on the political and socio-economic transformation agenda of transitional polities in Africa. Therefore, Africa needs Focused Structural Adjustment Policy Strategies [FSAPS] and "Servant Leaders" [SL} to pilot its transition from a third to a first world. Without an efficient, effective, productive, credible, professional and non-partisan, sustainable public service backed with comprehensive interface or constructive engagement between the private sector-civil society sustainable transition and development cannot be attained. The much needed aggressive, dynamic, confidence and vibrancy in both the public service and private sectors remain inadequate in many African countries which must constructively be beefed-up to accelerate its development process.

The public sector as the lead entity piloting policy-articulation, decision-making, implementation and development related activities is found wanting. A vibrant productive-private sector is lacking to back up the efforts of an effective, efficient and productive public administration in improving the quality of livelihood of the people. Reforming the public sector for the emergence of a developmental state in Africa requires, professionalism, servant leadership, detachment from the whims and caprices of political parties, and a democratic governance system among others. Without the emergence of a development state, Africa cannot be part of the globalised knowledge-base technological society of the 21st century.

The focus of the paper is an interface on capacity building [human and institutional], leadership and strategic policy priority choices within the broader objectives of effective governance and management as the modus operandi for navigating Africa from a developing to a developed society. The argument is that human resources development including in-house training is necessary in building the capacity for effective and efficient output services delivery under the canopy of "putting people first" in all developmental strategies. In this regard, the extended position is a call for a "servant leadership", "constructive state engagement", "good governance", "strong state institutions", a" productive and competitive private sector: and a "vibrant and responsive civil society," without of course, bypassing the role and impact of the international community. Africa is part of the global community and must engage with it.

It is a comparative analytical paper drawing examples from some newly industrialised countries in the South East Asian Regions - Singapore, Hong-Kong Malaysia among others. The paper equally addresses issues of building on the assets of potential partners - state-civil society-private sector - interface for quality service delivery [improving the living standards of the people].

The conceptual framework is construed within the premises of strength, weakness, opportunities and threats [SWOT]. How do we interpose SWOT within the experiences of some Newly Industrialised Countries? What lessons can be learned to put the continent on the right development path? How does Africa capitalise on its strength and exploit its opportunities? How does Africa convert weaknesses and threats into opportunities to better strengthen its developmental capacity?

It takes a historical perspective, retrospective as it charts prospective new ways forward for a new public service sector for the continent. Proactive strategic policy measures are advanced

Chapter 11 - The process of nation-building in post-colonial Africa has taken different dimensions – moving from "exclusion" to embracing quasi "inclusion". This calls for qualitative leadership and managerial skills. The paper provides an overview of the challenges facing African countries since the granting of independence and especially from the 1990s. It is set against a brief overview of the key aspects of post-cold war Africa and in the light of the continent's lost decade of the 1980s, and the challenges of meeting United Nations Millennium Development Goals [MDGs]. The first issue outlined is the massive democratic shift in the structure of African governments from monolithic to political party pluralism. The second underpins the development challenges in particular and interaction between the key stakeholders. The third question concerns the non-progress made after 15 years of the return to political pluralism in arresting poverty, corruption and poor quality service delivery? The fourth issue relates to establishing free, independent, professional bureaucratic machinery void of political party interferences, dictates and influence, but one ready to serve whichever political party legitimately elected into office. The fifth focuses on ways forward for an underdeveloped continent facing the forces of globalisation.

These developments underpin fundamental issues of political and managerial leadership for change and development in Africa. The paper looks at the absence of quality and visionary political and managerial leadership in the body politic of the state as serious threats to the progress of a nation. To what extent political and managerial leadership and democratic systems promotes or inhibits the level and nature of developments and change within a country? It argues for effective political leadership and strong government from the perspective of opening the political space as institutional imperatives necessary for rolling out and ensuring sustainable development. It demonstrates how effective leadership nurtures transitional politics to place these countries within the limelight of a developed polity.

My argument is that strong, visionary, effective and functional political leadership and managerial skills leads to "inclusive" politics as basis for constructing a developmental and sustainable nation-state focused on improving the quality of livelihood of the citizens. These implies meeting the development challenges of eradication extreme poverty and hunger, drastic reduction in child mortality, promoting gender equity and empowerment, control and eradicating killer diseases like HIV/AIDS, malaria, tuberculoses etc; putting in place radical measures halting the destruction and depletion of the environment, arresting corruption and wanton poverty among others. In short, poor leadership, poor managerial skills, bad governance and poverty constitute a threat to the development of the continent. The conclusion is, countries that have effectively demonstrated a unique combination of visionary, concerted, just and competent political leadership, managerial skills and backed by professional and impartial led public service, stand a better chance of achieving progress within a relatively short time frame in comparison to those lacking these attributes. Proactive policy measures are advanced.

Conclusions and Prospects - For the system of governance is to be well-suited to its task, the agents of the state should not just be induced to do things in he right way – which is the administrative perspective as well as impelled to do the right things, that is the those things the state leaders want them to do – which is of being a *"servant leader"* in the political chase game within the African context. There is breakdown between state, civil society and the private sector which has to be restored for progressive developments taking place in the overall benefit of the people. The armies of poverty stricken people must be brought into the mainstream of the development process. No doubt the improvement in the situation of the poor would weaken the standing of the few rich which is against the wishes of those controlling the realm of governance.

Africa's challenges, therefore, is to continue the democratisation, good governance and economic recovery programmes; promote greater and equitable growth, based on a strategic policy on poverty alleviation and empowerment. Power to the people with equal opportunities for all – *shared-government; shared-responsibility; shared-prosperity* – should be the catch word for *rethinking government and reorganising the state.*

Chapter 1

REFLECTIONS ON DECENTRALISATION WITH PRIORITY FOCUS ON GOOD GOVERNANCE AND POVERTY ALLEVIATION. LESSONS FROM CAMEROON: CHALLENGES AND OPPORTUNITIES[*]

ABSTRACT

In recent years most governments have increasingly engaged in what they refer to as partnership with the private sector and civil society in order to hasten the achievement of national development goals and those imposed by the international community – for example, United Nations Millennium Development Goals (MDG). This idea underpins both a national and global contract to improve the social environment and quality of livelihood of the people. The crux of the matter is that centralisation over the years has failed to produce a balance social construct in society; rather it spreads wide manifestation of disillusionment, exclusion and foster greater divide between the centre and periphery. There is an urgent need to narrow the divide – between central administration and local communities, between male and female gender, between the urban and rural areas or hamlets, and between the "haves" and have-nots" to ensure sustainable development for present and future generations.

The magnitude of development problems facing transitional polities like Cameroon cannot be over-stated. Much of the blame for these outcomes, however, is attributed to the centralisation of administrative machinery. Poor governance, crony capitalism and ethnic hegemonic forces in various ways combine to accelerate the divide in social and economic inequality in the society. The paper argues that centralisation is an impediment to development when not properly controlled – and decentralisation accelerates the development process: "power to the people and equal opportunities for all" constitute a level playing ground for all to be participants and partners in the development process. It is imperative for the state with its centralised administration to relinquish some of its inherent powers to the people, local communities and private sectors in order to enhance and accelerate quality service delivery to better improve the living standards of the population.

---

[*] Paper presented at The First Departmental Seminar, Department of Political Sciences, University of Buea on the Theme: "The Challenges of Governance and Development in Cameroon". 8th – 9th June 2006. Buea Cameroon.

To achieve these goals, the paper argues, that human resources development and institutional capacity building are necessary implements to promote democratic governance. There is need for modifying government by changing structures, including the relationship between the public and private sectors as well as bringing on board civil society. Thus a multiplicity of suppliers providing a range of choices or consumers, public-private partnership (PPPs) and a maximum of local autonomy are advocated to achieve improvements, for example, schools and hospitals that serving their communities.

The paper rejects the "top-down" approach: advocates the ideological approach of "bottom-up" strategy, and creating an enabling or people-focused rather than a "bureaucratic" approach backed with promoting technological innovation, building competitive enterprises and the use of market forces with a human face to achieve public ends. With this approach value is added to the rich natural resources of the country. The conclusion centres within the simple and essential elements of empowerment of civil society and community institutions as well as giving the private sector a larger role in public life. Inputs and outputs of activities should operate on the basis of partnership, participation, accountability, responsibility and equitable benefit sharing for the common good.

Keywords: Decentralisation, governance, partnership, participation, benefit sharing, stakeholders, empowerment, resources management, democratisation

INTRODUCTION: SITUATING THE PLACE OF THE STATE

"Civil society" is a political concept because it is essentially about power, the power of no-state actors to participate in making decisions that have impact on them. [Leslie Fox].

"It is by the people's effort that colonialism is routed, it is by the sweat of the people's brow that nations are built. The people are the reality of national greatness. It is the people who suffer the depredations and indignities of colonialism, and the people must be insulted by dangerous flirtations with neo-colonialism" [Nkrumah 1964:103]

The state is a response to demands from society, invented as an instrument for improving society's collective capacity. In addition, major changes in the economic and political realms have influenced the design of state structures. These structures tend to be enduring with strong imprint on the organisational and cultural configuration of society. While the catchword today is globalisation, liberalisation, the structural functioning of the world is dominated by the activities of strong and centralised national governments. Caught in the web of centralised governance, development seems to have grounded to a stand still. Other ways of doing things are needed to give new impetus to the development of the nation and continent. The state in Africa emerged as the major producer and provider of basic needs. Yet the state lacks the capacity and human resources to undertake these valuable tasks of meeting the essential needs of a rapidly increasing population as well as facing the challenges posed by a rapid changing hostile international environment.

We are confronted with the triple issues of *democracy, governance and development* [DGD] with the ultimate goal of providing quality living standards for the population. Issues of democracy, governance and development constitute problems areas with many and varied political interests – struggle for power –as well as undertaking effective public policies as an inherent of the obligations of state commitment or social contract with those who elected the governors. In short, the governor and governed must tango in unity if the genuine completion point – *quality living standard for all* – is to be attained and sustained. The African state structure due to its construction and its evolution is laden with many drawbacks that impinge its proper functioning. Seen in this light, policy-makers and scholars are equally troubled by how much importance should be attached to the state and its institutions targeted or focused on the role of values and attitudes in the modernisation process. As transitional polities depart from the contours of a traditional or agricultural to an industrial society, the process of modernisation weights heavily on state institutions that have emerged with relatively no experience to start tackling issues characteristics of a post-industrial society, especially now that most countries are becoming bedfellows of the service delivery bandwagon, and a global knowledge economy.

The position of this paper is clear. It does not break any new academic background not known for the past decade or so. But judging from the conventional view of international development theorists like Ferguson [1999], it argues for *more less government and more community participation* in the process of nation-building and development. We need to understand more carefully and appreciate the assessment of the international imperatives necessary for rolling out development at the local community levels. The position of the paper is that while the State should be an important player, it should not be only the sole actor in the chase game of development. It is neither possible nor visible to discard totally the input equation of the state. Therefore, the state as the major trigger for development requires concerted, progressive and comprehensive inputs from other actors. The state apparatus is inadequately configured for implementing a developmental agenda. What is needed is putting in place the fundamentals and institutions that can facilitate pro-poor or community action-oriented development initiatives that benefits the people. One of the processes is to seriously embark on the process of devolving power to the people and communities to drive the development process.

No wonder fragmented African polities or societies are confronted with a number of crises that impact on establishing stable political systems, which can better, propelled them to the completion point and to consolidate its attainment. The completion point is the devolution of power from the centre to the periphery. These crises are all appearing simultaneously in emerging polities, with governments struggling to use the distribution crisis to resolve the identity, penetration and legitimacy crisis among others. Given that transitional polities are embedded in confusion due to the fragmented nature of its politics, and people do not share common ideological orientation toward political action, it is imperative to articulate common socialisation platform from where to pilot the affairs of the state. That common dominant political culture can be conceptualised under the umbrella of *'democracy'* or *'democratic governance'* as the road map for quality services delivery and sustainable development.

Just as the colonial lords were hesitant in sharing powers with citizens of their dependencies, the new custodians of power, the current centralised state system, is reluctant to devolving power to the periphery, local councils and other institutions. We see the old colonial masters reflecting their tentacles of non-power sharing through the current state formation, where the new custodians of power and authority have failed to understand the practical realities and relations of democratic politics within their own confines. Failing to understand the realities of their environment vis-à-vis the hostile international community, the belief is that politics should revolve around personalities rather than on democratic politics ideologies and principles. This constitutes the first giant step to the poverty of the continent – a poverty woven around the non-adherence to the basic tenets of democracy. Stretching the issue further, in these transitional polities, the clash between administrators and politicians reinforces the latter's suspicion of particular interests contra the views of the ruling party. This suspicion in some cases gave birth to the one-party system making the bureaucracy to depart from its traditional role of impartiality and serving whichever political party assumed office. The politicisation of the civil service makes the bureaucracy not to be identified with the aspirations, needs, and predicaments of the people, especially the local and rural populations. The non-adherence to the basic *'principles of democracy'* or the *'democratic values'* is a starting point of exclusion. The state excludes other actors in the development process.

Working towards an open society, involving the people is above all, a test to statecraft. Establishing effective administration in developing countries constitute a fundamental problem in these societies. Here lies the basic argument of the paper. Borrowing from Lucian Pye [1966], *"firm rule and efficient administration need not be seen as the composite of democratic development, but rather authority and participation must go hand in hand in the building of modern states"*. There is urgency for stressing the need and advantage of expanding democratic participation to limit the practical liabilities of democracy by taking government much closer to the people and getting them involved. Seen within this context, is the suggestion of expanding popular participation as a priority factor in nation building? Decentralisation should be recognised as a vital matter of administration and governmental rule in building an effective modern state. Having democratic governance requires having a government and ordered authority with the people's participation.

This underscores crucial input factors of solving part of the crisis of integration, penetration and distribution among others, which are crucial in building effective modern states, and ensuring checks and balances in the function of the system. The devolution of power or *'local people-oriented'* approach widens the horizons of development within the society. Citizens are encouraged not to be dependent on government as the magic wands for resolving their predicaments. Encouragement that should also ensure their voices and opinions being incorporated in decision-making and implementation of development related activities and processes. In this connection developing the human capacity of the people is vital in pushing forward the smooth transfer of power to the local population and communities. Trickle-up development approach requires a sustained financial and human capacity

DEMOCRACY AND GOVERNANCE: THE VITAL BUT MISSING LINK

Democracy can be a key component but it is not a sufficient condition for good governance – as can be seen from its absence in many transitional societies. Good governance should never be shackled with theories however attractive and logically elegant. Africa's worst performance since independence are cases not *of failed democratisation but have failed centralised and authoritarian rule* unable to meet the needs and aspirations of the people. Uncontrolled centralised and authoritarian government breeds room for bad management, i.e. many African countries have entrenched themselves in *"wrong management"* of the State where institutions designed to govern relationships between citizens and the State are used instead for personal enrichment of public officials and the provisions of benefits to the corrupt" {Mancham 2003:21]

Undoubtedly, democracy matters because it promotes human rights, freedom and liberties as well as it protects and preserves human dignity. Democracy is vital because it helps in addressing crucial and challenges issues of peace, development, and economic growth as part of state duties in advancing the well being of its citizens. However, *"a missing link exists, as African states are not developing stronger links between representation and participation: grass roots are not involved: the top-bottom approach prevails over the "bottom-up approach, which should trigger partnership, participation, and representation in the development process. So far, poverty challenges democracy in Africa. Seen within this context, democracy in Africa has failed to address the problems of the silent poor and rural majority. The governance system in place centralised as it is, enhances and sustains affluence for the few"* [Forje 2002].

Many factors contributed to the entrenchment of centralised authoritarian governance system in Cameroon. First, there was a *"clash of cultures"* between the politics of *"assimilation"* and *"indirect rule"* with the former triumphant over the latter, the out come of numbers. It was a contest between the Napoleonic and Republic governance system. Second, attributed to the prevalence of the *"Cold War"* and the fear by western democracies of *"Communist"* penetration into the African continent. Yet most of these countries tolerated and permitted the structural-functionalism of Communist Parties in their backyard. Strong and centralised governments were advocated as countervailing forces to communist entrenchment within Africa. Third, related to the demise of colonial rule creating a vacuum in the struggle for power and leadership within the new polities. Fourth, building on the sentiments of the euphoria of independence, the centralised nature of authority in traditional societies was evoked by the new custodians of power as a rallying point for reconstituting, reconstructing and as the instituting instrument for nation building. Resources were to be pulled together for the common good, to create a sense of belonging and national identity/unity. The emergence of the one-party system can be attributed to this line of thought. Nationalism was the goal to compress the legacy of colonialism in the process of manufacturing a new brave society. Unfortunately no new brave society was created.

The ideal of reform and reconstruction after many years of colonial governance was good but never genuinely realised. It fell on the wayside as other forces overtook the noble ideal of moulding a sense of belonging, cohesion and unity. Unfortunately, essential checks and balances to ensure accountability, participation, answerability and benefit sharing soon disappeared in place of nepotism, ethnic hegemonic rule and exclusion. Chaos not cohesion reigned. Ethnic conflicts, political instability, economic crises and secessionist tendencies being more pronounced. To gain favour from the centralised administration, localities and individuals embarked on the *"Politics of Motions of Support and Ethno-Regionalism"* [Mbuagbo and Akoko 2004:241-258].

Cameroon moved from what could be seen as a *"mission-driven"* noble ideal of constructing national unity and sense of belonging to a kind of *"rule-driven"* governance system with ethnic hegemonic and exclusive forces taking centre stage. Devolving power to the people constituted a challenge and threat to existing ethnic hegemonic centres of power. To achieve and sustain this mission, *patron-client relationship*, the *politics of exclusion and marginalisation* took precedence over the *politics of inclusion and benefit sharing*. The devolution of power to the periphery is considered a serious threat to established order. Mbuagbo and Akoko [2004:255] asserts: *"The ideals of national integration have been jeopardised by ethno-regional jingoism, fanned and sustained by the fact that in public policy, priority is given to group membership first, and the nation second, and the notion of citizenship is therefore bound to suffer from a geo-ethnic delimitation and order".* Instead of a non-partial public service administration, the country puts in place an *"ethno-party hegemonic and partial"* pubic service sector that caters for the specific interests that establishes it.

Critical opinions agitating for more open government and inclusive politics are often silenced or considered non-patriotic to the national course, or as enemies in the house. It must be imposed, not participatory governance system of *"top-down"* approach, or the State forcing down the throats of the people policies envisaged as best for them. The State emerges as an instrument of repression and not one advocating the freedom, equality and liberty of the people. By and large, African politics and state system exhibits a remarkably high potential for conflict. One factor often adduced in explanation thereof is the heavy dependence on the state; the occupancy of State office furnishes the golden road to social and economic advancements, for which few prospects otherwise existed.

An embedded centralised and authoritarian governance system conceals and perpetuates activities contrary to quality service delivery, revealing the complexity of political dynamics and the governing function of satisfying the needs, wants, and desires of the people and communities. The out come is failure on the part of *"government in facing the challenging reality of optimally utilising resources in an inventive and cost-effective manner in the attempt to address the multitude of needs that exist"* [Jonker 2001:242]. More often than not, the Head of State or Government is directly or indirectly high jacked by ethnic hegemonic forces and sentiments initiated through "various ethnic, cultural and religious associations," ruling elites, and other strong forces {business tycoons, hawks} within the party. Cameroon practices the most absolute form of the Napoleonic system. Bear in mind that a Presidential system of the Napoleonic type does not permit any form of power sharing with other constituencies. A republican presidential system would to some degree permit and tolerate the existence of other constituencies of power.

It is vital translating democratic principles into making grass-roots democracy a reality – power o the people – at the local or grassroots levels. It entails constructing institutions that are transparent and accountable ensuring that the poor and excluded can engage in collective actions, decision-making and protecting the rights and liberties of all citizens. Reconstructing and reforming the state means building and promoting democracy – democracy not just in name, but also in substance. An important and significant step in eliminating poverty is increasing the influence and involvement of local communities and the poor in decision-making, articulation, implementation and evaluation of development projects

A RETURN TO REASONING

In the mid 1980s, the returning to conscious reasoning was initiated from the top echelon of state machinery following the publication of Communal Liberalism {Biya, 1987], with the slogan of *"democratisation, liberalism and rigour"* designed to uplift the country out of its existing doldrums of inertia, economic decline, total political and administrative impasse in the structural-functioning of government machinery. The President in 1985 drew strong support from the population when declared that the chasing of flies would soon be a thing of the past. It was healed as a breakthrough for a transitional polity. The vision of *"Communal Liberalism"* died immediately even though it became a household slogan used to cement the spoils of the one party system. Centralisation was intensified, corruption institutionalised and ethnic diversity promoted and made a liability instead of an asset for forging ahead the prosperity of the nation. Pockets of the democratisation process were initiated within the ruling CPDM party against some descending voices and opinions against political changes in the country. The status quo was to be maintained at all cost. The strategy has paid off in the past twenty-five years.

Events in Cameroon were overtaken by external developments. The collapse of the Soviet Union triggered an avalanche of developments throughout the world especially in Africa, where the single-party centralised governance system had taken hold. One of the conditionalities of the imposed World Bank Structural Adjustment {SAP} strong emphasised the issues of democratisation and good governance. The forces of re-democratisation process could no longer be stopped. The ideals in Communal Liberalism [as a forerunner] was injected with a new lease of life to re-engage in the democratisation process of the country, by {i} returning power to the communities and people – decentralisation: {ii} initiating pluralist democracy – the demise of the one party system was eminent: {iii} liberalisation of the economy: and {iv] the rise of a vibrant civil society as the true custodian of the peoples' power. The emergence of civil society in the body politic of Cameroon is captured in many scholarly discourses noted in the early 1990s. [See Monga 1996, Nyamnjoh 1999, Bayart 1973, 1993].

Eventually, Cameroon jumped on the democratisation bandwagon, without a deliberate and planned transfer of power and resources from the centre to the periphery. Decentralisation was actually not envisaged even though the 1996 constitution creates room for devolving power from the central institutions to peripheral institutions. A decade down the road, the country is far from the envisaged target of power transfer and bringing other stakeholders as active participant in the process of governance and service delivery. The process towards decentralisation has been slow in Cameroon. Scholarly discourses concerning the progress, problems and development ramifications of decentralisation highlight issues like, {a} lack of political will, {b} fear of loosing power and the benefits these entail; and {c} the argument that communities lack the requisite human and institutional capacities. Thus the state remains the most appropriate source of the flow of power, direction and guidance for establishing national unity and ensuring sustainable economic growth. A state or government mission-driven developmental approach is envisaged.

Fundamentally important with a mission-driven government approach is only achievable if policy guidelines are unambiguous and clearly spelled out parameters within which functionaries are expected to operate. In addition, it requires organisational structures that are conducive to quick decision-making and clearly defined areas of responsibility [Jonker op cit]. This government is not providing as the spoils of patron-client ethnic hegemonic tendencies hold the State hostage in its output functions. The rescue came from the Bretton Woods Financial Conglomerates through its imposed Structural Adjustment Programmes {SAP] with all the conditionality of democratisation, good governance, devolution of power, and economic liberalism. What are the implications of these? First, the centralised nature of governance is now subjected to external scrutiny. Second, Government operates according to the dictates of the Bretton Woods Financial Institutions and other donor bodies. Third, SAP had no human face as it affected mostly the marginalised. Fourth, the declining level of living standards in Cameroon {70% salary reduction, employment stop and forced retirement}, the many hungry faces the world over and the plight of the poor forced some sense of returning to reasoning by the external donors. Fifth, it necessitated the bringing on board other stakeholders as inputs to accelerate the outputs of state functions to the society in a humane and equitable way. So far this has not been achieved.

To begin with, policy-makers are some how blinded to the revolutionary structural transformation of devolving power to the communities and people that are needed over the next decade to meet key aspects of the Millennium Development Goals {MDGs}, for example, drastic poverty reduction which is closely related to the realisation of other development goals, and to achieve successful transition to sustainable development and quality living standards for the people. To a large extent, centralised governance and conventional approaches to development have left the country as deprived as ever, with prospects of a better tomorrow mixed and bleak for more than half the population. A new weapon is needed to initiate and accelerate these required revolutionary and evolutionary changes.

DEVOLUTION OF POWER AND AUTHORITY: THE NEW WEAPON FOR DEVELOPMENT

For Cameroon to make significant changes and to realise the vision envisaged in the MDGs of halving poverty by 2015, it is imperative that existing centralised and authoritarian governance system be dismantled. New structures put in place vested with the appropriate insignia of power. It cannot be gained said that taking government to people, sharing power with civil society and the private sector will established significant avenues for participation, partnership and responsibility sharing including equity in the distribution process. Unleashing the power of the people is necessary in alleviating poverty and ensuring sustainable development. It is a question of tapping into the knowledge and potentials of the people as instrument for constructed development. Two fundamental points being the issue of knowledge and resources, which are best, exploited by empowering the people from the grass roots.

Fighting poverty must be tackled at all fronts. Here the underlying issues of the Cameroonian Knowledge Economies [CKE] and the Cameroon Ethnic Societies [CES] and the Cameroonian policies for sustainable development [CPSD] through democratic governance must feature significantly in the process of reconstructing and reforming the country. The country's potentials must be linked to as well as tap from existing global knowledge of information and communication technologies. Abundant but untapped knowledge exist in the rural areas and among the marginalized population, which should be exploited for the common good. Here Maharaj and Ramballi [1998:114] asserting the situation of Durban, South Africa, state: "…in the Third World, local dependence and competition between localities have shifted the responsibility for economic development from the central state to the local state". However, this is not enough, as the communities and localities must be actively involved in the governance of their areas. Non-involvement may lead to serious impediments that fail to tackle issues set out to address. An environment of institutional poverty and exclusion is put in place to the detriment of society.

Devolution of power and democratisation are convergence of poverty alleviation. The World Bank Poverty Reduction Strategy Papers [PRSP] will only make the necessary impact when the localities are mobilised at all levels and forms to impact on the expected outcome. Critics of devolution of power fear of an escapist mode by the state in fulfilling its obligations. It should be noted that the marginalisation of the poor from the core administrative or institutional systems and resources of government is one of the key dimensions of persistent and chronic poverty. Thus centralised authoritarian rule breeds' corruption and institutionalises poverty and underdevelopment.

Against this backdrop, the question how development is possible, and poverty overcome when the consent of those concerned is not involved and voices listened to? Or, when government policies are such that limited capacity develops within local communities for implementation and enforcement of development activities as a result of centralised administrative machinery. The existence of a Ministry of Territorial Administration and Decentralisation does not translate into reality the practicalities of the Ministry. The decentralisation component remains a theoretical ploy or skeleton requiring flesh to be added and for the people to feel the real impact in changing their life style. Decentralisation should play the vital role of empowering the people and communities in promoting development in their areas, job creation and boosting the local economy. It should also lead to investing in the basics by promoting good quality cost-effective services by making the rural areas and communities' areas a pleasant place of labour. In short genuine devolution of power and democratic governance should promote local economic development [LED] as well as provide special economic and social services.

Building a sustainable society is a complex process that involves a broad definition of local and national economic development: centralised and decentralised authorities all working in partnership with people and private sectors to ensure that all the citizens become beneficiaries in the process. Creating a development strategy is not only a political commitment and economic engagement but also a process that must rest on the social commitment of the people and administrative systems that facilitate economic growth and participatory democratic governance. It is a process that must engage other spheres of state and local government including the corporate sectors in a developmental approach to governance. Devolution of power is a critical route to popular participation and good governance is a topic that remains on the political agenda of the country for many years yet. The role of civil society another important area is connected with strengthening rural communities and moulding public opinion for governance system of checks and balances, accountability and transparency.

In a society still embedded in traditional authority, the risk of conflicts and tensions between tradition rule and local community authorities cannot be ruled out Currently, with traditional authorities as auxiliary of the state administration, devolution of power would have to take into consideration *"The developmental role of traditional authorities in Africa is also often overlooked when investigating decentralisation issues. The potential schisms between traditional political authority with its social hierarchies, and the 'new men and women of state-led decentralised local government, may de-rail the whole decentralisation process* [Binns et al 2005:24]. *The 'decentralised despotism of customary authority and ethno-*

clientelism, together with the colonial legacy of indirect rule, must not be ignored. The argument posed by Mamdani [1996] *"that the failure of political reforms aimed at democratisation to empower ordinary Africans can be firmly associated with the lack of recognition of the potent role of decentralised despotism"* is interesting in this context.

ADVANTAGES OF DEVOLUTION OF GOVERNMENT

The advantages of power devolution to the local communities will include the following:

- It encourages more contact between state, representative and participatory democracy;
- Decentralised institutions reflect the needs and aspirations of the people, and are far more innovative than centralised institutions:
- Devolution of power to the people will promote greater accountability, checks and balances and services delivery with the well-being of the communities properly promoted:
- Institutions are better placed to respond rapidly to changing circumstance and customers needs:
- Whatever existing bottlenecks or weaknesses of existing local government units, as administrative institutions that exist must be addressed by the partners concern to give greater vitality to the people to be partners with the state in the development process.

Success is assured only when the centralised authorities in the process of devolving power to the localities ensure that constant and adequate financial resources and responsibility are established:

- That the transfer is not short-term but long-term focused and oriented within the parameters of the citizens taking full control of their decisions, actions and destiny.
- The people are totally committed in ensuring the sustainability of the process by either contributing financially or otherwise to locally initiatives.
- The devolution of power to local communities and the people must be an ongoing process, not one-time shot process.

Devolution of power should induce a sense of nationalism, local democracy, and not boredom in even the most politically interested citizens. The word devolution of power or empowering local government authorities outside Unity Palace can arouse intense passions among die-heart supporters of the system where they benefit. Part of the problem is that local government is often defined simply as the powers and activities of an existing county, district councils and these are complicated, highly circumscribed and apparently of no great significance. This is a very limited view of local government. It under estimates the difference local government empowerment can make in the development process. Devolution of power should go beyond this narrow conception, be holistic, encompassing and highly committed to the virtues of cooperation, closing niches in skills development among others.

BY WAY OF CONCLUSION

Is devolution of power possible in an authoritarian presidential system? Does the Napoleonic system permit many centres of power and authority? Is Cameroon ready to adopting a republican governance system? These and many other questions have to be reviewed to understand why centralisation is part of the hegemonic governance system in Cameroon: and why there is need for change to a governance system that is more accommodating and responding to the needs of the people. The last decade of the twentieth century saw Cameroon's entry in the new century with a considerable shift in the economic and political equation. Cameroon is now bound to ride on the "elephant of democratisation, power devolution and economic liberation with a heightened degree of internal integration. The rural areas have to be integrated into mainstream national political and economic development, as the country guns for regional economic and political integration at the continental and global levels.

The argument is that without democratic and participatory governance system, the frontiers of poverty cannot be pushed back. It is only through advancing the process of participatory democracy and power sharing, wealth creation and equitable distribution such that wealth can enable the people construct a healthy society. The underlying areas of tackling the enabling state and role of the public service in wealth creation under the auspices of governance, equity and public management focuses on issue areas such as:

- More efficient, people centred government;
- An expanding economic opportunities for all, particularly the rural poor and marginalised population;
- Pushing back the frontiers of poverty, exclusion and eradication poverty as well as curbing the escalating rate of corruption;
- Creating and enabling environment and ensuring the functioning of democratic governance at all levels and capable of meeting its obligations;
- Creating an enabling state [i.e. open and encompassing] remains the only way forward for sustainable development and wealth creation. A possible future is better assured when factors inhibiting efficiency, ethics, productivity and virtues of the basic tenets of democracy are adequately and contumaciously addressed, system that upholds all the values and virtues of ethics and management and sharing power with the people.

The conclusion is that without the state providing the necessary legal, economic, political, institutional framework and safeguards against predatory tendencies and forces, democratic governance, and sustainable development can hardly come the way of the people. Devolution of power remains imperative without which Cameroon will be stuck on the runway for forever. Local communities must take their share of responsibilities ensuring the practice and prevalence of open governance, the rule of law, fundamental human rights, basic liberties, and accountability among others. Who says the future is not bright with intense representative and participatory democracy.

Communal Liberalism was the first step towards giving Cameroon a new focus to proper development. Greater decentralisation, devolution of power and authority, and visionary leadership can contribute towards the emergence of entrepreneurial government that places more emphasis on the role in *'steering'* rather than *'rowing'*. The position taken by the Bishops Conference of Cameroon in a recent report about democratic changes in the country is praise worthy. What is important is for the government to accelerate the decentralisation process especially with the Ministry of Territorial Administration and Decentralisation in place. The test is to see whether this will be fully realised before the 2007 parliamentary and local council elections. The way forward for Cameroon is to marry Communal Liberalism and the Bishops report, to ensure full implementation of views expressed in these two publications; and to better chart a new course for the country. What a wonderful country Cameroon will be when the views expressed in the two publications receive the blessings and "political will" of positive action of those in power for effective implementation.

The argument can also be advanced that devolution of power does not necessary lead to the creation of genuinely democratic, participatory, bottom-up decision making processes. Centralisation paves the way for authoritarian governance, corruption and all the ills that it entails: and devolution or decentralisation of centres of power paves the road to peoples' participatory and representative governance and development, accountability, transparency is assured. Revamping the process of decentralisation and good governance addresses the issues of poverty and underdevelopment, as democratically elected government is made accountable to its citizens. The country stands to gain much through the devolution of power to the periphery. Failed governments or banana states are avoided. It curtails the rise of ethnic hegemonic state systems camouflage as democratic governance system

REFERENCES

Binns, Tony, Gina Porter, Etienne Nel and Peter Kyei [2005] "Decentralising Poverty: Reflections on the Experience of Decentralisation and the Capacity to Achieve Local Development in Ghana and South Africa", *Africa Insight*, Vol. 35. No. 4 December 2005, Pretoria, South Africa.

Biya, Paul [1987] *Communal Liberalism.* Macmillan London.

Bayart, F. [1973] "One Party Government and Political Development in Cameroon", *African Affairs,* 73:125-144.

Bayart, F. [1993] T*he State in Africa: The Politics of the Belly.* Longman, New York.

Forje, John W. [2002] *"Rethinking Poverty by Supporting Democratic Governance: Critical Issues and Policy Choices",* CARAD Yaoundé, Cameroon.

Jonker, Alan [2001] " Challenges and Imperatives Facing Modern Government: in Jonker et al. [2001] *Governance, Politics, and Policy in South Africa,* Oxford University Press, Cape Town, South Africa.

Mancham, R. James [2003] "Africa "Falling Behind" The Rest of the World", in Forje, John [2003] *Consolidating Democratic Governance and Quality Management in Africa:*

Building New Strategies for A New Century and Extending the Benefits of Development to All, Carad, Yaoundé.

Maharaj, B. and Ramballi, K. [1998]"Local Economic Development Strategies in an Emerging Democracy: The Case of Durban in South Africa", *Urban Studies,* Vol. 35, No. 1.

Mbuagbo, T. Oben and Robert M. Akoko [2004] "Motions of Support" and Ethno-Regional Politics in Cameroon" Journal of Third World Studies {JTWS}, Selected Papers - *Twenty-First Annual Meeting Association of Third World Studies,* Shreveport, Louisiana, November 6-8, 2003. Edited by Harold Isaacs and Kathryn L. Zak.

Monga, C. [1996] *The Anthropology of Anger: Civil Society and Democracy in Africa.* Lynne Rienner, London.

Nkrumah Kwame [1964] *Consciencism.* Panaf Nooks, London.

Nyamnjoh, F. [1999] *"Cameroon: A Country United by Ethnic Ambition and Difference",* African Affairs, 98: 101-118.

Pye, W. Lucian [1966] *Aspects of Political Development. The Little Brown Series in Comparative Politics.* Boston, USA.

Chapter 2

WHITHER AFRICA: RETHINKING PUBLIC ADMINISTRATION IN A GLOBALISED WORLD. NEW SOCIAL SCIENCES PERSPECTIVE FOR DEVELOPMENT IN AFRICA[*]

ABSTRACT

Five decades after attaining independence, Africa is still equated with underdevelopment, failed states, mismanagement, corruption, conflicts and wars. Whatever indicators applied (per capita income, economic growth, debt statistics, debts etc.), the conclusion is inescapable. Africa finds itself within the plethora of a chronic crisis, political instability with the politics of exclusion over-riding that of inclusion. We need to understand why Africa is in such a mess? What are the remedies? However diverse the thinking has been, there is an emerging consensus that conventional theories of development have been callously implemented with the net effect that the quality of livelihood of the vast majority of the population is far worse today than four-five decades ago. One begins to question the structural nature of independence handed the people: second the kind of development theory forced down the throat of the new colonies: and third, to seriously questioning leadership role in the process - the extent to which their political skills helped marginalized or bleed their respective countries to death.

It could be argued that social science (political science, sociology and anthropology) failed to give the right signals in reconstructing Africa, with the contextual slogan "seek yeh the political kingdom". This failure helped in derailing the first wave of democratization process that mainly focused on attaining independence at all cost. The concept of seeking the political kingdom gave a wrong view of democracy: it failed bringing on board the idea of economic empowerment, participation, and public-private sectors–civil society interface. The absence of a functional public sector embedded with credence of quality services delivery enhancing and improving the livelihood quality of the people added to the woes of the people.

Political empowerment did not lead to economic empowerment, efficient public service sector, hence the status of failed, collapsed, and banana republics glittering the

---

[*] Paper prepared for 27th International Congress of Administrative Sciences, on the Theme "Global Competitiveness And Public Administration: Implications For Education And Training" Sub-Theme, Macro Effects Of Globalisation 11 Abu Dhabi, {United Arab Emirates} 9-14 July 2007.

continent. The root causes could be traced to the failure of development from above and imposed from outside. The practice and discipline of public administration ignored its enriching past becoming prisoners in accelerating the process of a knowledge-based economy of the 21st century. A new holistic, valuable alternative for African public administration paradigm shift is necessary for proper functioning within the global political and economic space.

Keywords: Scientific inquiry, human development, cultures, underdevelopment, communication, anthropology, social sciences, institutions, public policy

INTRODUCTION:
FACING THE CHALLENGES

"Honest and effective government, public order and personal security, economic and social progress did not come about as the natural course of events" [Lee Kuan Yew]

The ethnocentrism of Western cultures or industrial civilisation dominance in structuring the development process pervades the sustainable socioeconomic transformation of these countries. Given that society is the social science laboratory an interdisciplinary approach to development becomes imperative for a viable development strategy. The attainment of independence heralds the crucial need to change the colonial system of administration and to fashion a new system of governance with focus on nation building. The emerging states were compelled to create conditions that would meaningfully and constructively fulfil the aspirations of the people. Consequently, it required a new system of public administration, that called for reorganisation and restructuring the machinery of government in line with the requirements of the emerging new order. Obviously, reforms within the civil service could not be ignored in view of its key role in energising and sustaining the functioning of the machinery of government. At the same time pressure was mounting on government to meet rising aspirations, popular uprising or revolutions among other demands precipitated the need for administrative reform including restructuring the political system to address societal demands.

This view of development approach has significant and profound implications for democratic practice in Africa. The ideals of globalisation is driven mainly by two ideological orientation – {a} the way economic, technological, military, political and cultural forces and mechanisms *'become global'*, or anchored in institutions at the global level: and {b} the way interests and institutions at the global level *exert down-ward pressure* upon those below, especially national governments and their citizens, reducing the latter's freedom of action and instructing what to do [Smith 2006:2]. Becoming less local and more global. The forces of globalisation driven mainly by the prospects of private sector profit maximisation and the tenets of market economy engage and at times collide with international, national, regional and local systems of governments, with important consequences and lessons for the discipline and practice of public administration, and for an accountable and competent civil service.

Africa is plagued by rapidly expanding, inefficient, corrupt and politically laden public services sector unable to deliver quality services to the population. The paper questions [i] the conventional approach and its failure: [ii] the correlation between imperialism, underdevelopment and leadership; [iii] development has not been Afro-centric: [iv] the role of social sciences in African development; [v] the conspiracy nature of the international community under the guidance and dictate of the 'big brother' and [vi] the need for an African Renaissance as the way forward in facing the development challenges of the continent. There is call for a theoretical paradigm shift from the failure of the conventional approaches, imperialism and underdevelopment to searching for an authentic new approach addressing the plethora of problems plaguing the continent. The last few years have seen very rapid changes in Africa, which provide food for thought and discussion. Africa needs to make strategic choice for is transformation.

A new development paradigm, {an integrated interdisciplinary social sciences approach construed from} 'development form below upwards and from inside" is imperative. Such approach has to be backed with explorable, comparative, regional and global dimensions in the social sciences In short; a multidisciplinary approach to theorizing development should be adopted. Drawing from Pitt [1976:13], "it seems obvious that more realistic development thinking and more appropriate avenues for the anthropology of development lie in increasing the lines of communication between disciplines, institutions and cultures. But in order to achieve this, and ultimately, in order to achieve greater development success, it is first necessary to develop a much more flexible and more realistic model and method capable of multidisciplinary usage."

Social sciences, though universally agreed, should reflect practical realities and incorporate the cultural values of the people [Ball et al. 1989]. Seen within this context, it is argued that democracy got off the ground on the wrong note or premises hence the state of decay in Africa. Ake {1993} argues that the second movement towards democracy in Africa since 1980s was fuelled by the 'desire of ordinary people to gain power and material improvement". Therefore, African democracy should be different from liberal democracy on at least two counts: [a] stressing concrete economic rights, at the expense of abstract 'political rights'. Nkrumah's slogan of *"seek yeh first the political kingdom"* failed to materialise economically for not "giving the belly kingdom to all the people". The slogan was good as a political tool in the process of self-determination and the granting of independence' but failed as a developmental tool due the greedy attitude of the ruling elites and those operating the political and public service sectors.

The second aspect of Ake's vision of democracy in Africa lies in the *contrast between the individualistic atomised society of the west, and the more communal nature of African society*. Closely linked to this are different perceptions of participation in the political process. Ake maintains that participation is not competitive and often conflictual relations with other individuals. Rather, they participate as social beings in a society, which operates as an organic whole. With focus on political parties, the postulation is that political parties could hardly be the appropriate vehicles for economic empowerment. Taking into consideration that the essence of development is participation, research and theory on development in Africa should focused on strategies to maximize participation or inclusion with civil society, public and private sectors playing increasing functional roles in delivering quality services to the people.

The role and teaching of social and political theory must evolve from other premises but within a holistic globalise scientific inquiry of contributing to knowledge and human development. There is urgent need for the rebirth of critical social sciences within the framework of theory and development. Social sciences in Africa must challenge development stereotypes and clarify, with evidence, the position of their different disciplines in the development matrix of the African continent for example, and show why development has gone wrong in a region that held much hope at the time of the granting of independence. Experts have opined that, given the competitive nature of globalisation and its focus on the bottom line and profit making, it may not have the transformative impact that its advocates proclaim. Transitional polities are caught in a difficult situation – holding together crumbling traditional societies and catapulting these societies within the pathways and dictates of the forces of globalisation without the necessary human capacity, scientific and technological know how.

Development administration as an academic field has so far remained the handmaiden of Western comparative public administration. A number of African countries, especially Eastern and Southern African countries, including some Western African countries, Ghana, Nigeria, Gambia among others are making significant strides in breaking loose from its old moorings that ghettoed the development process. A number of nongovernmental or inter-governmental organisations like African Association of Public and Administrative Management {AAPAM], Development Policy Management Forum [DPMF] have embarked on a crusade for a New Public Management [NPM] for best services as a cure-all approach for the ills in both the private and public sectors. While NPM continues to be the best offer for transitional polities, it can only be effective when forces are put to work within the framework of the mechanisms of an institutionalised democratic governance system. The carrot and the stick must be brought to bear if a functional, effective and quality delivery services sector is to be part of the development process of the country. Least it be noted that the successes of these alternatives require new approaches and cooperation in North-South relations as well as a comprehensive interface among the various key holders within the country. Without a strong, independent and efficient functional civil service sector, it is difficult to improve on the delivery services of the state.

GENEALOGY MOTIVATING ADMINISTRATIVE REFORMS

The political situation in Africa at the end of World War II intensified new social movements and political resistance to colonial regime forms demanded new discourses on democracy and governance different from the colonial one. Many inter-related factors - political, economic, social and technological - combine in different dimensions propelling reforms for example: the attainment of independence, adoption of a new constitution, advances in science and technology, introduction of national planning, changes in the availability of resources and other environmental input factors require far reaching changes in the administrative system to meet new challenges. The Makerere School {Bujra, Mkandawire, Mazrui, Mafeje, Mamdani, Hyden, Rodney, Shivji and many others} championed the drive for comprehensive social and political changes and a developmental state within the emerging African state.

Box 1. Genealogical Pathways to Administrative Reforms in Africa

- Political changes, including changes in political status and changes in political systems;
- Changes in state functions, including growth of government generated by expansion of its functions and the assumption of new state responsibilities;
- New knowledge and new technological or modern management techniques;
- Drastic decline in public service delivery system
- The growing degree of poverty in society and corruption within the public sector, leading to dissatisfaction with governmental policies and development related activities.
- Growing divide between North and South
- Blind copying of foreign models of development, including poor judgement in timing;
- Resistance from vested interests within the bureaucracy;
- Poor leadership including lack of clarity in focus and content;
- Rising tide of governing elites.

Immediately after independence, the African state drifted into what Fanon [1966:152] calls *"pitfalls of national consciousness"*. Box 1 depicts some transitional motivating pathways and failures that characterises set backs within the public sector in meeting the needs and aspirations of the people. To a large extent, qualities that had made intellectuals the kingpin of nationalism became the original sin in the post-colonial era. The capacity of intellectuals to 'speak truth to power', and their penchant for puncturing myths, which was prized in the struggle for independence, were now perceived as divisive and thus inimical to the new nation-state [Mkandawire 2005:3]. The pre-colonial states lost their freedom, and the new European powers determined how society would b governed and ordered. Many African scholars have generally interpreted this loss and Marxist advocates in tragic terms, one connected with slavery to retard Africa, to counter a pro-colonial interpretation that glorified the period as a creative, powerful engine of positive transformation. Nevertheless, colonialism gave birth to a nationalism that destroyed it. Africans resisted many aspects of colonial rule and struggled for their freedom. It is a question of translating that freedom into improved quality service delivery and enhanced quality living standards.

Unfortunately the post-colonial era has been characterised by a number of disappointing factors. The modern African state exhibiting lapses and failings, namely:

- Government and leadership failed to acquire credibility, and in most cases the basis of power legitimating lies in violence, hence the public administration deployed to sustain such illegal regimes in office:
- Power has been used primarily to steal from the state. Political leadership is characterised by corruption and mismanagement. Public administration construed and function on clientelism, with political leaders rewarding their supporters with positions and money. Corruption looms on large scale compromising the

management of the state, and destroying morale values and ethics, which wrecks the fabric of society;

- Absence of an effective and transparent way of regime change as rulers refuse to relinquish power or click to power through illegitimate elections or by military force;
- Military leadership being above reproach; alternative opinions discouraged or punished, the press restrained and opposition parties not tolerated, even in the wake of political party pluralism;
- No commitment to the rule of law

Building a viable nation-state became more difficult than had been envisaged. It was chaos, disorder, environmental degradation and dependence on the departed colonial master. The public service sector was used to fan some of the chaotic situations. There were limited mechanisms to build consensus and resolve conflicts, cohesion of the different groups could not be realised due the politics of exclusion instituted by the regime. To a large extent, independence was seen as a colossal failure, with the expected gains not accruing to the majority of the population. The failure of the nation-state was apparent.

THEORIES OF TRANSITION AND DEVELOPMENT

The end of World War 11 and indeed changes following the end of the Cold War constitute sources of radical transition in the development of African states. These developments compelled African social scientists to rethink the governance process of the continent. Some scholars hold the opinion political changes result from internal struggles between warring factions of the regime in power, or that they are the legacy of a new president or a consequence of political liberalisation. According to Bayart *et al* [1992:17] "grass-roots or popular political action are the main causes of the democratic explosion in Africa, sparked from within the sub-Saharan political systems themselves. Discourses of the nature of African political systems and the impact of the international system {*dependency theory*} is fuelled by analyses of the impact of the entry of a subordinate imperialism, neo-colonialism in African states, the social class system, and the structures of patronage or repressive systems [Amin 1993]. The failure of the emergence of a developmental state in Africa can be traced to some of the controversies surrounding transforming the economic, political, social and intellectual visage of African states.

Ongoing debate about state failure in its delivery services is also a crisis in our understanding of how this has changed the epistemological approach to understanding the reality in Africa? To a large extent, a recipe for chaos and underdevelopment is constitutionalised. Hence poor institutional performances as a result of captured special interests and poor institutional capability including the ability to mobilise resources and available knowledge for developmental activities: The biggest challenges facing governance in Africa is that of the pervasiveness of corruption attributed to the state's role in the economy, exclusion of other political opinions and social tolerance for corruption.

In this light, Diouf [1998:3] states: "examining civil society, culture and traditions, discourse on identity, irredentism and extremism of all kinds, in their complex, contradictory and/or complementary relationships with democratisation and institutional restructuring is insufficient if not to say imprecise". Currently, we seem to be headed down the same path committing the same mistakes, or deploying the views of Shivji [1990], "the prioritisation of rights" and to seriously rethink democracy instead of settling for a 'compradorial democracy." Therefore, African social sciences must gun for the creation of a functional democratic public sphere of "inclusiveness", and taking into consideration prevailing socio-cultural realities [Ball *et al* 1989] of the continent without compromising the basic tenets of the virtues of democracy. Simply stated, governance should be participatory, responsible, accountable, transparent, efficient, legitimate, consensual and inclusive with the objective of promoting and sustaining the rights of citizens, public interest, welfare and social justice and sustainable development.

To address some of the issues, the following hypothesis are advanced, from the perspectives of not turning our backs on the state, but to confront squarely the difficult task of creating an effective state that is embedded with legitimacy and capacity to provide development, and is responsive to the needs of all, especially, the forgotten poor majority. It is clear that the state no longer can exclusively go alone in this task, but in dynamic engagement with civil society and the private sector.

HYPOTHESIS

- The absence of democratic governance as a major contributor to declining public service delivery:
- Political party interferences or the politicisation of the civil service, contributes to poor output functions:
- The lack of professionalism in administration and institutional support constitutes significant constraints as this encourages "muddling through" rather than a disciplined and technical sound approach to articulating and aggregating reforms addressing the plight of the marginalised population.
- Political leadership with versioned and focused ideological orientation backed with a responsive civil society remain essential in promoting public services delivery in a society.
- Positive responses from the international community towards the envisaged goals of the nation.
- The absence of a vibrant private sector is serious impediment to service delivery within the society.

The proliferation of the literature on governance and administrative reforms in recent years reflects the rising concerning with this question in many circles. The policy prescriptions by various international bodies and funding agencies, the conceptual and theoretical interventions advanced by social scientists, and the role of various non-governmental organisations to improve the quality of governance provide evidence of this. Against this backdrop New Public Management {NPM} implies civil service reform and public service delivery, along the lines of democratic governance, decentralisation, the politics of inclusion, reform of the judicial system and extreme emphasis on anti-corruption initiatives with strong emphasis on quality management. These changes are important to highlight the most pressing governance concerns. Niraja Gopal Jayal [2007] of the Jawaharlal Nehru University, New Delhi notes: 'social scientists share a broad agreement on the fact that the governance approach is less about institutions and more about processes and outcome, so that institutional design becomes a means rather than an end in itself. The presence of actors other than government on the landscape of governance suggests less a concern with official structures, and more with the ways of enhancing citizen participation in policy deliberations, or creating the conditions for greater transparency and accountability, or enlarging opportunities for citizens to demand and obtain responsive governance'.

It is evidently clear that the absence of democratic governance compromises the chances of quality service delivery as it infringes on the rights of the people to make choices. From a governance perspective, the relationship between government-civil society-private sector partnerships is important. The central issue in governance is improvement in government especially its output functions in terms of efficiency and quality public service delivery. To a large extent, most African governments have failed in this respect. Admittedly, rapid population growth and falling world prices for the export of raw materials and rising prices for imported finished goods, contribute to some of the problems. But should not be the excuse for failing to improve the living conditions of the population. It is not surprising that the issue of governance remains a pressing academic concern in many African states a ranged of social science disciplines. The people are preoccupied with issues of how and where the next meal could be obtained. Civil society is disenchanted with widespread dissatisfaction concerning the actual quality of governance in every thing ranging from high levels of corruption to poor quality service delivery. "The significant point here is the recognition that the state alone lacks the full range of capability that is required to meet the ever-complex needs of contemporary society" [Ayeni 2006: v]

The continent is besieged by interferences from all corners. Political party interferences constitute a major drawback to quality services delivery. The institutionalisation of the one-party system failed to draw a distinction between the activities and structures of the ruling political party and the structures and functions of state bureaucracy. The return to multi-party political pluralism has not altered the situation. The governing party especially in francophone African countries, are yet to realise current trends in plural political dispensation. In Cameroon, for example, the civil service is seen as an extended structure of the ruling Cameroon People Democratic Movement {CPDM} party.

Given that governance is about creating effective institutional complements for providing sustainable development and good quality of life for the people, it goes without saying that efficiency; integrity and professionalism must constitute the cornerstone for democratic governance in the country. The lack of professionalism and technical skills in administration pervades the proper functioning of the system. The system is hijacked by clientelism and patronage relationship at the expense of professionalism, credibility and skilled human capacity. It encourages a mediocrity rather than a disciplined and technical sound approach to formulating and executing administrative related activities. Institutional support is often lacking to push ahead much needed administrative reforms. Very often ad hoc bodies are established without clear focus. Seen in this context, administrative reform programmes fail due to ill conceitedness, lacking clarity in the definition of objectives and poorly planned. An administrative reform is a continuous and changing process requiring sustained attention that the short-lived ad hoc bodies cannot provide. In addition, the following factors impede the process of restructuring that should aid quality service delivery: {a} poorly staffed institutions and lacking necessary the requisite professional and technical skills: {b} lack of cooperation and linkages with other institutions: and {c} non-involvement of other key partners in the process of effective and meaningful decision-making processes.

Human and institutional capacity buildings are essential input factors that should set the tune and direction for productive mobilisation and utilisation of resources, enhanced by the processes of institution capacity building and strengthening in the public service to raise and improve standards of performance to support sustainable human-centred development and a new social order aimed at poverty alleviation. Simply stated, the performance capacity of the public service should be rehabilitated and strengthened to support meaningful policies and other related activities that should enable people to enrich their capabilities in economic, social, cultural and political fields without compromising the resources needs for future development [Bentil 1994].

Africa is facing serious crisis of leadership with focused visionary ideological orientation and direction to inspire and mobilise the people towards a common goal, especially that of improving their quality of livelihood. Africa needs leaders that can successfully pilot their countries from a "Third World to First World" within a generation. Countries less endowed with natural resources, like Malaysia, Singapore, Turkey, Thailand and South Korea have accomplished this fate. What prevents Africa from attaining the same success stories of the Asian Tigers? The quality of Political leadership is fundamental to nation building. Some African countries like Botswana, Mauritius, Seychelles and South Africa have made significant progress in this direction. In respect to the cultural, economic, political and social transformation of societies, "leadership is cause; everything else is effect" [Adei 2004:10]. Improving leadership in Africa within a democratic set up is imperative to drive, and shape a national agenda, including making it extremely unsafe to embezzle public funds and ride on mediocrity.

Certain criteria must be set upfront. For example, the people must be committed to a number of principles of legacy-building leadership, namely: character, competence and care. In addition, people must be involved in articulating and elaborating a national agenda that should move the country from a Third to First World within the shortest time possible. In line with the aforementioned factors, people must be willing and committed to challenging and fighting the negative tendencies that hold back Africa such as corruption, nepotism, poor work habits, undemocratic governance and bad management among others. Developing quality leaders backed with positive responses from society to grow the economy must be an inherent commitment of the people. Development entails a paradigm shift and significant break from the past failures and mistakes. Past failures and mistakes should be the beacon to forge ahead from a positive direction and solid background

The exclusion of vital stakeholders – civil society and the private sector. The notion of collaboration and partnership is distant from the governance and managerial process of many African countries. Yet no nation can overcome the challenges of development if quality public service delivery can be attained in transitional polities. The absence of a vibrant private sector and the exclusion of the civil society impede functionally defined services delivered through public bureaucracies. Therefore, "collaboration is now central to the way in which public policy is made, managed and delivered throughout the world" [Sullivan and Skelcher 2002]. Without a vibrant and productive private sector, research results cannot be translated into consumer goods. Economic development requires certain public institutions, such as effective and secure property rights backed by an effective judicial system, accountable and predictable systems of authority, and the provision of basic public goods.

Last but not least, lays the issue of the kind of responses from the international community towards the policy and developmental strategy of the country in question. Positive responses from the international community towards the envisaged goals of the nation are a crucial input factor in the sustainable development of transitional polity. To achieve this, both developed and developing polities must be able to trade on the politics of consensus, give and take and mutual respect of the sovereignty status quo of each other, and inevitably need to draw on a wide range of perspectives, expertise and resources far beyond the traditional role of government. Given the special effect to the nature, problems and challenges African countries face in fostering inter-institutional collaboration and partnership for sustainable governance, the need for positive responses from the international community remains vital inputs for the development of the region.

The speech by World Bank Vice President for Africa, Edward V.K. Jaycox [1993:1} opens the Pandora box on the continent's role, place and responses within the international community: "In the last 20 years, Africa has had to face a very hostile general economic environment and most of the crises have been generated by the inability to respond. Other countries that are also primary producers, if they had a slight edge in capacity, were able to weather these storms better, and in fact, they have done better. When you lack capacity, there is a tendency to substitute rigidities and rules and arbitrary activity to compensate for it"

Many African states have abandoned the project of human-focused development and become a predatory state lacking legitimacy but promoting mediocrity and authoritarian rule. There is growing lack of political will to reform emerges as the main culprit. To a large extent, we can rightly question the one-size fits all design of administrative reforms. Here we can suggest that political and economic reforms and globalisation present both an opportunity and a challenge for effecting substantive change in the administrative system. To improve on democratic governance and service delivery, all activities must relate and be integrated with the national social economic plan and should be consistent with the over all development programmes

CHANGES, CHALLENGES AND RESPONSIBILITIES

Concerns about public administration in Africa are deepening. The poor performance of this sector contributes to poor service delivery and the rising tide of failed states that has gripped the region. Public administration is widely recognised by governments the world over as the substitute or surrogate government uniquely responsible to keep afloat state machinery and its obligations to the people. Hence regimes in the established democracies - UK, USA, Sweden, Germany, France etc. - recognise the role of public administration in the smooth functioning of the state: hence appropriate measures of ensuring that their civil service sector remains continuously efficient, effective and readily responsive to discharging their responsibilities are taken. This is not the case with many African countries. Many inter-related factors are responsible for the stalemate in the role and functioning of public administration providing quality service delivery to the citizens. Political interference and politicisation with different intentions and interpretations interface have been destructive to the place of public administration in the development of the state. The solution requires democratic governance of total participation and involvement of the state, civil society and private sector.

Back, in December 1948, Resolution 200 of the United Nations General Assembly, Third Session recognised inter-alia, that lacking expertise and technical organisation were serious factors impeding economic development, and social progress in transitional polities in Africa. More than six decades after, African countries continue to suffer from scarcity of trained manpower capacity in all sectors to effectively and efficiently manage the different sectors and responsibilities of government. In the same vein, the keynote address during the inauguration of AAPAM by Wu, C.Y. [4 November 1971] the then Director of UN Public Administration Division, noted: "In order to increase the administrative capability for development, the challenge at this stage is for the professionalisation of the Civil Service and development of modern management techniques. Without such capability, no government could cope effectively with the ascending complexity of the problems of development". The Economic Commission for Africa {ECA: 1973} re-echoed this in a publication "Administration and Management in Africa - Localisation of Professional Qualifications in the fields of Administration as a Measure for attaining Administrative, Managerial and Executive Effectiveness'.

These and other publications significantly raised issues pertaining to human capacity development and the role of social sciences in the development process. The burden is on social sciences to craft a new development approach most suitable for the continent. Sixty years after, the issue remain current and pressing, calling on social sciences to revisit the situation. The development approaches adopted by African countries were they the right type needed by the continent? Apparently, it is clear that the structural-functional governance system should be looked into and from a holistic perspective that includes issues depicted in box 2.

Intellectual discourses following the granting of independence pivoted on *'dependency theory and modernisation theory'* where scholars argued about the physical subjugation of societies under colonialism with intellectual imperialism reinforcing western dominance and dictates. For a good summary of the intellectual arguments of the *dependency/modernisation* theorists, see [Leys 1996]. The *Eurocentric* modernisation model embedded with the contention that the path of development followed by Europe should ultimately be the same path African countries had to traverse to become civilised and developed. Of course, the process failed to take into consideration the cultural and other shortcomings in the societies of those continents rather calling for closer links between the developed and transitional polities to facilitate the diffusion of modern values from the former to the latter. The establishment of national, regional and continental research bodies like universities, the Council for the Development of Social sciences Research in Africa {CODESRIA}, the Organisation of Social Science Research in Eastern and Southern Africa {OSSREA}, Association of African Political Scientists [AAPS], African Association of Public Administration and Management {AAPAM} and others should revisit the kind of development path needed for the continent in light of past experiences. *"It is important that knowledge of Africa must reflect on Africa's reality not as constructed through Eurocentric prisms, but through a deep understanding and immersion in Africa's popular social realities"* [Obi 2001]. Africa's dependency on knowledge imported from the North has serious implications for the African people's self image and pride in African institutions and practices. Importantly, those who lack knowledge see their fate shaped by others in the light of their own interests, notes a UNESCO [1981] publication. Similarly, societies lacking knowledge are doomed to perpetual manipulation by others. Of course, this demands that knowledge production be married with knowledge consumption or else it has no meaning for the continent.

The issue of human capacity development remains a nightmare in Africa's development prospects needs. This requires serious and critical attention by governments. Zeleza [2003] contends that higher education or tertiary educational institutions, specifically universities, colleges, and polytechnics, play a major role in the training of minds and generating knowledge that could be utilised in addressing societal needs. Universities, in generating knowledge that could be of use in the policy-making process, are critical players in the knowledge industry and therefore deeply involved in the business of generating knowledge for development [World Bank 2002: Stone 2002. Hallak 1990]. African countries have made significant progress in the sector of developing and improving human capacity. However, the process has been constrained due to poor governance that failed to propel social development.

Generally, it can be argued that the African condition expresses not the absence of policies, but rather policy failure. Policy failure, especially in the education and, therefore, social development front can be attributed to institutional and structural deficiencies within Africa and its relationship with the global community. With the latest neo-liberal economic paradigm subjecting Africa to harm experimentations by multilateral financial conglomerates through their economic structural adjustment programmes, it is more than necessary for African alternatives to be advanced through African prisms. More importantly, it is imperative for African scholars to fashion independent but truly African social sciences tradition to enable proper reflections on African problems, addressing the changes, challenges, and responsibilities confronting the continent.

To have a productive, efficient and effective public administration requires trained human capacity, a functional democratic governance system and with the international community responding positively to the aspirations and needs of the people. Therefore centres of excellence for nurturing, vetting and testing critical national issues and serious contributions to the development debate must be established. The political environment of the past is partly to blame for the muted public reflection of academics and intellectuals. There is now a need more than ever before of the scholars of the Makerere School of Social Sciences and others who made intelligent, decisive and contemporary contributions and strongly advocated for a scientific and objective path to and integrated national development approach. Given the return to political pluralism, with society embracing the democratic governance situation; as it improves and is consolidated, alternative avenues to improving the quality of livelihood will eventually emerge. Eventually a functional [public administration will be put to place to pilot these changes.

The African academia is confronted to seeking the right path to the weakest link and /or missing links to the development of the continent's *modus operandi*. Therefore scholars need to rethink, re-conceptualise and re-strategise some aspects of the development process from within a purely African perspective while taking into consideration that the region is not an isolated island.

Box 2.

- The kind of developmental approached to be crafted by African countries;
- Disparity between the orientation of educational and vocational training
- systems, the skill needs of the public sector and private sectors
- The structure and role of public services, civil service practices and rapid changes in skill requirements
- Absence of a well-developed educational system tuned to the pressing
- needs of African countries:
- The involvement of civil society and private sector in the process of development.
- The impact and influence of scientific and technological changes

Note: See UN Public Administration Division – Public Administration Newsletter, Issue No. 50 [March/April 1973:1], Forje 2003.

CONCLUSION AND WAYS FORWARD

Africa s confronted with a plethora of public sector reform to improve service delivery. The Millennium Development Goals MDGs acts as incentives towards that direction. The public service sector needs coherency and free from politicisation to be effective and efficient in terms of achieving overall improvements in poverty reduction and service delivery improvement. There should be a convergence point for all public sector reform activities implemented in African countries. Structural reform of the public service sector is needed. The sector should move from a strategic change and shift from the former mechanical model of public and development administration towards a more organic, integrative and adaptive model of corporate governance and taking into cognisance the role and opportunities offered by Information and Communication Technologies {ICTs].

It has been argued that African scholars need to articulate new *'social science'* approach to its development debacle. One that is independent and truly African social science tradition to better enable them reflect on African problems, address challenges plaguing the region, but without departing from the main stream of scientific inquires, objectivity and discourses projecting scholarship on the continent for the solutions of its pertinent problems. The diversity of culture across the continent may present difficulties but can be surmounted provided the political will exist and rightly deployed.

The realisation of intended objectives is, in many African countries constrained by the prevailing political environment, management culture and incentive framework. Many of the decision-makings have yet to shrink and shy-away from old practices that prevailed in the days of the monolithic one party and authoritarian governance system. Old habits die-hard. But the times are changing, offering new challenges and opportunities for comprehensive turn-a-round towards an entrenched public administration responding to the needs of the people. In view of issues discussed, the following recommendations are advanced as ways forward to crafting a functional, efficient, effective, responsive public administration. It is reasonable to conjecture that partnerships - state-civil society-private sector interlude – will emerge as the core public sector activity and as mainstream forces promoting quality service delivery much needed in Africa.

Box 3. Recommendations

- Reforms to enhance good governance, accountability and transparency
- Decentralisation, local government and institutional pluralism to promote service delivery
- Harnessing Information Technology {IT}
- Professionalisation of the public service and human capacity development
- Incentives and pay/salary reform as essential input factors for curbing corruption and other malpractices within the system.
- Implementing, measures to reinstate ethical conduct, integrity and credibility of the public service
- Sustainable interface/linkages between the state, civil society and the private sector
- Decentralisation and devolution of decision-making powers
- Strengthening managerial responsibility and accountability for results
- Democratising internal work procedures, exhibiting accountability, transparency
- Ensuring participation, partnership, responsibility and benefit sharing among the key stakeholders, state, civil society and private sector.
- Communicate and share information and lessons learned in an effort to raise greater awareness and seeking the best solutions for the country.
- Engendering gender empowerment and promoting competition, which serves the people.
- Incorporating civil society and the private sector into the governance process
- Developing team work, linkages, cooperation and coordination across the board
- Rest for the rule of law, social justice and responsibilities
- Making public service institutions and officials accountable to the citizens
- Developing a national think-tank capacity and a national development or future institute to guide development efforts.

REFERENCES

Abdi, A. Ali, Korbla P. Puplampu and George J. Sefa Dei (eds.) *2006 African education and Globalisation: Critical Perspectives.* Lexington Books.

Adei Stephen [2004] *The Promise of Leadership. Combert Impressions,* Accra, Ghana.

Ake, Claude [1993] "The Unique Case of African Democracy", *International Affairs,* vol. 60. No. 2.

Amin, Samir [1993] *Itineraire Intellectuel.* L'Harmattan, Paris.

Ayeni O. Victor [2006] Editor – Foreword, Special Issue: Fostering Collaboration for Sustainable Governance in Africa. *African Journal of Public Administration and Management.* Vol. XVII, No. 2. July 2006.

Ball. Terence, Farr James and Hanson, Russell L. {eds.} [1989] *Political Innovation and Conceptual Change.* Cambridge University Press, Cambridge.

Bayart, J. F, Mbembe, A: Toulabor, C. [1992] *La politique par le bas en Afrique noire Contributions a une problématique de la démocratie*, Karthala, Paris.

Bentil A. Michael [1994] "Institution Capacity Building for Rehabilitation and Reconstruction", *Paper presented at AAPAM's 16h Round-table Conference on Mobilisation and Utilisation of Resources for Effective Performance in the Public Service,* 27th November – 3rd December, Nairobi, Kenya.

Diouf Mamadou [1998] *Political Liberalisation or Democratic Transition:* African Perspectives. Codesria New Path Series, No. 1, Codesria, Dakar, Senegal.

Economic Commission for Africa [ECA] {1973} *Administration and Management in Africa - Localisation of Professional Qualifications in the fields of Administration as a Measure for attaining Administrative,* Managerial *and Executive Effectiveness'.*

Fanon, Frantz [1966] T*he Wretched of the Earth.* Grove Press, New York.

Forje W. John [2003] *Consolidating Democratic Governance and Quality Management in Africa.* Yaoundé - Cameroon.

Hallak, J. [1990] *Investing in the Future: Setting Educational Priorities in the Developing World.* Unesco/International Institute for Educational Planning/Pergamon Press.

Jayal Nirajan Gopal [2005] Review Essay: On Governance. In *Current Sociology,* Vol. 55. No. 1. January 2007, pp126-135.

Jaycox, V.K. Edward [1993] *Speech at the African-American Institute Conference on "Africa Capacity Building: Effective and Enduring Partnership",* Renton, Virginia, May 20, 1993, USA.

Leys Colin [1996] *The Rise and Fall of Development Theory.* James Curry, Oxford.

Mkandawire Thandika {2005} Introduction. In Mkandawire Thandika {ed.} *African Intellectuals: Rethinking Politics, Language, Gender and Development.* Zed Books, London/New York and CODESRIA Books, Dakar, Senegal.

Obi Cyril [2001] "Beyond 'Isms' and 'Posts'": Imagining Epistemology in Africa in the Age of Globalisation", *The Journal of Cultural Studies,* Vol. 3. No. 1 2001.

Pitt, David, ed. [1976] *Development from Below: Anthropologists and Development Situations.* Mouton Publishers.

Shivji, I. [1990]"*The Pitfalls of the Debate on Democracy: in Ifda Dossier,* 79. Oct/Dec 1990, pp55-58.

Smith Dennis [2006] *Globalisation: The Hidden Agenda.* Polity Press, Cambridge.

Stone, D. [2002] U*sing knowledge: The Dilemmas of 'bridging research and policy.* Compare, 32(3), 285-295.

Sullivan Helen and Skelcher Chris [2002] *Working Across Boundaries – Collaboration in Public Service.* Macmillan, Palgrave.

UNECO [1981] *"Domination or Sharing: Endogenous Development and the Transfer of Knowledge,* Paris, France.

World Bank [2002] *Constructing Knowledge Societies: New Challenges for Tertiary Education.* The World Bank, Washington, DC, USA.

Zeleza, P. T. [2003] *Rethinking Africa's Globalisation.* Vol. 1. The Intellectual Challenges, Africa World Press, Trenton, New Jersey, USA.

Chapter 3

RETHINKING POVERTY IN THE MIDST OF PLENTY. WHAT LESSONS, OPTIONS AND PROSPECTS FOR THE FUTURE

ABSTRACT

After half-a-century of independence, and many decades of limited successes in eliminating abject poverty, new ideas about sustainable growth and development are emerging which transitional societies should adopt in addressing their predicaments for the nation to move forward. Eliminating the poverty cankerworm, which is gradually, destabilising and even disintegrating the society calls for vigilant, concerted and comprehensive policy strategies encompassing the state, civil society, the private sector and the international community?

The paper adopts the conceptual approach of the quality of livelihood as the new development strategy for the continent. It argues that the politics of exclusion and the absence of good governance and quality service delivery are major contributing factors to

The increasing state of abject poverty and misery in the midst of plenty. Development has to be more human focused and oriented, targeting the poor by placing the poor first, and the affluent or rich last in the development continuum. It takes a crosscutting edge approach to multiple deprivation and social exclusion.

The conceptual approach further builds on issues of exclusion, marginalisation, ethnic hegemony, misuse or abuse of power, inequitable resources distribution or wealth sharing and responsibilities. It advances proactive strategic policy measures for providing and sustaining quality livelihood for the vast majority of the poor and excluded population. Though the focus is on Cameroon lessons and experiences from other regions are incorporated as we mover deeper and deeper into the realities of the unstoppable forces of a global village of the 21st century and beyond.

Based on the conceptual framework of the quality of livelihood, the conclusion is that in designing poverty-related activities or programmes, it is more prudent to respect the vision of poverty articulated and aggregated by the poor themselves. In doing so, priority should be reducing variability of income, as well as strengthen women's participation and autonomy politics of inclusion should replace the existing one of exclusion. Above all, the poor and vulnerable should be placed on the plus, and not minus side of the development continuum in improving and creating conducive environment for the participation of the poor in the development process. Fundamentally important is to build on the politics of partnership, participation, responsibility, and of course, equitable wealth sharing.

Keywords: Poverty, exclusion, partnership, participation, gender empowerment, and wealth sharing

INTRODUCTION: ANTHROPOLOGY OF POVERTY

The Holy Scriptures sanctions the state of poverty. Drawing from the books of Mathew, those who have, more shall be added....' The anthropology of poverty while building on the inherent impact of the Mathew effects also argues looking at certain principles underpinning poverty analysis. First, we should never forget the hardships and tragedy that lie behind the horrifying figures of the state of poverty in Africa. Second, we must grasp the meaning of the multidimensionality of poverty. The different dimensions of poverty interact in ways to reinforce each other; this constitutes a crucial insight from social exclusion. The poverty trap is as much a social phenomenon as an economic and political one. The poor have become social outcasts. The very presence of poverty removes this category of people from the social support systems. Politically they are disenfranchised, on the one hand, and on the other, the political leaders acquire extra external funds that never trickle down to the poor but rather swell the bank accounts of the political powerful in society for their personal use. Thus a number of qualitative interrelated factors underscore the state of poverty and human development in Africa. Anthropologically, was the human being born to be poor or has he/she made her/him poor? The human being was not born poor: the Garden of Eden was at his/her disposal. The human being faulted and lost the right and privileges of the fruits of the Garden of Eden.

Poverty today is the outcome of man's created acts – the politics of greedy values. The failure of collective sharing values contributes to the state of growing poverty in the midst of plenty. Individual greed value belief systems creates the conceptual situation of the poor, because they are poor to begin with, and conversely, the rich are rich because they rich to begin with. Whether rich or poor, the entire issue is linked too much broader inter-related factors. It is imperative to see poverty within the wider framework of national policies, cultural norms and household behaviour. Underscoring these factors lays the issue of democratic governance currently absent in many African countries.

Critical alternative views of poverty exist in other cultures where the emphasis is not simply on money, but on spiritual values, community ties and availability of common resources. Some would regard the West as deprived of the most basic human needs of spiritual fulfilment. Similarly, others would consider the West impoverished for her loss of the extended family and sense of community belonging. Critical views have emanated from within Western society also. For example, it has been asserted that Western emphasis on monetary values has led to the creation of a system of production that ravishes nature and a society that mutilates man' (Schumacher 1973).

Since the end of World War II, the meaning of poverty has been homogenised and even universalised. Poverty is seen as economic condition dependent on cash transaction into the market place for its eradication. An economic yardstick is used to measure and to judge all societies and peoples. Poverty has widely been regarded as characterising the third world, and it has a gendered face.

In the last decade or so, global figures on income poverty have not changed significantly – there are still over 1.2 billion people living under a dollar a day. Sub-Saharan Africa has the largest share of people living below income poverty line. Poverty is a major challenge facing African countries and its eradication is fundamental to achieving sustained growth and development. Poverty is the interplay of a number of factors and tackling these through encouraging sustained and broad-based economic growth, improving productivity and production capacity, creating employment opportunities and ensuring food security, remains a priority. Given the fact that today's global economy is driven by rapid technological change, there is need for African States to accelerate and improve on whatever endogenous technological capacity they master. Without this improvement or adaptation process the continent will continue to suffer from an ever-widening technological gap between themselves and the rest of the world. Faced with severe budgetary constraints, limited science and technological personnel and an inadequate managerial or organisational culture, African states remain ill equipped to take advantage of new technologies. Hence the need for African cooperation to fill existing missing gaps and to focus on the agricultural /agro-industry sector to re-justify that agriculture is the mainstay of the economies of these countries. Agriculture can help to promote economic development in Africa.

The paper is concerned with process issues around poverty reduction and eventual eradication, and is not producing new evidence but highlighting and stressing on existing hard facts on either the dimension of poverty or on poverty outcomes. It starts from the presumption that there exists some clear sense of what the objectives of policies for poverty-reduction consist of. What can and should be done. How to proceed and so forth. Within the African region, some considerable progress in information collection about poverty levels, characteristics and tends and increasingly, an attempt to find mechanisms to ensure that the evidence on poverty informs the design of policy.

It is evidently apparent that issues and dialogue around reform is not adequately informed regarding the clear identification of the poor. The stress is on improved state performance for quality service delivery for the entire community and, particularly meeting the needs of the vulnerable and marginalized in society. Measuring progress against poverty is not friction free. Problems may often arise depending on the kind of indicators one goes after. However, it is necessary to gain and maintain public support for the overall reform process. The people must be part and parcel of the process from start to finish.

What mechanisms are governments putting in place to ensure a comprehensive and concerted eradication of poverty and to promote quality service delivery? Has the public a say and confidence in the government pro-poor poverty eradication policies, strategies and agenda? Are civil society's responses to State's policies positive? What are the attitude and input mechanisms of the industrialised countries and international community towards a poverty-reduction strategy by the government? Is there a national development strategy? Is poverty reduction an integral party of the strategy and what priority allocation is given to it?

The paper advocates that a poverty-reduction strategy is a necessary precondition for inclusion in all projects. And that mainstreaming poverty eradication within the linked processes of national development planning and budget allocation is extremely necessary. Poverty reduction prioritisation should remain an inherent part of development and budgeting process implementation. For example, income and consumption poverty are conventionally measured using measures advanced by Foster-Green and Thorbecke – the so-called F-G-T measures that enables a calculation to be made both of the head count, i.e. number of people below the poverty line, and poverty gap, or short-fall of the poor below the poverty line. The latter provides a measure of the resources required to eliminate poverty.

Policies and actions need to be articulated and aggregated in this respect. In other words, defining and measuring poverty barely kicks off the game. Only by understanding causes can the main business begin of designing, implementing and evaluating interventions. By improving the governance and legal systems or strengthening women's autonomy and empowerment, things will no doubt begin to move in the right perspective and directions internally, as well as canvassing and generating external input measures. Seen within these perspectives, the believe is that wider application or reviewing the poverty reduction focus of policy processes and actions remain imperative. That initiative must come from within. The failure of SAP should be a lesson for both the government and external donors not to bypass the consultation process of involving the people affected or whom they want changes to occur in their environment.

It is not sufficient to have policies but most importantly to forge ahead with positive actions that addresses the needs and meets the aspirations of the vulnerable groups in society. This paper has its value if only in unionism with contributions from others assist in drawing the lessons from different experiences and assists policy analysts and policy-makers in government and the international community in improving performance on poverty reduction. Without which we would have failed in our mission.

CONCEPTUAL FRAMEWORK

The conceptual framework builds on (i) a dominant mainstream or orthodox approach which provides and values a particular pattern of development; and (ii) a critical alternative approach which incorporates other more marginalized understanding of the development challenge and process. Box 1 attempts a brief differentiation of the two contrasting positions on poverty, development and hunger.

The complexity of measurement mirrors the complexity of definition, and the complexity increases where participatory methods are used and people define their own indicators of poverty. A mixture of conceptual framework is adopted. Beginning with Robert McNamara's celebrated speech to the World Bank Board of Governors in Nairobi – Kenya in 1973 and the subsequent publication of Redistribution with Growth; backed with Runciaman and Townsend's redefinition of poverty, not just as a failure to meeting minimum nutrition or subsistence levels, but rather as a failure to keep up with the standards prevalent in a given society, through ILO's pioneering work in the mid 1970s, poverty came to be defined not just as lack of income, but just as lack of income, but also as lack of access to health, education and other services.

Terms often used to situate poverty include:

Box 1.

Alternative Perspectives

Poverty: being a situation encountered by
People not able to meet their material and
Non-material needs through their own
effort

Purpose: Creation of human well being
Through sustainable societies in social,
Cultural, political and economic terms.

Process: Bottom-up, participatory, reliance
And appropriate often local knowledge and
Technology, small investments in small-
scale

Orthodox Perspectives

Poverty seen as a situation suffered by people
lacking the financial means to buy food and
satisfy other basic material needs

Purpose: Transformation of traditional
subsistence economies defined as 'back-ward'
into industrial, common defined economies
defined as 'modern'

Process: Top-down, reliance on expert
knowledge, usually Western and definitely
external large scale capital investments in
projects; protection of the commons. large
projects; advanced technology; expansion of the
private sphere

- Income or consumption poverty;
- Human [under] development;
- Social exclusion;
- Ill-being;
- [Lack of] capability and functioning;
- Vulnerability;
- Livelihood unsustainability;
- Lack of basic needs;
- Relative deprivation;
- Undemocratic governance system.

The concept of basic needs inspired policies like integrated rural development. New layers of complexity were added in the 1980s. This included amongst others, Chambers (1997) on powerlessness and isolation, inspiring the participation, interest in vulnerability, and its counterpart, security, associated with better understanding of seasonality and, of course, the consequences and impact of shocks, disasters and droughts. The Brundtland Commission on Sustainability and the Environment added yet a new approach broadening the concept of poverty to a wider construct, which popularised the term sustainable livelihood.

Theoretical work by Amarty Sen strengthened his earlier conceptual framework of food entitlement, or access, by emphasising that income was only valuable in so far as it increased the 'capabilities' of individuals and thereby permitted 'functioning' in society. The rapid increase in the study of gender shifted and strengthened the debate from a focus on women alone (women in development (WID) to wider gender relations (gender and development (GAD). Poverty (under) development goes hand in hand. This calls for policies to empower the vulnerable in society – women, child, the aged etc. and to find ways and means to underpin autonomy and participation.

For the past two-three decades, one sees further development in the poverty concept, with concomitant emphasis on how poor people themselves view their situation. This aspect has to be further developed and strengthened. Inspired by Sen, the United Nations Development Programme (UNDP) articulated the idea of human development; 'the denial of opportunities and choices to lead a long, healthy, creative life and to enjoy a decent standard of living, freedom, dignity, self-esteem and the respect of others.

FAULT-LINES – THE HARSH FACE OF REALITY

The barrages of concepts no doubt remain embedded with fault lines in the poverty debate. It will continue to be so. Notwithstanding these fault-lines which arise as a result of definition, interpretation, and indicators deployed in the analysis be it objective or subjective perceptions of poverty, the underlining fact is that poverty exists and most be radically addressed if the continent is to be part of the evolving globalise world of this century and beyond. The use of participatory methods has greatly encouraged an epistemology of poverty, which relies on local understanding and perceptions. For example, exposure to domestic violence may be seen as important in one community, dependency on traditional structures in another. What is important is to find common grounds and answers to the existing epidemic. The answers are best provided by critical research on institutional and structural and process issues in national poverty policy that should create enabling government actions to improve the quality of public expenditure and allow the economy to respond to sound macroeconomic management.

Government policies should ensure a new political will and conditions which facilitate 'pro-poor poverty policymaking and positive actions. Some of the possible areas being (i) National development planning, budget allocation and expenditure management addressing the needs of the vulnerable in society; (ii) Government policy towards economically productive sectors; (iii) Approaches towards the social sectors and safety nets; (iv) Restructuring relations among levels of government; (v) Listening to the poor and making them partners in the development process; (vi) An international community responding positively to the genuine aspiration of the vast majority of the disadvantaged in society.

By examining changes from Africa's lost decade, 1980 to 1997, the full gravity of the situation becomes evident. Africa started the period with a very adverse situation. Since it should be easier to improve on a bad situation than a good one, Africa's results over these two decades might have been expected to be better than average, as compared to South Asia for most indicators. So far Africa has not been able to meet up with the rest of the developing world. Instead Africa's relative position has deteriorated. For example, estimates of the number of people with incomes equivalent to less than USA $1 a day in 1987 and 1998. Nearly 300 million Africans – almost half of Africa's total population – were below this poverty line in 1998. Poverty has increased most rapidly in Africa, causing its share of total income poverty to rise sharply over the period. In many countries in Africa, it is not hard to find the opinion that life is in many respects harder now than 20 to 30 years ago.

The harsh reality of the faces of poverty in Africa is depicted in Box 2.

Box 2. The Harsh Face of Poverty in Sub-Saharan Africa {approx. estimate}

- The estimated total population of Africa in 1995 was 580 million.
- Of these 291 million people had average incomes of below USA $1 per day in 1998.
- 124 million of those up to age 30 years were at risk of dying before 40.
- 43 million children were stunted as a result of malnutrition in 1995.
- 205 million were estimated to be without access to health services in 1990-95.
- 249 million were without safe drinking water in 1990-95.
- More than two million infants die annually before reaching their first birthday.
- 139 youths and adults were illiterate in 1995

Source: United Nations Development Programme UNDP, Human Development Report 1998.

There is no doubt that the Africanisation of world poverty has continued in the 1990s, and has probably accelerated, and there is every prospect of a continuation of this trend. It should be recalled that many African countries were far ahead in the late 1950s and early 1960s of most of today's East Asian tigers. Why has this kind of development take place? Could it be attributed to the intensity of colonialism and its legacies in Africa compared to Asian countries? What measures are taken to redress the situation?

LOFTY TARGETS – MISSING LINKS

Following Africa's lost decade – the 1980s and the sudden collapse of the Soviet Union or the end of the Cold War, there emerged a climate of optimism that heavy expenses on weapons of mass destruction would at least be deviated to addressing socially related problems. In the 1990s, world conference and Summit meetings emphasised the urgency of eradicating poverty, enhancing women's participation and promoting democracy and good governance.

Unfortunately, the lofty targets set by national governments and the financial and moral commitments pledge by the international community of reducing poverty have failed in making a dent and significant progress in poverty eradication. The question that comes to mind is how national governments can and the world community tackle poverty in a way that is systematic and sustainable? And how can poverty eradication programmes more effectively impact on the lives of the poor and excluded? The author holds the opinion that the answer may in part lie in linking poverty eradication with democracy promotion – the politics of inclusion, partnership and participation should replace existing policy strategies of exclusion, monolithic, ethnic hegemony lording it over the rest, and, that of individual greed value cultures that pervert the smooth functioning and stability of the society. The dominance of individual greed value culture inhibits government from articulating and aggregating policies that improve the welfare of all. Citizens do not participate in decision-making at all levels of society. The poor, traditionally excluded from political participation, must have a voice in issues that affect their lives and well being to ensure that their needs are adequately addressed. Therefore, an important step in eliminating poverty is empowering the poor and increasing their sphere of influence and decision-making capacity.

Rethinking poverty means a concerted and comprehensive need and focus on making democracy work for all. African countries should go beyond building or reforming the institutions of democracy to ensuring that democracy becomes a real tool for empowerment and participation. The need to make institutions more responsive to the needs of the poor – to make them 'pro-poor' – and to ensure poor people's meaningful participation is as relevant for established democracies, where social exclusion is a pressing problem, as for new democracies.

The politics of dispossessing the disenfranchised of their inalienable rights to existence by the affluent group must stop. This could also be seen from the perspectives that poor countries produce in the main raw materials and agricultural products, suffer persistently in the terms of trade with the industrial lands. Hence people in the developed countries of the poor have most often made the explanations of poverty. But a lesser current explanation runs from the poor countries to the rich. Of these explanations the legacy of colonialism is the most important. Colonial ruler deliberately enforced industrial backwardness for reasons of commercial interest, destroyed self- confidence, created habits of dependency. All this explains the present misfortune of the poor.

What is not explained is why this effect was so diverse and highly adverse in some parts of Africa and Latin America but much less so in other parts of these continents. We can as well equally question for how long this explanation can be made to some and be used as the escape route of mismanagement by the current custodians of political and economic power. Is the legacy of colonialism still valid as a force? Or should we be addressing the afflicting effects of neo-colonialism or 'black colonialism'?

Africa has had at least half-a-century of independence. Even though some will argue that it is a short period compared to the many decades of the independence of the United States and other western countries. What has the continent achieved during this period? Is it the eradication or increasing state of poverty or, the rush to stocking the peoples' wealth in foreign banks by the powers that be? While the causes could be traced to colonialism, the penetrating impact of neo-colonialism cannot be ruled out. How much have the new custodians of power embezzled in the last half-a-century – those bleeding their countries to death – but hiding under the canopy of colonialism.

In Africa any improvement in income is nakedly exposed to the pressures of consumption, and these pressures needless to say, poverty makes infinitely more urgent. The poverty of the poor country denies its people the means for improvement. And when this become available, there are built into structures of poverty, the social and biological forces by which improvement is aborted, the poverty perpetuated. There is a consensus between colonialism and neo-colonialism on ensuring that poverty prevails. That grand coalition has expanded through the imposition of the structural adjustment programme (SAP) by the Bretton Woods Financial conglomerates. Africa needs a programme that can best destroy the infrastructure of poverty, dictatorship and bad governance. Such a programme can only be manufactured through a genuine collaboration between the State, Civil society, the Private or productive sector, and the participation of the international community.

SITUATING CAMEROON: IN THE NAME OF PROGRESS

Because Western Governments are more or less representatives of their citizens, and because gross abuses of state power – such as persecution of minority groups or the innovation of martial law – are rare occurrences in the old democracies, we tend to equate a country's policies with its people. We may as well extend this topic to undemocratic regimes at our peril. When a government is as unrepresentative of its people as is the case in much of the Third World, Cameroon, for example, or when a leader acquires power over a country's legislative, judicial and other institutions, what further the plans of the national government may bear no fruit, or bitter fruits for its people.

From the late 1960s to early 1980s, Cameroon had one of the fastest growing economies in Sub-Saharan Africa. Since the mid 1980s, Cameroon has witnessed a severely contracting economy, ending up with the classification as the most corrupt nation in the world 1998 and 1999, following Transparency International Corruption Perception Index.

Cameroon's economic reversal can be traced to the concentration of government power that allowed privileged individuals and groups to use the government to promote their private interests through a variety of instruments including loans without guarantees, misuse of funds and outright embezzlement of funds and government properties. The government embarked on the ambitious programme of bringing development to the people, especially through the instituted Five Year Development Plans. But the idea of a better economic future soon took a nosedive as projects to enhance the quality of livelihood for the vast majority of the people turned into grandiose enterprises without concern for the economic viability and the future of the common people. Individual greed value culture replaced the collective need interest culture. Those in authority were independently pursuing their interests. The populace in Cameroon has never played any important part in formulating the State's plans and in shaping their personal goals. The populace was used to enhance the functioning of the monolithic party structure that dominated the political landscape of the country from 1966 to 1990. As a result, the national plan for the better economy collapsed and poverty escalated to heights never known in the country.

In the remote rural parts of Cameroon, the good times cannot come when the national economy is depressed, the national debt growing, imported commodity prices are high and exported raw materials low, and when quality management is non-existent; basic services essential to the livelihood of the people are not available. The larger part of the country remain enclave to the extent that villages can neither get their produce to markets, of if they do, transportation costs are so high that these prevents them from bringing their produce to a large consumer public.

Another effect of the national crisis leading to the state of poverty, which is so apparent, is the issue of good governance, transparency and ethnic harmony. The absence of these bleeds the nation into disintegration and confusion, creating a political time bomb ready to explode any moment from now. Studies show that more than fifty percent of the population live under the basic poverty line. Government is seen to be administered by the Bretton Woods conglomerates rather than by the elected people of the country. The Structural Adjustment Programme has failed to produce the required result. Instead, it has heightened the state of social discord and poverty in society. The reason here is simple. SAP was not drawn up in consultation with the people. It is imposed on them. Instead of the policy improving on the livelihood of the suffering masses, it has only enriched the few. A few cases will illustrate the state of dehumanising the human being following the introduction of SAP in Cameroon. To begin with, for twenty years, there has been no salary increase in the country. Rather, during this period the people have been subjected to a 70 percent reduction in salary; a hundred percent devaluation of the CFA franc; employment stop: and workers forced into early retirement. In the majority of case, retirement benefits not paid to the retrenched workers. Social and other basic needs services are no longer available to the people.

A foreign-imported strategic policy has only worked to the detriment of the poor. No matter the good intention of such imported policy strategies like SAP, they will always break down because the institutional framework and structures including the good will and skills required to maintain and see through the smooth implementation of the policies are not available. Even if there are present, the governance system perturbs the true realisation of the intended policies. Thus the millions received from donor agencies and the international community has had little impact in moving the country forward but feed into the dreams of the ruling elite. The existence of 'have-money-must-lend' constitutes one of the main causes of the sad state of economic affairs in Cameroon. Because they are in league with spend-drift politicians in Cameroon, a country rich in both natural and human resources is classified as 'a highly indebted poor country. The standard of living has fallen far below the pre-debt era. The leaders have mortgaged the future of present and future generations.

International financing that is given to unrepresentative governments or governments where the rule of law is replaced by the rule of force may harm more than the national economy; it may harm large numbers of people, since allocated monies are never put into projects that enhance the quality of life of the vast majority of the population. The leaders in partnership with external financial institutions put in place an agenda of marginalisation. This explains why poverty is so widespread in Cameroon.

THE FAILED POOR

An outstanding cause of poverty and poor growth in Cameroon should be attributed to government failure. Existing political systems have contributed to economic stagnation, exclusion, leading to abject poverty like the slave trade; governments now use the politics of exclusion to enslave the population. The spirit of optimism and aspiration ushered on the eve of independence and reunification in 1961 had disappeared by the mid 1980s. The competence of the government largely eroded by both major and petty corruption, democracy abandoned in favour of monolithic one-party system state; and accountability greatly undermined by reliance on ethnic hegemony

Ake (1994:15) points out that 'to inherent the colonial state rather than transforming it in accordance with the democratic aspirations of the nationalist movement. Inevitably they went out with their fellows and became repressive. It was not the military that caused military rule in Africa, it was the character of politicians and the nature of politics practiced iced in the continent. Africa leaders used traditional institutions and notions of consensus to justify one-party systems without drawing attention to the traditional process of consultation and participation which produced consensus.'

Box 3.

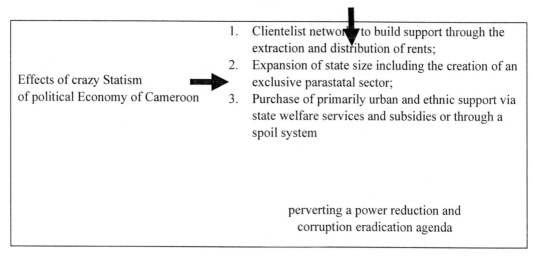

It is not astonishing to note that since independence the policy agenda of the political hierarchy has been one of the imposition of control from top rather than from the mobilisation of support from below; exclusion instead of inclusion, ethnic harmony and national integration instead of ethnic hegemony and supremacy has prevailed because the predominant or institutionalised relationship between Cameroon rulers and their citizens does not evolve on the same platform. It evolves on much strained platform that what existed between the colonial masters and their subjects. Personality cultism takes control over popular will and participatory development process. Adedeji (1993:8) catalogue this as the 'personalisation and monopolisation of power' in leading to a 'marginalisation process which has been further aggravated severely by SAP. The cumulative effect is a state set apart from its society in which 80 percent of the population is in the margin.

The underlying reality and argument is that elites in Cameroon pretend to absorb the Western Development transformation paradigm construed on western values and experience. This is what marginalizes the population since the paradigm 'takes hardly any interest in Cameroon and its culture. The result is their total self-alienation. Thus Cameroon needs a new development paradigm – improving the prospects of putting back development into the hands of the people – especially the grassroots population without of course, closing the window of opportunity necessary for sustainable development.

Since reunification and the establishment of unitary state in 1972, the dominant form of political economy became a crony statism consisting of a number of inter-related characteristics as depicted in Box 3.

To a large extent the ruling class in Cameroon has been enemies of progress. The siphoning of funds is not carried out by the 'buy and sell' class but by those in top hierarchical positions of the administrative set-up. This attitude enhances the problem posed by the difficulty of crystallising a development agenda that expresses the aspiration of the people and can therefore elicit their support. The policy of the ruling class during the past two decades has been one holding back poverty reduction in several ways but propelling all the basic tenets of corruption. To begin with, the state has failed to deliver growth; rather, it has delivered stagnation and decline. Growth has not been part of its agenda; at the best it has failed to provide the stable framework it requires. Second, the state has not addressed the needs of the poor, which has been manifested in various ways, such as poor quality management and skewed service delivery (see Callaghy 1991). Third, the leaders believe in society serving them and vice versa.

Rethinking poverty in Cameroon highlights the fact that the State has promoted stagnation and decline, instead of growth and equitable wealth sharing, as a result of:

- State collapse – the absence of democratic governance and poor quality management. There has been a privatisation of the administration;
- The rise of corruption enhanced by ethnic hegemony – the criminalisation of politics;
- Absence of a stable legal and institutional framework for economic activity – i.e. the rule of force and ethnic hegemony replacing the rule of law and ethnic harmony;
- Implementation of controlled economy policies that were amenable to rent seeking and detrimental to growth;
- Adoption of ad hoc instead of consistent and comprehensive short, medium and long-term development policy agenda. The abandonment of the five years development plans has been detrimental to a state of balanced and short term development process in the country. What is seen is favoured development in certain areas which further fans all kinds of disintegrating tendencies and promoting corruption.

Over the years there has been a lack of minimum function of the State providing a legal and institutional framework to facilitate the economic life of the population; the rule of force has replaced the rule of law and with the absence of the rule of law, creates a state of insecurity to both life and property. Insecurity scares potential investors. In short, 'government as is known in the West does not exist in Africa. One expects at a minimum a government to be responsive to the basic needs of the people, or at least to perform some services for its people. But even this most basic requirements for government is lacking in Africa (Ayittey 1998:150)

Cameroonians are exposed to all sorts of treatment internally and externally as a result of the absence of a functional democratic governance system. Resources for the Heavily Indebted Poor Countries initiative [HIPC] do not to reach the target audiences. As noted by Fombe (2002:7) many citizens are still astonished by the feet dragging over the use of such a colossal sum of money {CFA 71 billion} for the purpose for which it is meant. Certainly no palpable change has been noticed in the lives of Cameroonians. It may be too late if speedy measures are not taken to get the projects going and efficiently. Is the government out for the interest of poor or addressing the needs of the rich? Is the amount kept to be embezzled or what?

PRIVATISATION OF ADMINISTRATION AND CORRUPTION

Poverty has many facets. It has been argued that the State has deep roots in the country. It equally remains true that public administration and institutions in the country are indeed weak and captive due to the rhizome-like nature of the State and the organisation of public power. Ethnic hegemony and political party interference has rendered the administrative set up weak and corrupt. The poor pay the price. With the State bureaucracy functioning as the administrative wing of the governing party or as an extended master voice of an ethnic group, it gets exposed to all sorts of influences and spoils systems. The erosion of administration – existence of institutional weaknesses and other administrative shortcomings, in combination with an ongoing economic crisis remain particularly disastrous for the country. In this respect, the needs of the poor cannot be adequately addressed. Rather it gets worse.

Corruption is bad for both growth and poverty reduction in several ways. First it is the equivalent of directly or indirectly drawing resources from the poor to the rich. Second, high-level corruption erodes the good will of the population, the business community, and the donors, encouraging exist. Third, corruption diverts the attention of state employees and the activities of the state away from the tasks that need to be undertaken to achieve growth, especially if it is to be of a pro-poor variety. Fourth, the abuse of State power for personal enrichment is so wide spread in Cameroon as to constitute a 'Criminalisation of the State', (Bayart et al (eds.) 1999). The escalating nature of abject poverty in the country is a reflection of the weakening of State control and not only the ability of the state to provide the basic needs of the masses, but also its ineffectiveness in controlling and coordinating its excessive interventionist programmes or policies.

However, measures so far taken by the government following pressure from the Bretton Woods Financial Conglomerates include that of establishing a National Programme on Good Governance as conditionality for further funding of activities in the country. A recent report of the National Programme on Good Governance notes that 'at the economic level, the serious crisis the country experienced for nearly a decade had serious consequences on the economic and social fabric. It was especially reflected through {i} drastic drop in the incomes of the state, enterprises and households, and a drop in agricultural income; {ii} the closing down of many enterprises and essential infrastructures; {iii} the drop in the supply of basic social services and essential infrastructures; {iv} the cut in the salaries of State employees and the reduction of private sector salaries. In this context, the living conditions of the population deteriorated considerably and the phenomenon of poverty spread wider and worsened. Similarly, deviant behaviours including the scourge of corruption increased.

The plight of the disadvantaged group in Cameroon has to be properly addressed not only in this period of election and canvassing for votes, but above all, in the years ahead. Importantly here is to incorporate the vulnerable group. The poor themselves certainly have the will and motivation to defeat their poverty. Anyone who has ever set foot in a slum area in Douala, Yaoundé, a poor village or shanty-towns knows what ingenuity; skill and effort go into the daily struggle to survive. Experience shows that the successful grass-roots development programmes are those, which respond to national needs through local action and involve both men and women, rich and poor. It is on this that the State should draw valuable lessons, reconstruct the functioning of the administration and tailor its new development agenda for the 21st century.

GENDER FACTOR – TOWARD EMPOWERMENT

The position of the lower income groups in Cameroon has severely deteriorated over the past decades owing to [a] the failed state as a result of the policies pursued by the government; [b] the international economic developments, including a high international debt; [c] the state of increased poverty leading to malnutrition and high child mortality rates. In this regard, gender inequity in Cameroon operates alongside conditions of dare poverty and ill health.

Turning to the 1998 Poverty Status Report, Gender Growth and Poverty reduction in Africa, there are synergies between positive outcomes for women's well being and pro-poor growth. Hence the fight against poverty requires a concerted effort to understand the cultural mechanisms that create uncertainties and dependency. Unequal relationship between women and men create high levels of dependency and low-levels of self-esteem among women who lack the power to make decisions as well as constrained the numerous cultural taboos. The female gender form more than fifty percent of the total population of Cameroon estimated at 15-16 million. There has been no censor since 1987 and the figures were highly contested. The results of the census conducted in 2005 are still awaited. Must it take two years to have a preliminary result given that 2007 is election year in Cameroon for parliamentary and municipal elections? Women constitute an extremely important development factor in the country, but are always sidelined and marginalized in all aspects concerning decision-making, representation both in the local and legislative assembly; posts within the administrative set-up and in government. A country cannot develop when more than half of its population is excluded from the decision -making organs of the country; or go to bed hungry in the midst of plenty; have no access to education and yet bear the blunt of household activities.

Thus education, healthcare and balanced population growth, with special attention to the status of women are the keys to modern development. They also form a basis for the elimination of poverty and protection of the environment, as well as giving development a dimensional face. Indeed, African poverty is deeply embedded in social attitudes and structures, and female poverty is manifested according to cultural context more than male poverty – 'they are less able to turn labour into income, income into choice and choice into personnel well being (Whitehead et all. 1999). Some of the obstacles confronting and imprisoning women within the poverty brackets include, see Box 4.

Box 4. Obstacles confronting and Imprisoning Women within the Poverty Brackets

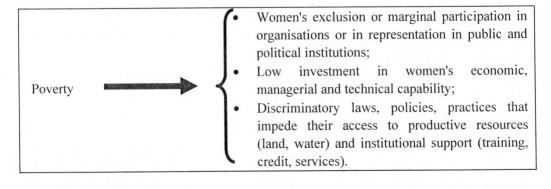

Poverty
- Women's exclusion or marginal participation in organisations or in representation in public and political institutions;
- Low investment in women's economic, managerial and technical capability;
- Discriminatory laws, policies, practices that impede their access to productive resources (land, water) and institutional support (training, credit, services).

Reversing this negative attitude calls for activities and policies focusing on empowering women - policies and action plans designed to alleviate the conditions of poverty as well as putting in place measures increasing the capacity of women in all aspects of governance and development. This involves articulating as well as promoting a systematic strategy directed at:

Building and empowering women's organisation and enhancing their participation in the mainstream policy and decision-making bodies:

- Eliminating legislative administrative, socio-economic, cultural and attitudinal barriers to women's access to assets, land, technology and capital;
- Putting in place the necessary support mechanisms that will encourage men to be more responsive to the changes, to cope with their new responsibilities;
- Improving on the level and skills and productivity of the female gender [rural and urban] through investment in basic education, literacy skill acquisition and other related training programmes.

Box 5.

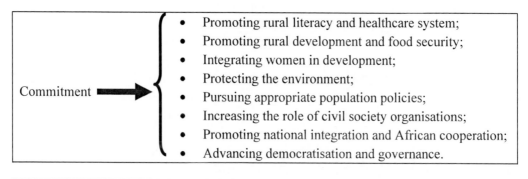

Commitment →
- Promoting rural literacy and healthcare system;
- Promoting rural development and food security;
- Integrating women in development;
- Protecting the environment;
- Pursuing appropriate population policies;
- Increasing the role of civil society organisations;
- Promoting national integration and African cooperation;
- Advancing democratisation and governance.

Action or Policy →
- Political reforms, concentrating on good governance and democracy;
- Economic policy;
- Human resources development;
- Creating an enabling environment for the private sector, with increasing attention to the quality of financial intermediation practices and the role of the informal sector;
- Protection of the environment;
- The integration of women and rural communities in development;
- The participating of civil society organisations in development;
- Strengthen Regional Corporation;
- Accepting people of different cultures and diversities as human beings.

Rethinking poverty and development thus imply a number of inter-related commitments, political will and comprehensive actions. See Box 5 on commitments and actions on policy.

The underlying factor and effort is the formulation and implementation of reform policies and programmes especially by African countries and, of course, the need to receive the blessings and backing of the industrial nations and the international community. A further vital input factor for Africa to sustain any of the necessary investments in education and other infrastructures require curbing, at least, four fundamental development challenges, namely:

- Ending extensive arm conflicts;
- Reversing the HIV/AIDS pandemic;
- Reducing or controlling fertility rates;
- Institutionalising a democratic governance system that is accountable, transparent, credible, and efficient with a functional capacity to serve the people;
- Creating a sense of developmental awareness in the society.

Armed conflicts have intensified expenditures on weapons of arm destruction. In many countries the military budget ranks highest of all government expenditures. That trend has to be redressed. Furthermore, ongoing conflicts in the region have caused as well as contributed to massive human and economic devastation. At least, one African in five lives in a country severely disrupted by conflicts and wars. These conflicts are often caused by bad governance system that leads to the exclusion of the people in the development process. It is estimated that one million people died between 1990 and 1994 because of conflict. In 1998 more that 20 million Africans were either refugees or displaced. Restoring democratic governance, peace and stability in the continent is thus an urgent priority for poverty eradication and development.

Presently, the continent is hardest hit by the HIV/AIDS pandemic. Africa is host to the largest number of AIDS patents in the world. The hardest affected age group being children and those in the productive age. In relation to this are other killer diseases, like malaria which cure has yet to found. By killing people in their most productive years, the pandemic is destroying the social and economic fabric of nations. Reversing hard working human development gains, replacing education and health sectors staff lost to AIDS and other related diseases, providing education to AIDS orphans, and integrating AIDS education into school curricula are urgent challenges, unplanned rapid population growth consistently frustrates efforts to achieve universal primary education and other development activities in the society.

Given the development challenges facing African countries and in light of widespread failure of current policy approaches in all sectors to deliver the desired results, the respective governments must respond decisively, urgently, and clearly. This is best done when there is functional democratic governance system; a government that sticks to the basic tenets of democracy; one that respond to the aspirations of the people; that serves the people and not for it to be served by the people. The wind of democratisation has yet to reach the shores of the African coastline and implant itself within the fabric of the society.

To move forward, a number of comprehensive policy priority measures or dimensions must be fashioned out by the respective governments in respect of and bearing in mind that:

- Creating a concerted and integrated framework for reform necessitates bold policies, which must be sustained over time and implemented in broad unionism or partnership with civil society;
- In view of the continents diversity of contexts, the process of identifying strategic priorities will have to be country specific and even local / rural specific;
- In order to make significant strides in all national development activities, this can only be achieve and sustained only where efforts are underpinned by a genuine commitment undertaken by clearly sets of guiding principles, visions, focus and human-face oriented;
- Designing investment activities must take place and require fundamentally changes in managing finances transparently, accountably and efficiently.

Human resources development remains primordial in the eradication of poverty. It must be recognised and appreciated that without equitable, high-quality and efficient educational systems, Africa cannot meet the development challenges and changes of the 21st century. Underlying all these changes and challenges is the issue of democratic governance that should contribute to development. Political institutions are important source of incentives (positive or negative). Political institutions can either become a vehicle to mediate and manage conflict, or, quite often, a source of conflict or stalemate them. But without the political will things cannot move forward as desired. Only through sustained development can poverty be adequately eradicated and contained.

There are more challenges ahead, and bigger ones. But as the continent looks forward the voices of the poor must be the compass. Yet time is not on our side and is short. But this generation has a serious obligation. It must be the first to look ahead and forge a new code of ethics and conduct – of redressing the poverty pandemic in an ever shrinking and more complicated and connected planet. It is imperative for African countries to hit hard at poverty without which there can be no stable and peaceful continent. Future generations of Africa will inherit the continent we create today. The future of future generations is being shaped by the decisions we make now.

A GROWING PRESENCE OF CSOS

Development is no longer a state prerogative. The dominant role played by the state has not brought forth the expected results. New approaches are needed. And in searching for new solutions to the underdevelopment and poverty crisis of the continent other stakeholders should be incorporated – for example, the active participation of civil society organisations [CSOs] to highly learned academic groupings. The advantages of CSOs over the mainstream development institutions in fostering development and eradicating poverty at the local and national levels remain imperative and in advancing the politics and strategy of inclusion. CSOs remain an important vehicle for development. Their resources and capacity should be adequately tapped particularly in advancing the course of:

- Women's empowerment;
- Agricultural development and healthcare;

- The democratisation process;
- Conflict management and résolutions;
- Advocacy and bridge building roles.
- Knowledge acquisition and skill development;
- Self-awareness and self-confidence;
- Perspective change and behaviour change.

Experience shows that the successful grassroots development programmes are those, which respond to national needs through local action and involve both men and women, rich and poor. For national policy to succeed, effective and appropriate services must be delivered locally and at family level. Even more important, families and communities must be involved in the policy-making and management process. There is considerable scepticism today about the ability of government's ability to involve communities in decision-making, although in most countries this has scarcely been given a fair trial. Where governments are committed the experience has certainly been that services such as education, healthcare, family planning, agricultural extension and even housing can be delivered with community cooperation.

Civil society has been at the forefront on the issue of people and the environment. Leonard {1989:6} notes that the interaction of poverty and environmental destruction sets off a downward spiral of ecological deterioration that threatens the physical security, economic well-being and health of many of the world's poorest people.' The human factors responsible for this degradation are becoming increasingly apparent. High rates of population growth destroy the land and our future capacity to respond to the world's needs. Environmental problems are not new. Human societies have long had a major impact on their environment. Rapid population growth and growing demand for better quality of livelihood puts greater pressure on the environment. Hence the urgent need for conservation and protection for the benefits of present and future generations.

Human tendency to exploit resources as if it were an inexhaustible resource has repeatedly led to disaster, sometimes leading to the loss of entire human communities. However, the poor and vulnerable are always held responsible for the depletion of the ecosystem, leaving the big forest exploiters and large industries responsible for the depletion of the ozone layer untouched, since this group of persons wield enormous economic and political power and can easily influence policy-makers.

However, the process leading to over-exploitation and environmental degradation are intimately linked to broader political and socio-economic processes, which themselves are part of a national and global political economy. Thus it is widely recognised that the causes of most environmental problems are closely related to the generation and distribution of wealth, knowledge, and power, and to patterns of energy consumption, industrialisation, population growth, affluence and poverty. What is fundamental is the issue of poverty particularly on the part of the poor who are always marginalized and deprived from all social amenities and other basic needs.

To ensure ecosystem sustainability, to cure poverty, heal the poor visionary leadership is imperative. And this also implies the following policy measures and actions:

- Advancing democratisation and governance and curbing all forms of corruption;
- Integrating and empowering women in development;

- Protecting the environment;
- Pursuing appropriate population policies;
- Promoting rural development and food security;
- Increasing the role of NGOs as well as promoting partnership between various stakeholders, state, civil society organisations, the productive sector and the international community;
- Ensuring a positive international community responses to the aspiration and development efforts of the people in Africa / Third World in general

The most fundamental environmental management constraint the country/world faces is not lack of resources, but lack of leadership and management skills. Natural resources in Cameroon and other parts of the world are under great pressure. For example, many states in Africa are classified as water-scarce or water-stressed. Forests are disappearing at a rate of 100000 square kilometres per year. Nearly 70 percent of the world's fisheries are over exploited. Soil degradation affects many millions in Africa. Millions more of rural people are at risk from desertification and dry land degradation. The Sahara desert is fast expanding its borders ????

Natural and man-induced disasters remain high. The poor are most affected, as they are forced to live in vulnerable areas not fit for human habitat. Almost as shocking as these different environment horrors are, is our abysmal ignorance of what we are doing to the ecosystem. Key contributions are needed to help build a more sustainable ecosystem and have eradicating poverty. The overarching concern is to help the state make the policy and institutional choices that benefit poor people most and facilitate equitable and sustainable growth. The international community and in particular, the Bretton Woods Financial Conglomerates and other donor agencies/nations should facilitate the means of provide the necessary funds and give greater priority to the issue of promoting good environmental governance and democracy in most developing countries in Africa. They equally stand a good chance of promoting partnership and participatory actions focused in addressing the issues of poverty and environmental degradation. The need to support the sustainable management of natural resources – land, water, forests – to enhance poor people's livelihood today and in the future should take prominent place in their action plans for a better world. Empowerment of the poor and society in general remains the best hope for improving the quality livelihood of the vast majority of the population currently lavishing in abject poverty and misery.

CONCLUSION AND RECOMMENDATIONS

Drawing together the main-strands of the foregoing discussion in order to establish how the ever-increasing contact with the rest of the world has affected transformation of hierarchical relations and, how it has exaggerated the unequal distribution of wealth, it is clear that poverty stands as a major impediment in the way of development in the region. The structure of the political system and form of governance in African states facilitated the development of an ever more apparent discrepancy between rank and class, on the one hand, and some socio-political position and wealth on the other.

This tendency accelerated not only during the colonial but also in post-colonial era. Moreover, socio-economic status was increasingly manifested as an independent dimension of inequality, especially with the rise of a category of educated and economically oriented people who now replaced the departed colonial masters, labelled 'been to's' or 'Oxbridge's' and the new men from the 1960s onwards dominated the emerging political, administrative, economic and social landscape of the new nation. Today, market forces have, therefore, increasingly influenced the nature of inequality in the African society.

In the pursuit of an explanation of the concentration of wealth in a small number of persons, we discovered that the newly acquired power, wealth and position in the public institutions encouraged the privatisation and ethnicisation of public offices enabling a few ethnic constellations and minorities to enter the spiral of an exceptionally rapid economic growth. Some of these ethnic groups judiciously used the windows of opportunity created by the new political dispensation to consolidate their position with the society. Yet even within the rank and file of such group's politically privileged factions lies the irony of a vast bastion of poor, and poverty smells.

For two decades, this ethnic group has controlled the realm of power. There emerged thus an elite group within the ethnic hegemony that has hijack the political, military and bureaucratic power but still unable to manage the economy. Having dominance in the political, administrative and military sphere enhances their economic power through ill-gotten wealth, thus reflecting the fact that though the Cameroon society or any other African country has, however deeply been penetrated by market forces; the control over state policies and resources by a particular ethnic group has proved to be much more important than market-based entrepreneurial activities.

The acceleration of socio-economic inequality since Cameroon's independence, and especially since 1982, is a factor of peculiar development which has only plunged the country into the status of the most corrupt and highly indebted poor country in spite of its rich and vast natural resources potential. Before 1980s, Cameroon was ranked as one of Africa's success story in terms of economic growth. Most obviously, the shift from national government to tribal or ethnic government clearly involved a shift in the constitution of the ruling class. And most members of the inner circles of the ruling party are only used as window dressings, wielding no political power of significance. Power lies within the inner ethnic circles of the governing party. Furthermore, the resources, accumulated in the political centre are conditioned by different factors and used in very different ways in different historical contexts. Similarly, the persistence of a large majority of poor is not only a superficial reality and matter of historical continuity. To a large extent, the majority of the poor are always excluded from the flow of distributive resources; they are made to content with the resources of production – i.e. supplying the needed labour for producing the wealth of the nation but never benefiting from it. This explains why there is an ever-increasing army of the poor in the country several decades after independence.

There are several major interdependencies underlying the hierarchical politico-administrative relationships and the rapid socio-economic stratification of the Cameroon society. Generally, those who control the realm of power in the newly independent states in Africa, apply all kinds of administrative, political and economic forces and machineries to marginalize those who are outside. Factors, which exacerbate this trend, are readily apparent in the country. The institutionalisation of the monolithic one party system in mid 1960s made things even worse. The return to political party pluralism has not altered the status quo. Most

African countries continue to operate within the dictates of one party system under the disguise of political pluralism.

The critical fact of recent and modern times is the rise of the State and the consolidation of control through military means (Satzman 1981:731) or through an ethnic cult. In reality, the political economy of Cameroon rests and springs from the western Province not from the ethnic group controlling the administrative and political machinery. These two divergent poles of forces foster socio-economic stratification. Inequality is intrinsic in the society due to the impasse existing between the economic and political powerful groups – one group in government: the other out of government. Second, the ruling ethnic elite occupy and retain almost all senior political, bureaucratic and military positions but unable to trigger the kind of economic development needed to move the society forward Incidentally, 'the concept of elite cannot be a substitute for the concept of class {Magubane 1976:194}; and that in post-colonial Africa, there do not exist a class that could be described as an African capitalist class or bourgeois. The evolving Africa elite populated the new government institutions and, because of the externally generated capitalist policies, could take advantage of a variety of career opportunities

Magubane also argues that the social stratum of salaried elites, which is not the owner of the means of production, faces a cruel paradox. It cannot ensure its privileged material position as long as it serves foreign monopolies {op cit. 192} and political interests. Accordingly most of the post-colonial political-economic history of Africa has been concerned with the failure of African elite interests to manoeuvre in this highly problematic environment. And the poor continue to suffer: just as the ruling elite continues their exploitation of the poor and the nation.

Although there is considerable antagonism between those who prosper and those who remain poor, the growing stratification in Cameroon has not yet manifested itself in any social protest or ideological expressions of an emerging class-consciousness. In view of the extremely skewed distribution of essential productive resources, it is inadequate to attribute the absence of political protest to the fact that there has always been an unequal distribution of wealth in the country. The time bomb for protest will be triggered by political factors, which embody significant control measures that would most likely be activated in the event of any attempt to mobilise the poor politically. Whether the June 23rd 2002 twin elections – Council and Parliamentary – will trigger such a move remain unknown. It is a question of 'wait and see' especially with the rigging machinery put in place by the ruling government well ahead of the elections.

In respect of policy, it should be noted that participatory processes could facilitate social development, specifically the ability of a society to reconcile competing interests in a non-violent, non-coercive fashion. They do so by helping to create a sense of community and trust or in academic parlance, by building social capital.

Africa as a whole is falling behind the rest of the world in the prevention of poverty, and in some respects the problem is getting worse. The proportion of global poverty attributable to Africa is rising, and the likelihood is this will continue unless there are radical and urgent changes to policies and performance. The manifestations of poverty blight the lives of many millions of Africans, causing huge suffering and diminishing the possibilities of progress. Although poor performance in reducing poverty has many causes, analysts agree that action is needed on both the domestic policy and external assistance fronts. Judging from the analysis, at least five main conclusions about poverty from the perspectives of the poor can be drawn, see Box 6.

Rethinking Poverty simply implies a critical alternative view and approach to development. The process of development should be one of the turning corners from bleak prospects to a hopeful future. Democracy, though still fragile in the region, has during the past couple of years taken some concrete roots. With democratic governance gaining more and more significant grounds, accompanied by positive economic growth and relief measures for the poor and vulnerable groups, backed with more political freedoms and the participation of the masses in the development process, a brighter future could be attained by for all.

We are confronted with poverty, which seems to be institutionalised. Definitions abound and have been advanced. But the question remains, is there a right answer to the issues of poverty? Obviously 'no' single definition can be applied or taken to be correct. But certainly we have to build on whatever simplification that exists. To begin with, there is no philosophical disagreement with the statement that poverty needs to be understood first and foremost as a problem at the individual rather than the household level. Of course, it has moved from the individual level to the national and eventually is now a global problem. Second, many researchers or students of the discipline would include income obtained from common property and state provides commodities, especially social welfare payments, though not always health and education provision. Third, relative poverty and relative deprivation are accepted as relevant, at least in theory. Fourth there is little dissent from the view that people move in and out of poverty, and that seasonal, cyclical or stochastic shocks are important.

Beyond these areas or agreement, there are different views on whether assets should be counted in a poverty matrix, on the importance of vulnerability, and on the relative prioritisation of monetary and non-monetary variables. Some indicators are inherently more quantifiable than others, and more decomposable, in the sense that they can be subjected to statistical manipulation. The bottom line of all this is that poverty is a reality and a serious problem in Africa as well as in many parts of the world which must be quickly addressed to ensure the sustainability of Planet Earth for present and future generations. Finally, measuring poverty is not the same as understanding why it occurs. Serious interventions need to tackle causes not symptoms.

Box 6. Perspective of the Poor

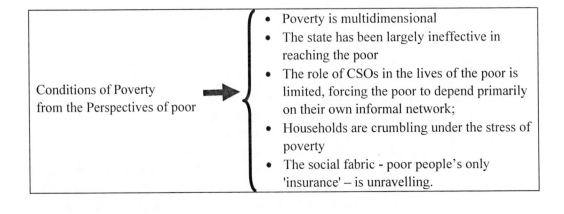

| Conditions of Poverty from the Perspectives of poor | • Poverty is multidimensional
• The state has been largely ineffective in reaching the poor
• The role of CSOs in the lives of the poor is limited, forcing the poor to depend primarily on their own informal network;
• Households are crumbling under the stress of poverty
• The social fabric - poor people's only 'insurance' – is unravelling. |

It is clear that the dimensions of poverty include [a] lack of opportunity which leads to low levels of consumption and income; [b] low capabilities and this leads to no improvement in health and education indicators especially amongst a particular socio-economic group; [c] low level of security, as most of the vulnerable groups are exposed to risks of various kinds, income shocks etc; and [d] empowerment being the capability of poor people and other excluded groups to participate in, negotiate with, change, and hold accountable institutions that affect their well-being.

These situations call for priority action areas by the public sector (State) which should include amongst others the following measures; {i} improvement in governance, including public sector financial management; [ii] appropriate sect oral policies and programmes; [iii] macro and structural policies to support sustainable growth in which the poor participate; [iv] realistic costing and appropriate levels of funding for the major programme; [v] the need for the people to seriously take development into their hands by mobilising domestic resources, human, financial and natural and [vi] ensuring a valuable and reliable monitoring and evaluation system – accountability and transparency should be watch word or slogan underlying policies to address the current state of poverty and underdevelopment in Africa.

1. Need-oriented (material and non-material)
2. Endogenous {coming from within a society};
3. Self-reliant {in terms of human, natural and cultural resources};
4. Ecologically sound, i.e. ensuring the sustainability of the environment;
5. Based on structural transformation (of economy, society, gender, power relations;
6. Construed on the agenda of the politics of inclusion, partnership, participation, responsibility and equitable wealth-sharing;
7. Adopt emerging technologies within the framework of encouraging endogenous technological capacity and know-how;
8. Making significant efforts to diversify the economy;
9. Encouraging and providing resources for civil society organisations, participatory role in the economic take-off in all countries in the region;
10. Placing women and the vulnerable group on the plus side of the development continuum – in short, empowering the weak especially women;
11. In designing poverty – related programmes, it is essential and most proper to respect the vision of poverty articulated by the poor people themselves – follow Chambers slogan of 'putting the rich last and the poor first – remain a significant sign post approach on rethinking poverty.
12. To mitigate adverse effects of SAP on the poor and vulnerable groups, programmes have to include the phasing of price adjustments and decontrol measures, as well as of public sector retrenchment. This should also include specific policies aimed directly at improving the terms of trade for agricultural and other products, in order to benefit the majority of the poor who live in rural areas. Such measures or programmes should incorporate social safety nets measures for the poor, income transfer, public works and welfare programmes;
13. The need to articulate and aggregate policy strategies to improve efficiency, transparency and accountability in public management.

Box 7. Some Steps toward achieving the Goals of poverty eradication

- Promote fast, sustainable growth that benefits the poor and reduces inequality;
- Strengthen participation of poor people in political processes and local decision-making;
- Reduce vulnerability to economic shocks, natural disasters, ill health, and violence;
- Invest in people through education, healthcare, and basic social services;
- Promote gender equity and eliminate other forms of social exclusion;
- Forge effective partnerships between civil society, governments, and international agencies;
- Encourage public discussion of the goals and the means of achieving them.

Source: World Bank {2002} Perspective on Development. Washington D.C. USA.

The last word is to adopt proactive measures toward achieving the goals of eradicating poverty which should include issues depicted in Box 7.

REFERENCES

Adedeji, Adebayo (1993) 'Marginalisation and Marginality' in Adebayo Adedeji (ed.) *African Within the World.* Beyond Displacement and Dependence, Zed Books, London.

Ake, Claude (1994) 'The Marginalisation of Africa' Note on a Productive Confusion,' *Paper prepared for the Council on Foreign Relations, African Studies Seminar, 18* February 1994, New York.

Ayittey, George B. N. (1998) *Africa in Chaos. Macmillan Publishing House,* Basingstoke, UK.

Callagry, Thomas M. (19941) 'Lost Between State and Market: The Politics of Economic Adjustment in Ghana, Zambia and Nigeria', in Joan Nelson (ed) *Economic Crisis and Policy Choice.* The Politics of Adjustment in the Third World, American University Press, pp 257-70.

Cameroon Government (2001) National Programme on Governance. *Comprehensive Strategy for the Implementation of the National Programme on Governance and The Fight Against Corruption.* Yaoundé.

Carney, Diana (1999) *Approaches to Sustainable Livelihoods for the Rural Poor,* (ODI Poverty Briefing Paper), UK

Fombe, George (2002) *'Poverty Alleviation: Making Hay' Cameroon Tribune,* 2 April 2002, Sopecam, Yaoundé, Cameroon.

Forje. John W. (Forthcoming) *Cameroon Without Poverty.* (Dove Publishers, Yaoundé – Cameroon.

Forje, John W. (Forthcoming) *Signs of Despair or Hope.* Dove publishers, Yaoundé - Cameroon.

Bayart, Jean-Francois, I. Stephen and Beatrice Hibou (eds.) 1999. *The Criminalisation of the State in Africa,* James Curry, Oxford, UK

Kabeer, Naila and Ann Whitehead (1999) 'From Uncertainty to Risk Poverty, Growth and Gender in the Rural African Context', *Background paper* 5, World Bank.

Klugman, Jeni (ed.) 2001 *A Source Book for Poverty Reduction.* Washington, D.C.? World Bank.

Magubane, B. (1976) The Evolution of the Class structures in Africa' in P.C. W. Gutkind and I. Wallestain (eds.) 1976 *The Political Economy of Contemporary Africa,* Sage Publications, London.

Schumacher, E.F. (1973) *Small is Beautiful. Economics as if People Mattered.* New York, Harper and Row.

World Development Report, 2000/2001, World Bank USA.

Chapter 4

CONSOLIDATING DEMOCRATIC GOVERNANCE AND QUALITY MANAGEMENT IN SOUTH AFRICA: CHALLENGES AND FUTURE PROSPECTS*

ABSTRACT

Politics and governance cannot be completely value free. No government can function efficiently and effectively without a set of directives that will steer it in the direction which society expects it to move. Although governments have different cultural, political, and administrative environments, they often confront similar democratic, ethical challenges and responses in their ethics management show common characteristics. How are democratic governance and quality management in South Africa explained and what can be conjectured about the challenges as future prospects?

This paper looks at the salient features of the political economy of the rainbow Nation viz the intense internal constraints in light of the growing fragmentation that plagues the continent: poor leadership, poor performance in economic development, political instability, corruption, genocides and the growing politics of divide and rule between ethnic communities, and social classes.

What is it that has brought South Africa to it current status? What must be done to consolidate its democratisation and quality management prospects? What factors internal and external that impact in slowing or accelerating the process of consolidating democratic governance form a decade after the collapse of the apartheid system? Is South Africa setting a course for the rest of Africa to follow? What are the challenges and future prospects?

The paper argues for a dedicated effort in consolidating the democratic process through the realm of expanding the 'politics of inclusion, partnership, responsibility and equitable sharing of the wealth of the nation" among the key actors. To sustain and improve on its newly won democratic freedom, the politics of "exclusion" must be avoided, rejected and buried. It is only through reconciliation, consensus and ensuring the reign of and values of human dignity and solidarity that the country can best consolidate the pursuit of social justice and quality livelihood for all.

---

* Paper Prepared for Presentation at the Annual Conference The South African Association of Public and Administrative, 24-27 November 2004, University of Western Cape, South Africa.

INTRODUCTION: BRIDGING THE DIVIDE

"The challenges facing South Africa is to instil in the consciousness of people sense of solidarity of being in the world for one another". *[Nelson Mandela, 2004. Speech delivered at the Fifth Steve Biko Lectures, University of Cape Town, 10th September 2004]*

"We were not ostracised by the ANC or the Black majority in 1994 but we have been doing a fine job ostracising ourselves since then. In 10 years we have not managed to create a political presence that is credible positively oriented and not rooted in the old South Africa. How must this look to the Black majority?" *[Don Lindsay, Henley-on-Klip. The Sunday Times, 12 September 2004, p.19, Johannesburg]*.

"The integrity of politicians and public servants is a critical ingredient in democratic society" *[Alice Rivlin]. Vice Chair, Federal Reserve System, United States]*.

Ten years of democracy is a short period in the life of a nation that many decades suffered under the yoke of the apartheid system of exclusion. However, since the political transformation of South Africa in 1994, expectations not only in Africa but elsewhere have steadily grown on the country's transformation to majority rule – the shift from a close system of apartheid to a plural, open and more inclusive system of governance. So far, South Africa has identified itself as a genuine 'rainbow nation" and embracing the ideals of democratic governance. It is now facing the challenges of consolidating its newly won freedom with the vision of ensuring that quality management trickles down to improving the living conditions of the people.

Breaking the chains of apartheid, and meeting the basic needs of the people, calls for a policy of inclusion, open government, sustainable economic growth and equitable distribution of national wealth. It is the submission of this paper that to achieve quality livelihood requires a political process of reconciliation, consensus, partnership, participation and responsibility sharing between all the stakeholders. The paper addresses the issue from three broad based perspectives, namely, political, economic and social, not of course excluding the responses of the international community towards the country's efforts in building a new and caring society.

From the government of National Unity through the Truth and Reconciliation Commission to the African Renaissance Agenda, a vision emerged to address issues that continue to plague many African states beset by different facets of neo-colonialism and economic imperialism as hangovers. According to Kwame Nkrumah [1965: ix] *"every independent African state in theory is feasted with the trappings of international sovereignty. In reality, its economic system and thus its political policy is directed from outside"*. The prices of exported raw materials from Africa and finished products from Europe are determined not in Africa but in Paris, London or New York. Inequality in trade relationship has to redress for developing countries to have a say in the world market and trading system.

South Africa is no exception to this, for many reasons. First no country is an island of its own. It must interact with other countries. Second, the shackles of apartheid are still there to impose certain conditionalities consciously or not. Third, there is greater expectation from the excluded silent majority that was subjected to the tyranny of the minority for a rapid and sustainable improvement in their living conditions. These development and perceptions in different ways put pressure on the state to deliver the goods as quickly as possible. The passage from apartheid to a renaissance South Africa constitutes a process of "liberating ideology" which calls for a paradigm shift and a concerted and conceptual redefinition of South Africa as a Nation: "Africa is a continent and Africans as a people and how Africans see themselves and in the world [Maloka 1998]. Adding his voice to this perception, a close aid to President Mbeki, Mavimba Vusa see the Renaissance Agenda as *"the need to empower African Peoples to deliver themselves from the legacy of colonialism and neo-colonialism and to situate themselves on the global stage as equal and respected contributors to as well as beneficiaries of all the achievement of human civilisation"* [Nieuwkerk 1998:43].

In fairness to ourselves, the problems and challenges facing South Africa and Africa in general cannot only be attributed to apartheid and colonialism. The existence of pervasive corruption, bad governance, skewed income distribution; social divide and the prevalence of conflicts are largely to be blamed on African themselves. Colonialism and apartheid laid the foundation. The new custodians of power have done nothing to show that colonialism and apartheid constitute the greatest crime ever committed against humanity. To a large extent, legacies of these policies are being executed in post colonial/apartheid Africa. The continent's inextricable linkage to the global economy cannot be rule out. Laying blame is not the answer to the problem. The underlying factor here is how to resolve existing problems. Without this soul searching of us, efforts for change will only be futile. Time spent on laying blames on colonialism should instead be directed at looking at the causes and objectively addressing them from a holistic perspective.

The position taken by Johan Van Zyl [2002:21] is fundamental in this context. Negative criticism, he states, *"alone will achieve nothing. What needs to be done is more positive thinking in three areas: {i} a sane and sensible economic and political assessment of the basic weakness of fault lines in the present economic situation in South Africa – with a sharp focus on the core reasons involved: {ii} a brief outline of some key propositions of the new paradigm or vision of economic progress internationally much discussed today, namely, sustainable people-centred economics, with its strong emphasis on greater self-reliance and less dependency: {iii} a number of pertinent policy proposals for changing things around, even if some of these might appear to be rather radical in conventional economic terms".*

No doubt, the continent was subjected to colonialism and apartheid. It is still subjected to the tentacles of neo-colonialism and globalisation. The forces of 'new-colonialism' and its bedfellow 'globalisation' are with use. But we must move forward. And move forward by demonstrating that colonialism and apartheid was evil and wrong. What do we put in place to win the war of poverty, dependence, corruption, mismanagement and ensure that quality service delivery exist to improve the living standard of the vast majority of the population? In short, how can we materialise Johnson's [2002] *"people wars"* metaphor of ensuring quality public service, the battle to win the hearts and minds of government workers as well as make people feel they are part of our articulate process of change designed to better their pattern of life. Above all, that no one is left out in the ongoing process for change.

Consolidating democratic governance and quality management in nutshell presents an overview of people management policies and initiatives in a young democracy like South Africa with its compound, complex and complicated historical past. Seen in this light, the paper builds on a number of issues, namely: {i} policies, {ii} leadership, {iii} performance, {iv} management and responses. Larry Elowitz [1992] states: "Policies represent the finally authoritative allocation of values". Dunn [1981:46] defines public policy as "along series more or less related choices including decisions not to act, made by government bodies and officials". Government provides essential services and products that are related to the well being of citizens. Public institutions that are governed by national legislation provide these services and products. It therefore reflects the outcome of policy-making process. Legislation occurs within the wider national and international political, social and economic context (Niekerk et al. 2002:57].

Both public and private actors and their interest, a framework of beliefs and attitudes toward a policy proposal shape policies, and formal rules and institutions ingrained in the democratic process. The new democratic political process in South Africa in light of the new constitution makes room for citizens to influence the political process by exercising their civic duties through free and fair elections. Exercising these rights are parts of the process of consolidating democratic governance, and for those so elected to uphold and ensure the supremacy of the constitution and the rule of law, equality and the advancement of human rights. Governance, as noted by Fox and Meyer [1996:665} is possible only as long as governments manage to enforce their will through the establishment of government structures within the context of a state: to ensure that services are rendered to communities to ensure their general welfare and quality of life are promoted". The South African democracy is fairly new and young but getting vibrant and giving rise to a variety of new channels and processes for public participation and partnership that should ensure its sustainability and consolidation. With a decade of universal suffrage and access to political power by the once marginalized black majority is ample justification for assessing the consolidation of democratic governance in the country. Importantly, the people should not let this golden opportunity slip by but ensure that the culture of democratic governance remains in tact within the body politic of the society.

The constitution of the Republic of South Africa {Act 108:1996} creates an empowering environment within which the various structures of the state are constituted for the execution of its output activities. Every one is obliged to contribute towards a system of good governance. Issues contributing towards achieving a system of democratic governance in all sphere of government of South Africa do require: {i} openness and transparency; {ii} adherence to the principles contained in the Bill of Rights: {iii} capacity to act and deliver: {iv} answerability and accountability: {v} efficiency and effectiveness: {vi} distribution of State authority and autonomy: {vii] positive and constructive responses to problems raised through the process of constructive engagement between government, civil society and the private sector: {viii} influencing the way in which politicians address essential problems and needs: {ix} keeping a check on government activities to ensure accountability and answerability – checks and balances at all levels of the state: and {x} cooperative government open to inputs from all sources of society.

These and other related activities legitimately articulated within the constitution stipulates pattern of authority, responsibility, accountability and the bond of relationship between the key actors designed to provide functional, effective and efficient services delivery to the people. Taking its share of responsibility in this respect, government policy oscillates on three fronts, social, economic and political {SEP} with the focus of:

- Ensuring and meeting its obligations to the people:
- Promoting partnership, participation and responsibility sharing between the key players
- Ensuring equity in sharing the wealth of the nation:

- Ensuring its legitimacy and confidence building, trust and support from the key players.

A concerted social, economic and political agenda is vital to consolidate the democratic process, spur growth by addressing pertinent societal problems and exerting the necessary political will of translating words into actions.

THE RENAISSANCE AGENDA

The collapse of apartheid led to a Government of National Unity {GNU}. The Truth and Reconciliation Commission {TRC} reinforced a sense of national unity in diversity. It created the necessary platform for putting the past behind the people. It equipped them to forge ahead for a better future devoid of hate and revenge. The 1996 Constitution laid the framework for a sense of national unity and security in its wider context. From the 1994 to 2004 elections, a culture of democracy has emerged. But it has to be sustained and institutionalised as an inherent and integral part of the life of the people and body politic of the nation. That of "inclusion" has replaced the politics of "exclusion" under apartheid. This politics requires a completely new approach and attitude to development – that of "people-focused/national unity or cohesive oriented development agenda. In short, a South African Renaissance Agenda (SARA) should be exported for other nations to restructure within their own political environment and context.

The Economic Growth Employment and Redistribution Strategy {GEAR} constitute the embodiment of government agenda for economic empowerment: to better address the inequalities of the past in its entire facet and to promote quantitative and qualitative economic growth as the key to progress. The first responsibility of any government is toward its own citizens. This is an obvious yardstick of democracy that must be reinforced in a young democracy like South Africa. In effect, it strengthens the wings of national government to follow the basic tenets of the democratic guidelines for a functional and effective administration in the best interest of the people. It should be noted that the "trickle-down" effect failed in the past and the new development approach is that of self-reliant or "bubble-up" activities initiated at the local levels of economic activity for the good of the currently marginalised majority.

Seen in this respect, the 1996 Constitution lays the political and legal framework and creates a new political order. President Mbeki asserts: *"the new political order owes its existence to the Africa experience of many decades which teaches us as Africans that what we tried did not work – that the One-party states and the military governments will not work. The way forward must be by what is after all, common to all African traditions – which the people must govern"* [see Le Pere 1998:35]. Adding further that "given the direct, obvious and well-known relationship between poverty, community degradation and contact crimes, all who are engaged in the fight against crime have to find ways to motivate even the most depressed communities not to impose additional pain on themselves by allowing a permissive atmosphere that encourage crime" [The Citizen, 4 October 2004:16].

These and other related statements across the broad political spectrum of the South African constituencies set the democratic agenda for the country to move forward and be the new architect of democratic governance in Africa. South Africa's development suggests a desire for progress, unity, freeing of the creative spirit, and ending of old ways and a beginning of a new and progressive chapter for all. The role of what is seen as the fourth estate – "state bureaucracy" is vital. It is only through a non-partisan functional public administration that democratic governance and quality management can be assured. The key actors in the South African body politic must ensure the following: {i} input capability: {ii} conversion capability: and {iii} output capability is not derailed by either tribulations of the past or the self-interest of the new elites in power. The bureaucratic way of doing things must be improved to accomplish the tasks of South African Renaissance Agenda of "inclusion, partnership, participation and responsibility-sharing, including equity in the distribution of national wealth.

Policy Acts or mitigating measures are required to bring about a just society. The *"politics of the belly"* [Bayart 1993} for the individual must change to a *"collective politics of the bellies"* for every one in society. Government mitigating measures should be seen within this context and direction of ensuring that no one is left out of the battle for better living conditions for all. Policy acts should be geared to a "collective belly politics: for the collective good of all.

GOVERNMENT MITIGATING MEASURES

Policy Acts or mitigating measures are required to bring about a "just society". Most governments in Africa – South Africa inclusive – are facing the challenges of inadequate human capacity or capital. The lack of these critical human masses impedes adequate quality management and service delivery. An output function of the government fails in providing the essential needs of the people. Human capital is not developed over night. It takes time and capital. Without developed human capital, it will be difficult to give added value to natural resources, to address the debilitating effects that skill shortages are injecting into public sector performance and delivery services in South Africa. Sustainable delivery service can better be assured through the participation of civil society and the private sector in legislative related activities and public participation in the integrated development planning, execution and evaluation processes. A holistic public and state participation in the democratic governance in South Africa could no doubt set the tune for consolidation democratic governance in other parts of the continent. The continent needs this kind of positive spill over effects.

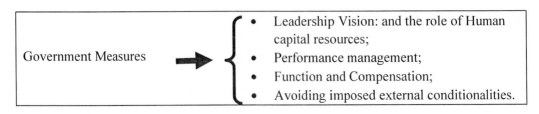

Figure 1. Mitigating Measures for Good Governance and Quality Management.

Investment in human resources is vital. "Knowledge" we are told is "power," and 'power rules the world'. The absence of the *"technology of knowledge"* means Africa can neither rule the world nor give added value to its abundant natural resources base. It will for a long-time remain dependent and subjected to the dictates of the industrial countries. What are the mitigating measures adopted by government to bring order and harmony in meeting its goals and obligations as well as satisfying customers' needs? Figure 1. – Mitigating Measures for Good Governance and Quality Management depicts some of the approaches that government can adopt. Sense of direction by political leadership remains vital in piloting the ship to an envisaged destination. It is a necessary compass or road map for development, sustainability and progress but requiring positive responses from the people and the international community at large. Civil society plays an important role in the consolidation of democratic governance. This is spelled out and recognised by the African National Congress {ANC} in its policy document, the Reconstruction and Development Programme {RDP} in 1994. which states: Reconstruction and development requires a population that is empowered through expanded rights, meaningful information and education, an institutional network fostering representative and indirect democracy, and participatory and direct democracy [ANC, 1994:120]

HUMAN CAPITAL AND LEADERSHIP

The movement from closed to open government since 1994 saw the emergence of plethora of policies, legislation and other initiatives taken by the government to give new impetus to human capital development {HCD} and institutional capacity building {ICB}. Typical among these are measures such as {a} Government White paper on the Transformation of Public service {WPTPS}: The Public Service Act {1994}: The White paper on Public Service Education and Training (August 1998): Skills Development Act {1998}: Public Finance Management Act {1999}: Public Service Review Report {1999-2000}: Local Government Municipal Systems Act {2000}: Public Service Regulations {2001}: Framework Agreement for the Transformation and Restructuring of the Public Service {January 2001}: National Skills Development Strategy {February 2001}: Human Resources Development Strategy {April 2001} (see Ambursley 2002: and Government Publications).

Ambursley [2002-407] points out: *"a coherent analysis of the institutional legacy of apartheid, the White paper on transforming Public service {WPTPS} called for the creation of a "people-centred and people-driven public service" characterised by equity, quality, timorousness and a strong code of ethics ... detailed proposals and guidelines were enunciated with respect to issues such as restructuring, institution building, affirmative action, service delivery, accountability, human resources development {HRD}, labour relations and promotion of a professional service ethos"* {see also Republic of South Africa, White Paper on the Transformation of the Public Service, 1995 para.2.1}. According to the Batho Pele Report [1997:30], *"it does not promise the impossible. It asks public servants to commit themselves to the limits of what is possible and then to push on to the next goal. If the initiative is to achieve its aims, public servants at every level, from the top to the most junior, must understand it and support it. Batho Pele must become the watch word of the New South African Public Service."*

Leadership role is important. This can make or mar the system. Poor leadership has been the source of conflict, corruption and underdevelopment in many African countries. The government does just the opposite of what the law states or what is stipulated in official documents. The significance of leadership role is illustrated in the following Commission Report: *"if within the Presidency, letters are not answered or even acknowledged, and if priorities of policy and programme cannot be judged independently or effectively co-ordinated, not only is the Head of the State and Government let down, but a signal is being sent throughout government"* [Folscher 2001]. Leadership role is necessary in restoring confidence, trust and building a better society. In his weekly Internet message, President Thabo Mbeki noted: *"by any measure, the decreases in some crime categories constitute good news for all. There is national agreement on the need to improve the safety and security of the people as an inherent important part of the pursuit of the goal of a better life for all"* [The Citizen, 4 October 2004:16]. That statement instils confidence, hope and trust in the people. That top political leadership is focused on the quality and livelihood of the citizens restores confidence and is a motivating factor for a joint approach between the state and civil society to forge ahead with good governance and quality service delivery in the best interest of the nation.

PERFORMANCE MANAGEMENT: FUNCTION AND COMPENSATION

The government documents mentioned are designed to improve management performance. How to measure performance is a different thing? Output functions constitute some of the indicators that can be used to access the state of management performance. How long doe it take to process a file, pay a bill or book an appointment with a top official? What are the delivery services like, the mailman for example? What is the state of electricity supply and failure rates? What form of services exists at the hospitals or any other public establishment? These are issues that need to be looked into.

Are the right people given the right jobs? Are the workers well paid? What future exists in their career? The 1997 World Development Report [World Bank] eludes to the fact that countries with poorly paid public servants tend toward higher corruption. The case of Cameroon is typical example. Poor input functions in respect of low salary, bad working environment obviously would lead to poor output functions: corruption and poor delivery services for example. Poor pay leads to corruption [see Rijckeghem and Weber 1997]. Improving the level of public service pay should be kept in policy agenda of the government. Taking an example, like Cameroon, where there has been no salary increase for the past 24 years, it is not surprising that the country tops the list as the most corrupt nation in the world. Rather, the public service sector suffered a salary cut of about 70 percent in 1993 and a 50 percent devaluation of the CFA francs in 1994 [Forje 2003]. The situation of Hong-Kong and Singapore show a sharp departure "where the wage policies are to a large extent responsible for a low corruption levels recorded in these emerging markets" [Ambursley 2002:417, and see Wei, 1999:19].

The salary gap between the public and private sector should be bridged in order to maintain skill human resources within the public sector. This will also help the state to reduce its dependency on external consultants in undertaking some of its activities. The fear expressed by Pile [2001:46, cited in Ambursley 2002]. *"State outsourcing has a cash cow as skills continue to drain from the public sector to the private sector. State entities are finding it hard to attract and retain skilled staff, particularly to administer treasuries. Legislative requirements are also becoming more onerous for accounting officers, who can be liable for breaches of internal controls: hence the growth in outsourcing to private companies"* is very pertinent. With some of the structure put in place through: The Labour Relations Act [1995]: Government Basic Conditions of Employment Act [1997]; The Presidential Review Commission Report [February 1998]; National Skills Development Strategy [2001]: Public Service Review Report [1999-2000] create some basis for addressing the issue of salary scale within the public service sector, It is vital that these acts are rigorously implemented to establish security and confidence in the sector.

CHALLENGES AND FUTURE PROSPECTS

The challenges facing South Africa are many and varied, taking into consideration its historical past and the current desire to right the wrongs of that past from the platform of consensus and reconciliation building in order to establish a strong, united and progressive nation for all. No doubt, this will raise eyebrows in some quarters First, those who think government is not doing enough to meet the aspiration of the once excluded and marginalized majority. Second, those of the old establishment who do not want change to obstruct their existing status quo. Here we find a "clash of cultures", the fear of the old and conservatives giving way to a more radical objective present. It is imperative that mechanisms be put in place to address either sides or make things fall apart. Government's effective presence is necessary. Such a presence must be guided by the rule of law, social justice and legal instruments restraining the tyranny of either the majority or minority.

For a young democracy emerging out of the shackles of apartheid to one of "inclusion" is not a simple task. It requires commitment from the entire key actors, serious shift in mindset to adjust into their new positions of consensus and reconciliation building for a particular objective: that of ensuring national cohesion, equity, and unity in diversity for the common good. And seeing diversity not as a liability but as asset to the reconstruction, reformation and advancement process of the country. The Truth and Reconciliation Commission {TRC} laid the foundation for *"shifting position"* towards the common good. Ali Mazrui points out that in South Africa *"bridges needed to be built not only between races, but also between genders and across generations. Relations between men and women had been disrupted by repression, by ways of liberation and labour migration. And relations continued to be strained by anger and radicalisation generated by apartheid"* (1993:918].

The challenges are that individuals constitute "agency and action" which in turn develops process and institutional character. How individual change determines as well as sets the pace and structural framework for the country to solve its inherent problems of underdevelopment, exclusion and inclusion? Thus, the crystallisation of history, traditions, institutions and the future lies in the vision of South Africa's Renaissance Agenda on economic, social and political transformation of the society to meet present and subsequent challenges and changes. What is most required is not to betray the confidence, aspiration and hopes of the people especially those who were placed at the fringes of poverty and marginalisation by the apartheid system? The views of Houngnikpo [2000:30] are relevant here. *"Through a vibrant and educated civil society, Africans can and should demand transparent and accountable governments. Africans should prevent vampire states and leaders from continuing to seek their blood. Catalyst and facilitators are need in every community and village to foster attitudes that could redress the misfortunes of Africa's social fabric. Both followers and leaders will have to cooperate to find solutions for the continent's problems."*

Admittedly, South Africa has emerged from a complicated and complex historical past but with a difference compared to most African states. The positive side of the vices of apartheid {if one can catalogue it that way} can be nurtured into a virtue for the positive good of the people. Saying there exist a positive side of the vices of apartheid does not imply my approval of the apartheid system but streamline on with what could be viewed as the positive sides, for example, the quest for survival by the minority white population – the technology of violence and mobility marrying the technology of knowledge which today puts South Africa at the forefront of the growing global knowledge-based economy as far as Africa is concern. In this respect, we can talk of the benefits of apartheid in a way or with a difference. How to convert the technology of mass destruction into one of mass development for the common good?

The other aspect of the process of change and challenge can be seen in the process to mobilise indigenous South African experiences and aspirations – "The Mandela's Democratic Doctrine" as a creative attempt to use acquired resources, popular experiences for existing institutions to expand opportunity and consolidate success (see Nash 1999). An efficient, functional and delivery public sector in South Africa will be an input to the country's scientific, economic, technological advancement and political stability of 10 years down the democracy line, as it constitute a major contribution to democratic governance and economic development in other Africa countries. The views of President Mbeki need to be taken serious in this context: *"..improved governance and socio-economic conditions in Africa are also the extension of the frontiers of human dignity to all humanity"* [Hadland & Rantao, 1999:182].

The behaviour of civil servants should be placed in a certain political context, particularly to evade the risk of corrupt practices within the system that will contribute to malfunctioning of the system leading to failure in quality services delivery to the people. The recent corruption practices within the police and other departments of government raise doubts in the minds of the people. Government's quick response is imperative in restoring confidence in the people. Issues of salary increases and better working conditions remain a major a nut to be tackled. If not adequately addressed will be a major input factor to corruption and instability. The trappings of corruption become greater when the environment lacks the basic tenets of the democratic principles. The absence of this would hamper quality service delivery as well as erode confidence among the people

Indeed, the democratic process in South Africa is a good course. It has to be consolidated without which, true political transformation; tolerance, reconciliation and nation building would elude Africa. It will be a serious setback for democratic governance and quality management to take hold in the rest of the continent. As stated by Molokge [2002:447] there is a need to intensify these efforts to unite the different sections of society as much as possible to avoid divisive references. This will give the people a sense of belonging and ownership and encourage cooperation in the building of their provinces and the whole country. It is also important for those in positions of power to realise and accept that real power belongs to the people and is the ability to persuade others to work together to realise common potentials, not the capacity to control and be served.

Prospects for the future are clear: institutionalise democratic and ethical governance and respect human rights in its totality. Alice Rivlin, Vice Chair of the Federal Reserve System of the United States of America, states: *"The integrity of politicians and public servants is a critical ingredient in democratic society"* Future prospects will demand an ethical governance system so as to establish formal mechanisms and to utilise possible remedies to highlight the issue of human rights and values that incorporate the following crucial areas: *honesty, humaneness, justice, freedom, decency, truth, integrity, order, fairness, reasonableness.*

The promotion of ethical governance constitutes issues of critical significance for government, politics and civil society to ultimately inculcate moral choices and value judgement in the input-output functions of government. Since democracy prescribes certain rights and freedoms to individuals, individuals must reciprocate to uphold these moral choices and values in their daily activities. It is the responsibility of government to promote ethical conduct by meeting its obligations to the people: by putting the necessary infrastructures in place. Unethical conduct manifests itself through political corruption, election fraud, official violence, and institutional misconduct. To combat such manifestations appropriate mechanisms must be put in place and appropriately utilised by both the state and civil society. Such measures should include {a} open and transparent government, {b} political leadership with a vision: {c} accountability – adhering to rules and regulations as stipulated in the constitution, legislative acts, statuary guidelines etc: {d} respect for the rule of law, and independent judiciary, free press: and {e} the use of the stick and carrot measures without fear or favour.

The various policy acts by government are designed to bring quality services to the people. It is therefore the place of public servants to translate and implement these mitigating measures in a transparent and accountable way. It is also the place of government to give encouragement to the civil service for job well done. The statement by President Mbeki could be seen in this light: *"The SAPs, the Community Police Forums, Business against Crime, and other activists in the struggle against crime deserve our congratulations. The improvements in the crime situation are consistent with the progress the country is making in other areas. For those genuinely interested and involved in the national effort to improve safety and security, the crime statistics must indicate that more work needs to be done to prevent the commission of these contact crimes, especially in their areas of concentration"* [The Citizens, 4 October 2004:16]

SOME TENTATIVE CONCLUSIONS: THE WAY FORWARD

South Africa's passage from apartheid to majority rule, [from exclusion to inclusion] under the auspices of the Government of National Unity, supported by the Truth and Reconciliation Commission, and now with the Renaissance Agenda has not only been received with enormous enthusiasm world wide but remains a beacon for a continent still struggling under the yoke of dependency and marginalisation and the quest for a new global order of knowledge-based market economic – globalisation

Obviously, the political stake around these changes calls for an efficient and effective Civil Service Sector {CSS} to ensure the smooth transition from a close to an open governance form and to sustain the momentum for development as well as ensure that the benefits of development and progress trickles down to the people, especially those at the fringes of exclusion and poverty. It is not an easy task to remake or reconstruct the new South Africa. To promote the politics of "inclusion" which should ultimately lead to a balance development pattern and growth equitably shared by all in a pattern that addresses the historical injustices and grossly inequitable structures and lost opportunities which constituted the legacies of the past – and to forge ahead in building a more inclusive present and future.

To ensure progress requires functional democratic governance and respect for human rights, a democracy that rejects both the tyranny of the minority and majority. The country is faced with the challenges of change and continuity in ensuring a progressive economy. Since 1994, South Africa has conducted what could be described as Africa's best and most outstanding free and faire elections, backed with the 1996 constitution the country is well armed to enter the annals of democratic governments of the world. To a large extent, this puts greater pressure on the rest of the continent to accelerate their reform processes. As the country looks north of the Limpopo, pressures for change at home could lead to unrest. However, hope and not despair remain strong to pilot the democratic progress in the country that in a way is a new export commodity.

So far, South Africa remains the beacon for democracy and quality management in Africa. This has been made possible through committed leadership rooted in a successful domestic transition to the socio-economic and political levels that gives it the basis on which to forge a new era of cooperation and community with the rest of the continent. The hosting of the Pan-African Parliament {PAP} and the New Economic Partnership for African Development [NEPAD] strengthen that drive for a New Renaissance African Order {NRAO} to championing the continent in the age of globalisation. A functional public service is required to ensure the proper realisation of these goals. The "consolidation of democracy in South Africa thus entails achieving higher and higher levels of public participation in the political process and the development of institutional channels that enable effective public participation. Monitoring the evolution and consolidation of this new democracy must include, among others, the evaluation of progress in establishing participatory and direct democracy". [Houston 2001:3]

A new reconstruction process that stretches above the Limpopo is emerging. For it to succeed requires strong, impartial and efficient public service sector devoid of all the trappings of malpractice in service delivery to the people within and beyond the national frontiers of the country. It requires a vibrant civil society and a productive/progressive private sector to back up government initiatives in the process. South Africa's policy must continue to build on a bureaucratic re-organisation and re-orientation awareness creation strategy – the move from the apartheid past to an era of black majority rule and that of encompassing the socio-political and economic situation of the continent. In this process of change and continuity, the problem of bureaucratic over-load must be addressed so as to better address policy changes in domestic and foreign policy alike. It becomes vital for the country to engineer changes in the machinery of government and to establish and implement new policy priorities agenda. A decade after the historical collapse of the apartheid governance system,

South Africa has made significant strides. What is required is to improve and consolidate the achievements of ten years of democracy and management

Ensuring the integrity, fairness, effectiveness and accountability of administrative decision-making through the democratic process and representative political institution constitute the fundamental basis for good ethical governance, and in many cases an effective instrument to deal with corruption. Cleaning up government is a complex and lengthy process, requiring political commitment and determination to see the process through a successful conclusion. There is no other way for government to restore confidence and trust in the people than ensure the openness of the administration. The voices of the people must be head and their complaints well looked into. Recent revelations about corrupt practices in some public service institutions – the police and home office – show how much is required to clean up. The South African Broadcasting Corporation {SABC} programme showed how police officers from Rosebank and Bramley Police Stations routinely threatened to arrest sex workers and clients unless they paid a 'spot fine'. They also threatened to expose clients to their wives. The spot fine was in the form of a bribe of between R6000 and R10000, which is paid to the crooked policeman in return for the person's freedom. A crew from Special Assignment, went undercover, armed with hidden camera and pretending to be a prostitute and her client…" [Kcosana 2004:2] Government prompt action is vital to restore confidence and credibility in the system

Anna Cox [2004:1] writing under the caption, "Top Metro Cop in Hot Waters" calls for disciplinary action to address crisis in city *policy department. The Report recommends that five disciplinary charges be brought against Johannesburg Metro Police chief and the Head of Human Resources". Importantly, prompt government actions into these developments indicate government resolve to be at the services of the people".* In this connection, Kcosana {2004:2] praise for "swift action over alleged bribes solicited from sex workers and clients."

To ensure an open and clean government of accountability and responsibility, democratic governance must reign. Such mitigating approaches exhibits good leadership and performance management that the people come first in the battle of 'winning the people wars in government' [Johnson, 2000: Ambursley 2002:405-425]. A number of Key Capital Initiatives have been put in place by government since 1994 in order to bring sanity by creating a 'people centred and people-driven service'. The Batho Pele Report – The White paper on human resources management in the Public service, 1997 for example, states: *"The vision is that human resources management in the Public Service will result in a diverse, competent and well-managed workforce, capable of and committed to delivering high quality services to the people of South Africa."*

As an emerging democracy, South Africans have to commit themselves to building a stronger sense of nationalism, the duties and obligations of democratic citizenship and a sense of democratic civility among citizens. Defeating apartheid was one thing, cultivating and sustaining the democratic values of equality, liberty and freedom {ELF} is another? Here lies the change and challenge to build a resilient popular commitment to democracy and quality management. As of now, the general belief is one that commitment to democracy is expected to improve their daily lives in concrete ways. Of course, quality living standard is all we expect and which should not be the preserve of a few. And so the conception of democracy as having more to do with performance than with procedures. Those committed to democracy tend to tie their commitment to satisfaction with how the government and economy is doing.

Commitment to democracy and legitimacy of its institutions should not depend on how a particular administration is performing. It should be a function of socialised norms and values. Consolidation requires the transformation of society to make it more representative of diverse population. It requires good citizenship – that is, informing us and ridding ourselves of the scars of apartheid, colonialism and military regime forms. While constructive criticism is an essential part of a functioning democracy, there is simultaneously space for our efforts to create a more equitable society. Therefore, redistribution is not just something governments implement but something that falls to us all, as citizens and as caring communities.

A bad functional administration derails good intentions. We need to remind ourselves of the skills, knowledge, know-how and expertise that now lies hidden in our communities. It is this inherent strength that needs to be captured and utilised. Hence, the slogan, "here the people govern with equal opportunity to all." In short, quality services delivery that should trickle down to the hinterlands. Consolidating our resources, and knowledge for the transformation of the society is what should remain paramount in the minds and actions of every citizen, with the government coordinating such activities.

Across Africa, the British left a legacy of colour superiority and the French a legacy of cultural superiority. The marriage between colour and cultural superiority could be seen through the apartheid legacy. These tow developments gave birth to the "culture of apartheid". These past attitudes have to be overcome: and that, the change process is now in our hands. It is here that we have to read deep into the miracle of the peaceful legitimate and negotiated settlements deal between 1990-1994, leading to the Government of National Unity. These developments paint a positive scenario for the future of South Africa as a country in transit and setting the pace for others to follow. Yet the country's transit is compounded by an external transit as globalisation brings changes in all countries. These changes impact on us all, calling for a sense of commitment, hard work under the common goal in the interest of all.

As of now, not just South Africa but the entire African continent is disoriented and perplexed. To a large extent, state institutions, the policies and justice systems are not providing the protection that citizens expect. Totalitarian and military regimes dot the political landscape of Africa, putting in place [permissiveness, lawlessness, corruption and disorder prevail. In this disorientation we grab at materialism. The maximization of profit has gone so far that it needs greater forces to call us to moderate profit, to think of collective politics of the belly not the individual politics of the belly as we have institutionalised it in the past many decades.

The rest of Africa needs to draw useful lessons from the success story of the rainbow nation in the past 10 years. What is crucial in any transition to democratic regime form is the management of the process. The social realities have been swept under the carpet over the years, and now they have to be faced head-on. The one-party state, military regimes, and the apartheid structure have left us with a corrupt legacy. The change, which requires serious management, has to be done sensitively and vigorously for the common purpose of ensuring democratic governance in the new political dispensation. Here we need an effective, efficient functional public service sector to protect the change movement. We dare not destroy or denigrate the past, nor dare we glorify the past. Yet we must disconnect ourselves from the old order by demonstrating the success of the new order requiring a paradigm shift that we must work to achieve. Mentality, attitude and behaviour changes remain vital to achieve envisaged goals. The crooks of the problem lie here. How to rid the vices of existing mentality, attitude and behaviour in the daily activities of the people? Poor output functions of government reflects the result of bad behaviour among citizens. It takes two to tango.

As there is need for a "clean-up" in government, so also the need for a radical clean up within civil society and individuals. Civil society is an intermediary entity standing between the private sphere and the state. An organised civil society serves as a check against the excesses of government, human rights violation, abuse of the rule of law, and the monitoring of the application of constitutional provision. In the absence of an engaged civil society, governments are left with unchecked powers, which over time corrupt the individuals in leadership and subsequently exposes, a country to politically motivated human insecurity. The presence of civil society increases the chances of participation and the use of the skills of all the various segments of society and instils a sense of tolerance, thrift, hard work, moderation and compromise among the various competing parties in the society [see Diamond 1995: M'boge and Doe 2004].

As of now, looking at the past and progress so far made, South Africa stands out different from most African countries which continue to have democratic governance and management difficulties. For example, of the first eleven African states to transform themselves into multi-party democracies, seven returned the old guards to power under a new guise. We are embracing a form of inherent tendency to centralised power – "presidents for life" are resurfacing under the auspices of plural political party systems, or in the name of "advanced democracy, in the pretext of preserving national unity which in reality do not exist in these countries. Can we talk of national unity when more than half the population go to bed hungry, have no shelter with any medical health facilities? This is what has derailed Africa since independence. The one-party was developed in the same of creating national unity. Unity in diversity. But a national unity never emerged. Political leaders used the concept of one party to bleed their countries to death; to sow seeds of division and not unity as was envisaged. It was a noble idea if it worked. The society was betrayed. That politics of betrayal must be avoided in Renaissance South Africa and the African continent in the 21st century. The challenge, therefore, is for all to work for the common good despite the disorientation. Coherence and not chaos remains the way forward. Mentality change across the board is required before Africa can claim the 21st century or be part of the evolving global world. Are we prepared to meet that challenge or is it business as usual?

RECOMMENDATIONS

The paper examines and underscores the role of public participation in the democratic governance in South Africa. Though South Africa is fairly a young democracy, it has within this space of time established itself as a fast growing democracy to be reckoned within the world. It remains a beacon for the African continent with most of countries struggling to get out of phobia of one-party governance system. There is still a long way to go, for democratic changes to be translated in concrete quality living standards for the vast majority of South Africans.

In sum, tremendous domestic changes and forging a new global image constitute challenges, which confront the New South Africa. To address these challenges, the emerging South Africa must continue on path of reconstruction, reform and democratisation and to forge ahead with the policy of good governance and rule of law. This "new political environment started the multi-party negotiation process {MPNP} in Kempton Park involving 26 political stakeholders with the fundamental element of "inclusivity" were every major political party and government administration in a negotiating forum for an interim constitution was followed by non-racial elections. The 1994 democratic election marked a dramatic change in the decision-making process in the country. The new approach to decision-making is aimed at strengthening peoples' empowerment to better ensure participatory democracy, accountability and transparency bringing about fundamental changes in the policy and developmental environment in South Africa. Here I can recommend the following:

- Continue to support and encourage efforts to promote good governance and strengthen the rule of law: enhance state capacity to undertake core policy and service delivery functions: enhance transparent, responsive and accountable Government: prevent corruption and address issues of abject poverty and ensure security to life and property: and unrestricted access to just for all. In short, power to the people with equal opportunities for all;
- Continue on the policy of reconciliation, participation, partnership, responsibility sharing as well as equity in the distribution of the wealth of the nation;
- Promote the "technology of knowledge" by reducing expenditure on the "technology of violence and mobility. – Ensure that the technology of violence or destruction is converted into the technology of human development";
- Promote n active and vibrant civil society as partners in development and as watch dogs for state activities – here the people rule – should be the guiding objective and philosophy;
- Recognise the need and measures to combat ethnic hegemony, racism and xenophobia, but promote unity in diversity, instil a sense of national belonging, one nation, one people, one goal, with diversity looked upon as asset not as a liability;
- Ensure an enabling environment for all – empowerment of the people is a vital tool in the democratic process and in nation-building.

REFERENCES

African National Congress {ANC}. 1994. *The Reconstruction And Development Programme*. Johannesburg, South Africa.

Ambursley, Fitzroy [2002] "Winning the People Wars in Government: An Assessment of Human capital Policies in the South Africa Service Since 1994" in Sipho Buthelezi and Elizabeth Le Rox {eds.} 2002. *South Africa since 1994: Lessons and Prospects*. African century Publications No. 8. Pretoria, South Africa.

Cox, Anna. [2004] "Top Metro Cop in Hot Water". *The Star,* 4 October 2004, p.1 Johannesburg, South Africa.

Cloete, J. N. N. [1998] South African Public and Administration and Management. *Pretoria,* J. I. van Schalk, South Africa.

The Citizens [2004] "Analysis – Vested Interest in Pessimism" *The Citizen,* 4 October 2004, p.16, Johannesburg, South Africa.

Department of Labour [2001] The National Skills Development Strategy. *Pretoria,* DOL. 2001.

Department of Public Service and Administration [1997] *White paper on Transforming Public Service Delivery* – {Batho Pele White Paper} Government Printer, Pretoria, South Africa.

Department of Public Service and Administration [1998] *White Paper on Public Service Education and Training,* Government Printer, Pretoria, South Africa.

Department of Public Service and Administration [1999] *Public Service Regulations,* Government Printer, Pretoria, South Africa.

Department of Public Service and Administration [2000] *Policy Statement on the establishment of a senior management Service in the Public Service,* Pretoria, South Africa.

Department of Public Service and Administration [2000] *Public Service Review Report,* 1999-2000, Pretoria, South Africa.

Department of Public Service and Administration [2001] *Public Service Job Summit Framework Agreement.* Government Printer, Pretoria, South Africa.

Department of Public Service and Administration [2001] *Public Service Regulations,* Government Printer. Pretoria, South Africa.

Diamond, L. [1995] *"Rethinking Civil Society"* quoted in Crossroads, USIS Newsletter, Lagos, February 1995:9-10.

Dunn. W. N. [1981] *Public Policy Analysis: An Introduction.* Englewood, Cliffs, Prentice Hall, N.J, USA.

Folscher, A. [2001] "Government needs to Spend More on Personnel" *Business Day,* 5 March 2001.

Forje, John W. [2003] Consolidating Democratic Governance and Quality Management in Africa. *CARAD Readings in policy, Governance and Management,* Vol. 2. Yaoundé, Republic of Cameroon.

Forje, John W. [2004] Cameroon Without Corruption. *The Search for a New Vision.* Neba Publishers, Bamenda, Cameroon.

Fox, W. and Meyer, I. H. [1998] *Public Administration Dictionary,* Kenwyn, Juta.

Houngnikpo [2000] *"Stuck at the Runway: Africa's Distress Call",* Africa Insight, Vol. 2, 2000, Africa Institute of South Africa, Pretoria, South Africa.

Houston, Gregory [2001] *Public Participation in Democratic governance in South Africa,* Human Sciences Research Council, Pretorious Street Pretoria, South Africa.

Johnson, M. [2000] *Winning the People Wars: Talent and the battle for Human Capital,* Prentice Hall, London, UK.

Kcosanan, Caiphus [2004] "Police Officers Fingered in TV Expose Behind Bars" *The State,* 4 October 2004. Johannesburg, South Africa.

Le Pere et al {eds.} [1998] South Africa and Africa. Reflections on the African renaissance, FGD, *Occasional Paper* No. 17. Johannesburg

Maloka, Eddy [1998] *"Africa Must arise A New,"* Sowetan, 14 September 1998, Johannesburg, South Africa.

Mazrui, Ali [1993] "Toward the Year 2000" in A Mazrui {ed.} *General History of Africa,* Vol. VIII, Since 1935, University of California Press, Berkeley, USA.

M'boge, Fatoumatta and Doe, Sam Gbaydee [2004] *African Commitments to Civil Society Engagement,* Compress, South Africa.

Molokoge, Benjamin, K. M. [2000] "In Pursuit of an Illusion. Political Transformation in the North West Province of South Africa since 1994," in Sipho Buthelezi and Elizabeth Le Roux {eds.} 2002, *South Africa Since 1994.* Lessons and Prospects. Africa Institute of South Africa, Pretoria, South Africa.

Nash, A. [1999] "Mandela Democracy" *Monthly review,* Vol. 50, 1999.

Nieuwkerk, A Van [1998] "South Africa's Emerging African Policy,' in G. Le Pere, A Van Nieuwkerk and K. Lambrechts {ed.} *South Africa and Africa: Reflections on the African Renaissance,* RGD Occasional Paper No. 17 Johannesburg.

Niekerk, D. Van, G. Van der Waldt and A Jonker [2002] *Governance, Politics and Policy in South Africa.* Oxford University Press, Southern Africa, Cape Town, South Africa.

Pile, J. [2001] *"Saki Finds Royalty in the Outscoring Business,"* financial mail, 23 March 2001, Johannesburg, South Africa.

Republic of South Africa [1995] *White Paper on the transformation of the Public Service.* Government printer Press, Pretoria.

Republic of South Africa [1998] *The Constitution of the Republic of South Africa,* Government Printing Press, Pretoria, South Africa.

Republic of South Africa [1999] Public *Finance management Act,* Act No. 1 of 1999, Pretoria, South Africa.

Republic f South Africa [2000] *Local Government: Municipal Systems Act* 2000, Act No. 32 of 20000, Cape Town, South Africa.

Rijckeghem. C, van and Weber, B. [1997] Corruption and Rate of Temptation. Do Low wages in the Civil Service Cause Corruption? *MF Working Paper* 97/73. Washington DC. International Monetary Fund, Washington, DC. USA.

Wei Shang-Jim [1999] Corruption in Economic Development. Beneficial Grease. Minor Annoyance of Major Obstacle? *Policy research Working paper WPS* 2048, Washington CD, USA.

World bank [1997] *Can African Claim the 21st Century?* Washington, DC USA.

Zyl, Johnan Van [2002] "Is there a Hopeful Economic Future fro South Africa" in Sipho Buthelezi and Elizabeth Le Roux {eds.} 2002. South Africa Since 1994: Lessons and Prospects. *Africa Century Publications Series No. 8.* African Institute of South Africa, Pretoria, South Africa.

Chapter 5

BREAKING BARRIERS: RETHINKING CIVIL SOCIETY AND GOVERNANCE FOR INTEGRATION AND SUSTAINABLE DEVELOPMENT IN AFRICA. WHAT PROSPECTS FOR THE FUTURE?

ABSTRACT

The focus of the paper is on the interface between the State, Civil Society and the Private Sector should play in advancing the process of African integration in light of the challenges of globalisation and the new political dispensation that emerged almost two decades ago. It focuses on and addresses common characteristics emerging in three different but inter-related trends, namely, the relationship between leadership, democratisation and civil society. The paper departs from the premises that the return to liberal democracy in Africa is witnessing a new jump-start riddled with much cynicism: how civil society organisations (CSO) are able to fit into the new political dispensation: and what is or are the response{s} from the State towards the new forces challenging its established hegemony partly born out of the monolithic State system that existed during the greater part of these former colonies. It questions the nature of African civil society and whether it exists at all. The paper addresses issues of empowering civil society through community development, and making it an instrument for socio-economic transformation and integration: while in the processes, the underlying issues of participation, partnership and responsibility sharing among other stakeholders are discussed.

The theoretical framework builds on concepts of democratic governance and civil society advanced by Ake (2000), Diamond (1998, 1997), Bratton and Walle (1997), Bujura (2003), Guy Peters (2000) among others. Without a deepening knowledge and understanding of the democratisation and governance process, state, civil society and the private sector cannot inject the necessary inputs so required for national, regional and continental integration necessary to uplift the quality living standards of the population currently lavishing in squalor and abject poverty.

Proactive strategic policy measures are advanced as the way forward for Africa in reconstructing governance and integration in the age of a knowledge based global society.

Keywords: Democratisation, integration, partnership, responsibility sharing, civil society, private sector, governance, state system, participation, interface, quality living standards

INTRODUCTION: TROUBLING ISSUES OF OUR TIME

"No political society, national or international, can exist unless people submit to certain rules of conduct. The problem why people should submit to such rules is the fundamental problem of political philosophy". *[E. H. Carr, 1984 (1939, second ed. 1946) 41]*

"There is nothing more dangerous than to build a society with a large segment of people who feel that they have no stake in it, who feel that they have nothing to loss" [Martin Luther King. 1968]

"Without good governance – without the rule of law, predictable administration, legitimate power, and responsive regulation – no amount of funding, no amount of charity will set us on the path of prosperity". *[Kofi Annan (cited in UNDP, 1997:20)]*

"The partnership between state, civil society and the private sector is not an option: it is necessity demanding each side to observe its obligations and responsibilities to the country. State-civil society-private sector interface should be a process of building bridges across existing divide that prevents the people from having quality living standards, peace, security and hope for the future". *[John W. Forje, 12 September 2005]*

This article is about big and troubling issues of our times. It addresses the framework underscoring the need for integrating civil society in the governance process to better achieve sustainable development, and quality living standards for the people. The current and ongoing initiatives involving civil society and other actors reflect a national as well as global trend away from treating poverty, corruption, and security and building peace issues as the sole preserve of the state. However, there is need for a stronger synergy between development building structures, both vertically (from national, regional organisations to the global level) and horizontally) between and across national and regional. To that end, a formal structural relationship is necessary.

The troubling issues of our time are poverty, racism, corruption, poor governance, absence of the rule of law, misuse of power, insecurity and the growing divide between affluence and abject poverty, and above all, the issue of not loving their neighbour as thy self to list but a few. We need to break barriers and create new hopes for present and future generations. Events leading to the September 14-16 2005 of the United Nations General Assembly as commemoration of its 60th anniversary celebrations show how far apart the existing gap is between the rich and poor, between the powerful and weak, and between the developed and transitional polities of the world. The current stalemate and existing gap between the rich and poor calls for a thorough rethinking of the role of state-civil society-private sector relationship within the context of development. It further brings into fulcrum the role and need for integration, the linking up of key actors in the process of a socio-economic and technological transformation of transitional polities.

It is clear the democracy and good governance is a missing commodity in many African countries, even though much progress have been made in Africa since the collapse of the communist regime form the late 1980s. Post Cold War Africa is caught between consolidating democratic governance form and of retreating into the old comma of monolithic governance system of the Cold War Era. The troubling issues of our time show the great divide between affluence and abject poverty, security and insecurity: food security and wide spread hunger: wars/conflicts and peace/stability; economic growth/economic decline; chaos and coherence; ethnicity, tribalism and national unity/integration among others. These troubling issues call for a critical analysis of the place of state and role of civil society and the private sector in the development process.

What is the nature of the African state? To what extent has the state fulfilled that role? What is the role of civil society? How does the state relate to civil society or vice versa? How can they cooperate to build a sustainable society for the common good? To begin with, the nature of the African state is such that it plays a most important role in managing development. This role has been ongoing since the attainment of independence. But the colonial powers did not see the state as the mechanism for providing development. For the colonial powers the purpose of the state was simply an instrument for promoting, upholding and sustaining law and order to better facilitate colonial hegemonic objectives – the exploitation of the colonies in all dynamics and dimensions.

However, the general expectation of the state after the attainment of independence was to ensure it playing a primordial and constructive role in the development process. In other words, the general impression given by the new custodians of power in post-colonial African was the extension of state authority and activities apart from that of law and order maintenance to one of being the engine for economic growth and industrial transformation. The state became the sole proprietor for development or the reconstruction of Africa after the end of colonial rule. African governments embraced the *"engine of development"* concept and responded differently, giving special justification of the "State" as the provider, producer and consumer in the development process.

Two ideological approaches quickly emerged, namely. (i) The minimalist: and adopted by leaders like Jomo Kenyatta, Tom Mboya and others who maintained a version of the African socialism that gave the state an important but not necessarily exclusive role in the development; and (ii) the "maximalists" inspired by the doctrine of Marxism-Leninism doctrine giving the state 'all exclusive' role in the development process. The adherents of this line of development included Kwame Nkrumah, Sekou Toure, and Patrice Lumumba among others. The reception or responses by the international community to the two ideological approaches equally differed. In some cases, Nyerere's *"Ujamma"* – efforts to create a development strategy deeply rooted in African culture and thinking received considerable praise from Scandinavian countries and other light minded European countries. The important consideration for the West was that this ideological thinking distanced itself from any form of alliances with the communist bloc. The *"Ujamma"* doctrine was more acceptable than the all out Marxist-Leninist ideology advocated by some states.

What ever ideological orientation adopted by African countries, the sad side which equally contributed to the failure of these approaches being the form of governance system that emerged. The non-distinction between state and political party activities made the state play a wrong role. The integration of political party into state bureaucracy contributed to gross mismanagement, inefficiency, corruption and ineffective service delivery. The dominant one part-party political structure equally penetrated into the structure and functioning of the private sector. For example, trade unions that should have defended the interests of workers found themselves as part of the mainstream trappings of the ruling political party. Private sector entrepreneurs became part and parcel of the top hierarchy of political parties. The state was converted into an exclusive garden whose fruits were for a certain category of persons.

The hegemonic nature of state power emerged from the legacies of post-colonial state structure in which the distinctions between civil society and the state tended to be blurred. The new governing parties were seen as popular movements, unthinkable or inconceivable that those who fought for it could question the newly won political power. Co-optation of civil society groups, e.g. trade unions, cultural associations, student unions, bar associations and women's groups was typical and widely accepted in the newly independent states (see M'bonge and Doe 2004:13). It is not surprising that this contributed to the state being unable to fulfil its obligations as the liberator of the people but subsequently degenerated to being the oppressor through the form of failed and weak state system that surfaced. A state of procrastination not progress eventually emerged.

Suffice it to state that Africa's over-underdevelopment is not attributable, merely to poor governance, rapacious and corrupt leaderships, protracted civil wars in too many parts of the countries on the continent; no democratic checks and balances on government borrowing and spending, excessive population growth, and the stubborn pursuit of economic policies which contributed to the relentless impoverishment of as rich continent for many decades, but equally has strong indubitably footholds played by the developed countries. Africa's crisis is severely exacerbated by several other reasons as well, including:

- A hostile and rapidly changing global environment led by the western industrial military complexes;
- Over-reliance on external assistance and dictates from the west;
- Unfair or poor terms of trade – in short, absence of a global new economic and political order ensuring social justice;
- Inconsistence policy strategies adopted by African countries, and lack of visionary leadership plunged the continent into its current of being a beggar region, constantly asking for debt relief and handouts from the West.

Following Africa's lost decade of the 1980s, backed with events behind the *'iron curtain countries'*, there has been a turn in the tide. Ideologically, there has been the shift away from treating the state as the sole engine of development. Nonetheless, the state should be seen as facilitator, providing the enabling environment for the smoothing functioning of the private sector and as a partner with other key stakeholders in the process of development. The focus, rather, is on the market as playing the key role as instrument of allocating resources. The neo-liberal ideology underpins Bretton Woods imposed structural adjustment programmes seeking to reduce the involvement of the State in development process but confining it to providing a policy framework within which the market and its autonomous actors can flourish. That new flourishing network has to bring other stakeholders on board. It should be noted that the governance system that emerged in the immediate postcolonial years quickly sidelined the role of civil society and the private sector in the governance process. An exclusive governance system emerged that plunged the country into a state of serious underdevelopment and global marginalisation. It created fertile farms for a selected few.

The commitment to promote an inclusive political system is not so much about the processes of party politics, elections or ethnic hegemonic governance attitude, but a commitment to let citizens from all segments of society benefit from the goods that the states provides and from the opportunities that participating in the political life of the society, e.g. bureaucracy brings to the people. There is need of bringing development back to the centre-stage by involving all key stakeholders to be supportive of the process or at minimum not harmful to, national development efforts.

CONCEPTUAL PREMISES OF DEPARTURE

Issues of civil society and governance have received broad scholarly discourses in recent. The public sector has come under scrutiny for failing to provide basic necessities to the people. At the same time there have been voices calling for greater input role from civil society and the private sector to be inherent partners in the structural and development process of the nation. Attempts to reform the state has focused on reducing the size, cutting costs and changing the structure at the centre with the fervent hope of rendering more efficient, cost effective compact and competitive quality services delivery to the people.

Diamond (1995:9-40) defines civil society as the *"realm of organised social life that is voluntary, self-generating, self-supporting, autonomous from the state, and bound by the legal order or set of shared rules. It involves citizens acting collectively in a public sphere to express their interests, passions, and ideas, exchange ideas, exchange information, achieve mutual goals, make demands on the state, and hold state officials accountable. It is an intermediary entity, standing between the private sphere and the state".* Civil society acts as the custodian of the peoples' rights vis-à-vis the state and protects the people from the exploitative profit making mechanism of the private sector.

Thus organised civil society acts as a check against the excesses of both the state and private sector. M'boge and Doe (2004:3) contend *"that in the absence of an organised and engaged civil society governments are left with unchecked powers which over time corrupt the individuals in leadership and subsequently expose a country to politically-motivated human insecurity".* It could further be stated that the presence of civil society increases the chances of participation and the deployment of the skills or potential of the various segment of society to map a sustainable development path for the country. Unfortunately, immediately after independence, civil society that had been vocal in the national struggle for self-determination suddenly drifted apart from the mainstream of the national development course. Or rather the relationship between state and civil society was blurred as state machinery soon co-opted the bastion, vanguard and custodian of the people's rights and liberties.

Kukah M. Hassan (2003:43) captures this disengagement with the following metaphor: *"The relationship between civil society and states in Africa seems to have some of the basic characteristics of a fortified city. In the fortified city, communication between those inside and those outside is severely restricted by the nature of the fort itself. So there are naturally outsiders and insiders. The thicknesses of the wall, its height, its impenetrability, are what make it a respectable fort. These characteristics are supposed to inspire awe and intimidation in the minds of observers...The result, of course, is that the fortified city is a barricade, a siege; those inside cannot come out and those outside cannot go in. When civil society feels completely locked out it begins to seek relevance by resorting to such alternatives as migration {exile}, informal economic activities, sorcery, witchcraft, cults, genocide, forced relocations, intra-and inter-ethnic, communal or religious violence, ethnic cleansing, etc."*

Governance according to Adejumobi (2003:6) is a process of steering state and society towards the realisation of collective goals". It points to the dynamic but problematic and often times contradictory relationship between the state and society (Pierre et al. 2000: Balogun, 1998:33; Hyden, 1999; Stoker 1998; Alcanter 1998). In all, the barricades that separate civil society from the state undermined Africa's state and national building but accelerated the pace for corruption, money laundering, poverty and underdevelopment. Consequently, the vices of injustices (political, economic, social) and exclusion took the upper hand, thereby breeding a sense of relative deprivation and popular discontent. The aggrieved produced by political exclusion turned against themselves with extremist, ethnic gangs and militia turning their villages, towns and cities into battlegrounds (M'boge and Doe 2004:7)

According to Houston and Liebenberg (2001:1) The notion of a role for civil society in democratic governance at all levels of the political system was recognised by the African National Congress (ANC) in its policy document, the Reconstruction and Development Programme (RDP) in 1994, as *"Reconstruction and development requires a population that is empowered through expanded rights, meaningful information and education, an institutional network fostering representative and indirect democracy, and participatory and direct democracy"* (ANC. 1994:120). It is widely accepted among scholars that public participation in political processes is a virtue on its own right, and a *sine qua non* of a democracy (Dowse & Hughes 1986:266). It goes without saying that a healthy democracy is one in which the citizens participate regularly in formal political activities. Though the hegemonic one party system did permit citizen's participation in the form of the people attending rallies, they were never involved in party decision-making, which often were left to small clique of ruling elites.

This attitude by the ruling elite corps implied that (i) meaningful and extensive competition among individuals for effective position of government power did not exist in the true sense: (ii) a high level of political participation n the elections could be accomplished but not in the decision-making process: and (iii) the monolithic party system did not permit civil and political liberties – freedom of thought, speech and expression and equality under a rule of law existed only on paper but never practiced. It is expected that politics in post cold war era should usher anew lease of life for equality in the rule of law, optimal levels of political participation, and above all, lead to the politics of 'inclusion' and listening to the people. In short, a system of *'here the people rule;'* thereby drifting away from the politics of one-dimensional rule and personality cult-worship. Civil society participation can be perceived from a wide variety of approaches. Thus, this paper examines political participation in democratic governance by civil society as voluntary activities by which members of the public, directly or indirectly; share in the processes of governance through democratic institutions.

The fundamental values of democratic life are universal to humanity as a whole. But no single kind of democracy is applicable to all societies, and no single culture enjoys exclusive insight into democratic truths. Democratic truth is holding on to the virtues of the basic tenets of democracy and consciously applying this in all facets of activities. Democracy in Africa is integral to, not consequential upon, the democratic reforms sweeping elsewhere throughout the world. African democracy must grow in African soil to create a sustainable governance system; that is capable of building bridges across existing divide that keeps civil society and the private sector from the governing process.

Reform – in the political and economic domain – must be fully transparent, answering to the interests and will of the African peoples. Conditionality, whether political or economic, must not be imposed, but rather agreed upon with the free consent of African leaders and citizenry. Africa is in the theorem of seeking and implementing popular participation, governmental accountability, and transparency of domestic policies. Unfortunately, the first major setback in the democratic process was the institutionalisation of the hegemonic one party system without creating room for constructive and objective debates among members of the groups. In the new political dispensation of the 21st century – post cold war politics in Africa, the nature of the state, as well as the role of the state in relation to civil society must be rethought. It means also that politics and democratisation goes far beyond the winning of political power through parliamentary elections. It should include empowering individuals and organisation outside the state {non-state actors} to participate in the decision-making process.

To a large extent, underdevelopment of the continent could be attributed to policy of the state turning its back to civil society, the greedy and overzealous attitude of governing elites in alliance with selfish western interests. These leaders knew too well that civil society provides the ambit and platform forces complimenting state actions by which post-independent Africa could succeed. The services of civil society or that of the private sector was never sought, or sought for the wrong purposes The issue is rightly stated by Mamdani (1996:12): *"the moment of the collapse of an embryonic indigenous civil society, of trade unions and autonomous civil organisations, and its absorption into political society"* destroyed the continent's path to sustainable development. Civil society became demobilised and political parties statised.

The assumption of this paper builds on the following propositions: -

- The statisation of political parties paved the way for corruption underpinning Africa Africa's current state of underdevelopment;
- The nature of the African civil society in colonial days if reactivated constitutes a significant force and with partnership with the state and private sector would a source for putting the continent back on the right path to the development of the continent;
- The state must create an enabling environment, bringing on board other essential key players (civil society and private sector) to accelerate economic growth;
- A robust democratic civil society will strengthen the social contract with the people mobilising them to be partners in the development process.

The sudden switch to democratic governance is not an easy task for those who benefited from the dictatorial system and are still in power. The challenges continue to persist and plague the continent. And solutions must be found particularly for some countries that fear regime and system change, as the following examples demonstrate, see Box 1.

Clearly, the pursuit of public and private sector partnership should constitute an integral part of sound economic policies. This is badly needed in Africa and why civil society must be an integral part of governance. Respect and practice of democratic governance, human rights contribute to increased economic, social and political stability and helps prevent setbacks to development from political unrest and civil conflict. There is no doubt that state-civil society-private interlude holds the key to a better Africa of tomorrow. That better tomorrow means in positive terms, a spectrum from representative democracy (polyarchy) to deliberative or participatory democracy and popular democracy as the minimum requirement for access to the levers of power in the state at national, provincial and local government levels by the citizenry. The question of active involvement is crucial. That active involvement entails a *"triple helix"* involving the *state, civil society and the private secto*r working in unionism for the common interest and welfare of the people.

Box 1. Plethora of Problems to be tackled

• It is sometimes difficult to separate governance issues from weaknesses in institutional and administrative capacity; • The plethora of national demands and meeting international standards and codes can be overwhelming and highly demanding of human and financial resources, and meeting them may overstretch the capacities of African countries; • Poor governance may not always reflect a lack of government commitment. Even with strong and honest political leadership eliminating corruptions, poor work attitude and behaviour in Africa will take time. Yet it is a task that must be accomplished; • A culture of democratic governance must be cultivated and nurtured without these attributes of transparency; accountability, responsibility and benefit sharing cannot be achieved. These attributes are necessary to ensure public and private sector participation. African countries must participate in initiatives to improve governance and transparency: sustainable development can only be achieved through abiding to these norms.

Forje (2002). Reforming the Public Sector, Karlstad – Sweden.

CIVIL SOCIETY AND GOOD GOVERNANCE: THE SYNERGY

What is the linkage theory between civil society and good governance? How can this be achieved? Redefining the role of the state implies that African governance system must focus attention on at least four areas, namely: (i) reducing the size of public sector: (ii) stabilising the macroeconomic situation: (iii) reforming the regulatory framework: and (iv) good governance. These four approaches simply means power structural shift from development from above to one of development from below. Here partnership and participation play a significant role, as development becomes *"people-focused"* or *"people oriented and driven".* It should go further by integrating the various actors – economic and political institutions - on the continent towards facing a common goal and in the general interests of the poor

Participation or development led from below in the wider political institutions involves some basic changes in local institutions, bringing and diffusing centralised governance to the people i.e. enacting local involvement to transplant participatory democratic governance form as the essential mechanisms for the new social contract for sustainable development and improved living standard. Redefining the role of the state, Box 2 captures some of the issues in question.

These issues should aim at introducing participatory democracy, accountability and transparency, bringing about fundamental changes in the policy environment on the African continent with goals of improving the livelihood of the people; being master of its development process; and not marginalized in the evolving global knowledge based economy of the 21st century and beyond. Importantly here is that of making economic restructuring to proceed in the direction of getting the private sector more and more involved; getting civil society to be a mobilising factor in generating, enhancing and the appropriate mobilisation and utilisation of domestic resources for economic and technological transformation of the society.

Box 2. Redefining the Role of the State, Civil Society and Private Sector

- Reducing the Size of the Public Sector: Requires withdrawing from commercial sector related activities and increasing state activities in providing public services: Unproductive and inefficient public enterprises should be privatised – the private sector is better equipped than the state to manage enterprises;
- Stabilising macroeconomic situation: Curb unproductive spending. Reduce fiscal imbalances and large balances of payment deficits need to be seriously contained;
- Reforming of the Regulatory Framework: Measures to liberalise economic activities and gun for free enterprise. The state should encourage healthy competition among business, while eliminating economic rents and mechanisms that legally confer a dominant position on a turn on economic agent;
- Good Governance; should be seen as the cradle for moving the nation forward and the pillar for institutional reforms. Opening the political space for active participation by all in the development process. This opening should involved: Transparent government: separation of powers: individual freedom and collective expression: fight against corruption and poverty through clean governance, accountability, independence of the judiciary; role and responsibility of civil society: and private sector acting in liaison with the public sector to provide the society with essential services. Inclusion and not exclusion;
- representative and participatory democracy;
- Encouraging the Private Sector: Encouraging the private sector to be partners in the development process. It is evidently clear that the state cannot be the sole catalyst in shaping the well-being of the people. The private sector has to play a significant role in improving the living conditions of the people. A level playing field is required. More opportunities created by the private sector to increase employment possibilities for all. Laws should be enacted that facilitate the process of creating the necessary climate for the smooth functioning of the private sector; just the private sector should be able to take its share of responsibility, commitment and obligations to the society.

The paper lays emphasis on integration as a way of the people getting to know and understand whom the other is. Presently, economic integration among and between African countries remains minimal. The focus is on external trade with the developed countries institutionalised under colonial rule. This focus on Western Europe could also be seen as contributing to the state of political conflicts and instability on the continent. Inter-African trade is minimal. The challenge is for AU and NEPAD to intensify the political and economic integration of the continent and for regional economic groupings to be the catalyst for such integration. Movements within and across national frontiers creates greater understanding among the various groupings, lessons tensions and conflicts, builds mutual understanding and cooperation across existing divide.

CONCLUSION

Both the national and international climate has changed in a major way over the last few years. The process and consequences of societal development are perhaps assessed more carefully and critically than ever before. This concerns grows partly out of the degree of ever increasing rate of poverty, corruption and bad governance, it left to its own devices, demonstrations carried out under the wrong auspices and often in an unregulated manners, i.e. not keeping to its virtues, will be self-destructive threatening the envisaged mode of political stability and governance, as well as the distribution of wealth and power in the country. For this reason, various institutions and instruments of governance are required, promoted and harnessed by the self-interest of ruling elites and other forces.

This paper considered at length (i) the impact of other stakeholder in the governance process, and (ii) the need from the state descending from its ivory tower and joining the rank and file in articulating conditions and producing mechanisms for providing better living conditions to its population. Sitting in the ivory tower resulted in the lost decades of development and lost generations of people. These years of effort have clearly resulted more in procrastinations than in progress.

First, the African continent and in particular Sub-Saharan Africa is at a point where there is no longer much argument about the need for significant political and economic reform. Every one within the continent agree on one common thing – in favour of good economic policies and good political governance with the failed experience of half-baked experimentation with various discredited ideologies behind them. It is clear the state lacks the capacity to be provider, producer and procurer of its activities, but can act as the facilitator by promoting sound economic policies, providing the necessary leadership, and creating the requisite political will, conducive and enabling environment for the smooth functioning of the society.

First, for any progress to occur in Africa that lack of clarity must be corrected sooner rather than later. Second, state-civil society-private sector inter-linkages must be intensified, and harnessed for the socio-economic transformation of the continent. Third, for the continent to learn the bitter lessons of being a victim of previous global disharmony and to move forward to a brave new African continent. Importantly, Africa is caught within the trappings of emerging ideologies which were alien to them, and now emerging from post-cold war into a complex and technological sophisticated global world, must endeavour to avoid a continent-wide economic and political failure of the past and construct a continent better than the present state of being a beggar continent, constantly asking for debt relief and other-handouts.

Of course, there should be no illusion of an overnight solution. But solutions must be sought by present generation of cognisant leaders even though it may take a couple of generations to benefit from. The generation born just before the collapse of the Soviet Union (post-cold war era), suffering enormous deprivation caused by the inflicted crisis of the period, are hardly likely to merge from it without the sense of direction and confidence that is imperative for Africa to regain and sustain incipient recovery

Given the relentless repetition of the failure of one government after another and the monotonous repetition of one disaster after another on the African continent – whether natural or man-made – has definitely resulted in the sense of fatigue and hopelessness taking hold in sympathetic handouts, that subjects the people to be classified as second class citizens, imperatively call for a new constructive and consensus mobilising building approach of domestic resources for the continents recovery efforts.

All these negative influences and development converging on the African scene should spur a turning point for better prospects for, and African commitments to, achieving real and durable political, technological and economic changes for a better post-cold war Africa. Political and economic integration provides a way forward, and through this concerted, comprehensive and aggressive engagement approach process of all the key stakeholders, better, democratic and accountable governance system that the continent can begin to win the respect and, heart and minds of the international community to be genuinely partners and not exploiters of the continent. Africa has the capacity to put its own house in order, provide the political will for the common good reigns supreme.

Since independence, African leaders carried away by foreign mores not properly understood created the general problem of dislocation between itself and the citizens. It is imperative to overcome the politics of disconnection by reconnecting with the key players in society, by rebuilding trust and confidence in the system. Here Philip Bobbit (2002) talks about *"The Shield of Achilles"* about the changing nature of the state. *"The story of governance becomes the story of personalities in conflict with the media itself, and the story of official evasion and incompetence unmasked by the investigative entrepreneurs of the news business."*

The paper draws attention to and for a governance system able to restore the sense of mission and challenge: how Africa in the 21st century can combine political and economic dynamics with social justice in a completely different, more complex and challenging world in respect of providing its citizens with good living conditions in respect of: -

- A new articulated vision and model of sustainable economic development for a high value added knowledge economy that provides employment opportunities for many not the few;
- New bonds of social contract, solidarity, consensus and active aggressive engagement of all key players in the prevailing fractured, culturally diversion society into a mode, vision of partnership, participation, responsibility and benefit sharing for the common good. In short, one of the politics of 'inclusion' must prevail over that of "exclusion' as the new progressive governance system much needed to rid Africa from its current mess;
- The need for the international system to respond positively to the aspiration, desires and needs of the people in building a sustainable society that meets the peoples' hopes, vision and future. There is a call for social justice at the international level as well.

The future depends on how we prospect the present to give light to the future. In doing that we should take into consideration an ardent reality: that the continent is still divided by huge economic and social disparities. We need to ask ourselves where they stem from and how we can overcome them. How are we going to overcome poverty, corruption endemic diseases etc.? Perhaps the answer *"lies in our ability to replicate the best elements of our society, at all levels and aiming all communities"* (Mandela 1999). The prospects for the future are bright provided we comprehensively address the many things currently plaguing the society – poverty, corruption, bad governance, poor service delivery, endemic disease, xenophobia, underdevelopment, absence of the rule of law, social injustice and inequities in society etc.

Prospects for the future are good if only the people and in particular, the leaders exhibit high sense of political will, vision and work in the broad interest of all. The common good and not individual self-interests should take centre-stage. Again, the words of Mandela (1999) should be a pointer in this direction. *"Inspired by the single vision of creating a people-centred society, we will drive the expansion of the frontiers of human fulfilment, and the continuous extension of the frontiers of freedom"*. That frontier of freedom implies achieving real and durable political, economic and technological changes to better improve the livelihood of the people. The other side of the frontier is for the international community under the leadership of the western industrial military complex extending a positive listening ear and responding to the needs and aspirations of the African people.

There has to be a reversal of the current perception harboured in the West about the continent and its people that *"too much of what has been given to Africa has been wasted and there is no reason to believe that giving more would result in a different outcome."* To a large extent they are right. Failed governments, corruption and other ills constitute the political landscape of the continent. Africa has and is a victim of previous global disharmony. Under these circumstances, and with past record in view there is neither the will of sympathy nor the energetic drive to support Africa in the same way. Africa therefore, has the only option of *"putting its house in order"* just as western democracies must be ready to take its own share of the blame and open up for sustainable partnership between the developed and transitional polities.

Future prospects depend on whether the right kind of structural adjustment is put in place in Africa now. The notion taking hold with confusing repetitiveness in emerging but obscure governance system as Africa countries are gradually drifting back to the old hegemonic status quo of monolithic party structure. Multiparty pluralist elections have been held: the conduct of these elections needs to be desired. Most Legislative Assemblies are fast becoming monolithic party structures. These disturbing trends in the governance system need to be swiftly corrected by remedies appropriately to and still in the culture of democratic governance and its sustainability in Africa.

These are challenges for the state. A number of changes are required at the state level: changes that place particular stress and obligations on the traditional role of the state, civil society, political parties and the private sector. The first concerns the distribution of power. The state is no longer seen as the sole powerhouse but as a facilitator that must work in partnership with other actors. The new powerhouse of politics consists of other actors that in unionism with the state would achieve change, identify where decisions are made by other actors to influence the process of decision-making. Government has to come down its ivory tower, dialogue, concert and partner with other actors. The development process has to change from *"top-down" to "bottom-up", from centralised to decentralised, and participatory.* The entire process calls for shared-responsibility among the stakeholders. Issues of development are blurring and interdependence is increasing. There are no longer any backyards where individual countries can do as they like out of sight of the rest of the world community. No government or country can ignore any longer what is going on in the rest of the country and the world. The local community being marginalized today may emerge as the centre of developmental change tomorrow. Today, everything is everybody's business. The effects of economic success and setbacks spread like ripples on the water. Underdevelopment, exclusion, armed conflicts, corruption, poverty, and terrorism are challenges that must be confronted by all the countries of the world working together not in isolation. We all have shared responsibility for our nation and the world.

Prospects for the future depends on the degree of active engagement, how the state is able to bring social changes through broadening the political space involving the state-civil-society-private sector intercourse: a relationship that can instil in the people the need for creativity, innovation, productivity and risk taking in our industries and in our public services. The future depends on the characteristics that will develop new solutions to old problems, allowing all stakeholders to take advantage of opportunities. Prospects for the future will also depend on a framework to encourage at the individual, rural, local levels and national levels with a necessary steering role for the centre. All the key stakeholders must be empowered so as to better transform the society for the common good. For progress to occur in Africa that lack of clarity must be corrected sooner rather than later.

Presently, it is not clear how African societies working together with the international community, can best bridge that yawing gap in mutually acceptable ways that do not offend a still insecure, but ever-present, sense of national pride and do not threaten legitimate concerns about sovereignty concerns which in the past have simply provided an excuse for African leaders and the elites which sustain them, to profit enormously at the considerable expense of their population and countries. But with political will and the interest of the people at heart, there is no reason why common grounds cannot be brokered for the welfare of all. Are the leaders willing to thread on this path or continue their selfish individualistic interests?

We have to manufacture new strategies, set new prerequisites for addressing ensuring challenges for sustainable national and global development. No doubts progress has been made in African countries since the demise of colonial rule. More people than ever before live in societies, which have made significant progress towards democracy and where they have a say in their own lives. But many are excluded from these developments. Over one billion people, most of them in rural areas, live in extreme poverty. May of them do not have enough to eat and lack access to clean drinking water, as well as access to basic health care, education and shelter over their heads.

There is urgent need for an open public dialogue on national development issues. Efforts should be exerted in make appropriate use of advances in science and technology Globalisation and national development issues are making increasing demands on knowledge and analysis which are important in political decision-making, but also for a constructive and open public debate. Information, communication and opinion formation are important tools for disseminating knowledge and stimulating public discussions about policy, articulation and aggregation. Existing barriers must be broken to ensure sustainable development: and the fruits of development are trickling down to all segments of society. Whatever governance system put in place must be able to face these challenges. Meeting the needs and aspirations of the people is a challenge good leadership should provide.

REFERENCES

Adejumobi, Said (2003) "Democracy and Good Governance in Africa. Theoretical and Methodological Issues" in Bujra Abdalla and Adejumobi Said (eds.) *Breaking Barriers, Creating New Hopes*. DMPF Addis Ababa, Ethiopia.

African National Congress (ANC), 1994. *The Reconstruction and Development Programme*. Johannesburg, South Africa.

Ake, Claude (2000). *The Feasibility of Democracy in Africa* (Dakar –CODESRIA).

Alcantara, C. (1998) "Uses and Abuses of the Concept of Governance", *International Social Science Journal*, No. 155. pp.105-113.

Balogun, J. (1998) "The Role of Governance and Civil Society in Africa's Development", *Regional Development Dialogue,* Vol. 19 No. 2 (Autumn), pp.32-50.

Bratton, M. and Walle, N. (1997). *Democratic Experiments in Africa: Regime Transition in Comparative Perspective.* Cambridge University Press, New York.

Bujura, Abdalla et al, (2003) *Breaking Barriers, Creating New Hopes.* DMPF Addis, Ethiopia.

Carr, E. H. (1984, 1946). *The Twenty Years' Crisis 1919-1939.* Macmillan, London

Diamond, Larry (1995) *"Rethinking Civil Society",* quoted in *"Crossroads",* USIS Newsletter, Lagos, Nigeria, February 1995, pp9-10.

Dowse, R. E. & Hughes, J. A. (1980) *Political Sociology.* 2nd ed. Chichester, John Wiley & Sons, New York, Brisbane, Toronto, Singapore,

Forje, John W. (2002) "Reforming the Public Sector – Restoring Confidence and Legitimacy to Public Authority: Lessons from Africa." *Paper prepared for the International Conference on Public and Private Sector Partnerships: Exploring Co-operation.* 12-15 June 2002, University of Karlstad, Sweden.

Houston, Gregory and Ian Liebenberg (2001). "Introduction." *Public Participation in Democratic Governance in South Africa,* Human Science Research Council< Pretoria, South Africa.

Hyden, Goran (1999), "African Governance Barometer: Measurement and Monitoring Issues", Paper Presented to the United Nations Economic Commission for Africa (UNECA) *Workshop on "Indicators for Monitoring the Progress Towards Good Governance in Africa,* September 20-22, Addis Ababa, Ethiopia.

Kukah, Matthew Hassan (2003) *Democracy And Civil Society in Nigeria.* Spectrum Books, Nigeria.

Mandela, Nelson (1999) Long Walk to Freedom. And see *"The legacy (2004) vol. 2. Emerging Voices*, p.12. The Nelson Mandela House, Houghton, South Africa.

Martin Luther King (1968), Sermon on Race Relations and Civil Rights in America. *The Martin Luther King Papers,* King Centre, Atlanta, USA.

M'boge. Fatoumatte and Sam Gbaydee Doe (2004) African Commitment to Civil Society Engagement. *African Human Security Initiative,* Pretoria, South Africa.

Pierre, J. and B. Guy (2000), Governance, Politics and the State. Macmillan, London,

Stoker, G. (1998) "Governance as Theory: Five Propositions", *International Social Science Journal,* No. 155, pp.17 -27.

Chapter 6

NAVIGATING LIBERIA TOWARDS CONSOLIDATING DEMOCRATIC GOVERNANCE, ECONOMIC GROWTH AND SUSTAINABLE DEVELOPMENT: BUILDING QUALITY LIVELIHOOD FOR THE PEOPLE[*]

ABSTRACT

The paper exams ways and means of putting war torn Liberia back on the path of sustainable development. Following years of conflict, Liberia now needs both domestic and external support for its recovery, reconstruction and development process on the basis of a platform that harnesses the resources of both domestic and international partners. The country is entering a new era and beginning which calls for total solidarity from different quarters in assisting the people build quality livelihood for themselves and future generations.

What measures are needed to improve international assistance as well as mobilising domestic resources to kick-start the long road to recovery and development? Obviously, the state must be reconstituted. For without a democratic governance environment it would be difficult to build trust and confidence as well as mobilise the requisite financial resources needed for the socio-economic transformation of the society from a war to a peace situation

The report ends by advancing recommendations for Liberia to engage in a new beginning from state failure to state building. This can only be possible when the people develop a new mindset of reconciliation and consensus building of give and take and healing the wounds of many years of conflict and wanton destruction that has taken away so many lives and destroyed property and caused untold human suffering.

INTRODUCTION

The focus of the paper is on the intriguing phenomenon of democracy and economic growth in Liberia just emerging from violent internal conflict. In short, Liberia is a country at

---

[*] Paper Prepared for the Conference of Former African Heads of State and Government on Mobilising International Support for Post-Conflict Reconstruction in Liberia, 28 October – 2nd November 2006, Pretoria, South Africa.

crossroads needing the support of the international community for its post-conflict reconstruction development.

Without sustained support to the newly democratically elected government, the prospects of "things falling apart" loom large and could once again be heightened with impunity, violence and social exclusion taking centre stage. We should not let the emerging hopes and aspirations of the people dashed into an unknown future.

If Liberia needs any thing now is the good will of the international community to ensure that peace, security and prosperity reigns for the citizens and neighbouring countries.

The underlying element advanced here is for the international community not to relent its efforts in sustaining the new leadership and government with the necessary windows of opportunities to reconstruct, rebuild and re-institute a democratic developmental state.

As a nation that has just returned to the fold of democratically elected government in grand style with a difference, but seriously charged with facing the challenges of reconstruction and development. The grand style and difference is that the leadership of the country is under Africa's first ever-elected female president endowed with a new vision and human touch for the people. The challenge of reconstruction and economic growth range from a pro-longed period of poor governance, economic declined and destruction, conflicts and wars and social exclusion that has crippled the economy contributing to massive abject poverty, insecurity and corruption.

The challenge{s} for the new government is manifold and must not be underestimated. Efforts toward reconstruction lie first and foremost in the committed spirit, will and efforts of the population to rebuilding the nation: and second, support from the international community towards the envisaged goal.

Presently, the government enjoys the promise of substantial financial and technical assistance from the international community. Importantly, Liberians must mustered concerted efforts and courage of building national capacity in innovative ways is of paramount importance. They should be masters of their reconstruction process while hoping and relying on external assistance at this initial stage of reconstruction efforts.

With present conditions unchanged, the people stand little chance of realising the ideals of the Millennium Development Goals {MDGs} without outside support. On the other hand, the international community has the obligation in the name of humanity not to allow Liberia return to its devastated past. There are obvious reasons for the international community to assist the country with its articulated Strategic Reconstruction Priority Development Agenda that should usher benefits and quality livelihood to the large marginalized population as well as extending the largesse to neighbouring countries.

Concerted national actions are required to restore confidence and hope in the people. This implies strategies to address long-standing problems of poor governance, corruption and mismanagement. A comprehensive effort to building national capacity {human and institutional} in an innovative ways is of paramount importance for Liberians to take charge of their lives.

For Liberia to mobilise and sustained support from the international community, it need to put in place a comprehensive Reconstruction and Development Priority Agenda Plan that appeals and attracts the various donors of the seriousness and intent of the people to put the past into the museum of antiquity and forge a head as a united body for a better future.

The paper adopts a holistic multidisciplinary approach based on the argument that Post-conflict reconstruction setting is fundamentally different from development under related activities under normal circumstances. Post-conflict reconstructions are designed to facilitate or to symbolise an end to internal conflicts. To a large extent, it could be linked to development after the struggle for "self-determination" with a difference. It means pulling the entire nation together at once with limited resources to quickly restore confidence, hope, and national unity and sense of belonging.

STRUCTURE OF THE REPORT

The paper is divided into the following sections. The first part gives a brief historical past of the country within the last two-three decades. Part two deals with reconstruction challenges. The third part treats cross-cutting issues. While part four looks at priority areas for action. Part five - the way forward - is a summary that includes conclusion and recommendations.

THE CONTEXT – THE CHEQUERED PAST AND UNDERLYING ISSUES

Liberian's past two to three decades constitute of a chequered historical setting pervading every aspect of recovery and development. The state of conflict defines the challenges the government faces in its reconstruction and development plans, highlighting the enormity of the problem the international community is called upon to grapple with.

The torturing and suffering of the people under the aegis of dictatorship, centralisation and misuse of power for over two decades is beyond description. The eminent outcome has been the collapse of the state. This can be traced through a confluence of historical, socio-cultural, economic and political conditions. It is imperative that the international community respond effectively and positively to the existing underlying socio-economic, ethno-political and structural roots of the country's protracted war and the emerging windows of opportunities for its return to the community of democracies. This is vital to ensure that Liberia does not relapsed into conflict that would again inflict serious consequences not only to the nation, sub-region but the entire continent and beyond.

The brutality of the war and the catalogue of atrocities suffered by the population were severe, from rape, mutilation, ritual killings, murder and massacre to destruction of infrastructure, child soldiers among others paint a bleak picture. These and other practices deepened the challenges of recovery and development as it necessitates greater attention to the process of healing, reconciliation, reconstruction, social justices and peace building.

Liberia has to start from scratch: to effectively muddle its way through the scourges of a collapsed state by reconstituting its social structures and political environment, building trust and confidence among the population and in government without which it could potentially contribute to en escalation of conflict with serious consequences beyond national frontiers.

Serious reconciliation process between the warring parties must take place to restore confidence and forge development in the country. Equally important is the issue of addressing the roots of the conflict that almost led to the total collapse of the country. This requires a carefully mediated process of reconciliation and the establishment of anew socio-political order that guarantees equality of access and opportunities to all groups and interests in the country. The question of the youth as an integral part of the conflict process is also vital to reconciliation efforts. A regime of good governance, capable of managing the resources of the country in response to the critical needs of society, is a *sin qua non*-to achieving these. Such societal needs include job opportunities, infrastructural development, economic growth and development, and a sustained regime of political order and stability. [Omotola, 2006:46]

Box 1. Some Characteristically factors Influencing Conflict-Ridden Nation. The Case of Liberia

- Monopolisation and inappropriate deployment of power
- Ethnic hegemonic tendencies and exclusion
- Inappropriate utilisation of natural resources
- Democratic governance that ensures the rule of law, social justice and quality delivery services
- Productive and competitive private sector
- Increase the middle class by reducing the growing poor
- External influence

- Crisis in Political development
- Identity crisis
- Legitimacy
- Penetration
- Integration
- Distribution
- Participation

Marginalisation, exploitation, disintegration, dependency, civil wars/ conflict, dependency, underdevelopment among many others. However, the sequences and pattern of development in a country depends largely upon the sequence in which the crisis occur and the ways in which they are resolved {see Lucian Pye 1966}.

Source: Forje [2007] Here the People Rule.

It is vital that a level political field be established just as it is important to ensure an independent judiciary system. For reconciliation and development to take place, and effectively carried out, there is need for a great deal of political will on the part of the state, adequate financial resources, institutional capacity such as human and social capital, a virile and robust civil society, and an environment of international cooperation and support. As of now, these requirements suffer fluctuating fortunes in Africa, given the declining capacity of the state as a result of years of abuse, and the continuing lack of interest of the West in

African affairs following the end of the Cold War. The effort to institute a regime of local ownership of the reform process by Africans offers some bold relief. This does not imply that international assistance and cooperation are not needed. Such efforts should be pursued as supplements, not alternatives to domestic or local initiatives. This is important given the sensitivity of security sector reform and reconstruction to sustainable peace, democracy and development in Liberia {Omotola 2006] as well as in other conflict regions in Africa, Sudan, Somali and Chad.

The country requires more than ever before an effective, holistic multidisciplinary broad based strategising approach for recovery and development [see World Bank 2005]. The historical and governance past of the country can be characterised by the gross absence of some issues shown in Box 1. Which plunged Liberia to disaster, destruction and destitution? These issues have to be addressed in post-conflict reconstruction development strategic agenda. Some are briefly discussed.

It is within this context that reconstruction, peace, security, social justice and development must evolve before the people can attain basic minimum level of quality living standard: and for the sustainability of the international community trust and confidence in injecting the necessary financial and technical support for the recovery of Liberia.

RECONSTRUCTION CHALLENGES

Democratic Governance

Developing effective and transparent governance structures is an imperative for the reconstruction and development of the society. The breakdown of government in Liberia resulted in large part from the failure of government being the liberator of the people, but emerged as the oppressor. Transparent and account systems of governance was absent. Previous constitutional set up assigned overwhelming power to executive domination of the legislature and judiciary and failing to create the necessary constitutional checks and balances Government degenerated into autocracy, greed, corruption and nepotism, with an ethnic hegemonic tyrannical minority in total control of the system. lording it over the silent and neglected majority. The repressive and predatory nature of the political ruling elite created an environment in which mismanagement and exploitation of natural resources, violence and predation were commonplace. As a consequence of the system of patronage, recruitment of employees was rife with favouritism and nepotism [Doss 2006].

Sources of conflicts in transitional polities {Liberia} for example, arise as a result of the presence of one or more of these crises within the social fabric of society. Poor distribution of resources, poor participation or exclusive policies promotes absence of a sense of belonging; legitimacy of the government is questioned as its policies can hardly penetrate the social fabric of the society. When civil society is uncertain over the appropriate rate of expansion and inclusion and new entrants are restricted, this is likely to create serious strains on existing institutions. Trust and confidence in the system is lost. The legitimacy of the regime is questioned. When government is limited in its demand in accelerating the pace of economic development and social justice and safety nets, by concentrating in particular regions and class of people, unable to reach other parts of the country, the issue of penetration becomes a serious problem. [Forje, 2006:9 chapters 2]. The nation degenerates into chaos and confusion. What the government need is an integrated development policy strategy, drawing from the Millennium Development Goals and the realities of the situation on ground to shape its reconstruction and development process that should include:

- Democracy, good governance and respect for human rights;
- Equality between men and women – especially women empowerment;
- Environmental protection ;
- Economic growth ;
- Social development ;
- Conflict management or rehabilitation of combatants.

Economy

Reconstruction requires sustained financial inputs. Liberia's prolonged conflict inflicted serious damages to its economy, infrastructure and human and resources and great damage to the environment. All these activities must be developed. The country stagnated and denied viable livelihood. Investors scared away imposing addition toll in economic activities and job creation, unemployment double many folds: Economic activity stalled small scale business activities providing subsistence occupation for women and other marginalised groups delivered a sharp blow to the living standards of women, children, the old and others. The society denied a viable livelihood. In addition, public mismanagement of public funds added more problems to an already depilated state of affairs.

Reconstruction implies putting the economy on its feet, which include, reinstating the following and making them functional.

- Transport, electricity, road, infrastructure ;
- Security, environment including a functional banking sector and proper financial management;
- Destruction of landmines, and creating the way for agricultural take off to ensure food security;
- Getting both combatants and non-combatants into gainful employment;
- Building human and institution capacity of the country.

Food Security – Agriculture

As an agricultural country, with the vast majority depending on subsistence agriculture, adequate measures must be taken for the country to re-dynamise the sector as a means of poverty alleviation and ensuring food security. Two issues must be simultaneously addressed, the problems arising out of poverty or the inadequacy of development itself, and the problems that arise out of the very process of development. The problems of the first category are reflected in the poor social and economic conditions that prevail in both the rural and urban areas. For a country like Liberia these are, by far, the problems of greatest importance

Building the agricultural sector is vital as it would provide opportunities for food security and gainful employment for all categories of citizens, especially women and the unemployed. Improvement in the agricultural sector will have to take into consideration many factors, the environmental setting, kinds of technology deployed, the issue of traditional versus modern agricultural development, environmental side effects that have been known to accompany, in varying degrees, the process of development in agriculture, industry, transport and human settlement. Some of the side effects would include: {a} resources deterioration: the deterioration, for example, of mineral, soil or forest resources: {b} biological pollution: the pollution represented by agents of human disease, and by animal and plant pests: {c} chemical pollution: arising out of air pollutants, industrial effluents, pesticides, metals, and detergents components and similar agents: {d} physical disruption: as reflected for example by thermal pollution, silting and noise or from prolonged conflict/wars like what the country has been subjected to: and {e} social disruption: of which congestion and loss of a sense of community are examples.

Reconstruction must take into account new opportunities for preventing some of these environmental hazards through proper planning and anticipatory action.

Human and Institutional Capacity Development

Developing its human and institutional capacity is vital for both the immediate and long-term reconstruction and sustainable development of country and for providing sustainable quality livelihood to the present and future generations. The educational system has to be looked into and ensure that education is tailored to the needs of the people. Strong emphasis should be directed towards science and technology and encouraging females taking interests in science and technology related disciplines. Training ex-combatants and the youths in acquiring technical skills and other forms of education is important for the reconstruction and development process. The approach should be seen from the perspectives of short, medium, and long-term proactive approach in addressing the literacy deficiency of the nation.

National Security

National security is at the heart of the reconstruction and development process and must be given top priority. Security to life and property must be assured to restore confidence in the population and to attract foreign private investment and assistance from donor bodies. People should feel safe to travel throughout the country and be assured of enjoying their fundamental human rights in its totality. Freedom of the press and speech are important to build confidence among the people.

Environmental Protection

It is significant that serious attention be paid to the environment and development. The twofold topic marks the recognition of the "link" and of the interdependence of issues and solutions concerning the reconstruction process of the nation. It is imperative that Liberia has adequate environmental space for its reconstruction and future development and to modify economic activities in such a way that the people obtain the required resources, technology and access to markets that would enable it to pursue a development process that is both environmentally sound and rapid enough to meet the needs and aspirations of its population.

Liberia will also need to adopt a comprehensive strategy for its environmental protection and to detest from any part of the country becoming a dumping pit for hazardous waste from the industrial countries as a prelude to receiving financial and technical assistance in its reconstruction and development process.

Building an Industrial Base

Reconstruction requires building an industrial base to improve on the unemployment situation and to process as much of the resources locally as possible. Liberia has an advantage in so far as it can learn from he experiences of developed nations. However, it should not be blindfolded in accepting offers of industrial plants that would great hazards to it socio-economic and environmental situation. It should in the process of reconstruction give careful consideration to the question of location of industries and formulate concrete guidelines in the context of its national reconstruction situation

The political economy of war precipitated by the miss-governance of the military government of Samuel Doe in the 19980s offers a good starting point to an understanding of the deepening crisis and contradictions of Liberia's industrial and infrastructure sector. Strong commitment and efforts are required to restore the infrastructure and to put the country back on the rails of reconstruction and recovery.

Cross-cutting Issues

A number of cross-cutting issues requiring consideration that the society must adequately address simultaneously in the effort to provide the population with democratically functional state institutions capable of meeting the quality living standards of the population remain imperative in the reconstruction priority policy agenda and approach

Policy strategies, projects and other related development activities must evolve in such a proactive platform of total engagement and to mainstream actions that further engages and improves the position of women, youths and other disadvantaged groups in society. Bearing in mind that women make up more than 51% of the population, and that youths constitute a greater part of the population and are the future hopes of the society, gender inequality and neglect of the Youth must be addressed to ensure a sustainable and balanced prospects of development.

Gender Inequality and Empowerment

Post-conflict reconstruction requires balancing the current imbalances existing between gender constellations in society. Balanced development should be promoted throughout the society so that no sector feels alienated. Women must be made integral part of the development process as they have much to offer. Neither the economy can be revitalised nor the democratisation advanced without the full involvement of women. Their continued marginalisation {exclusion} will hold back the process of reconstruction and development. Females have not been treated as equal partners in national development strategy. Generally, a new era of transition in Africa presents new opportunities and challenges for the goal of women's empowerment and emancipation. Women in Liberia should be brought to the forefront and mapping new futures for them in respect of:

- Inequality in power-sharing and decision-making at all levels;
- Insufficient machinery at all levels to promote the advancement of women;
- Adopting technologies favouring women to enhance contributions in the development process;
- Poverty discrimination and marginalisation ;
- Violence against women and inheritance/land tenure not favouring them.

Construction of a developmental state must not evolve on a restricted empowerment of the female gender, but addressed within the context of a national development strategy. Empowerment and equality becomes necessities for development and survival – the dreams of women are the dreams of their nations on which the construction of the democratic developmental state in Africa must build on. Gender in the construction of the democratic developmental state in Africa must remove women from the minus side to the plus side of the development continuum. Proactive strategic policy-measures are advanced.

Security and Peace

Security and Peace areas are vital cross-cutting issues in the reconstruction saga of Liberia. Both touch all aspects of society, creating the basis for sustainable investments and development. Security and peace must reign in Liberia to kick start development activities. The two remain the panacea for development and most be given top priority in all reconstruction process. Post-conflict reconstruction activities are conceived as an outcome of a process of social and political interaction in which social values and norms, collective identities and cultural traditions are essential [Wendt, 1992: 1999]. According to Art [1993] "to be secure id to feel free from threats anxiety or danger. Security is therefore a state of the mind in which an individual feels safe from harm by others". The people must feel secured to forge ahead.

Security in its total dimensions is vital for the reconstruction of Liberia. Currently, intra-state conflict, ethnic violence, landmines, human rights violation, gender inequality, crime, poverty, hunger, deprivation, genocide, disease and health hazards, environmental degradation, human capacity development among others impact on the reconstruction process.

Diseases – HIV/AIDS, etc…

Endemic diseases must be understood as log-wave event, which interacts with the long-term dynamics of development and social change. The situation of poor health of the people complicates and exacerbates the existing challenges of diseases, abject poverty, conflict and injustice by contributing to a complex set of inter-locking vulnerabilities.

Quality of life or livelihood vulnerability needs to be analysed in a holistic and context-specific way. Post-conflict reconstruction process of Liberia addressing the health situation of the country requires a comprehensive and empowering approach to social protection. The quality health status of the people determines the health of the nation and its output functions. The health of the nation [public and private] responses that reduce poverty, help individuals, families and communities protect themselves against shocks, and enhance the social status and rights of the most marginalized and vulnerable.

Apart from the already known endemic killer diseases, malaria, tuberculoses, polio etc, and the HIV/AIDS epidemic adds to the woes of the society, as the youthful population are victims of the pandemic. The health situation of the society must be addressed from an integrated perspective and within the context of the impact on the reconstruction development process and other institutional and political structures reinforcing sectoral boundaries and displacing research silos. The international community must not relent efforts in assisting the country in meeting its health and human capacity development challenges.

We need to see health systems as knowledge economies of regulated or mediated access to technology and expertise in society, which all the stakeholders should link up and engage more effectively, not only with one another, but also with these suffering from poor health. Improving the health of the people (citizens), empowerment, social change and accountability will have much to contribute to this area.

Priority Areas for Action

A policy strategic plans prioritising the priority areas need to be developed for action, short-term, medium-term and long-term purposes. Some of the priority areas may include:

- Expanding peace and security ;
- Rebuilding collapsed infrastructure and strengthening institutional capacity for providing basic services;
- Strengthening governance, rule of law and restoring trust, confidence, legitimacy to the state and its institutions;
- Getting the private sector and civil society as partners in development;
- Human capacity building ;

- Addressing the health status of the population and making serious efforts in containing endemic disease {malarias, polio, tuberculosis etc} and attacking head on the pandemic killer disease HIV/AIDS, STD among others;
- Revitalising the economy.

Taking a few examples, it is crucial for the country to broaden the peace and security space, and to ensure ex-combatants of their role in the reconstruction process. It is equally imperative for peace and security to reign throughout the country in order to attract foreign investment and for donors to be assured of the impact of their contributions are making on the lives of the people, and for them responding positively and courageously in ways that contribute to a constructive shift in power and opportunity needed to accelerate Liberia's return to the community of democracies.

All these activities cost money, time and efforts and cannot be realised overnight. But the first step must be taken in the right direction, here and now. Efforts that must involved all the stakeholders. Any financial contribution or technical assistance in this direction counts in moving the process forward. All avenues must be positively exploited to the advantaged of the people of Liberia.

Reconstructing the security sector for economic and social activities including the establishment of legislative and civil society oversight and accountability mechanisms is crucial and must be linked to the over all national recovery strategy. Returning to a state of peace and security will facilitate the growth of small and medium-size enterprises development, empowerment of women, create employment opportunities, alleviate poverty and improve on the quality of livelihood of the population.

Rebuilding infrastructure and revitalising economic activities. Liberia requires a broad-based poverty-reduction and sustained economic growth recovery and development with a big thrust on employment, human capacity building and institutional development including the rehabilitation and construction of infrastructure like roads, electricity, ports and other public structures to facilitate the smooth transfer of produce, goods and service. These infrastructures are necessary to creating opportunities and stimulating employment and revitalising economic growth.

National pressure management and protection of the environment and its resources is vital as booster to agricultural activities. Farmlands and forest areas must be cleared of all landmines and made safe for people to undertake economic related activities that should provide food security and employment opportunities for all. Liberia needs a global action Marshall Plan for its reconstruction and development efforts. This should be articulated and aggregated under the caption "Global Marshall Plan of Partnership for Sustainable Development for the total benefit of the people of Liberia.

I see the meeting of *Former African Heads of State and Government* constituting the ground-breaking space for such a noble course – *"A Marshall Plan of Partnership for Reconstruction and Sustainable Development"* for the ultimate benefit of the people, especially the disadvantaged groups in society. The necessary *political will* is required to drive the project through. Can the international community provide that vital ingredient? Are the people prepared to take their share of responsibility?

THE WAY FORWARD

Synopsis

One way to mobilising international support in *Post-Conflict Reconstruction and Development* in Liberia is through consolidating democratic governance and promoting growth and sustainable development. It is imperative that an environment of reconciliation, consensus, partnership, participation and responsibility-sharing be cultivated among the various stakeholders

Liberia needs a concerted and comprehensive strategic priority approach agenda to determine and implement a national model for recovery and reconstruction which should incorporate among others that include the following issues: {i} the magnitude of the problems and challenges to be overcome: {ii} the way: {iii} the participants and {iv} the objectives.

1. The Challenges: Confronting National Problems

[1:1] Only Liberian's know best what their problems are and these problems threatened by poor governance issues raised in box 1: development crisis: deterioration of the environment: poverty: lack of security in all its dimensions.

These problems are inter-related and cannot be solved only by Liberians but requiring some form of foreign assistance under what can be described *"mutual interdependence of all human-beings"*.

[1:2] The problems of Liberia and solutions are those of Liberians but must be approached, analysed and solved within a regional, continental and global context – hence, "Mobilising International Support for Post-Conflict Reconstruction And Sustainable Development".

[1:3] Seen within this context, navigating Liberia to the Community of Democracies and Quality Livelihood should be examined holistically within the framework of a short-term, medium-term and long-term effects taking into account, and as lessons for other nations in similar situations.

2. The Way

[2:1] Building national consciousness and choices made with intuitive knowledge and respecting the basic tenets of democracy and good governance.

[2:2] Solutions to the problems must be first sought from within but requiring external inputs {assistance} financial, technical and otherwise

[2:3] Open debate in the politics and technology of the "Baobab Tree" underlining the values behind decisions, unity of the people, individuals and society increases the value conflicts are dealt with from a holistic perspective

[2:4] Instituting a culture of democratic governance system will help cultivate a sense of belonging and participation.

3. Participants: Power to the People with Equal Opportunities for all

[3:1] The participants are state, organisations, individuals and the global community

[3:2] The entire nation should be involved in the reconstruction process. The politics of 'winner takes all' will not lead to a constructive post-conflict reconstruction process: but fan situations that caused earlier conflicts.

[3:3] Partnership, participation, benefit and responsibility-sharing among the stakeholders – state, civil society, private sector including the international community.

4. *Objective. Sustainable Development and Quality of Life with Dignity for all*

[4:1] Resolving national problems and securing the future of the citizens can only be achieved through joint efforts and a policy of sustainable development is economically sound, and viable, technologically feasible and socially just and is capable of broadening the basis for inclusion, leading to national cohesion and balanced development

[4:2] The reconstruction and development processes must be inclusive

[4:3] A Coalition Government {CG} or Government of National Unity {GNU} is advocated as the way forward for Liberia to reconstitute, reconstruct and regain itself as a Nation-State that cares for its citizens and working for peace, stability and progress of the sub-region, the continent and the world.

CONCLUDING OBSERVATIONS AND RECOMMENDATIONS

Some observations from a broad perspective of the post-conflict reconstructions are made. The paper demonstrates the Hercules task facing the newly democratically elected government is charged with. It has to launch and implement a robust economic and democratic governance intervention with a strong commitment of getting the people out of the ghetto of abject poverty, misery, exploitation and underdevelopment and to provide an opportunity for better quality livelihood for the population. All hands must be on deck in the post-conflict transition of a state to stable peace and sustainable development. In so doing, the peoples' efforts must be backed by greater international willingness and commitments for Liberia's return to the community of democracies.

The efforts by the African Forum {AF – a policy forum established by former African Heads of States and Government, chaired by Joachim Chissano} to convene a meeting of Former Heads of State and Government is a welcome move to be supported, and constitute a committed process showing the concern and "Africanness" required in addressing the problems of an African country. This concern must receive the support of the people and their determined willingness to respond accordingly. The initiative and effort, which is timely, should open windows of opportunities for the new government to make conscious progress necessary to realise the rights of its people. Here lies the challenge for the new government.

First the government must not betray the trust and confidence entrusted on it by the people. Second, the government must endeavour to uphold the good will and confidence shown by concerned individuals, organisations, and states to bring back Liberia to functional democratic governance. Third, the people of Liberia must work towards national reconciliation and consensus as the best possible options for reconstruction and development. Fourth, the Opposition and other factional groups must learn to accept defeat, just as the government must not embark on a policy of *"winner takes all"* in the reconstruction and development of a functional developmentalist state. Fifth, sustained engagement, dialogue, unity and inclusiveness are precondition for robust reconstruction and development intervention. Unity among the international community is equally vital in ensuring that financial and technical assistance needed are maintained. Sixth, the government must put in place a functional communication strategy in outreach and awareness-raising concerning the magnitude of the problems and support received. It would equally assist in mobilising domestic or indigenous support as well as contributing to establishing a supportive public environment. A general information campaign effort on the significance of governance for peace, reconstruction, sustainable development and prosperity for Liberia would go a long-way in establishing a supportive public. Liberia needs this support in its reconstruction and development efforts.

Seen within this context, the following recommendations are advanced as proactive strategic policy agenda for the rebirth and growth of Liberia. The reconstruction process must be guided by existing realities and the strong and firm commitment not to disappoint the people of Liberia in their efforts to rebuild a devastated country.

RECOMMENDATIONS

- Cultivate and nurture the culture of democracy and good governance with the impression that the virtues of this form of governance has to come stay;
- Restore confidence in themselves, the governance systems and state institutions;
- Reconstruction and development must evolve from a holistic, integrative and inclusive perspective;
- Wage a conscious and vigorous effort in the fight against poverty, corruption, mismanagement and unequal economic standing within the country. Integrated and balanced development should be the key approach;
- Ensure that sustainable development is socially just, equal, ecologically and economically sustainable, political and culturally free, innovative and inclusive;
- Reconstruction and Sustainable development geared towards *putting the poor first*, and that future generations will have the same possibilities of well-being;
- Gender empowerment is vital and creating room for the youths to be partners in the development process, without bypassing or forgetting other disadvantaged groups in society.
- Cleaning up the environment from weapons of destruction planted during the conflict period, stopping the depletion and misuse of human and nature resources, and the destruction of the environment;
- The international community responding positively to the aspirations and needs of the people is vital for the success of the reconstruction and development process;
- Establish a Liberian Marshall Plan Fund for Reconstruction and Development {LMPFRD}.

Source: Forje [2006].

REFERENCES

Art, Robert [1993] "Security" in Krieger, Joel {ed.} *The Oxford Companion to Politics of the World.* Oxford University Press, New York, pp 820-822.

Doss Alan [2006] *United Nations Common Country Assessment for Liberia,* 11 June 2006 {Draft} Liberia CCA.

Dwan, Renata & Laura Bailey [2006] *Liberia's Governance And Economic Management Assistance Programme* {GEMAP}, The World Bank – Fragile States: The LICUS Initiative, Washington.

Forje, John [2006] *Here The People Rule: Political Transition and Challenges for Democratic Consolidation in Africa.* Yaoundé – Cameroon.

Forje, John [2001] "Mapping New Futures for Gender Participation Towards Sustainable Development. *Lessons from Africa" in Futures Research Quarterly*, Spring 2001, Vol. 17, No. 1, pp 4959.

Omotola J. Shola [2006]"Post-Election Reconstruction in Liberia: The Challenges of Security Sector Reform", *Conflict Trends*, Issue 2, 2006, South Africa, pp 42-46.

Pye W. Lucian [1966] *Aspects of Political Development.* The Little Brown Series. Boston, Massachusetts, USA.

Wendt, Alexander [1992] "Anarchy is what States Make of it. The Social Construction of Power Politics", in *International Organisation,* 46, 2:391-425.

World Bank [2005] *"Towards a Conflict-Sensitive Poverty Reduction Strategy".* Washington, June 2005.

World Bank [2005] *Liberia: National Transitional Government of Liberia.* Washington.

Chapter 7

THE WIND OF CHANGE:
A JOURNEY THROUGH AFRICA'S POLITICAL
LANDSCAPE AND A SEARCH FOR AN ALTERNATIVE[*]

ABSTRACT

The Wind of Change – A Journey Through Africa's Political Landscape – is a simplistic and descriptive travel through memory lane, concerning Africa's transition from colonialism to the global knowledge-based age of the 21st century. The sub-theme of the paper "In Search of An Alternative' draws inspiration from Prof Archie Mafeje's book titled "In Search of An Alternative – A Collection of Essays on Revolutionary Theory and Politics" published by SAPES in 1992. The paper address issues concerning "The National Question and African Unity", Gender Empowerment", and the "Politics of Exclusion and Inclusion" among others. Many questions are raised, for example, why is Africa poor in the midst of plenty? Why has chaos prevailed over coherence? Why ethnic hegemony over national unity?

It departs from the premises of the 'politics' of the trinity of technology and the baobab tree' and how the technology of human destruction can be converted into the "technology for human development". The trinity of technology encompasses three inter-related factors, namely, the "technology of violence, the technology of mobility and the technology of knowledge", which contributes to South Africa's triple heritage, for political and socio-economic transformation. It calls for a new vision with the politics and techniques of the "baobab tree", forming the cornerstone for African integration, African Renaissance and African Transformation before the continent can claim the 21st century.

Africa needs genuine structural transformation by breaking out of its existing colonial mentality, to innovate itself out of the scourge of poverty and marginalisation, by making the best use of its human and natural resources. It is time for intellectual, economic, political and natural resources of the continent are put at the disposal of the marginalised majority and excluded poor of the continent.

---

[*] The Archie Mafeje Lectures: Paper Presented at the Conference Hall of The Africa Institute of South Africa, Pretoria, South Africa, 16 November 2004. John Forje was among the first recipients of the Prof Archie Mafeje Fellowship.

INTRODUCTION

"The values of human solidarity that once drove our quest for a humane society seem to have been replaced or are threatened by crass materialism and pursuit of social goals of instant gratification". *[Nelson Mandela 2004]*

"Government is a trust, and the officers of government are the trustees: and both the trust and trustees are created for the benefit of the people" *[Henry Clay 1829]*

"They want you, their elected representatives to help them change their material conditions so that they escape from the jaws of poverty and their countries and continent from the crunches of underdevelopment: They want to know whether you will help them realise their dreams and hopes – and give birth to the humane Africa that has eluded all of us for so long". *[President Thabo Mbeki 2004]*

"We have no eternal allies, and we have no perpetual enemies. Our interests are eternal and those interests it is our duty to follow". *[Lord Palmerston 1848]*

LOOKING BEYOND THE PAST

When Harold Macmillan made the statement, "wind of change blowing across the African continent", ardent colonialist took it for joke. A joke it was in their minds. They never believed in any change of status quo, for, The British Empire was one that the sun never set. Britain commander the waves and the Union Jack could not be lowered in any part of the world, not in Africa, the *'chop farm'*. The world is not static; it is evolving and "the wind of change" is seriously blowing across a continent that has been subjected to the worse crime of human indignation and suffering ever known in history – The Slave Trade. The world never talks of the *'African holocaust'*. Why? Are Africans not human beings and God's creation?

As we enjoy the fruits of our newly won independence, let us not in this hour of glory and jubilation forgets the thousand of our father, mothers, uncles, brothers, sisters and friends who in different ways sacrificed their lives for the freedom and liberty we today enjoy. It has been a *"Long Walk to Freedom"* [Nelson Mandela]. A long walk encompassing the deployment of weapons of human destruction. A long walk that opens new frontiers and a beacon of hope for the continent. A long walk towards the journey's end of overcoming abject poverty, institutionalise corruption, and wanton underdevelopment. The blood that watered the freedom tree must continue to be the corner stone, guidance and guarantor for our future struggle to sustain peace, security, happiness and progress for present and subsequent generations.

Our diversity must remain our strength and golden heritage; and our heritage the pathways to Africa's unity, strength and courage to fight the multi-facet odds of poverty, underdevelopment and global dominance that subjects Africa to destruction and destitution. Our diversity in unity should pilot us through the turmoil and shackles of globalisation, abject poverty and terrorism. Indeed, the virtues of our cultural diversity and heritage must push African countries to act together, to extend freedom, democracy, hope and quality livelihood to all corners of the continent currently gripped by the forces of tyrannical leadership, deprivation, marginalisation and exploitation.

The sub-theme of this paper *"Search of an Alternative"* is influenced by Prof Archie Mafeje's book with the title "In search of an Alternative – A Collection of Essays on Revolutionary Theory and Politics" published in 1992. In the foreword, The Executive Director of SAPES Trust, Prof. Ibbo Mandaza states: *"For Archie Mafeje, The search for an Alternative is but this search for that lost identity, the inner self; The Alternative should be implicit in the methodology that we use to analyse and understand our social reality. As one of the first generation of Africa scholarship, his essays constitute an important message for the committed African scholars of our era and even for those of subsequent generations"* {Mandaza 1992].

About four decades ago, he wrote an article with the title "The Ideology of Tribalism" with the basic argument that in modern African politics, 'tribalism' is deployed as an ideological ploy". This situation has not changed. Ethnic politics, tribal violence conceal the vibrant and analytical mechanisms deployed by political leaders and the ruling elites even with the return to political pluralism and democratic governance system. Archie Mafeje looked at democratic pluralism as a reaction against monolithic government and partly-structures. A decade and a half through the re-democratisation process many African governments have failed to translate words into actions, to accept the underlying principle of "Here The People Rule", which should be a check on government and to better consolidate the principles of open and participatory government. We seem to be gradually returning to the one party governance system, with a difference, may be.

The problem is that of finding common grounds to build consensus and coherence to achieve the National Question and African Unity. However, this requires a higher degree of building sustainable political alliances and of political consolidation from the Cape to Cairo, and from Banjul to the Horn. We should move from misconceived ethnic hegemony to facing the national question; from narrowed minded nationalism to consolidating African Unity or Nationalism without, of course destroying our cultural heritage, but giving it a new lease of life within the context and realities of the prevailing contemporary geopolitics of the time. We must stop jogging for ethnic hegemony to embracing the Africa identity through an Afro-centric policy, which the African Renaissance vision is advocating.

Standing at the forefront of Africa's second democratisation wave, South Africa is held as a blueprint for the continent's future. The death of apartheid has given way to an emerging, inclusive civilian rule with extended social justice and peace for all. Its leaders are pioneering new inclusive developmental strategies that should make political scientists rethink and rewrite new theories of development, as we become partners in constructing a new brave continent and world in the 21st century. Is South Africa indeed the new model for Africa, the Third World and the global community, the character of its historical past hold important lessons? At first glance the picture we have is a pessimistic one. There are all reasons to hold that view. But digging into the virus of the apartheid system like its senior brother, 'slavery' emerges a new and challenging picture – soul searching into our consciousness and the re-birth of a new vision of optimism to challenge the vices of the past in order to construct a new and better tomorrow.

My paper offers bearing testimony of these hopeful assumptions of optimism for the birth of a new brave Africa – one with a political climate of "inclusion, cooperation, equitable redistribution of wealth, respect, participation, pragmatism, growth and progress, stability, ethical values and moral rectitude etc. designed to foster effective, efficient and functional political institutions, democratic governance system and a strong civic traditions for the common good. To attain that noble goal, the imperatives of positivism of the technology of violence must be married with the technology of knowledge, or what may be fashioned as the trinity of technology and the impact of the politics under the baobab tree.

THE TRINITY OF TECHNOLOGY AND THE BAOBAB TREE

The underlying element of my optimistic view is construed within three inter-related factors: Call it the *"trinity of technology"*

- The technology of violence and destruction
- The technology of mobility, and
- The technology of knowledge.

The link, which established itself between political, power and military technology in Africa, was present at the very beginning when the politics of colonialism and apartheid took control in Africa. What gave the advocates of these policies the capacity to subject so much of South Africa to European power and dominance? A fundamental factor here is that of the European technological breakthrough. Two types of technology were particularly important at the early stages in ensuring the necessary superiority of the white minority. One was the technology of mobility: the other, the technology of violence. Later, the technology of knowledge added new dimensions with significant importance for empowerment and development. The trinity of technology is what makes South Africa stand out different from the rest of the continent. And why South Africa can claim its place within a competitive world as compared to Chad, Sierra Leone, Liberia, DRC, Cameroon, Somalia and others. Saying so does not imply an approval of the policies and politics of apartheid. The vices of apartheid must forever remain condemned.

What do I imply by these forms of technologies? To begin with, these three branches of technologies were particularly important in giving South Africa's apartheid regime system the necessary superiority. The technology of mobility gave the country a capacity to traverse and make precise calculations on the activities of these agitating for an inclusive governance system. The technology of mobility made it possible for apartheid's policy of 'hot pursuit' of freedom fighters. It thus constituted a critical variable in the establishment of white minority hegemony in the region. The second was the 'technology of violence'. Basically this concerned the invention and improvement of weapons of human destruction, from the handgun to the machine gun, from the cannon ball to tanks, and B. 52s [Marui 1977]. The brave African freedom fighters with their bows and arrows, or their spears, stone throwing techniques, soon discovered the real truth with the massively conclusive argument of gunfire. In spite of this, it did not deter their quest for self-determination and independence. The third. 'Technology of knowledge' equipped the people with skills necessary to overcome their status as a minority population capable of dominating the silent majority.

With this, they could withstand adversities, become creative, innovative, productive and competitive. Priority was given to human resources development and centre's of excellence established which made South Africa an internationally competitive manufacturer and supplier of goods and services. With this, it was possible to forge ahead with the application of technology to improve the living standards, health, welfare and other opportunities for an inclusive white population, which also began to trickle down to the excluded black majority. That trickle down process is today's virtues, which gives the new political dispensation in South Africa a comparative and competitive advantage in global politics. A virtue, which must be positively exploited to advance the socio-economic and technological transformation of the continent.

There is a kind of biblical cord linking the *"trinity of technology"* with *"the politics and techniques"* of the *'Baobab Tree'*; to produce the effects of the *"politics of inclusiveness"* It is this politics and techniques of the 'Baobab Tree' that paints an optimistic future. This places South Africa in the limelight of building a new democratic culture and political dispensation for Africa. In my opinion, this is South Africa's new found export commodity which must be nurtured, consolidated and given added values at all cost and for the common good. All Africa may not jump on the bandwagon of Truth and Reconciliation Commission {TRC}, but the process and outcome constitutes valuable political lessons that each country draws from and tailored to its needs. When President Paul Biya of Cameron published Communal Liberalism [1987]. It was seen as a political breakthrough on the annals of political development on the continent. It was ahead of Russia's Troika. Unfortunately, the issues of liberalism, democratisation, and moralisation, vigorously propounded in the book never materialised. That vision died and Cameroon today is ranked as one of the most corrupt nations in the world.

South Africa like most colonised territories is engulfed with "3Cs" – a compound, complex and complicated past which we cannot dismiss lightly. Mafeje [1992:93] asserts: "Politically, economically, and racially, South Africa is more complex than other African countries. This is so much that South Africans of either colour are inclined to think that what applies to other countries does not apply to them" That view has to change now. A past that inherently links to the politics and technology of mobility and violence. But one that materialised a decade ago through a conscious attempt in over coming the terrible legacies of apartheid through the ascendancy of neo-liberalism as a way of addressing a host of social and economic issues. That the Government endorsed a policy of "growth from redistribution": i.e. a strong state and a strong market expected to serve as vehicles for generating growth reducing poverty and inequality. The Government of National Unity {GNU} thus embraced a standard neo-liberal strategy as central piece of policy agenda for reconstruction, growth, poverty alleviation and development.

For many, this is seen as 'contradictions' between a progressive social policy on the one hand, and the implementation of aggressive neo-liberal strategies of privatisation, liberalisation and democratisation on the other, to stimulate the economy and create more employment. To a large extent, it is a positive blending of the "technology of violence and destruction and the technology of mobility in order to optimally achieve and sustain the technology of knowledge for socio-economic transformation. Converting the technology of human destruction into the technology of human development constitutes the greatest challenge. President Nelson Mandela [2004] sees this challenge as "the values of human solidarity that once drove our quest for a humane society seem to have been replaced or are threatened by crass materialism, and pursuit of social goals of instant gratification. In short, what Bayart [1992] calls "the politics of the belly" which is institutionalised in the body politics of African states with all its vices?

Why is this approach necessary? To begin with, South Africa is a very unequal society, consisting of a highly developed 'first world' sector on the one hand, and an underdeveloped 'third world' sector on the other. Racial and class differences generally coincide: most members of the wealthy minority are whites, and most members of the poor majority are blacks {Cheru 2001:505]. A similar situation exists in other parts of Africa, the ruling elite contra the suffering silent majority. This can be seen as reinforcing the "Matthew Effect" which in the words of President Mbeki [1998:143] "represents a scale of human suffering and wretchedness which by any standard is impermissible"

Reinforcing the virtues of the technology of knowledge requires that "economic growth should be translated into redistribution of incomes and opportunities through appropriate social development programmes, and economic growth, and the deliberate promotion of employment creation" [Government of South Africa, 1998:53]. The Triple Heritage of South Africa – technology of violence, technology of mobility and technology of knowledge – enhances and harnesses the human and natural potentials of the society for political development and social transformation. That there is a "Rainbow Nation" is no surprise. No one is more explicit on such an excellent summation of South Africa's dichotomous nation in playing the role of 'victor; victim, vanguard and villain" \, than one of Africa's greatest scholar and prolific writer, Prof Ali Mazrui as outlined in his key note address during the panel discussion at the Ten Year's Conference organised by the Africa Institute of South Africa early this year.

Another reflection of the triple heritage could be seen in the Government of National Unity [GNU] as the most important force for the realisation of social, economic and cultural aspirations of the new nation-state. With the collapse of the apartheid system and the prevailing social and economic structures of exclusion, emerged the development of a new social contract and order of "inclusion" with the larger communities, wider social inter-relations and linkages that fostered feelings of nationalism, in respect of:

- A new agenda for fostering the process of nation-building was put in place;
- Emerging sentiments, attitudes and consciousness of belonging to one nation;
- A new movement with political goals for the attainment and maintenance of the status of 'nation' and all that it implies, including organisations, institutions, activities designed to achieve those goals, and;
- A new doctrine or ideology placing the nation and people at the centre of its concern, seeking and consolidation the nation's autonomy, sovereignty, unity an identity.

Simply stated, consolidating its newly won freedom and transplanting it to others could be seen in Kwame Nkrumah's vision for Africa. The political independence of Ghana has no meaning without the total independence of the entire continent of Africa. A position reiterated by General Yakubu Gowon of Nigeria. "The survival, security and independence of Nigeria cannot be assured as any part of Africa remains under colonial rule or an apartheid system [1970]. In other words, the Government of National Unity through its Truth and Reconciliation Commission signified the opening up of a new political landscape and dispensation process for Africa to claim the 21st century. A new challenge of restoring the politics and dynamics of the "Baobab Tree" {consensus building}, reshaping and upholding the basic tenets of the democratic doctrine of individual freedom, equality before the law, universal voting rights, political participation and equality, popular participation and majority government, popular sovereignty and respect of minority rights. Fundamental here being that the tyranny of either the majority or minority is to be avoided and evaded at all cost [see Ranugu 1996:34; Le Duc, Noemi and Norris].

The collapse of apartheid, the formation of Government of National Unity gave birth to the African Renaissance – the economic upliftment and democratisation of a poor continent. According to President Thabo Mbeki, (architect of the African Renaissance Agenda), "the African Renaissance is upon us." An issue re-echoed by President Nelson Mandela in a speech at Oxford University July 1997, "the creation of a new world order that involves the reconstruction of countries through regional economic associations capable of successfully competing in the global economy. Or what President Robert Mugabe referred to "as a rebirth and renewal that is reshaping not only African societies but also African relation with the rest of the world" [Africa News Online, 1997]. What does the African Renaissance entail? This could be seen under the following areas amongst others, namely:

The economic recovery of the African continent as a whole as can be seen from revamping the Lagos Plan of Action {LPA} that was derailed by the economic crises of the 1980s – Africa's Lost Decade: and through Bretton Woods Financial Conglomerates imposed Structural Adjustment Programme {SAP} which in reality turned out to be nothing *but Socially Added Problems {in respect of salary cuts, retrenchment of workers, cuts in social services sector, price hike, devaluation of currencies, employment stop etc. etc.}* to the establishment of the New Partnership for African Development {NEPAD}. I hope this new initiative will not be derailed to become *Never Empower the Poor to Accelerate their Development*

- The establishment of political democracy on the continent, which can be seen from converting the lame duck OAU, conceived under the Cold War into the African Union in post-Cold War era that is now being terrorised by the "The Politics and War of Terrorism and Oil. Will the African Union and NEPAD be derailed by the found politics of Terrorism and Oil? The other aspect has been that of the return to multi-party politics {political pluralism} and pluralist elections even though the rigging machinery and other electoral malpractices are yet to be adequately addressed to ensure fee, fair, competitive and transparent elections;
- The total mobilisation of the people of Africa to take their destiny into their own hands, thus preventing the continent being a place for the attainment of geopolitical and strategic interests of the world's most powerful countries. Significant here is to avoid West, Central and South-west coast (Gulf of Guinea) becoming a victim of the new politics of oil and terrorism like the ongoing carnage in Iraq, the Gulf Region and the Middle East;
- The need to break neo-colonial relations between Africa and the world's economic powers and to create a border free continent;
- The development of a people-focused, people-driven, people centred economic growth and development aimed at improving the quality of livelihood of all citizens;
- How best to contain the HIV/AIDS pandemic and other killer diseases that impact in slowing the economic recovery and growth of the continent.

As of now, African economies are 'disarticulated' and economic exchanges between the various sectors of the economy are externally oriented with an over-dependence on export earnings and foreign aid: the political system is still authoritarian and centralised with rigged and flawed elections; president for life phenomena prevails thereby preventing a governance system of "Here the People Rule", "Power to the People" is still far of the shores of many African countries. Without translating these slogans into concrete political action, the continent would not be able to make progress.

Extrapolating from this situation is the urgent need for an African Renaissance? The African Renaissance should be given new impetus of a concept, a policy and vision so as to restore Africa's political and economic independence. It should be that of seeking first and foremost the *"political kingdom"* for the common and not *"seeking the belly kingdom"* for individual interest and a select few. Let us all jointly and honestly seek the *"belly kingdom"* of all and for all.

The second agenda of the New Renaissance Movement should focus on rebuilding African societies by purging it from the stigma of foreign domination and control. We have become more French than the French, more British that the British at the expense of destroying our cultural heritage and values. In short, we are neither British/French nor Africans. Who are we? We have destroyed the real, and authentic African social values, we have copied capitalism without abiding to the basic fundamental principles and tenets of capitalism: hard work, time and duty consciousness, investment and risk taking, quality service delivery, and profit making. What we are good at is profit making by siphoning state finances into private accounts: living a life style beyond our means: destroying the very essence of our cultural heritage and values – solidarity and socialism: and used by external forces in destroying ourselves.

A recent study based on a survey of African countries by the United Nations Economic Commission for Africa UNECA, raking 28 African nations on good governance show that these countries fall short on areas like corruption, political representation, economic management and respect for human rights. Angola, Cameroon, Kenya and Nigeria are ranked as the most corrupt of the 28 countries. Citizens in most African countries do not have trust in their law enforcing authorities, the police, prison services, justice system, and other public institutions. It shows the need for African governments to operate transparent governance systems, be more democratic as well as build strong, functional and responsive institutions promoting the public interest through quality service delivery

Africa is identified by its high degree of democratic deficits which include {i} party system and political parties in Africa remain weak and frail and above all, construed on ethnic hegemony and not national hegemony: {ii} flawed electoral systems and lack of credible, transparent and competitive processes: {iii} governance – lack of accountability and transparency but engraved with institutionalised form of corruption: {iv} weak and passive civil society: {v} lack of civilian control over the military: and {vi} absence of the separation of powers between the various branches of government – legislative executive and judiciary, including the challenges conflicts pose to democracies.

Can we blame our underdevelopment to colonialism fifty years after the shackles of colonialism were taken off on the Accra Polo Grounds? Though fifty years is a short period in the life of a nation, we must begin to rethink, deconstruct our mentality and attitude, as well as reconstruct the New Pan African Reality within a rapidly changing and challenging global context.

The hosting of the African Parliament by South Africa should be an added value to the country's new found export commodity – of reconciliation, consensus, inclusion, reconstruction, development and good governance. The request and appeal to South Africa is to judiciously nurture this commodity as the engine that will empower Africa to claim the 21st century. As we journey through ten years of democracy, let us not over celebrate and allow things to get out of hand. South Africa should learn from the mistakes of other African countries to strengthen and dynamite its independence. Let things not "Fall Apart" as eloquently analysed by Chinua Achebe. Let the ten years not replicate a *"False Start"* but a most genuine attempt to foster the spirit of partnership, participation, responsibility and equitable sharing of the national cake by all the key actors – state, civil society and the private sector, with the hopes of anticipating *positive responses from the international community* in enabling the people attain their needs and aspirations.

In claiming that future, we must ask ourselves the question Henry Kissinger did in his book: "Does America need a Foreign Policy"? Africa, Kissinger maintained, "is destined to become the festering disaster of our age". Must the New Wind of Change allow the continent to be a festering disaster of the 21st century? My answer like yours is a big 'No'. No, because the time is nor right for us to convert the technology of human destruction into the technology of mass human development {MHD}. Apartheid was bad and remains bad. But let us equally look at the other side of the coin. It did create some form of development, even though at the expenses of human suffering and lives lost. We should try to look at the legacy - vices and virtues - of apartheid in a more positive perspective. We have the resources. We only need to add the technology of knowledge to our resources. But that technology of knowledge must be developed, nurtured and properly utilised.

We only need to exert more political will to give added value to our wealth of natural resources. It is up to Africans to create the necessary conditions for that to occur. No one can do it for us. For the wind of change to contribute to our progress, we require institutions that can guarantee and strengthen political parties, accelerate the process of development; provide quality service delivery; ensure credible electoral processes, democratic governance; the rule of law and property rights, security to life and property; investment in education [and with greater emphasis in the areas of science and technology], investment in human capital development, improved healthcare services; improved communication infrastructure and reduction of policy distortions that make investment excessively expensive, reduction in corruption, poverty and wasted consumption expenditures and bringing women from the minus to the plus side of the development continuum to list but a few

Fifty years of Africa's independence have yield results far different from those anticipated by the architects of freedom. The wind of change blew in different directions. Africa disintegrated. The new wind of change "Africa Renaissance" should usher the re-integration of the continent. A period of unity, continental consciousness, a period of Re-ordering of the State and people of Africa – which the new wind of change should bring a New World Order, with Africa finding its rightful place in the security Council of the United Nations and other global decision-making bodies.

What vision of African politics emerges from issues discussed, or as we celebrate "10 Years of Democracy" and Fifty Years of Independence? How does this image differ from the conventional wisdom of the anticipation of the founding fathers, Kwame Nkrumah, Julius Nyerere, Jomo Kenyatta, Sekour Toure, Nnamdi Azikiwe, Kenneth Kaunda, Hasting Banda,

Nasser, Patrice Lumumba, Hale Salesse, Tafawa Balewa and many others of the early years of independence? What are the areas of interpretive consensus?

To begin with, a journey through the politics of human destruction show that political processes in Africa over the years displayed a complex image of government enfeeblement, growing societal activity beyond the reach of the state and heterogeneous forms of political is reordering. There is a rapidly changing but hostile international community attitude directed towards Africa. The conglomerates of the Bretton Woods Financial Institutions have become part of the international conspiracy to cripple the continent. And cripple the continent it has done. We need to restructure ourselves, but not through the structural adjustment of social added problems imposed on Africa by the International Monetary Fund {IMF} which has turn into *"Impoverishing Many Families"*. Africa and especially the poor is more and more being abandoned to itself. An abandonment that should forge greater unity among African countries. Africa's diversity is its strength and on that it must build its unity to deepen the democratic process and accelerate the sustainable transformation of the society.

The Cold War is over, but has ushered the era of the "War Against Terrorism" and the "New Politics of Oil" which may further destabilised and colonialised fragile polities. The Atlantic Coast of West, Central and South-west Africa {The Gulf of Guinea} would not surprisingly be the new target region after Iraq. The Next Gulf War will be the Gulf of Guinea. Has Africa the "fundamentalist" to fight the war to protect the interests of the poor? We are fighting more wars today than we did under the Cold War period. The Berlin Wall like Apartheid has collapsed: yet we are constructing higher walls of social injustice, exclusion and division. This remains one of the depressing features of Africa getting poorer and poorer for every passing day. These issues need to be revisited. Why are we poor in the midst of plenty?

Unfortunately, we are not fighting the war of *"exclusion and poverty"*. Internationally and under the guise of the *"big brother"* we are intensifying the politics of the 'technology of violence and mobility for human destruction" rather than building a global consensus for converting "weapons of human destruction" into weapons of human development and prosperity for all. The "Matthew Effect Syndrome" must be sustained at all cost, according to forces within the corridors of power in the West and their counterparts in Africa. A kind of ganging-up that destroys the aspirations and needs of the poor in society. Africa should not allow itself to be dragged into sustaining the politics of "exclusion". For it's the politics of exclusion that has transformed the continent into "failed states", "weak states", "rouged states" "banana republics", "president for life syndrome, which has weakened the continent, making it a laughing stock. Why is Africa poor in the midst of plenty? No other continent beats the natural resources potentials of Africa. Yet, no continent is so underdeveloped and exploited like Africa. And exploited for the socio-economic well being of other people. Where are we?

FIFTY YEARS ON

Africa fifty years on should begin with the conversion of weapons of human destruction into one of human development. The disaggregating of inherited structures and institutions are fast giving way to the articulation and aggregation of concerns in innovative ways and in redesigned areas of socio-political and economic integration – The Africa Union {AU} and the New Partnership for African Development {NEPAD} and return to political pluralism for example. These emerging institutions constitute guiding political currents in different countries, suggesting that existing analytical approaches for more thorough review to better reflect the realities of Africa to reclaim its place in the 21st century and beyond are put in place here and now. It is a million dollar question. Predicting into the future is a crystal contest given the very nature of the human being. It could go either way: hope and progress, or frustration and regression and decline

The past fifty years have been clouded with failed states, genocide, corruption, poverty, diseases and now the HIV/AIDS pandemic. Multiple so-called survival mechanisms surfaced during the period, further calling into question the utility of conventional development strategies – Highly Indebted Poor Countries {HIPC} strategy {which simply implies, Helping Increase People's Calamities} is a booster to the Matthew Effect Agenda. These mechanisms only aggravated the plight of the poor –as economic performance, marked at best by economic growth rates have given way to corruption, external neglect and mismanagement – to pervasive poverty and total rejection of Africans in the North. During the past decade, we have seen some form of more viable pattern of political realignment taking place. Africa's indomitable lions are back on the pitch to map out a new future for human development, by converting the weapons of destruction into one for human development. The conversion process has as its weapon, "The technology of knowledge", "and The politics of the Baobab Tree and The Politics of Political Will". The new version therefore, presents new obligations and challenges, at the same time as it assails old conventions. Bad habits die-hard. What are the implications of these shifting political perceptions for the study of politics or social sciences in Africa?

The refreshing return to political pluralism and democratic governance offers some hope but the absence of political will to see through genuine changes places political science in a more confused situation. We are faced with the task of piercing together the different development path that the continent has been subjected to. For over fifty years there was no apparent detachment of State and civil society, the lack of inclusion of all groups into the polity. At the end of the past fifty years – a new political dispensation emerged: political pluralism, the call for the politics of inclusion – which obviate careful treatment of modes of articulation, and analysis. Fifty years on, we would be confronted with political analysis of change. In other words, conceptual analysis must be combined with dynamic discourse and specific events placed in proper historical perspective. It is difficult if not impossible to insinuate what the future would be. Yet, it is only us that can construct that future.

We should not run from historical past, no matter how shameful it may be. But deploy it as a serious working tool to address future issues and challenges. As students of social sciences, we should be well armed to look at fifty years on from empirical, analytical, theoretical, conceptual and programmatic perspectives. Here we are bless that the icons of this continent, Ali Mazrui, Archie Mafeje, Claude Ake, Chinua Achebe, Mamdani Mahmood, Fantu, Bernard Folon, Adebayo Adeedji, Joseph Ki-Zerbo, Ngugi Wa Thiong'o, Thandika Mkandawire and many others have left their marks on the sands of time. We need to build on their scholarship to restore the lost glory of the Universities of Legon, Ibadan and Makarere amongst others so as to better address the problems of the continent. We all have the right that the wind of change of the African political arena to express genuine frustration over our ability to advance the continent in a better way. As conditions in Africa deteriorate, the malaise mounted. We must not relent the struggle for political pluralism, democracy and social justice on the continent. Today, we begin to see the light at the end of the tunnel, yet haunted with the failures of the past. And uncertainties by the actions of "big brother" of the North.

South Africa is currently "at the forefront of critical African politics aimed at transforming the continent. By hosting the Pan African Parliament, South African can influence Africa in the principles of democracy and good governance, given that most parliaments in Africa are merely rubber stamps. Hence, this is the time for Africans to come into their own, to take ownership of the continent, with all its conflicts, famine and, of course, it's many riches" [Tromp 2004:13]. African countries must now set their own priorities and agenda based on their own realities, experience and needs, rather than those imposed from outside through the barrel of foreign aids.

Has the wind of change answered our questions? No. For many questions remain open and many areas of analysis are yet to be exploited. The message emanating from this primary endeavour is that in order to grasp the full meaning of the wind of change of 10 Years of Democracy and Fifty years of independence, of state vagaries and state mutations, it is important to leave the state and its environs and to focus more squarely on power and politics in broader space if only to come back to the state and its potentialities better equipped in the future and with the tools placed at our door steps by scholars of greater repute. From this alternate vision new possibilities emerge, and these may permit greater options and more choices. Here lies the challenge of African politics for it to claim its place in the 21st century.

The New Wind of Change should usher a new era of proactive approaches to redressing the predicament of the people, namely:

- Mission-driven or oriented government;
- Mission-driven Parliament, bureaucracy, mass media an independent judiciary;
- Mission-driven civil service void of partisan politics;
- Mission driven civil society;
- Mission driven political parties;
- Mission driven leadership embedded with three Cs –[Character, Competence, and care] and with three Ms [model, mentor, and minister];
- Mission-driven private sector, even if it seeks to make profit with less investment, but with the benefits trickling down to the people.

It needs to be acknowledged that mission-driven or oriented is only achievable when society takes upon itself the responsibility and exert the necessary political will to ensure changes that brings optimal benefits to all. Because of the failures and frustrations of the past, expectation for a better tomorrow runs high. But can only be attained when we develop a mission-driven agenda and attitude. The quality of life, which we perceive as the end goal, cannot be considered to be static. It is for this reason that governments are continually challenged to find new and innovative ways of addressing the needs of their communities. And for communities to positively respond to policies oriented towards ensuring that sufficient opportunities exist for people to expand their choices; sufficient and basic public services exist, and are effectively and efficiently rendering quality services to the community;

people can live in safety and security, and that the physical environment is sustainable exploited to meet the needs of present and future generations.

The nations of the continent have common problems, which require collective solutions. Hence the need to transform the way in which government functions and civil society response to such measures. We must avoid transferring inequality to the next generations. National consciousness has been thrown over board. Yet without that sense of belonging we cannot construct the kind of political, technological and economic landscape to pilot Africa in the 21st century. Ethnic diversity and conflicts over-rides national unity; exclusion over inclusion; affluence over poverty and these vices continue to shape the destiny of the continent to the advantage of invading forces. From the Biafran War through Congo {DRC}, Sierra Leone, Liberia, Rwanda, Burundi, Mozambique, Angola, Somalia to the current Dafur crisis in Sudan, unravels the fact that we have not learned from our past mistakes.

Our future depends on our political will and priority strategic visions to address the causes of potential instability on conflict before it is too late. A New African Strategic Bargaining and Development Agenda are needed. One that extends the politics of the Baobab Tree to all corners of the continent and particularly in those areas where the seeds for future conflict lie. We need to look at cultural diversity as an asset not a liability and how to harness nature's precious gift "cultural diversity" as a recipe for development, oneness, strength and growth. We should not in this hour of a Renaissance Africa permit the clash of cultural diversity disunity us and dominate and pilot the process of development. In the end, there will be no development but conflict and regression. Cultural diversity should forge a new partnership and sense of belonging for A New African quality livelihood for all. But these changes cannot take place without a serious change of mentality, attitude and greater love for the nation/continent by every African. We all continue to behave as we are passing: as if the country/ continent does not belong to us. Others have to tell us how to clean our backyard. Decolonising our mentality, behaviour and attitude constitute a major task that has to be addressed before we can claim the 21st century.

BY WAY OF CONCLUSION

Creating a new society out of the ashes of apartheid is a process, not a fait accompli. South Africa's political triumph in 1994 was just one victory; many more are required. South Africa has taught a sceptical world a lesson how reconciliation can happen across the racial divide. How people can live in peace and harmony despite the racial divide. Can South Africa bring a similar miracle of reconciliation to close the economic divide between the "have and have-nots"? This remains the central challenged facing the young democracy [Goodman 1999]. It is a question of how best South Africa can make use of its triple heritage – using knowledge to convert the technology of destruction into the technology for human development

Unmaking the technology of violence and mobility is like unmaking apartheid. It can be done and must be done provided we all exert the necessary political will and change of attitude, turn our back against exclusion and embrace inclusion. When we all feel passionate about our continent, there is nothing that will stop us from reaching the mountaintop. We all need to develop a common silver lining – a depth of conviction and a passion for our land, our country, our continent, and our freedom. This takes me to a speech to the South African Parliament, by President F.W. De Klerk on 2nd February 1990. He said:

> "Let us put petty politics aside when we discuss the future during this session. Help us build a broad consensus about the fundamentals of a new realistic and democratic dispensation: Lt us work on the plan that will rid our country of suspicion and steer it away from domination and racialism of any kind".

As South Africa looks above the Limpopo, so also the urgent call for the Mahgreb States to look south beyond the Sahara desert. The new politics of human development cannot be successful if divisions continue to exist from the Cape to Cairo, from Banjul to the Horn and when the politics of exclusion remains the corner stone of development in many polities in Africa. The new wind of change hopefully, should create a detailed and unified blueprint not of words but actions for meeting the social and economic aspirations of the peoples.

The cross of Africa should go from Nigeria to Kenya, from South Africa to Egypt converging in the Democratic Republic of Congo, which unfortunately has known no peace since the assassination of Patrice Lumumba. With Abuja as the pull factor for West Africa, Nairobi for East Africa, Cairo for North Africa, DRC for Central Africa, and Pretoria for Southern Africa, a capacity to secure the welfare of an economically active population and politically united people should be established to promote human dignity and quality of livelihood for the people in Africa. It is a right and challenge for us to achieve that for our own good and the common good of all humanity. It is a challenge for continental reconstruction, development, equitable redistribution that cannot be achieved without policy dialogue between the governors and governed. Africa must establish its priorities, processes and concerted actions as the only way forward for a better and brighter tomorrow.

What emerges from the above is that there is a new awakening in Africa. President Nnamdi Azikiwe's "Renascent Africa" has been reborn with new dynamism, vision and leadership style to address the scourge of Africa's predicament. It is my contention that the emerging third generation of African leaders to craft an indigenous African development paradigm in the light of the continents own perception offers hope for the future. Here President Mbeki [1998:212] asserts: "The new political order owes its existence to the Africa experience of many decades which teaches us Africans that what we tried did not work – that the one-party states and military governments will not work. We need to embark on a new struggle for political pluralism and democracy throughout the continent The way forward must be informed by what is after all, common to all African traditions – that the people must govern" or, "Here The People Rule" perception.

We need to come out of the syndrome of fake elections by accepting the will of the people as the top priority and way forward. Respect of the ballot box through free, fair, competitive and transparent lections establishes the right basis for democratic governance, giving legitimacy, credibility, to those so genuinely elected to govern the people until the next elections. Lack of peaceful mechanisms for the transfer of political power from one individual or groups (government) to another has been one of the most common triggers for political repression, violence and even civil wars, leading to failed, collapsed or banana states in Africa. Africa deserves better. It is the place of those who have taken over the political leadership of each country to practice the very basic tenets of the paraphernalia of democratic governance, checks and balances, independence of the judiciary, political liberties such as freedom of speech and association, free and fair elections among others. It is the place of these leaders to ensure a holistic human security perspective.

Admittedly, democratisation does not immediately eliminate human security threats but if a democratic system is given time to root itself in strong institutional safeguards and if the principles and values of democracy become internalised among the political elites of a country, then violent power struggles would become a thing of the past. A properly functioning democratic system is one that takes power transfer out of the realm of security and into the realm of ordinary politics. However, the emphasis is on proper functioning of state institutions. The road to democracy is a risky one, and can lead to chaotic and violent conditions if key political actors do not play by the rules [Hammerstad 2004].

We can best attain this goal by establishing genuine, functional and stable democratic systems throughout the continent in which the legitimacy to govern and sovereignty must reside with the people. The challenge for this and subsequent generations is to build and improve on the footprints of our first generation political leaders and scholars by resisting " all forms of tyranny; oppose all attempts to deny liberty by not resorting to demagogy, repulse the temptations to describe African life as the ability to live on charity; engage the fight to secure the emancipation of Africa women and reassert the fundamental concept that we are our own liberators from oppression, from underdevelopment and poverty, from the perpetuation of an experience of slavery, from colonialism, from apartheid, and from dependence on alms" [Mbeki 1998:35-37]. Where there is a will, there is a way. That way needs committed political actions here and now. And "can only succeed with the spread of civil nationalism" [Kofi Annan] and love for the continent. Field Marshall Jan Smuts [1940] was not wrong when he stated: "If we wish to take our rightful place as the leader in Pan-African development, and in the shaping of future policies and events in this vast continent, we must face the realities and the facts of the present and seize the opportunities which these offer. All Africa may be our proper market if we will but have this vision and far-sighted policy will be necessary if that is to be realised".

The centrality of African unity must be consolidated. From the All African Peoples' Conference {Accra-Ghana 1958} to the establishment of the AU, and with South Africa hosting the African Parliament, the new leaders must not weaver in facing current and future challenges for a real and genuine Pax Africana. The greatest task of that burden rests on the shoulders of Africa's twin giant nations – The Abuja –Pretoria Connection – that should more than ever before be committed to a strategic alliance and with the rest of the continent seeing through the reality of the African Renaissance. The African Renaissance will have no meaning and impact if it is not converted into an ideology with grassroots foundation. It should be a national issue like the struggle for independence. It is not enough when it remains under the canopy of Heads of states. And when some of these Heads of State lack political legitimacy in their respective countries.

From Abubakar Tafawa Balewa, Nnamdi Azikiwe to Olusegun Obasanjo, all Nigerian leaders have maintained consistency in Afro-centrism as depicted through the views of General Mohammed Murtala three decades ago. "Africa has come of age. The fortunes of Africa are in our hands to make or mar. The time has come when we should make it clear that we can decide for ourselves. That we know our interests and how to protect those interests; that we are capable of resolving African problems without presumptuous lessons in ideological dangers which, more often than not, have relevance on us, or for the problems at hand"[1976].

The emerging African Renaissance is here. What is new about it? It is born in a New World Order Context backed with critical soul searching by Africans themselves to take command of their development and destiny in the turbulent world of the 21st century. The second aspect is the consistency of African scholarship, which has never, and should not weaver in guiding the newfound course of development. While the first generation of African political leaders were true nationalist and led their countries to independence, the second generation of political leaders {The Men in Khaki} betrayed and destroyed the ideals of the founding fathers. We ended with Odinga's reality of "Not Yet Uhuru" [1964] and Achebe's [1958] Things Fall Apart. The second generation of political leaders worked hard in bleeding their countries to death instead of giving water, bread and life to the people. While the found fathers can be faulted in many ways, they did their best given the prevailing global politics of the period in ensuring that the spirit of the Pan African Movement and Unity and the struggle against colonialism was kept intact. Thanks also to the dedicated quest for African identity by the first generation of scholars. I will be doing injustice to name only a few.

African scholarship has stood its ground in spite of the odds faced, namely: First, the adverse effects on intellectual life arising out of the malaise of the post-colonial state in Africa: banning and imprisonment of intellectuals. Second, the role of donors who invariably politically and ideologically motivated, are hostile to, or at best suspicious of independent-minded African scholars and often accuse them of "ideological bias". Third, the attitude of intellectuals in the Northern Hemisphere, who rationalise their own desire to control and dominate by imputing that most of the research proposals by African radicals or non-conformists are unscientific or "below standards". However, this Northern arrogance and prejudice did not and should not deter the existing community of African scholarship from playing their roles in ensuring and sustaining scholarship, knowledge creation and whistle blowing to constantly keep political leaders in check. The power of the pen must prevail over the power of the sword. It is here that the technology of knowledge should be the guiding principle and priority area for Africa to claim the 21st century. The wind of change has to recognise the role of those in the Diaspora and the female gender as significant input factors in the development process.

TAPING FROM THE DIASPORA

Unfortunately, the continent is not taping from existing human potentials found beyond the frontiers of the region. How do we bring the wealth of talents outside to accelerate the transformation process in the African region? The brain drain needs to be converted into a brain gain phenomenon. But to benefit from the Diaspora requires the establishment of an enabling environment for all to operate without harassment. Striving for good governance is a prerequisite for the sustainable transformation of the continent. The knowledge of the Diaspora wealth of knowledge lost, just as the failure to give added value to existing natural resources. Once a system of good governance is put in place, the Diaspora will respond positively in the reconstruction of the continent. The challenge to emerging generations of African leaders is to put in place a functional and democratic governance system that assures among others, the following:

- Openness and transparency;
- Capacity to act and deliver quality services to the nation;
- Adherence to the principles contained within the Bill of Rights;
- Distribution of state authority and autonomy;
- Efficiency and Effectiveness;
- Answerability, transparency and accountability;
- Separation of powers;
- That the interest of the people counts – putting the nation first and as the ideological rallying point. Give those in the Diaspora a chance to be part of the process for change;
- Bring them on the development bandwagon like our neglected female gender.

GENDER EMPOWERMENT

We cannot claim the 21st century when 51 percent of more of our population is excluded from the mainstream development process. In the fight for self-determination, from Mexico (1975) through Copenhagen (1980), to Nairobi (1985) and Beijing (1995), women have not wavered in their contributions to the political emancipation of this great continent. Their inputs to the political and economic landscape need to be properly documented and placed highest in the African political and economic hall of fame. Two thousand and four is indeed the year of the African woman. That the first President or Speaker of the African Parliament and the Noble Peace Prize goes to the female gender on the eve of the Beijing accord a decade after is testimony of their contributions in moving this continent forward. They need a complete their own triple heritage – An African Woman Head of State.

Women's empowerment and participation must be given top priority for Africa to claim this century. With children on their backs, heavy loads on their heads, under pouring rain and burning heat, at street corners selling their products to sustain their families, or farms, across rivers and mountains, women continue to bear the brunt of the increasing poverty of the continent. Unfortunately, they are not genuine participants in the decision-making process. This has to change. The wind of change must blow extremely strong in this direction to usher a new continent.

The wind of change gave the African woman the voting right but not the right in decision-making. According to the Inter-Parliamentary Union, women comprise only 9 percent of parliamentarians in Africa compared to the global average of 13.6 percent [Okello and Omale 2004:9]. Culture, religion, politics, economic structures among others has all been designed to favour men over women. As if to add insult to injury, about 70 percent of the poor in Africa are women. Key indicators of the famine face of poverty include high infant and maternal mortality rates, increased gender based violence, limited access and control of productive resources, such as land, financial credits, inaccessibility to social services and justice, and women's denial of opportunities to improve themselves. These are critical issues to the human security challenges that Africa faces [M'boge and Doe, 2004:69].

As already alluded to, there is an urgent need to move women from the minus to the plus side of the development continuum. We cannot talk of human security and sustainable development when 51 percent or more of the population consisting of women have no voices and choices in the decision-making process. Indeed, the failure of the constitution in many African countries to take a strong position for gender balance in the recruitment and appointment to public offices constitutes a major factor to the weak presence of women in positions of responsibilities and decision-making and in the public sphere as whole. The new wind of change must enforce a policy of equal opportunities for women and men and to develop affirmative action.

A few statistical data show why such affirmative actions are necessary to restructure the prevailing process of development. For example, women constituted only 8 percent of the membership of the First Parliament of the Fourth Republic of Ghana after the 1992 elections. IN 1994 women constituted only 2.9 percent of the membership of District Assemblies, 11 percent of judges and magistrates, 12.9 percent of senior officials of the Central Bank and 10.3 percent of Senior Academic Staff at the University of Ghana. In 1994, there were 4 women out of 25 members of the Council of State, 2 out of 19 Cabinet Members and 3 out of 35 ministerial appoint [NCWD 1995]. The 1996 parliamentary elections produced 18 women out of 200 members, representing just 9 percent of the total number. The 2000 elections produced a different picture, but still fell short in relationship to the role and contribution injected by women in the process of nation building. Of the 200 parliamentarians, only 9 are women, representing 4.5 percent: and 19 percent of ministers are women. Women's representation in local authorities stands at 24 percent as against 76 percent for men. Out of the 31 deputy ministers, 6 are women. There is no woman among the 10 regional ministers. Similarly, the statistics for women in other areas are as follows: 2 out of 21 cabinet ministers, 2 out of 10 Council of State Members, 24 out of 110 District Assembly Chief Executives, 2 out of 3 commissioners, 2 out of 11 members of the judiciary. There is no woman among the 3 metropolitan executives [NCWD – Ghana].

The case of Cameroon is not better either. Out of 180 members of parliament, less than 15 are women. There are 3 women ministers out of 50. There is no woman among the 21 Army Generals. No woman among the 10 provincial governors. Only one woman out of six Vice Chancellors of the country's six state universities. The list goes on. In Kenya, the 1992 elections saw the election to parliament of only six women; one was nominated, which in total constituted 3.5 percent of women in parliament. In 1997, four women were elected and another four nominated, making up only 3.6 percent of all the members of parliament. The 2002 elections saw the highest number of women elected to parliament since independence. Nine women were elected while eight were nominated – this translated to 7.6 percent [M'boge and Doe 2004:78]. The disparity between male and female can also be seen in the enrolment ratio at primary, secondary and tertiary levels across the continent. In Ethiopia for example, female tertiary students are only 30 per 100.000 [se Austrian Development Cooperation 2004].

It is vital to seriously confront the abuse of power: to ensure that abject and dehumanising conditions of poverty inflict on women are eradicated. The hurricane of poverty, inequality, injustice and exclusion remains a threat to the unity and socio-economic transformation of the continent and to civilisation. That terrorism prevails underscores the wretchedness of the world and of the poor in particular. The voiceless have no voice. We must empower the voiceless. For without that empowerment we cannot claim the 21st century. We will continue to be apart not a part of the evolving global dynamics. Africa should not stop at 2010, but go for the Olympics 2020 or 2024. Above all, how to sue sport as a uniting factor and basis for socio-economic transformation of the continent. When freedom is fragile, development is bound to be fragile too. Therefore, the continent has to build a system that can best provide, promote, strengthen and defend the freedom and liberty of the people. Democratisation in Africa is therefore, fluid and inconsistent, and this has in part, been the result in part of the fragile state of democratic governance and democratisation process in Africa,

Though the OAU is history today, nonetheless, it save the purpose for which it was created. Let the African Union remain a powerful and appealing image and force for the African people, and especially to political leaders in unionism search for concerted and comprehensive solutions for the complex and intractable problems that besieged the continent. Let the AU reconstruct the continent by drawing lessons from the failures and weaknesses of the OAU. Let the newly constituted body build on the founding anthem of the OAU:

> *Let us all unite and celebrate*
> *The victories won for our liberation*
> *Let us dedicate ourselves to rise together*
> *To defend our liberty and unity*

Making Africa the tree of life should incorporate all the basic tenets of democracy and - fundamental human rights, namely: "freedom from want, freedom from fear, and freedom of future generations to sustain their lives on this planet" [Annan 2000]. This calls for the marriage between formal or procedural democracy {free, fair, competitive, transparent elections, protection of civil liberties, separation of powers and the role of opposition parties as inputs in the democratisation and development process} and on the other, the strengthening of sustentative democracy {the ability of the state to be responsive to the needs and aspirations of the citizenry, to eradicate poverty, and ensure the effective participation of the people in decision-making process and addressing pressing issues of or poverty, corruption, poor quality service delivery and economic injustice.

A FINAL WORD

> *Let all us unite and work together*
> *To uphold our rights and fight the cause of freedom*
> *Let us dedicate ourselves to work together*
> *To build up strength in unity and peace*

Where do we go from here? Action not words should be the guiding factor. Africa needs a new democratic dispensation, and new leadership style backed with positive responses from the citizenry. Political science must reassert itself in the body politic of African countries. It should not be made a taboo subject. The theory of politics and governance should be related to practical output. Drawing from Jinadu Adele [2004:10], "political science requires a democratic environment to ensure and thrive: and that to thrive and be consolidated, democracy requires political science as its handmaiden, contrary to the uneasy tension that tends to characterise the relationship between political science, as critical political science and the totalising authoritarian tendency of the powers that be, even in a democratic state. Therefore, political science must be opposed to non-democratic political systems and must constantly subject even democratic regimes to critical searchlight and oversight".

A major threat to the sustainability of democracy in Africa is the problem of power struggle and the role of the military establishment to the pursuance of democratic governance. Military and dictatorial regimes are obstacles to deepening the democratic process on the continent. What the continent needs now is open, transparent accountable and responsive government. The key issue is arresting the state of conflict ands clashes of interests. Africa is a structural phenomenon; state power is all about contestation over control and distribution of resources and in situation where resources are scarce, then political contestation becomes even much fiercer since the rule of the thumb is survival of the fittest. What is important now is for Africa to start learning how to share and to put the people and the poor first. Shared responsibility should be the goal. Shared responsibility requires a harmonious interface between the states; civil society and the private sector which should be strengthen with participation, partnership and benefit sharing. The politics of the baobab three remains the gateway for a better Africa.

The preceding passage constitutes a thought provoking statement challenging civil society as the custodian of the people to rise up to its task; and ensure that the rule of law prevails throughout the continent. The men in Khaki should be brought to order. Cheque book politics has given politicians the chance to exploit the wretchedness of the people to the extent that the people seem no longer to have trust in politics and in public institutions. How to restore confidence in political leaders and state institutions is a major problem. Yvonne Galligan [2004] notes: "familiar questions focusing on ethical political values and behaviour are given a new framing, while fundamental concepts such as participation and representation are pen to being revisited and recast in the context of a modern discourse on democracy and its institutions"

> *Let all of us unit and toil together*
> *To give the best we have to Africa's*
> *The cradle of mankind and fount of culture,*
> *Our pride and hope at break of dawn.*

A New African Political and Development Thinking are required. And this should focus on the following:

- Crafting an encompassing constitution that ensures respect for human rights and dignity:
- Competitive political party system devoid of ethnic alliances or hegemonic tendencies;
- System of governance that shuns ethnic divide but builds on national unity, responsibility and partnership with all;
- A state system that delivers services to the entire society, not one that enhances division, ethnic hegemony, personal cult-worship and promotes either minority or majority tyranny;

- Democratic transfer of power from one party to another, and from one government to another;
- Strict respect of the constitution, independence of the judiciary and a non-partisan bureaucracy;
- Freedom and responsibility of the media industry including individual freedom of speech and association;
- Ensuring the sustainability of the environment and the equitable distribution of the wealth of the nation;

The problems of Africa are economic and political. Being political requires addressing constructive policy measures in the direction of electoral reform as a crucial component in the entire gamut of constitutional engineering for the deepening of democratic governance; addressing social cleavages that exist within the society from positive rather than negative perspectives. The wind of change should lead to a new and consolidated Africa. The future of democracy in Africa lies in transforming the continent's electoral systems, among other challenges and making sure that the general population as credible, legitimate and transparent process of electing public representatives sees the electoral process for electoral competition. The structure and functioning of the bureaucracy must be efficient, effective and devoid of ethnic or political part influence and affiliation.

In short, the will of the people shall be the basis of the authority of government, as expressed by exercising the rights and civic duties of citizens to choose and dismiss their representatives through regular, free, fair and transparent and competitive elections with universal and equal suffrage, open to multiple parties, conducted by secret ballot, monitored by an independent electoral authority, and free of fraud and intimidation. We cannot avoid democratisation. We must avoid westernisation. We must build on the African values within a changing and challenging world order of the 21st century. The Japanese adopted western technology but have not destroyed their cultural values and heritage. We can do the same.

> *O sons and daughters of Africa*
> *Flesh of the sun and flesh of the sky*
> *Let us make Africa the tree of life*

Catalogues of problems have been presented. Problems that have solutions if only the people should show the necessary political will to overcome their predicaments. What is required of us all is to focus discussion around civil society's passiveness, and the urgent need for civilian democratic control over the military be established and preserved. It is in this light that I look at the wind of change and with faith and hope for a better, stronger, progressive, and united continent of the 21st century. With this in mind, we would not have failed those who sacrificed their lives for subsequent generations and us. African scholarship must continue to be on the forefront of change, awareness creation and scholarship to save the continent and humanity from the bondage of destruction.

> *God Bless Africa*

REFERENCES

Achebe, Chinua [1958] *Things fall Apart,* London.

Africa New Online [1997] *Mugabe says "Renaissance" Taking Place Across Africa.* Online.

Annan Kofi [2000] "We The Peoples. The Role of the United Nations in the 21st Century. *Millennium Report,* 3 April 2000.

Austrian Development Cooperation [2004] Ethiopian Sub-programme: Gender and Democracy, Support of Gender Equality and Democratisation 2004-2006. Federal Ministry of Foreign Affairs, Austrian Development Cooperation. See also http://www. bmaa.gv.at (accessed 7 April 2004).

Balewa, Tafawa Abubakar [1960] Address to the House of Representatives, 20 August 1960, Lagos, Nigeria (See also, Idang G. [1973] Nigeria: *International Politics and Foreign Policy.* Ibadan University Press, Ibadan, Nigeria, p.7

Biya Paul [1987] *Communal Liberalism,* Macmillan Press, London.

Cheru Fantu [2001] "Overcoming Apartheid's Legacy: The Ascendancy of Neo-Liberalism in South Africa's Anti-Poverty Strategy", *Third World Quarterly,* Vol. 22 No. 4, pp 505-527.

Galligan Yvonne [2004] "Is democracy Working"? *Circular Note to the XX World Congress,* Fukuola, Japan 2006.

Government of South Africa [1998] *Poverty and Inequality in South Africa.* Office of the Deputy Vice President.

Hannerstad Anne [2004] *African commitments to Democracy in Theory and Practice.* Compress, South Africa.

Jinadu L. Adele [2004] "Political science, Elections and Democratic Transitions: Fragments of An Autobiography and Some Conjectures" *Presidential Address delivered at the 23rd Annual Conference of the Nigerian Political science Association* {NPSA}, 28 June 2004, Abuja. See also Newsletter – African Association of Political Science, New Series, Vol. 9 No. 2 May-August 2004, Pretoria, South Africa, pp9-15.

Le Duc L. Niemi and Norris (eds.) 1996. *Comparing Democracies: Elections and Voting In Global Perspectives*, Sage Publications, Thousand Oaks, USA.

Mafeje Archie [1992] *In Search of An Alternative: A Collection of Essays on Revolutionary Theory and Politics.* SAPES Books, Harare, Zimbabwe.

Mafeje Archie [1970] "The Ideology of Tribalism", Journal of Modern African studies, 9.2.

Maloka Eddy [2002] Africa's Development Thinking Since Independence. A Reader. *Africa Institute of South Africa,* Pretoria, South Africa.

Mbeki M. [1999] *South Africa – The African Renaissance.* Online. Mbendi.co.za/land/sa-ren.htm

Mbeki, M. [1998] "The African Renaissance" in *South African Year Book of International affairs,* 1998/9 Johannesburg, SAIIA.

Mbeki, Thabo [2004] *Speech at the Opening of the Pan-African Parliament.* 16 September 2004. See Pretoria News, Friday 17 September 2004:4 – "President Unveils PAP's New Home.

Mbeki Thabo [1998] *The Time Has Come.* {Cape Town: Mafube/Tafelber}

Mbeki Thabo [1998] Address to Corporate Council on Africa's attracting Capital to African Summit", Virginia, USA, 19-22 April 1997, see G. Le Pere, A Van Nieuwkerk and K.

Lambrechts {eds.} 1998. *South Africa ad Africa. Reflections on the African Renaissance. FGD Occasional Paper No. 17.* Johannesburg, South Africa.

M'boge Fatoumatta and Doe Sam Gbaydee [2004] *African Commitments to Civil Society Engagement.* ComPress, South Africa.

Murtala Mohammed [1976] *Speech at OAU Extraordinary Session held in Addis Ababa,* Ethiopia, 11 January 1976.

National Council on Women and Development {NCWD} 1995. "The Status of Women in Ghana 1985-1994. *Executive Summary of the National Report for the Fourth World Conference on Women,* NCWD, Accra, Ghana, 1995.

Nelson Mandela [2004] *Speech delivered at the 5th Steve Biko Lectures.* University of Cape Town, 10th September 2004.

Nkrumah Kwame [1965] *Neo-Colonialism: The Last State of Imperialism.* Thomas Nelson, London.

Odinga Oginga [1964] *Not yet Uhuru,* London.

Okello R and Omale J. (eds.) 2004. *A Journey of Courage. Kenyan Women's Experience of the 2002 General Elections.* AWC Features.

Ranuga T. K. [1996] *The New South Africa and The Socialist Vision: Positions and Perspectives Towards a Post-Apartheid Society.* Humanities Press, New Jersey.

Rothschild Donald and Naomi Chazan [1988] T*he Precarious Balance: State and Society in Africa.* Westview Press, Boulder/London

Seale T. [1997] "Mandela's Ode to A Rising Africa. *Daily News,* 16 July 1997.

Smuts Jan C. [1942] *Plans for A Better World: Speeches of Field Marshal Jan Smuts.* Hodder & Stroughton, London.

Tromp Beauregard [2004] *"Pan-African Parliament – A Feather in South Africa's Cap",* *Pretoria News,* Friday 17 September 2004, Pretoria.

Vale P and Maseko S. [1998] "South Africa and The African Renaissance (p.76) in Le Pere et al. [1998] South Africa And Africa: Reflections on the African Renaissance. Johannesburg, *FGD Occasional Paper* No. 17.

SOME RANDOM THOUGHTS ON VALUING INNOVATION SYSTEMS IN A RAPIDLY CHANGING GLOBAL KNOWLEDGE-BASED ECONOMY. WHICH WAY FORWARD FOR AFRICA IN THE 21ST CENTURY

INTRODUCTION

When in Africa we speak and dream of and work for, a rebirth of that continent as a full participant in the affairs of the world in the next century, we are deeply conscious of how dependent that is on the mobilisation and strengthening of the continent's resources of learning". *[Nelson Mandela 1998]*

"The promotion of an NSI as framework for social and economic policy maximises the possibilities for all parts of the system to interact with each other to the benefit of stakeholders and the advancement of national goals. The close co-operation between government, industry and research institutions is a pre-requisite for projects designed to produce growth and development in accordance with national goals". *[DACST. 1996:5]*

FACING THE REALITIES

The forces and legacy of colonialism and bad governance confronts many African countries with the process of socio-economic transformation, reconstruction and reconstitution of their ravage torn society. While science and technology are not the panacea for development, it is evidently clear those nations that have adopted a concerted and comprehensive science and technology policy backed with the necessary 'political will' are making rapid and significant headway in accelerating the process of socio-economic transformation, and eventually improving the quality of livelihood of their citizens.

Africa is still at the bottom of the innovation scale. Innovation and technological progress should lead to the advancement of global processes in the production of knowledge. How is Africa contributing and benefiting from this? Underlying this process is the vital input factor of *'human capacity building'* and the enabling environment for people to be creative, productive and competitive.

This discussion is based on an interesting, well focused scientific paper "Valuing Innovation Surveys: The International Dimension" presented by Professor Sunil Mani of the Centre for Development Studies, Trivandrum, Kerala, India at the International Workshop on "Measuring Systems of Innovation, Inputs, Flows and Outputs," organised by the National Advisory Council on Innovation {NACI} at the Sheraton Hotel, Pretoria South Africa, from 23-25 April 2006. In his presentation, Prof Mani drew and focused attention to a number of key issues such as:

- Ways of measuring innovation – conventional vs. new information;
- Diffusion of innovation surveys across the world: developed vs. developing;
- Specifications of innovation activity in the developing world;
- The four critical issues in innovation surveys;
- The Brazilian experience; and
- Lessons for other developing countries.

Where does Africa fit within this equation? Where and how does Africa fit in the area of "science, technology and innovation systems [STIS]?" Given the wide disparity between the developed and developing countries, the first issue that comes to mind, is simply, innovation for whom, how, and what purpose? On the African continent the divide exist for example, between countries like South Africa, Egypt, Nigeria on the one hand, and Chad, Benin, Cameroon, Gambia, and Mali on the other. Thus attempts to close the *"innovation Chasm"* even within the continent, and between the continent contra transitional economies like Brazil, India, Mexico, not to mention the first economies like USA, Britain, Japan, Germany among others, is a major uphill task to overcome. The variations between different countries systems of innovation are profound. One can simply not compare.

From Prof Mani's [2006] presentation, one is left with a *"lost African continent"* that cannot claim the 21st century. South Africa is the only country on the continent making effective and significant effort in Science and Technology Policy {STP} and in National System of Innovation {NSI} judging from the perspectives of the establishment of scientific institutes in the 1920s [see Kahn 2006, Marais 2000] and in light of the current state of the art [Pouris 2003; IDRC 1993; Government of South Africa 2002].

In terms of technological achievement index (TAI), South Africa ranks highest placed at the 39 position, with the following positions for the rest of the continent: Tunisia (51), Egypt (57), Algeria (58), Zimbabwe (59), Senegal (66), Ghana (67), Kenya (68), Tanzania (70), Sudan (71) and Mozambique (72). The rest of Africa is poorly classified in respect of the following:

- Technological Achievement (TA);
- Technological Creator (TC) – (patents, granted and receipts of loyalties and licence fees);
- Position of recent innovations: (Internet and high and medium technology exports);
- Diffusion of and innovation (Telephones, Electricity Consumption);
- Human Skills: (a) mean years of schooling: and (b) Gross tertiary science enrolment) (UNDP 2001-HDR).

Box 1. Level of Scientific and Technological Underdevelopment

Mauritius	63
Tunisia	89
Cape Verde	91
South Africa	94
Algeria	100
Egypt	101
Gabon	109
Namibia	111
Morocco	112
Cameroon	125
Congo	126
Sierra-Lone	160

Source: UNDP [2001] HDR - New York.

The score for the rest of the continent is extremely poor. Investment in technology creation which embodies (i) mean years of schooling: (ii) Research and development –R&D expenditure in respect of (a) as % of GNP: (b) in business and (c) scientists and engineers in R&D, we find the following statistics for the period 1987-1997, with Libya placed at the 59 position and with the other countries taking the following positions as depicted in Box 1. These statistics depict a scientific and technologically underdeveloped region that is not able to be competitive in global knowledge-based economy. Handicapped by these shorting comings, the region has to rely on external inputs for its industrial take-off. The Commission for Africa – Our Common Interest [2005] is clear on this issue.

The views of British Prime Minister Tony Blair are explicit on this issue. "Growth will also require a massive investment in infrastructure to break down the internal barriers that hold Africa back. Donors should fund a doubling of spending on infrastructure – from rural roads and small-scale irrigation to regional highways, railways, larger power projects and Information and Communication Technology {ICTs}. That invest must include both rural development and slum upgrading without which the poor people in Africa will not be able to participate in growth. And policies for growth must actively include – and take care not to exclude – the poorest groups. There should be particular emphasis on agriculture and on helping small enterprises, with a particular focus on women and young people. For growth to be sustainable, safeguarding the environment and addressing the risks of climate change should be integral to donor and government programmes": the statement reemphasis the need for Africa to build its human and institutional capacities [see Oketch 2006: 554-564]. The idea is further elaborated by Gordon Brown [2005:5] as his emphasis on growth and governance in Africa, constituting opportunities for the region to realise sustainable long-term development by investing, innovating, educating and developing skills, deploying science and technology, in the process of socio-economic transformation.

Though the statistics send a message, other factors have to be looked into to obtain a holistic perspective of the state of science, technology and innovation within the African continent. Contrasting this with the developed world shows how scientifically and technological vulnerable Africa is in facing the challenges of development and in providing quality livelihood to its rapidly expanding population. Johnson and Lundvall [2003:25] pinpoint five areas as crucial for constructing innovation systems in Africa. These areas need serious attention. They include the following:

- The role of nation states;
- Prerequisite for building education systems;
- Building social capital and local knowledge systems;
- Finding strategies for appropriate insertion in the world economy;
- Building strategies for appropriate insertion in the world economy.

Unfortunately, the African political landscape is not providing the appropriate and conducive atmosphere for knowledge creation, productivity and competiveness. Innovation is thwarted. Science, research and technology are not incorporated in national development agenda. How many Africa countries undertake innovation survey? What does innovation imply to these countries? How many African countries can boost of a serious industrial private sector? How many of these firms are involved in the promotion of domestic related research and development activities? What form of linkage{s} exists between these firms and the country's research and institutions of higher learning? What are government policies towards the private sector? Are government policies designed to promote competitiveness and production within the private sector? Or are government policies designed and oriented towards the provision of public goods? Is the government working in tandem with the manufacturing industrial to develop and implement comprehensive national industrial policies? In short, is there a national master plan for science, and technology {S&T}, research development and innovation {RDI}?

There is the absence of the political and the creative and risk taking spirit within the private sector. In some cases, the real *"private sector"* does not exist. Government assumes the functional role of a private and public sector, but lacking the capacity in providing the necessary services delivery functions. As far as *"valuing innovation"* is concern, Africa is at the periphery of the periphery. Why? Of course, it is easy to put blames on the *"legacy of colonialism"* and the rising wave of *"neo-colonialism"* that continue to thwart the aspirations and desires of the people. Many inter-related factors account for this deplorable situation. The bottom line being the absence of visionary political leadership, endued with a sense of direction, and a scientific community conscious as to what the priorities of the nation should be. And to mobilise resources towards in achieving envisaged goals. Of course, the rapidly changing international political and economic environment significantly contributes positively and negatively to the state of art within the region. However, the continent as a virgin territory offers brighter prospects and opportunities for research and development for key stakeholder - the private sector, higher education and government – to exploit and make a difference in the living standard of the people. Existing possibilities are not being explored and exploited, leaving the continent as an under-research region in the context of science, technology and innovation.

As a discussant to the paper, I would rather address the issue from a different perspective, but drawing from the areas of (i) four critical issues in innovation surveys, (ii) the Brazilian experiences, and (iii) lessons of other developing countries for Africa; situating this within the African context. And to lump this under the banner, where is African coming, where it is, and where it is headed as far as issues of science, technology, research and innovation are concerned? It may sound vague to downsized Prof Mani's scientific discourse in this manner. I do so for a better understanding of evolving technological change, research and development to better appreciate the need of innovation system within the national context contra the global scene. And why it is vital for the continent to get on the science, technology development and innovation bandwagon of this century. One has to see this approach from the perspectives of:

- Creating the necessary local linkages to promote creativity and productivity of new products, processes and management of activities related to local conditions and needs;
- Drawing from indigenous knowledge to build a critical mass in the domain of S&T, RDI;
- A policy and attitude of mastering and adapting imported technologies and transforming such technologies to meeting the needs of the people, as well as ensuring that these new technologies enhances the productivity, competitiveness of their products in the global market;
- Developing policies that stimulate as well as support the process of human capacity development, and promoting a continuous learning and innovation processes;
- Ensuring networking, interactivity as well as building trusts, confidence and cooperation with and among institutions and nations.

WHERE IS AFRICA COMING FROM?

The historical past of Africa is one where indigenous knowledge, science and technology capacity of the people was destroyed through the forces of slavery and colonialism. Even with the attainment of independence, the forces of neo-colonialism continue to thwart means of regaining the lost scientific, technological and cultural heritage of the people. Therefore, Africa is coming from a weak scientific and technological base. This can be seen within the context of Puplampu [2006:31] as the crisis of the African state within the past couple of decades, which severely curtailed its role in political, economic, and social development, with the result of human suffering in Africa often reported with 'ghoulish relish'. Africa has to construct a new image of it by ensuring that structural adjustment within the broad spectrum of activities takes place in a constructive and humane manner. It should be people –oriented

WHERE IS AFRICA NOW?

The euphoria of independence failed to trigger the reconstitution of the lost heritage and indigenous capacity and capability of the people in the field of science and technology, no matter how crude this was. As a result, failure to revamp and give new direction leaves the continent weak, fragmented and lacking coherence in its recovery strategy. Post colonial Africa failed in effecting a coherent national development plan and strategy where science and technology took centre stage as part of the national reconstruction and development agenda after many years of slavery and colonialism. It is a crisis-ridden region, having no focused science, technology and innovation policy, rising level of abject poverty, increasing degree of political instability and facing the forces of bad governance and all that it entails.

WHERE IS AFRICA HEADED?

Africa is headed for disaster if appropriate measures are not taken now to develop its human capacity, and refocus attention on improving the living conditions and standards of the population. The continent needs to re-institute, reconstruct, and reform through instituting democratic governance system that exploit and build on the ingenuity of the capacities of the people and its stock of natural resources. In this process it is imperative to develop the human capacity and skills of the people and to link this with global knowledge system. Though the rising tide of globalisation propelled by the forces of information and communication technology offers hope, the current state of science and technology and its poor human capacity constitute hindrances for the continent to benefit from the various advances made in the domain of science and technology.

By not focusing on redesigning the economy and reorganising the state, the continent is heading for disaster of the worse magnitude. The frontiers of existing poor infrastructure and poor human capacity must be reconstructed to ensure sustainable development with the ultimate goal of improving the quality living standard of the vast majority of the population. The poor must be brought into the process. This requires a *"bottom-up"* rather as against the current *"top-down"* approach that has only helped in widening the disparity between the rich and poor in society.

It is the place of government in partnership with civil society and the private sector to make poverty history and to put aside the destruction done by colonial rule, "which failed to integrate the continent or stimulate local industrial development" [Njoh 1997] and forge ahead in a constructive, and comprehensive pattern of prioritised strategic long-term development approach. In spite of this set back, there is hope in the form of science and technology through ICTs transforming the continent as noted by Oyelaran-Oyeyinka and Lal [2005]. A good example comes from Uganda which in 2001 was the first African country where the mobile phones exceeded land fixed phones; and the market expanded from under 20,000 users in 1993 to an estimated 18.2 million in 2003, But despite such phenomenal growth rates, much of Africa still remains disconnected from the rest of the world because of poor communication infrastructure and erratic electric power supply among other shortcomings [See Juma 2006; Hamilton 2003; Guislain; Ampah & Bescangon 2003; Lor & Bester 2006]

ABSENCE OF A NATIONAL POLICY

Most African countries lack a comprehensive national science and technology policy as an integral part of a national development strategy plan – NDSP [Forje, 1989, and see also various Unesco Reports on CASTAFRICA 1 and 2 1974 and 1987 respectively]. Without a coherent and compressive strategic policy plan, development evolves in harp hazard pattern, with no vision for the future. Many African countries have fallen backwards in the area of science and technology even though global advances have been recorded in the domain following the penetrating influence of Information and Communication Technologies (ICTs) and genetic engineering in recent years. While the structural adjustment programme imposed by Bretton Woods Financial conglomerates {World Bank, International Monetary Fund etc.} could be part of the slow down, governments have since CASTAFRICA II; Arusha (Tanzania) 1987 paid lip services to this vital sector.

Of all the continents in the world, Africa is the most in dare need of the potential benefits science and technology can offer in addressing issues of poverty, environmental degradation and disasters, the cruellest burden of diseases and other ills that continue to plague the region. It is imperative to understand as well as appreciate the patterns of existing innovation systems, and their limitations and to articulate and aggregate policy measures and strategies that can best deliver the basic needs and benefit the people of Africa. What crimes have African committed that they are treated with scorn the world over? Why have Africans leaders not learned from these treatments poured on the people? Will Africa continue the way it has done in the age of knowledge-based global economy?

The collapse of the Lagos Plan of Action [LPA] saw the decline of science and technology related activities in the region. There is the absence of the political will and the vitality of responsibility taking not only by the government but also by civil society and the private sector. The triple heritage of the state, civil society and the private sector must concert to move the continent forward. Moving the continent forward requires positive responses from the international community. In the global-knowledge based economy of the 21st century, no nation or continent is an island. But Africa needs to develop effective responses in the game theory of scientific knowledge, globalisation, production and competition. For this is the only way in meeting the numerous challenges facing the region.

We are, thanks to advances in science and technology inter-connected, yet disconnected, as the gap continue to widen between the few rich and silent poverty-stricken majority. The scale and reach of technologies are widening, such that their spill over affects increasingly cross-national borders. The Chernobyl nuclear power station disaster 20 years ago [1986] led to serious adverse environmental and human impacts is still haunting many today. Rapid deforestation in Central African Sub-Region or in the Amazon leads to climate changes that affect not only the countries within these regions, but the entire world. Climate change is no longer an issue of "not in my backyard" but one that requires both national and international solutions. This shows how globally we are interconnected. On the other hand, ICTs is significantly transforming the lives of people in many transitional economies. Kaplinsky [2005:12] notes: *"as technology and communications allows a widening of personal and social horizons, innovation and globalisation are a natural outcome of the curiosity of the human spices"*. Thus climate change and the ICT are connecting factors urging the world, rich and poor nations to seek common solutions for a common and interrelated future.

It is imperative for Africa to develop core functions of technology and innovation missions to better accelerate the process of economic growth and wealth creation in society with the ultimate goal of improving the quality of life of the people. Here the continent can draw experiences from other emerging economies. Drawing from the strength of existing natural resources potential, innovation will necessitate targeting and funding resources. It also requires improving on human capacity [building the necessary critical mass] to accelerate the transformation process – technological innovation, incubation of new businesses and building a network of knowledge workers at all levels. The Absence of a National Science,

Technology and Innovation Policy in many African countries is regrettable. These policies must not be articulated and aggregated in isolation but as inherent integral component of a national strategic development plan from a short-term, medium-term and long-term perspectives.

COMPARATIVE INNOVATION – IS IT POSSIBLE?

Is it possible to have comparative innovation given the variety and disparity in the level of science and technology in the world? As earlier mentioned, within the African context, there is the advanced South Africa and some other countries like Egypt compared to the poor technological countries like Chad, Central African Republic, Gambia and others. Yet the basic needs of the people are the same be it in the USA, Britain, South Africa, Cameroon, Democratic Republic of Congo, Kenya and others. Such a common silver lining in human basic needs constitute signposts compelling those countries with poor quality living standards to take appropriate measures, doubling efforts in improving the situation. In this regard, innovation should be approached from the synthesis of realism and pragmatism that create possibilities for essential activities in ameliorating existing conditions, namely:

- The way forward for enhancing quality of life for all;
- Means and possibilities for contributing to knowledge creation and capacity building efforts especially in developing countries;
- Facing the challenges of globalisation in respect of competitiveness, productivity and sustainable use of resources;
- How innovation gives added value to the continent's abundant riches in natural resources, so that the people are not poor in the midst of plenty, but able to build themselves into a position of strength within the global economy?
- Community innovation – how the communities are empowered to be part of the productive global community;
- Innovation at the firm level;
- Innovation at the university/research institute levels;
- Innovation at the community level, especially, the integration of indigenous knowledge system with the modern scientific knowledge system for products and service delivery;
- How to get the political establishment increase interests in science and technology related disciplines, respond to social needs, and face the ever increase and fundamental debacles of the second economy?
- While drawing experiences from other emerging economies like Brazil, India, Mexico and others, Africa cannot wave aside challenging questions and issues like:
- What are the linkages between the technical and social aspects of innovation?
- How do they relate to human capacity building and developing indigenous knowledge capacity of the people?
- What use they make of their skilled human capacity and the extent to which knowledge production is consumed?

- The creation of enterprises especially in transitional economies.
- Promoting service delivery and the general performance of the society.
- Getting the rural communities as part of the evolving global village of the 21st century.
- What role do we permit our institutions of higher learning to influence the process of socio-economic and technological transformation?
- How do we relate innovation to the informal sector, which is the largest employer in most developing countries in Africa?
- Marrying the technology of knowledge with the technology for development for the socio-economic and technological transformation of the continent.
- Where do we locate the marginalized, especially, female gender in the entire process and how do we enhance the creativity and ingenuity of the local people.

BUILDING KNOWLEDGE CAPACITY AND KNOWLEDGE CONSUMPTION

First, the knowledge and innovative capacity of Africa is low. Second, the private sector is passive in the development process. In some countries, the private sector does not exist in the true sense of the word. Third, creating an effective government science and technology system becomes an imperative. Of course competence building and innovation takes places at different levels and stages on the continent. But this requires a coherent and integrated approach involving all the stakeholders, with the state and private sector injecting new and vigorous inputs in building the knowledge base of the society.

A triple linkage should evolve between the state, civil society and private sector, with roots firmly and deeply rooted within another triple heritage of university-research institute-private sector interface to enable training, research and research results converted in consumer products by the productive private sector. That interface is necessary for the advancement of innovation and improving on the quality of living standards for the masses. It is not sufficient to build human capacity and knowledge production. It is important that such human capacity and knowledge production should be consumed. Africa is currently weak in these two areas. As knowledge production is intensified so also must appropriate use be made of human capacity and knowledge consumption intensified at all levels, from primary, secondary, tertiary levels of education and among civil society.

A reading public is a knowledgeable, powerful and productive society. Knowledge is power as the old age adage goes. A reading public is a knowledge society equipped with the necessary tools to face odds and improve the living standards of its population. That is the image Africa must cultivate and inculcate in the minds of present and future generations. Engendering and empowering the youths and especially girls is extremely vital in this context. Africa must transcend the body of knowledge in its socio-economic transformation so that poverty and misery can become an issue of the past. Without which, the continent cannot take leave from the ghetto of underdevelopment and embrace the luxury of quality livelihood enjoyed by countries possessing far less the rich natural resources potentials of the continent.

Africa cannot claim the 21st century when it remains poor and human capacity is underdeveloped, when the technology of knowledge is not incorporated in the development process, and "when neo-classical economic recipes alternate with the human and social face of the same paradigm" [see Mammo 2003:355]. Drawing lessons from other countries, we need to incorporate a holistic and interdisciplinary approach by {i} creating science, technology and development infrastructure and innovation system, including a vigorous and conscientious expansion of tertiary education with greater emphasis on science and technology related disciplines: {ii} development of indigenous knowledge and capability and the encouragement of production of goods in a wide variety of areas as well as ensuring that these goods are competitive globally: {iii]creation of the scientific and industrial innovative potential to compete globally: and {iv} implementation of an agricultural policy of food self-sufficiency.

It should be noted that a national innovation system must be accompanied by technological accumulation backed with significant progress in building its human capacity basis and promoting high growth performances within the industrial sector. There is need, therefore, to a better build and a strong private industrial sector that should be linked with the activities of universities and research institutes directed towards improving the living standards of the citizens. The linkage of state-university- private sector interfaced is urgently needed in Africa to build an industrial base and promote the well being of the people. There is an urgent need in reorganising the State in Africa and Redesigning African Economy. This is best achieved through vital developmental processes, instituting democratic governance and promoting the role of science and technology in the development process.

Current investment in infrastructure is low in African countries that impede their strategic starting point for building capacity in science and technology related disciplines. The views of Amsden [2001] are clear on this. This can also be linked to that of Gerschenkron [1962] the advantages of a latecomer'. One of those advantages is making use of strategic opportunities that ICTs offers; through it is not the panacea for development. The panacea for African development rests with the people through self-reliant development and by- mobilising their domestic resources. Foreign aid or external assistance should be treated as a catalyst and in complementing efforts on the ground.

In redesigning African economies, we require stronger cooperation among African countries. Regional integration is vital in promoting intra-national trade. Existing regional integration groupings like ECOWAS, CEMAC, and SADC should be strengthened as the basis for a continental economic integration – An African Common Market like the European Union. The New Partnership for Africa Development [NEPAD] should play a leading role in forging the economic integration of African nations. Juma [2006:13] situating the position and role of engineering in the transformation of the continent notes: "a common feature of African regional integration agreements is their recognition of the importance of engineering in sustainable development. The integration of engineering is based on the recognition that individual African economies are small and poorly endowed with the human, physical and financial resources necessary to develop and harness engineering capabilities. The cost of building science and technology infrastructure often appears to be an overwhelming task for the national economies, especially in smaller and poorer states".

WAYS FORWARD

The development of the continent lies in the hands of the people themselves, who must articulate and aggregate the right policy strategies to overcome existing predicaments. They must also oscillate within the contours of an international environment that is not friendly to the Africa predicaments. The basic foundation of our institutions of learning, teach research and services to the community must be incorporated in development-oriented policy strategy.

They can tap from the globally knowledge of modern science and technology to improve on their indigenous knowledge capacity.

Improving tertiary education is a necessity, and building a culture of science and technology within the educational curriculum is imperative. The process must begin from the early stages of schooling and nurtured at the tertiary educational level and sustained throughout the span of our existence on planet earth.

Importantly, science and technology and its related disciplines must not be a preserve for the male child. Females must be encouraged to develop interest in science and technology related disciplines – mathematics, physics, chemistry and engineering subjects

Africa has only itself to blame for not making attempts to claim the 21st century, given global advances in science and technology within the past couple of decades. Windows of opportunity offered by information and communication technologies should be exploited

While colonialism played a role in contributing to the plight of the continent and its people, Africa should not continue to live in the past but moving forward by exploiting existing possibilities and harnessing its resources for the common good.

Good governance and visionary leadership is needed for the continent to pull itself together and give added values to its abundant wealth of natural resources. Good governance requires inputs from society. A passive civil society constitutes beacon for disaster in the long run.

Reorganising the state by creating the necessary basis for the structural-functioning of democratic governance remains in complete without adequate attention paid the continent's greatest virus, - the pandemic of corruption and poor quality services delivery [see Quest 2004]

Adopting a policy strategy of *"people focused"* can make the difference. Therefore, priority strategy of concerted and comprehensive structural adjustment agenda with a human face, incorporating science, technology, research, innovation and development [STRID] provides the way forward for the continent The continent must develop the capacity and ability to develop, operate as well as maintain infrastructure and services. It must be self-reliant to a large extent.

There is urgent need to intensify knowledge production and to promote knowledge consumption. Building the requisite human capacity necessitates building a critical reading public. The culture of reading in Africa is currently weak. A critical reading audience is needed to sustain knowledge production and advance innovation. Knowledge production must be married with knowledge consumption to have serious impact on the scientific and technological development of the continent.

Tapping on the expertise of the Diaspora. Efforts should be exerted to encourage Africans in the Diaspora to return home or invest home. Therefore, African governments must embark on an elaborate strategic policy offensive of inducing their citizens to return home by designing programmes and offering incentives as well as creating the necessary enabling environment that enables their citizens to contribute to national efforts. In short, a policy of converting "brain drain" into "brain gain"

THE GUIDING PRINCIPLES

The Commandments of Leadership for a New and Brave Africa

The people of Africa like any where in the world have in their service leaders at every level who possess the skills, abilities and attitudes [SAA] that will enable them to successfully execute the responsibilities incumbent to their office. It goes without saying that African leaders must learn early in their mission to serve the people certain basic qualities and have opportunities to mature in them.

Seen in this light, and in order to skilfully lead our nations and continent, we must have leaders who possess, among others, the following essential qualities, which through experience become mastered skills.

- Loyalty: The leader must be loyal. Disagreement is not necessarily disloyalty. A leader, who, in the best interest of his/her people, disagrees, should be listened to. On the other hand, a leader who actively participates in or encourages actions that are counter to the good of the people is disloyal.

- Courage: The leader must have courage, fearless and have the fortitude to carry out assignments given him/her - the gallantry to accept the risks of leaders. Africa leaders must not urge at the sight of obstacles, nor must they become bewildered when in the presence of adversity. They must be able to withstand the inherent periods of loneliness, despair, ridicule and rejection. They would be periods where the leader must be long-suffering in their duties – they must have the courage to act with confidence and to excel in times of uncertainty or danger as well as in times of prosperity.

- Emotional Stamina: -Each succeeding higher level of leadership places increasing demands on the emotions of leaders. As citizens, we must ensure that our leaders at every level have the stamina to recover rapidly from disappointment – to bounce back from discouragement, to carry out the responsibilities of their office without becoming distorted in their views – without losing clear perspective, as well as the emotional strength to persist in the face of seemingly difficult circumstances.

- Desire: - Few people will sustain themselves as leaders without a strong personal desire – an inherent commitment to influencing people, processes and outcomes. Weak is the leader who does not want to be one.

- Physical Stamina – Each nation must have leaders who can endure the physical demands of their leadership duties. Leaders cannot leader from their bedside, nor from a state of drunkenness. A body not properly tendered for becomes abused. A healthy body supports a healthy mind. Our leaders must be strong in body and mind in order to lead the charge.

- Empathy – Our leaders must develop empathy – an appreciation for and understanding of the values of others, sensitivity for other cultures, beliefs and traditions. However, empathy must not be confused with sympathy, which may result in unwise consolation at times when, above all others things, the good of the people or nation must be pursued with adroit diplomacy or battlefield action.

- Decisiveness – Our leaders must learn to be decisive, knowing when to act and when not to act, taking into account all facts bearing on the situation and then responsibly carrying out their leadership role.

- Anticipation –Learning by observation and through instincts sharpened by tested experience, our leaders must anticipate thoughts, actions and consequences.

- Timing – Essential to all acts of leadership is the timing of recommendations and actions. There is no magic formula for developing a sense of timing. One often gains this leadership skill by applying the lessons learned through failure. Knowing whom you are dealing with, their motives, characters, priorities and ambitions are critical elements even when seeking approval of the simplest recommendations.

- Competitiveness – An essential quality of leadership is the intrinsic desire to win. It is not necessary to win at all time; however, it is necessary to win the important contests. Our leaders must understand the competition inside and outside our nation/continent is strong and not to be taken lightly. A leader without a sense of competitiveness is weak and easily overcome by the slightest challenge.

- Self-Confidence. - Proper training and experience develops in leaders a personal feeling of assurance with which to meet the inherent challenges of leadership. Those who portray a lack of self-confidence in their abilities to carry out leadership assignments give signs to their subordinates, peers and superiors that these duties are beyond their capabilities. They become, therefore, weak leaders.

- Accountability - Learning to account for personal actions and those of subordinates is fundamental to leadership.

- Responsibility – Leaders are only necessary when someone is to be responsible to see that actions re carried out in directions followed. No king or subordinate leader should ever be allowed to serve who will not accept full responsibility for his/her actions.

- Credibility – Leaders must be credible. Their words and actions must be believable to both friend and foe. They must be trusted to have the intelligence and integrity to provide correct information. Leaders lacking in credibility will not gain proper influence and are to be hastily removed from position of responsibility, for they cannot be trusted.

- Tenacity – The quality of unyielding drive to accomplish assignments is a desirable and essential quality of leadership. The weak persist only when things go their way. The strong persist and pursue through discouragement, deception and even personal abandonment. Pertinacity is often the key to achieving difficult assignments or meeting challenging goals.

- Dependability – If a leader cannot be depended upon in all situations to carry out his roles and responsibilities, relieve him of them Leaders should understand that serving the nation is a sacrifice, a call to service and trust in their ability to lead, and they should be proud of being entrusted with such responsibility That trust must not be abused.

- Stewardship – Our leaders must have the essential quality of stewardship, a caretaker quality. They must serve in a manner that encourages confidence, trust and loyalty. Subordinates are not to be abused; they are to be guided, developed and rewarded for their performance. Punishment is to be reserved as consequences of last resort and sparingly applied only when all other attempts have failed to encourage the rebellious to comply. Without a flock there can be no shepherd. Without an army there can be no generals or leaders, Leaders are, therefore, caretakers of the interests and well being of those and the purposes they serve.

These qualities of leadership simply take time, learning and experience to develop. There are few who will find shortcuts. Importantly, Africa needs leaders who can give a sense of direction as we have moved from colonial rule {colonial status} to local or home-grown administration {independence}. Such a transition implies the rule of governors to that of the representatives of the people. It is necessary to stress the importance of dynamic leadership in conquering development crises plaguing the continent. Since independence African leaders have been faced with some of the cruel dilemmas as they seek to establish effective governmental institutions that can blend parochial traditions and international standards. Modern communications through 'shrinking' the world force people to recognise that they are different from others. But as people learn about other systems and norms, which seem to govern them, they often become more critical of the assumptions that uphold their own systems of authority and governance pattern.

The relative success of existing institutions of government and leaders in carrying out the essential functions of the political system remains the most decisive factor in determining the ability of a new nation to resolve its developmental problems. Africa suffers from the growing state of accumulation of problems without comprehensive solutions. And the consequences of the accumulation of problems are many. First, the overlapping of too many problems makes each harder to solve. Second, problems raised in the various performances are interrelated with each other. Where there is a way there is hope for Africa to overcome its development predicament.

REFERENCES

Amsden Alice [2001] *The Rise of The Rest: Challenges to the West from Late-Industrialising Economies*. Oxford University Press, New York.

Brown Gordon [2005] "Toward" in Calestous Juma, (ed.) 2005 *Going For Growth: Science, Technology and Innovation in Africa.* Smith Institute, London.

Britz J. P. Lor, Coetzee, J. I. and Bester B. [2006] "Africa as a Knowledge Society: A Reality Check", *International Information & Library Review,* Vol. 38. No. 1 (March 2006), pp.25-40.

Commission For Africa [2005] *Our Common Interest: Report of The Commission for Africa,* Commission for Africa, London.

Forje, John [1989] Science and Technology in Africa, Vol. 10, *Longman World Series on Science and Technology, Essex, Longman Publisher Group.* United Kingdom.

Gerschenkron Alexander [1962} *Economic Backwardness in Historical Perspective.* The Belknap Press of Harvard University Press, Cambridge, MA.

Government of South Africa [2002] *South Africa's National Research and Development Strategy*, Pretoria.

Guislain Pierre, Ampah Mavis, & Bescangon Laurent [2005] Connecting Sub-Saharan Africa: A World Bank Group strategy for information And Communication technology Sector Development, *Working Paper No. 51.* (World Bank, Washington, DC.)

Hamilton Jacqueline [2003] "Are Main Lines and Mobile Phones Substitutes or Complements? Evidence from Africa," *Telecommunications Policy 27,* Nos. 1-2 (February/March 2003), pp.109-133

IDRC [1993] Towards a Science and Technology Policy for A Democratic South Africa, *IDRC Mission Report,* July 1993, Ottawa: IDRC.

Johnson Bjorn and Bengt-Ake Lundwall [2003] "National Systems of Innovation and Economic Development", in Mammo Muchie et al {ed.] 2003 *Putting Africa First: The Making of African Innovation Systems,* Aalborg University Press, Aalborg, Denmark.

Juma, Calestus [2006] Redesigning African Economies: The Role of Engineering in International Development. The 2006 Hinton Lectures, *The Royal Academy of Engineering,* London, DFID.

Kahn, M. [2006] "After Apartheid: The South African National System of Innovation; From Constructed Crisis to Constructed Advantage?*" Science and Public Policy,* Volume 33, No. 2 pp125-136.

Kaplinsky, Raphael [2005] *Globalisation, Poverty and Inequality.* Polity Press, UK.

Mammo Muchie et al {Eds.] *Putting Africa First: The Making of African Innovation Systems.* Aalborg University Press, Aalborg, Denmark.

Mani, Sunil [2006] "Valuing Innovation Surveys – The International Dimension", *Keynote Paper presented NACI International Workshop on Measuring Systems of Innovation:* Inputs, Flows and Outputs", Sheraton Hotel, Pretoria, South Africa, 24-25 April 2006.

Mani, Sunil [2003] "The Role of Government in Shaping the National System of Innovation: The Case of South Africa since 1994" in Mammo Muchie {eds.} 2003. *Putting Africa First: The Making of African Innovation Systems,* Aalborg University Press, Denmark, pp201-216.

Marais, H. C. [2000]. *Perspective on Science Policy in South Africa.* Pretoria: Network Publishers.

NACI [2006] "Draft Literature and Policy Survey: *NACI International Workshop on "Measuring Systems of Innovation: Inputs, Flows and Outputs",* 24-25 April, Sheraton Hotel, Pretoria, South Africa.

Njoh Ambe [1997] "Colonial Spatial Development policies, Economic Instability, And Urban Transportation in Cameroon", *Cities,* Vol. 14. No. 3, June 1997, pp 133-143.

Oketch Moses [2006] "Determinants of Human capital Formation And Economic Growth of African Countries", *Economics of Education Review,* Vol. 25. No. 5 October 2006, pp 554-564.

Oyelaran- Oyeyinka Banji & Lal Kaushalesh [2005] "Internet Diffusion in Sub-Saharan Africa: A Cross-Country Analysis, *"Telecommunication Policy,* Vol. 29, No. 7. (August 2005), pp.507-527.

Pouris, A. [2003] "South Africa's Research Publication Record: The Last 10 Years", *South Africa Journal of Science,* 99:425-428, September / October 2003.

Puplampu P. Korbla [2006] "Critical Perspectives on Higher Education and Globalisation in Africa", in Ali A. Abdi, Korbla P. Puplampu & George J. Sefa Dei [2006] *African Education And Globalisation: Critical Perspectives,* Lexington Books, USA.

Quest Robert [2004] *The Shackled Continent: Power, Corruption, And African Lives.* Smithsonian Books, Washington, DC.

Chapter 9

THE CHALLENGES OF POLITICAL LEADERSHIP AND CENTRALISED-BUREAUCRATIC AUTHORITY IN TRANSITIONAL POLITIES IN AFRICA: EXPERIENCES FROM CAMEROON[*]

ABSTRACT

The issue of leadership is a world wide problem, but more acute in transitional polities, Cameroon in particular and Africa in general. The absence of a democratic developmental state can be attributed to the kind of leadership practiced in country. Thus where quality leadership exist, political leadership looms highest in the minds of many for a number of very important reasons, namely that of shaping the national vision and overseeing priority strategic policies for change and development for the common good.

Referring to Cameroon, one can demonstrate, however, that a country can undergo fundamental transformation process within a relatively short period of time if quality and visionary leadership exists, and especially when such political leadership is strong, dedicated and backed by high professional and performing managerial and bureaucratic structure capable of independently and apolitical articulating and aggregating effective quality service delivery to the people. Cameroon has been success story within the central African Sub-region. What lies behind this? What factors impede further success? It is believed that "leadership is cause: everything else is effect". How does this relate to the Cameroon situation? What lessons can other nations draw from the Cameroon experience?

The paper further penetrates into issues of democratic governance being fundamental as this advertently or inadvertently promotes or undermines effective and complementary roles of the political and managerial leadership. The paper identifies a number of leadership secrets and how the principles of leadership can be applied to ensure sustainable change and development. The conclusion builds on the fact that the kind of leadership to propel Cameroon or most African countries from the state of underdevelopment to a developed polity must be qualitatively different from what currently exist. Proactive strategic policy measures are recommendations are advanced.

[*] Paper presented at the 29th AAPAM Annual Roundtable Conference on the Theme: Political And Managerial Leadership For Change And Development in Africa, 3-8th September, 2007, International Conference Centre, Manzini, Royal Kingdom of Swaziland.

Keywords: democratic governance, service delivery, leadership skills, developmental state, change, affluence, poverty

INTRODUCTION: IN SEARCH OF A LEADER

"What has emerged from this demarcation and definition of jurisdictions is a strong executive and a weak legislature, both of which draw their democratic legitimacy from the same source since both are elected by universal suffrage. Can exercise of legislative power serve as a means of control of the executive in such a constitutional arrangement is the question this study seeks to answer?". *[Kale Ndive Kofele 1998]*

"The ensuing struggles punctuated by tribal wars and exacerbated by the stave trade, could only be restrained by compelling systems of peaceful-coexistence, initiated and promoted by some of the emerging nationalists in their respective milieus to install and advance self-rule. This was the forerunner of modern democracy in pubic governance." *[Atogho 1999]*

"We left the governor's office feeling satisfied. We, however, still ran the risk of being arrested, of becoming political prisoners. We were then not conscious of the risk we were running by openly criticising an autocratic regime and its government and through them the President of the Republic himself. We had forgotten that we were of Anglo-Saxon culture, with its very highly developed sense of freedom of expression, and that we were facing people of a culture that was different from ours". *[Christian Cardinal Tumi: 2006:32]*

"I think that what ever African leaders do, they should think of the people they are leading, because leaders are to serve their citizens. They must look after their welfare. They must accept defeat during elections and they must not do anything to stabilise the country". *[President Olusegun Obasanjo, 17 May 1999: Interview during a visit to Yaoundé, Cameroon; as cited in Atogho, 1999:98]*

Leadership is the privilege to have the responsibility to direct the actions of others in carrying out the purposes of the organisation or society, at varying levels of authority and with accountability for both successful and failed endeavours. It does not constitute a model or system No model of system of leadership behaviour can anticipate the circumstances, conditions and situations in which the leader must influence the actions of others. An evaluation of leadership principles is an effective base upon which to build other skills that may be important to success in specialised fields.

The paper looks at leadership and democratic governance in terms of the imperatives of power and within the Cameroon polity context given that power involves the exercise of a wide range of influence and pressures to determine and implement official policies in society Aseka Eric [2006] notes: "leadership is an influence relationship that is intended to realise real changes in accordance with the mutual purposes. What seems to lack is a well-theoretical epistemic basis in the fact that influence can be both ethical and unethical and predatorily is simply unethical exercise of power. It is at the root of the typical African vampire state. There is need for a rational perspective to put sense in the leadership crisis and its consequent socio-economic effects on Africa". [see also Israel, 2001; Bewaji, 2003]

In short, leadership is maximising the capability of people to fulfil purpose through the development of character, the development of traits and dispositions, which can spearhead the exercise of various competencies in rendering effective and strategic leadership. It entails confronting problems and offering endurable solutions as opposed to predatorialism practiced by the political elites with no other strategy than reaping the riches of their countries and their international linkages or what Bayart [1993] aptly gives an in-depth analytical exposure under the concept of the "politics of the belly". Leadership vacuum is the cause of the tragic and intractable problems of Africa, notes Israel [2001], while Burns [12978] adds: *"there is no school of leadership, intellectual or practical and we lack the very foundation for knowledge over the phenomenon we call leadership in the arts, science and politics":* and yet, "the leadership process is a phenomenon that touches and shapes our lives. Without such standards and knowledge we cannot make vital distinctions between types of leaders: we cannot distinguish leaders from rulers: from power wielders, and from despots. Africa has had its share of despots from time immemorial but the post-colonial era has seen weird regimes presided over by dictators" [Aseka 2006; Burns 1978] of various kinds.

Politics and administration constitute mediums of exercising and legitimising control of power and authority that remains the channel through which contradictions are expressed and resolved [Staniland, 1985:152]. The control of power demands the development of the right political character given that character education and development apart from political education is critical in the development of leadership competence. Both are supposed to generate mature leaders and citizens who can both advocate and carry out appropriate political actions to protect and further national interest [Remy 1980:1; Aseka 2006].

The return to political pluralism and the intensification of the democratisation process in Africa in post-cold war era intensify the issue for quality leadership in the transformation process. Political leadership takes the upper hand in the process of reconstruction and development. Politics is mainly about the solution of problems plaguing the country. This requires the coordination of power expressed as authority for the common good. Politics is not only about liberty, freedom enthronement and control of the market. Politics is about leadership because it empowers one's access to formal leadership positions in the public domain and political leadership is a matter of exercising the right competencies in the management of public affairs [Aseka 2006; Little, 2002: xii]

Africa needs leadership that holds promise, hope, inspirations and the capacity of uniting people and other forces within society. Seen within this context, Kotte [1999] states: "leadership is the development of vision, and strategies: the alignment of relevant people behind those strategies: and the empowerment of individuals to make the vision happen despite obstacles". Therefore, good leadership embeds people who exhibit ethical and moral integrity: with moral integrity resting on the virtues that Aristotle and his adherent Arendt extolled in the exercise of power under demonstrable, intellectual, emotional, creative and reactive competence for the common good.

Even in this regard, and tied to grazing national goals, Adei [2004] looks at four crosscutting marks of leadership, namely, the ability to:-

- Elaborate and communicate a desirable vision and goals that give direction to national development efforts;
- Mobilise people who are excited about changing national fortunes;
- Put together effective growth strategies translated into policies and programmes that, overtime, enable the realisation of national goals; and

- Manage the difficult change entailed in transforming economies including the ability to respond to internal and external shocks.

Given the geo-political, geo-economic and geo-cultural nature of the African society, transformational leadership is required to bridge through prophylactic policy initiatives, make best decision and effectively implement national integration and developmental projects as well as be capable of making good and productive decisions for their societies. Tied to Adei's perception of crosscutting benchmarks of leaders, Bass [1995; 1990; Bass & Steidmeier 1998] identify three ways in which leaders transform their fellows:

- Increasing their awareness of task importance and value;
- Getting them to focus first on team or organisational goals, rather than their own interests; and
- Activating their higher order needs.

Political leadership role in Cameroon in variance combines these attributes to foster both national and self-interests. For this reasons, apolitical, professional and independent public service institution is often thwarted to attain the maximum individual and collective benefits from the system of governance. This is done through the holy or unholy marriage between the structures of the ruling political party with that of the structural-functional system of the public service. This explains why in an autocratic-centralised- bureaucratic-administrative system, the ruling party becomes an inherent and decisive instrumental structure within the public service administration. It is assumed and even made compulsory once given a post of responsibility; you automatically become a member of the ruling party. There are cases where people with no political inclination or adherence to the ruling party when appointed are conditioned to join the party or loose their appointments.

Appointments are no longer on the basis of meritocracy but mediocrity. Your rise and fall within the administrative system depends on the degree of allegiances to the ruling party. Public bureaucracy is political party oriented: not apolitical and independent in serving whichever political party that assumes office. In this regards, he civil service will thwart any structural-functional policy agenda designed to usher quality livelihood to the masses when such policy strategies are against their current harvesting spree within the system. Which mouth bites the finger that fees it? This explains why change is slow to come to those countries that have embarked on a centralised-autocratic-bureaucratic administrative governance system.

It further highlights the fact that centralised governance systems cannot ensure social justice and equity and creates room for disorder, mismanagement and exploitation of the weak by the strong, since the system thrives on disorder and confusion paving the free way for corruption and disrespect for the cardinal principles of open government and respect for the rule of law. The country needs serious reflective approach to democratic values and practices, just as professionalism, work ethics remain important, are you a cashew nut worker, council worker, administrator or a president. There is need to encourage more independent and reflective reasoning that includes a wider understanding of the role of moral concepts, principles and ethical evaluation in democratic development. The purpose is to encourage reflective, ethical and objective scholarly discussions and reflections on issues of leadership, values, value conflicts, citizenship responsibilities, and moral dilemmas we face in our daily lives as well as on our rights and responsibilities. It is imperative that issues such as democracy, human and civil rights, development, equality and justice be openly discussed to create greater awareness among the population. Bear in mind that these concepts inevitably vary in different cultural and linguistic contexts. It is a believe that the only way to empower people and give them the basic intellectual skills needed in order to fully participate in the political, economic and social affairs of their respective communities, and to develop their nation towards a direction that benefits everybody, not just a few.

CONCEPTUAL FRAMEWORK

The conceptual framework is o on the "Epistemology of the Theory of Leadership Qualities" which builds on the structural basis those nations, tribes and other bodies rise and fall on the strength of their leaders and the ability with which their leaders carry out their responsibilities of office – "seeking first the good of the people". The underlying factor is that of "leadership as call to serve". Service to the nation should remain the paramount goal and the responsibility priority scale of good leadership role. It is also conditioned by the constitution and its right interpretations. How this is accomplished depends on individual skills, purpose and intensions. To skilfully lead a nation, leaders are needed possessing among others, the following essential qualities which experience become mastered skills. The epistemology of leadership role is an embodiment of various inter-related qualities among which are:-

- Stewardship or sense of purpose and direction;
- Responsibility of seeing that right actions are undertake according to directions;
- Credibility, the degree to which the policies are articulated and aggregated to be believable to both friends and foes:
- Accountability relating to how the leader accounts for personal actions and those of subordinates;
- Ethical, moral rectitude and sense of justice, with complete adherence to the rule of law.

The basis of departure further builds on the concepts of *"culture, integrity, honesty and "manipulation"*. Culture is the socially transmitted pattern of human behaviour that includes thought, speech, action, institutions, and artefacts. Culture constitutes a fundamental factor in societal building. A society or person without a culture is nothing short of a living dead. Integrity as defined by the Oxford Illustrated Dictionary entails wholeness, soundness, uprightness, honesty. It is the unimpaired state of honesty and purity. The synonym for integrity is honesty. Honesty entails uprightness, truthfulness. Being honest implies fair and upright in speech and act, not lying, cheating, or stealing; sincere, good, worthy; showing uprightness of gain earned by fair means, unadulterated, unsophisticated and so on. Manipulation entails in nutshell, to control or influence by artful, unfair, or insidious means, especially to one's own advantage.

Therefore, honesty and integrity *constitutes "essential qualities for leadership because they define and infuse clarity of purpose. In the context of public life, it asks and answers the question: why am I seeking to be appointed to public office? Correct answer: To serve the common good. A man of integrity does not see his appointment to public office as an opportunity to get rich from the public purse by abusing public office. A man of integrity does not get to bat an eyelid he has littered the entire place with his 'country' people. It is integrity, together with competence that anchors good governance"* [Chia 2007:8].

These concepts juxtapose key roles in situating political leadership in the Cameroon political system discourses construed mostly on the bureaucratic-authoritarian-centralised system, where {a} political leaders create and cope with the problems of disorder, and with the leaders perceiving politics as the exercise of power and authority by the state institutions: {b} bureaucratic-authoritarian-centralised regimes supplying the integrated administrative framework enabling the ruling elites (especially those in the public service) to retain their power or expand economic growth and wealth at the expense of the suffering masses: and {c} besides the domestic politico-economic pressures, foreign institutions reinforcing the bureaucratic-centralised-authoritarian system through the colonial system or neo-colonial system or economically, through the hegemonic influence of financial conglomerates like the World bank and its agencies (structural adjustment programme {SAP} without a human face), tied financial aids from western governments and other financial institutions.

The Cameroon political landscape is entangled with strategies, tactics and manipulative attitude of a Machiavellian leader pitted against a shroud charismatic cultural and traditional leader within a transitional society craving for modernity. Since independence, leadership style has been engraved with the virtues and vices of authoritarian and centralised governance system. Atogho [1999:78] asserts: 'leadership in many African communities is symbolised by a traditional ruler or chief. Chiefs do not view dead bodies because they are like excrement. Any action that deviates from a set of goal is like going for the excrement". So far, Cameroon is going through the second republic ensuring some degree of stability, as change from one leader to another transpired through serenity, mutual understanding and not violence. This remains a blessing for the country. Political leadership should tap on this to build a stronger nation. May be this is what motivated the ideals behind the new rallying slogan of *"great achievements"* that has yet to manifest within the developmental struggle of the country.

It can be pointed out that the two leaders either by design or accident seem to have developed a *"lust for leadership"* or it bestowed on them, or forced by circumstances to assume leadership role. Both leaders showed variance for or lack of commitment in responsibility as leaders. Too often, the leadership of many nations falls to people who lack the ambition, sense of direction, courage and capabilities to function as leaders. Even if they have these qualities, certain events can help divert what was seen as original good intentions. Others may be influenced by the spectre of 'power'; and get carried by the sweetness of the institution and all that it incarnates. As the old adage goes, 'power corrupts, and absolute power corrupts absolutely'. Unfortunately, absolute power is not used to the buttress the common good but selfish ends.

Committed leaders are those who with a lust for leadership, sense of direction, and willingness to serve. Will, however, is distinguishable by their wisdom, sincerity, benevolence, authority, charisma and courage. They will have a human quality and a strong commitment to their cause and those they serve. Paul Biya (incumbent Head of State) crusade under the slogan of a *"New Deal Governance System"* with the virtues of *"democratisation, moralisation and rigour"* initially held hope for the people. It captured the aspirations and desires of the people. He became the *beacon of hope* and a *redeemer* after almost a quarter century of Ahidjo's rule described as dictatorial and oppressive. For many, a new messiah was born to take the people out of bondage and enslavement. Biya's authority was not challenged since the realm of power, {the baton of state authority} was voluntarily passed to him {and latter won the presidential election} by one considered a dictator and tyrant.

Paul Biya could be classified as possessing an intrinsic desire to achieve substantial personal recognition and willingness to earn it in all fairness, bearing in mind that he had been Ahidjo's adherent and top civil servant for almost two decades, and emerging with a new vision distant from his predecessor. It was a courageous move but which turned out to be deceitful in the long run. In this light, he could be regarded a "mobilising political leader", just like Ahidjo can also be classified as a mobilisation leader following the euphoria of *"reunification"* of British and French Cameroon in {1961} and the *"peaceful revolution"* of {1972}, instituting a unitary governance system, abolishing the Federal system established in 1961. The Cameroon society does not suffer from incipient or actual instability. Emerging instability could be seen as a carry-over of the patterns of leadership developed since the reunification of the territories. There is conflict between the forces and style of inherited colonial administration and also internal strife among the leaders. Is should be noted as earlier pointed out that the 'country' is an artificial creation of the colonial powers and in partnership or cognisance with the United Nations in establishing one administrative unit.

Gap exists between the two parts of the country. Also one can state gap existence between the styles of administration adopted by the two heads of state though under a common centralised-authoritarian-bureaucratic system. This leads to an imbalance in the country's economic development and other features. In a sense, one may characterise the regime of the first president as 'traditional elites' and that of Biya as 'modernising elites'. This may actually be a series of differences – in the social background, in orientations toward change, and linkages to the mass of the population. There are more educated Cameroonians today than in the early stage of independence. The modernising elite tend to be urban and educated, overtaken by corruption and the exigencies of prevailing global life style. The new elites control the technological skills that are vital to the nation's development, greedy in the process of implementing these skills for the benefit of society. The old or traditional elites were committed towards building a developmental state but lacked certain capacities. The traditional elites who took over from the departing colonial powers exhibited signs for development; hence Cameroon's rapid development spree under the first regime. Under this circumstance, the first regime could be regard as a *'mobilisation and modernisation'* governance system

To an extent, the *"mobilisation political leadership system"* can be deplored in situating certain aspects of Cameroon development. The purpose of mobilisation system struggle is to attain rapid, fundamental transformation of government and society. The fundamental principle of a mobilisation system focuses on the following:

- Active mass involvement to view events in political terms;
- Concentrate on general, common concerns;
- To link their individual interests with the well-being of the whole society;

- Struggle for a public good – national independence, industrialisation, mass literacy, a healthy society {virtues of quality livelihood} becomes an intrinsic end and a means to resolve private problems;
- Through ideological exhortation, political organisation and heightened mass participation, mobilisation leaders attempt to realise wide-spread societal changes for the common good;
- By articulating and implementing an all inclusive and comprehensive policy agenda – promoting policies for human resources development, quality healthcare services, mobilising activities at the grassroots level and society in general in wagging war against social inequalities and underdevelopment, poverty and corruption.

For mobilisation leaders, politics involves steering state and society towards ideological goals in a conflict-laden environment. Sometimes mobilisation can promote conflict and struggle. Instead of negotiating bargains, they exploit value conflicts. Polarisation, not accommodation, becomes the dominant style in the mobilisation policy process. Dedicated to an ideological cause, mobilisation systems try to arouse mass passion, faith, and emotion needed to defeat political enemies. The nature of the bureaucratic-centralised-authoritarian and mobilisation systems creates a confused and complicated atmosphere exploited by the shroud political leadership in enhancing the behavioural features that reflects the dominance of the individual, the party-state accord over society. This explicitly portrays Cameroon's political landscape. The application of both the 1972 and 1996 constitutions depending upon which aspects of the constitution that suits the government and ruling party is a typical example. Leaders will exploit whatever existing advantages in either or both systems in advancing their leadership role.

When an authoritarian-centralised bureaucratic system collides with a vibrant citizenry, the clash or chemistry may not be pleasant. Will such a clash surface? What will its intensity be? What is the country's preparedness and shared-commitment towards resolving conflicts of interest? As the society continues suffering from the incipient or actual political and administrative impasse, leaders remain exposed to exhibiting a high-sense of alertness and committed desire. During the struggle independence, the people were promised heaven on earth. These promises remain unfulfilled. The same messages are voiced every five or seven years when the leaders come seeking for the people's vote. A discrepancy between form and reality is frequently the product of a combination of insufficient administrative output, leadership role, fear, acquiesce and passiveness. There is a pending clash of conflicts of interests: centralised – authoritarian-bureaucratic versus a passive citizenship looming in the horizon. There is an ongoing clash between underdevelopment and development; between abject poverty and affluence. It may not be easy to contend when it eventually surface. Are leadership, the political system and governance form and the conversion process of the administrative system strong enough to address pending crisis?

UNDERSTANDING CAMEROON'S POLITICAL ENVIRONMENT

The political configuration of Cameroon is woven within the parenthesis of *5C's*, namely: *"complexity, confusion, complicated, centralised and challenging"*. It is a society with more than 273 ethnic groups and languages excluding the two official languages of "English and French". Mfoulou [1981:7-8] states: *"since the rulers were interested only in running the countries they used tribal divisions to impose authority. Lugard's British policy of "indirect rule" and the French ideologies of "decentralised administration and cultural assimilation" did not try to create a feeling of togetherness among their subjects".*

It is a nation glued together by two different and opposing cultures underpinning the politics of *"assimilation"* and *"indirect rule"*, bounded by the *"common law system"* and *"civil law system"* though from 1st January 2007 a harmonised criminal procedure code [Government 2005] came into force. The New Code has yet to make significant impact in judicial interpretation and implementation particularly within French speaking sections of Cameroon, where the civil law system has been an integral party of the system. The absence of *"togetherness and inclusion"* remains a dark cloud in the political dispensation of the country. This will continue to haunt Cameroon for a very long-time impeding the common march towards genuine national integration and unity. This according to Ndzana [1992:190] *"is the typically Cameroonian scourge whereby the least reality is generally given a distorted interpretation depending on the ethnic group to which one belongs or does not belong. Or whether{s} he is English or French speaking".*

The diversity of the country also constitutes its strength. Diversity as a set comes from what may be fashioned successive modifications and appellations. The name of the country tells it all. Starting with Fernuado Po's christening of the Wouri Estuary – "Rio Dos Cameroes" or "The River of Pawns", Cameroon has thus tasted the virtues and vices of the Portuguese [Cameroes], Spaniards [Camerone], Germans [Kamerun], British [Cameroon], Nigerian [Cameroon], and French [Cameroun] and United Nations trusteeship Council, and perhaps the holy or unholy interface of Cameroonians on both sides of the Mungo (see Atogho 1999:61 and others). No single tribe has total monopoly over the other. Certain comparative advantages exist but out-played by other disadvantages favourable to other ethnic groups. Therefore, shifting alliances must be constructed across ethnic divide from time to time to build a political basis in order to secure a majority or monopolistic situation on various issues.

Seen within this context, there is no state tribalism in Cameroon as aptly noted by President Biya on 4 May 1983: *"The most sectarian of our compatriots should be aware of this reality that no single tribe can pretend to dominate the others; that no tribe should pretend to be invested with any form of legitimacy to rule others, and it will be a vain and dangerous illusion to pretend to do anything whatsoever that is profitable and durable for the nation by relying on a single ethnic group or particular region"* [cited in Tumi, 2006:117]. What cannot be hidden is the Anglophone problem or Anglophone-Francophone divide – the result of cultural differences existing between Southern Cameroon and French Cameroon. The unresolved issue of failing to adhere to the *"gentleman's agreement"* as the foundation for the reunification of the two Cameroon and the marginalisation of one by the other stands as serious barrier to national integration. It remains a source of serious political contention within the political landscape of the country.

Since reunification, Cameroon has had two Heads of State: President Ahmadou Ahidjo *[1961-1982]* and the incumbent President Paul Biya *[1982-to-date]*. Political transition from Ahidjo to Biya evolved under an atmosphere of serenity. Ahidjo voluntarily resign and handpicked Biya as the successor in line with the existing constitutional provisions of the time. Cameroon remains a peaceful and stable country within a conflict-ridden turbulent and unstable Central African Sub-region. The country is the political and economic powerhouse of the sub-region. It is the gateway to Chad and Central African Republic. So, far, the two leaders have been French-speaking. An English-speaking head of state as of now remains an unthinkingable dream.

While President Ahidjo functioned under the immediate post-colonial, reunification and cold-war era with all the mechanisation and ramifications in international politics and spill over in national politics that entailed: the latter assumed power towards the collapse of the East-West conflict and on the heat of the rising euphoria of the "democratisation" bandwagon. The two different periods testify that governance system could not be the same. Each leader being conditioned by the environment of the period and personnel trait of leadership, backed by the commitment to persevere even in the face of serious opposition and challenge: sustained willingness to work hard, and to temper the lust to lead with preparation, experience, turbulence and opportunity. Both national and intellectual factors contributed in determining the successes and failures of the two leaders. The indications are both leaders have positive and negative sides to account for their stewardship. "The tension that presently surrounds 1st October each year in Cameroon leaves the false impression that the people of the former Southern Cameroon can only remember 1st October – their independence Day – if they separate from the 1961 union…Patriotism is about rising above ourselves and striving for more than individual, selfish goals. Nationalism on the other hand, is one of the burdens of humanity. As with every evil, it hides itself, living in the shadows and only pretending to be product of love for one's country. It is in reality, the result of anger and hatred towards other people and towards the portion of one's own people which does not share nationalistic views' [Asonganyi 2007:4].

GOVERNANCE SYSTEM

By virtue of either the 1961, 1972 or 1996 constitution, Cameroon operates a *"bureaucratic-centralised-authoritarian governs system"* [BCAGS], which confers executive powers to the President, with limited checks and balances by the legislative and judiciary branches of government. The country operates a single chamber legislature. The 1996 constitutions provides for a second chamber which has yet to go operational. The same constitution provides for the constitutional court. For now the Supreme Court acts in the place of the constitutional court. In addition, the colonial state created a centralised political power structure which centralises power and authority in the capital city. The famous statement by the president *"when Yaoundé breathes, the rest of the country lives"* during the hectic days of the return to political pluralism testify to the centralised nature of the governance system. The only place that matters is Yaoundé – the seat of government. The rest of the country can go to hell. Leadership must embrace all acting as a shield and protecting the dignity and rights of its citizens. Such statements depict poor quality leadership.

The leader is not just for one province or a select number of provinces or ethnic group{s} but for the entire country. Hamilton in The Federalist Papers [1961] acknowledges the role and importance of administration, giving it a second rank below the presidency. He goes on to argue that the president should control the appointments of administrators and should be responsible for their supervision. *"There is an intimate connection between the duration of the executive magistrate {i.e. the president} in office and the stability of the system of administration".* While acknowledging the importance of administration, he sees the presidency as a greater concern than the administration. *"...we cannot acquiesce in the political heresy of the poet who says: For forms of government let fools contest - That which is best administered is best-, yet we may safely pronounce that the true test of a good government is the aptitude and tendency to produce a good administration'* [The Federalist Papers No. 68].

A bureaucratic, centralised authoritarian administrative structure of trained civil servants, centralised tax collection with no sense of accountability and transparency incorporates the economy into a global capitalist market system with all the difficulties bound to arise. In addition, a sharp political distance separates the behaviour of rulers and ruled in the bureaucratic-centralised-authoritarian system. While the bureaucratic-centralised-authoritarian elite dominates the policy process, the masses remain passive, griped by the phenomenon of *"Fear"* and *"Appointments"* which the authoritarian system implants and incarnates in the people. The people sell their rights and consciousness on the alter of the *"politics of promotion and appointment".* Since very Cameroonian is waiting to be *"appointed"* to a post of responsibility, critical and objective discourses even within the citadel of knowledge [University] is shelved. Recruitment and promotion depends mainly on personal contacts with superiors, not on merit and technical achievements. Personal ties triumphed over rules and role requirements of the official position. Often the *"flagship of regional balance"* is injected to justify the issue of recruitments or appointments. The recruitment of the first batch of students into the medical school of the University of Buea in 2006 is a typical example. Incidentally, regional balance is not invoked concerning recruitments into other universities and institutions of higher learning east of the Mungo.

Political parties remain impotent, playing a restrictive role except for mobilising party adherents during elections. Very often, bureaucratic elites constrain party activities. Either the party, especially *"opposition parties"* operate within restricted political confines or are banned under very obnoxious excuses. Open and decentralised governance, under the caption "Here the People Rule" [Forje 2007] is replaced by an *"authoritarian presidential monarch system"* providing the personal initiative and flexibility in propelling the impersonal, exclusive, rigid administrative mechanisms of the system. Yet the country needs a professional civil service with the requisite expertise were {a}the state's administration's policies confirm with those of the aspirations of the people and government; and {b} government jobs are simple enough to permit frequent turnover without significant loss in expertise. This underscores the competence of a good structural-functional and professional public administration, which Alexis de Tocqueville in early 1830.s found as *"so much distinguished talent among the citizens and so little among the heads of government".* It is not surprising that in present day Cameroon, Andrew Jackson's [1829] strategy of *"the ablest men or women are rarely placed at the head of state affairs and it must be acknowledge that such has been the result in proportion as democracy has exceeded all its former limits"* is deployed for appointing and dismissing state employees on the basis of *"political",* rather than *"technical"* qualification [Quoted in Kilpatrick et al 1964:32].

Confronted by this elitist centralised behaviour, the masses remain political passive, apathetic, and fatalistic. Fear and coercive punishment usually dissuades the masses from revolting against totalitarian or dictatorial governance system. Or the reward system turns the people into sycophants: the legislative system into a hand clapping body and the judiciary dispenses injustices and not just rulings. Only when state coercive apparatus begins to disintegrate do the populace gain the efficacy needed to organise movements for change. The first sign towards change came with the granting of independence to colonial territories, followed by the collapse of the *Berlin Wall* that triggered serious political system change across the world. Civil society was active and vibrant in the early days of the emerging political dispensation – that saw *"Ghost Town"* activism which almost brought the collapse of the regime. Manipulation of the opposition parties by the government and the failure of the opposition parties to constitute a united front and chart a new course for the people have contributed to the growing state of political apathy.

Moving from a colonial territory to independence under the weight of the cold war politics into a post-cold war era, required serious political balancing acts which the two leaders played in different styles under different time periods, with the following facts acting in favour or against:

- First the Ahdijo era was constrained by the difficulties of independence and reunification – the merging of French and British governance system and culture was an uphill-task even at the time Britain and France could not unite under the European Economic Community, let alone merging their administrative systems;
- Second, the fear in the West of the spread of 'communism' throughout Africa intensified total grip by the colonial powers over the leaders of the newly independent countries creating dictatorial regime forms of one kind or the other;
- Third, Anglophone politician failed to read into the politics of assimilation, but working on the concept of 'good faith' and the 'gentleman agreement' which remains a distant aspect in French-Cameroon politics and especially looking at politics as a 'game of interests';
- Fourth, France's gripped over its former colonies pressurise leaders to work within the confines and dictates of their western protégées against the interests of their own citizens;
- Fifth, Ahidjo's longevity in office did not work in his favour: a similar fate faced by the current Head of State, particularly when the people do not feel the impact of economic growth but are subjected to misery and poor quality living standards;
- Sixth, both leaders have benefited from the existence of two factors – peace and stability in the country – within a turbulent Central African Sub-region: and the degree of food sufficiency, thanks to the "green revolution" initiated many years back;
- Seventh, for many, the Ahidjo era was characterised by authoritarian regime form, witnessed by the introduction of monolithic party system in 1966. While the period of Paul Biya is one related to the return to political pluralism, and democratisation [Biya 1987] with the ideals of democratisation, moralisation and rigour, which can be faulted in many aspects. Such assessment must take into consideration the existing global geo-political dispensation of the periods in question as well as domestic forces agitating for system change in situating the successes and failures of leadership in the country.

During the past decades, the notion of *'peace and stability'* has not attracted foreign investments in the country, implying something is wrong somewhere. One is the heavy-loaded centralised bureaucratic administrative system: the other is the high level of institutionalised corruption prevalent within the system, rendering poor, ineffective and inefficient service delivery. Such attributes can not attract investors. Peace and stability has failed to emerge as a pull attraction for foreign investment in the country. *"Creating an enabling environment for wealth creation calls for particular attention and reforms of two mean sectors in the governance programme, namely; {i} the public service; and {ii] the judiciary"* [Doh, 2006:21].Cameroon is entrenched with problems because representation through the choice of the people and the voices of the people are constantly thwarted [Forje, 2007:49].

The body politic of Cameroon is that of a minority Anglophone community fussed with a dominant French community and where the latter embraces the totality of the vices and virtues of France's overseas politics of "centralised administration", cultural assimilation, and the unchallengeable authority of the state. This implies that leadership and authority is *"top-down"*, non-contestable under the auspices of a supreme authority that must be obeyed wily Nellie. The former {Anglophone} is schooled within the confines of independent thinking, indirect rule/decentralisation, ethical values and virtues respecting the rule of law, accountability, and transparency. Under the political dispensation cajoled under the 1961 treaty for federalism, unilaterally changed into a centralised-integrated system within the body politic of the Republic of Cameroon, the virtues of democratic governance and management system no longer exists. It is this fear of total assimilation that the Senegal-Gambia Treaty could not hold for long. Anglophone Cameroon was caught between the devil and deep sea on the issue of *'reunification'* with either French Cameroon or *'integration'* with Nigeria. Anglophone Cameroon, some may say, made the better choice of two evils. Of course, they are paying the price of the choice (unification or integration) imposed on them by the United Nations.

The leadership style of the two presidents is characterised by a number of related and misrelated factors working in their favour or disfavour. *"Ahidjo exercised as Biya is exercising his elected mandate with the support of all the provinces, ethnic groups' religious dominations in Cameroon. Equally important in this context, is that there does not exist in Cameroon any legitimate, democratic and legal means of any one ethnic group (not to mention tribe) confiscating power. The President of the Republic receives power from a sovereign people and exercises such power in the name of the people"* [Tumi 2006:116].Developments show that in the practical exercise of these duties, power is confiscated by a tribe, and elections are poorly organised which could create conflicts and jeopardise the unity of the country. Strong and sustained political leadership and citizen support are necessary adverting such developments; and to transform the governance system into effective and responsible instruments for economic and social development. It is imperative that the necessary enabling environment be established for popular support, political leadership and attitudes of public servants, legislative and judicial backing be put in place to enhance the capacity of the executive and administrative machinery of the government including the expertise and competence of civil servants and other bureaucrats to implement comprehensive and concerted policy actions that improves the living standard of the people.

CERTAIN ENDURING CHARACTERISTICS

A number of enduring characteristics can be established in the leadership style of the country's two leaders. This in various ways impacts of the state of the society. One can question whether the leadership style evolves under the cardinal facto of "putting People and potential first and exploiting it to the best advantage of the society? What were their missions? Did they achieve their goals? What legacies can be traced?

Ahidjo operated a planned national economy [executed under the system of Five Years Development Plan) that brought prosperity and balanced development to the people. In his respect, he is popularly perceived as the builder. Most of the state own corporations apart from those inherited from the West Cameroon Government *(CDC, Market Produce Board, and Santa Coffee Estate etc.)* were created during his period. As a bureaucratic-authoritarian leader he was noted for operated a dictatorial governance system: restricted political activities and the suppression of alternative political views. As a mobilisation leader, credit is given for being an innovator as most of today's significant infrastructures are traceable to his tenure in office. *"With a buoyant economy poised to grow in leaps and bounds, there were no easy answers as to why Ahmadou Ahidjo had voluntarily relinquished power"* [Atogho op cit.]

Biya operates an inconsistent economic policy full of misery, disaster, and misguided priorities that intensify patronage, clienteles, and hegemonic tyrannical and cult worship governance system. He is popularly known as the *"seller"* of state properties or corporations. Even though as the initiator of a new political approach "Communal Liberalism" which was ahead of 'petroiska', he still argued that *"the phase of history of Cameroon does not permit the institution of a multiparty system. Our party is, therefore, responsible for the reduction of existing ethno-cultural divisions in order to promote national integration which is the pre-requisite for the institution of a pluralist democracy"* [Biya 1987:127]. In other words, plural democracy was forced down the throat of the head of state political party leader by the unstoppable circumstances of global trend for democratisation and good governance.

The recently conducted 22 July 2007 twin elections {Parliamentary and Municipal} affirm the desire for one-party state governance system. Asonganyi [2007:9] in a critical write up on the elections states: *"Government morality has been sacrificed on the alter of crooked electoral victories that have led to the loss of the respect of the people. Turning around to preach against corruption would only be comparable to a drunken person preaching temperance".* The United States, the Netherlands Embassies and the British High Commission issued a joint statement in which they declared that the 22 July 2007 legislative and municipal elections represented a *missed opportunity* for Cameroon to build public confidence in the democratic process in Cameroon. In clear terms this means that they did not consider the elections free and fair. The highly critical statement blames the government for deliberately refusing to apply recommended improvements from previous elections [see Ndien, 2007:1-2].

Freedom of expression and worship exists today than before. A check list shows that more political consultations - elections – have taken place during the reign of Biya than before, namely: {a] the 1992, 1997, and 2004 presidential elections; {b] the 1992, 1997, 2002, and 2007 Legislative elections, and {c] the 1997, 2002, 2007 municipal elections. Record also shows that Biya is an absentee landlord. Ahidjo was an ever present landlord and as a representative of the nation at international fora within and outside the African continent.

Cameroon's presence was felt in a much more positive way within the international community. Ahidjo never missed any of the OAU Meeting and other events of significant political and economic importance to Cameroon and the Continent. Of course, there was no Transparency International to score and rank the state of management at a global level. The chasing of files has not diminished. Unpaid salaries remain an issue to be addressed. Poverty is on the increase: quality of livelihood has deteriorated. Youth unemployment is high. Insecurity to both life and property has increased. Some strides have been made in the direction of instituting a good governance programme. Such positive strides are thwarted by officials within the centralised-bureaucratic administrative system seriously affecting quality service delivery.

Apparently, leadership and democratic governance in Cameroon has not evolved on a good footing. A good governance programme is in progress but over politicised. Nevertheless, progress made so far in this domain requires consolidation and perfection of what has so far been achieved. To do so requires a complete dislocation of the current political party and state bureaucratic marriage. A healthy independent professional public bureaucratic setup independent of the aprons of the ruling party is necessary to better move the hearts and minds of public servants in the direction of rendering quality and not political party indoctrinated services to the people. In this respect, the country is in daring need of a public bureaucracy capable of upholding the basic values and principles of good and effective administration. Seen this context, Cameroon should strive towards the following:-

- Public administration in the country must be broadly representative of the society and with manned by qualified and professional personnel;
- Public administration must be people-focused and development-oriented;
- Public service administration must remain apolitical, devoid of ethnic hegemonic tendencies and control, accountable, efficient, effective, knowledgeable with transparency and quality service delivery as the primordial goal;
- Good human-resources development and management, including career-development strategies and practices, must be cultivated to develop, maximise and utilise human potential to better give added value to the rich natural resources potentials of the country;
- Quality services delivery must be provided impartially, fair, accountable, equitable and without bias;
- Greater emphasis in the public service should be directed in reducing bureaucratic red-tap, to better get the economic off the ground; encourage investment; promote growth; employment and accelerate positive interventions that addresses the deep-seated economic inequalities amongst the most marginalised in the society in order that bridges be constructed between the rich and poor and between first and second economies of the world.

The mentioned principles and others are important, and the role of leadership in cultivating, harnessing and promoting them remain indispensable. Citizen participation is a fundamental tenet of good governance. Cameroon can draw positive lessons from other countries in this respect while building up its own approaches, strategies and implementation action plans. Taking administration to the people is one such way of good administration.

Political leadership must develop grassroots orientation; visiting rural and urban communities, communing with them and understanding their problems, aspirations and needs. Here lessons can be drawn from the South African experiment of *'Imbizo'* where the President and Deputy President visit rural and urban communities, make no speeches but listen to the grievances, and advices from these communities on governance and service delivery. These encounters are documented to ensure follow-ups by departments and municipalities. It paves the way for crucial features which include:-

- Sufficient fragmentation of administrative decision-making so that a limited group of individuals does not have the sole authority to make the important decisions for any sector of policy or parts of the society;
- Wide access to policy making machinery by citizens who can act through various institutions and make societal request of elected representatives or administrators, or who can exert concerted action through civil society group protest or civil disobedience;
- The interaction of leaders with individuals with different perspectives within the arenas in which important decisions are made;
- Adequate control of Administrative units by 'overhead' institutions that represent the electorate;
- Efforts to keep the personal interest of employees out of policymaking, perhaps by enforcing conflict-of-interest regulations or by a programme of profession training that socialise decision-makers into universalist as opposed to particularist norms.

National Imbizo Focus weeks are twice a year where the leadership of all three spheres of government participate. These are some of the mechanisms and other systems that can be put in place to ensure that the people's voice and the voiceless is heard given attention and bringing government to the people [see Levin 2007]. In addition, the strategy adopted by President Mbeki of bringing nearer to the people is paying-off in South Africa. *"We are determined to ensure that government goes to the people so that we sharply improve the quality of the outcomes of public expenditures intended to raise the standard of living of our people. It is wrong that government should oblige the people to come to the government even in circumstances in which the people do not know what services the government offers and have no means to pay for the transport to reach government offices"* [President Mbeki, 2003].

Contrast this with a system where people are brought from far-away places of over 1000 kilometres into Yaoundé to follow up their salary advancement, pension and other matters in the Ministry of the Public Service and Ministry of Finance. Here lies partly the cause of the institutionalisation of corruption in the country. It is an act created by government under the bureaucratic-centralised-authoritarian public administration system and giving a blind eye to those who commit the crime. Two features in Cameroon's bureaucratic-centralised authoritarian 'problems' can be distinguished, namely; *'pervasive corruption'* and a *'marked discrepancy'* between the forms and realities of administrative procedures. Corruption exists in the country's bureaucratic structure affecting both small and large decisions and involves proportionately minor and major resources. This includes the small bribes taken by officials in exchange for 'expediting' a decision on behalf of an individual or individuals; the willingness of officials to evade formal personnel procedures to hire their own relatives of fellow tribes people [ethnic hegemonic alliances and influences] and the massive bribes from foreign investors that assure a favourable decision about investment activities in the country, a utility monopoly or commercial concession. In Cameroon, these are known as 'kick-backs' with thirty or more percent of the amount involved. A cartel has been established in the Ministries of Finance and Public Services with the full compliances of workers in these ministries to exploit and live fat on customers. In many cases this corruption is so widespread and institutionalised and taken for granted that it is defended as *'part of the system'* without which officials could not justify their decisions. Nepotism and tribal favouritism is part of the system.

Discrepancy between form and reality is frequently the outcome of a combination of insufficient administrative resources and excessive aspirations. This is backed with the inherent aspiration created by government under the caption of 'appointments'. Everyone wants to be appointed. Government establishes procedures to resemble those observed in the capital city or wrongly copy what exists in cities of former colonial powers. That is why a centralised-bureaucratic system or what Riggs [1964:12] terms *'formalism'*, implying that announced procedures may provide no reliable guidelines about the service to be rendered. Formalism rewards those who lean the informal procedures of administration and frustrates those who rest personal aspirations on the public promises of the government.

The interface between leadership and the people is a means of stimulating greater participation in the governance process, encouraging investments, tapping into the indigenous knowledge, capacity and capability of the people. It is a way of encouraging local communities to be innovative. The South African experience shows a principle of building bridges and sharing knowledge of government with the rural and urban population. Bringing government down to the people, as well as it helps towards shaping stronger good governance and democratic partnership between the state and civil society. This kind of leadership role helps in increasing the effectiveness of a well-structured public administration, system of local government, strengthening its awareness of and capacity to respond to the needs of the people at all levels. Through an approach of this kind, many valuable integrating initiatives could develop whereby government penetrates deeper into neglected areas and in other sectors with quality service delivery action plans.

Currently, the issue of centralisation and decentralisation is on a perpetual pendulum swing seen from the creating of a Ministry of Decentralisation within the Ministry of Territorial Administration. The slowness in implementing policies on decentralisation clouds doubts about taking administration to the people and ensuring a process of democratisation. The 1996 constitution makes provision for Regional or Provincial Assemblies, a Constitutional Court and the declaration of assets by those appointed into high public office before and after assumption of office. A decade after, these provisions are yet to be effectuated. Government has been slow in creating the necessary enabling environment for good governance, and moving towards greater decentralisation of decision-making machinery for fear of power and authority evaporating under the process of *"power to the people"* or *"here the people rule"*. The fear of devolving power and authority in Cameroon is a major obstacle to the development of the country. Some features of the country's public administration may appear developed while others in the same country remain underdeveloped, non-productive, ineffective and no-delivery. It should be noted that a well-trained civil service with moral and ethical values is essential for the developmental goals of the regime, but then, given the centralised-authoritarian nature of the administrative, there is bound to be tension between the technical and professional, between those imbued with ethical and moral values and those who place ethnic hegemonic and corrupt tendencies and between zealous bureaucrats and politicians who insist on the primacy of nationalism and loyalty to the current regime.

The issue of devolution or decentralisation in Cameroon is more theoretical with little practical actions. The country's experience of decentralisation is mixed in many instances showing that leadership and management at the local level lack the capacity to develop and implement policies and that the bureaucratic-centralised-authoritarian is not willing to extend support to struggling provinces and municipalities. Devolution of power will erode the powers of the centralised-bureaucratic authoritarian system. The Cameroon Constitution of 1996 requires through Article 66 that public administration maintain and promote a high standard of professional and moral ethics. So far, government has failed to implement vital sections of the constitution. In essence, these constitutional provisions creates and establishes standards of ethics and moral values in conducting state affairs and in the acquisition of assets through legal means and processes according to applicable and ethical prescripts whereby a public service servant or leader must be beyond reproach and most set positive examples to those s{he}leads.

Corruption undermines the confidence of citizens in government and the state starts loosing its credibility and legitimacy. Of course, corruption is not peculiar to Cameroon; but hitting Transparency International Corruption Perception Index as the most corrupt nation in the world is no good news. Though the ranking has improved somewhat, stringent measures are required more than ever before to rid the society of the cankerworm and the perpetual perception of a corrupt African state. At the First African Forum on Fighting Corruption in March 2007, the Ekurheleni declaration, it was *"reaffirmed that African Leaders must reassert traditional communal, egalitarian values and ensure that these values are infused in all institutions of government and from the basis of a national integrity system in order to counter the rampant pursuit of individual gain"* [Ekurhuleni Declaration 2007].

Today corruption has quadrupled and institutionalised, often with a blind eye given to culprits. Legal actions are seldom taken against those found to have siphoned state wealth into private accounts. Attempts of retrieving funds are not made. Unorthodox habits and the nonchalant attitude of civil servants prohibit quality service delivery to the people. There are cases where imprisoned persons continue to construct skyscrapers from their prison cells. Justice cannot be used to justify and support the whims and caprices of the executive or incompetence of the administration. Doing business or investments, tax collections and payments, getting documents approved in Cameroon is as difficult as going through the station of the cross. The creation of National Corruption Observatory and other institutions to address this cankerworm has yet to make its impact in the eradication of the corruption and poor service delivery. Civil servants with all impunity out rightly demand motivations from the public to attain to submitted files for treatment. Corruption both in low and high places in Cameroon remain endemic. The sum total of such activities makes Cameroon occupy the envious position of being one of the most corrupt nations in the world.

A kind of silence clouds the entire legal, political and appointment processes as it is alleged that ex-convicts are appointed ministers, as critically analysed in what Chia [2007:4] quoted at length, aptly faults in looking at the recent cabinet changes of 7 September 2007 ;"The word 'razzmatazz' *is an attempt to situate the cold conspiratorial comfort being enjoyed by an unhealthy cabal, otherwise called the new deal government…..as governance, practical governance god governance that helps to bridge the gulf between the abstract promises of democratic theory and the practical reality of daily public management. There is a huge catalogue of public management failure in Cameroon and corruption stands in the midriff of our obstacle to attain the best we hope to be as people and a nation. Going by Biya's post July 22 election speech, whereby he practically invited Cameroonians without recourse to political affiliation to be part of his government, one thought that he had, at least, learnt some useful lessons in democratic accommodation or, simply put, the imperatives of good governance. And because good governance is about probity and accountability, a cabinet team at this time should have been tailored to address the pervasive culture of institutional corruption. A cabinet that is peopled by the likes of Nji Atanga is certainly doomed to further muddy the already thinking new deal Augean Stable"*

Apparently, there is no such thing as a perfect human-being, leadership, democracy or constitution. There can be no perfect society. But this does not exclude the continuous process of review, stock-taking and reform needed to help leaders, politicians, their advisors and lawyers, government officials and academic community fine-tuning political and legal instruments necessary to safeguard democracy in order to improve the quality of livelihood of their citizens. In democracies governed by the rule of law, people have a right to critic and participate in how they are governed [see UN 1948]. Therefore, popular sovereignty, granted to a leader or representative government through free, fair, transparent, competitive and periodic elections, endows a head of state or government with the legal authority to govern on behalf of others through a stipulated term of office. This fundamental principle of all democratic constitutions increases the odds that political change will take place peacefully, through rules direct accountability to the voters, open competition and transparent rules of the game.

On the other hand, citizens judge their leaders according to the degree of improvement in the status of their living conditions. Failure to provide basic needs may provoke constitutional crisis, driving the democratic legitimacy of the state to a precipice. At the edge of that cliff, political leaders/actors have a choice: either reconcile their competing demands in the interest of preserving democratic governance, or decide to break constitutional legitimacy and thereby precipitate a downward spiral of violent conflict, dictatorship, human rights violations, economic despair and civil war. To avoid the worst case scenarios, transitional polities and democratic political systems need a basket of measures to stimulate and increase the likelihood of quality leadership staying on the democratic path and delivering the goods so needed by society. Unfortunately, governments unable to fulfil their mandated terms in office are a common and troubling reality of contemporary democratic politics. No one advocates unconstitutional removal of governments. The legacy of the struggle for independence and situation in the Democratic Republic of Congo {DRC}, Niger, Cote d'Ivoire and others are pointers to Cameroonians to remain passive but suffering and smiling in silence.

Given the tangle of factors that give rise to political instability, lapses in democratic governance and coups, no clear-cut answer would be credible as Cameroonians are whitewashed with the existence of peace and stability within a turbulent sub-region. The issue of peace, stability and tranquillity ranks high in the political dispensation of the people, even in the face of deteriorating living standards, absence of the rule of law, increased centralisation, authoritarian, corruption and mismanagement. This constitutes both the strength and weakness of politics in Cameroon which political leadership manipulates and capitalises to its advantage. Starting from the basic premise of leaders serving the people not the other way round, we discover the following lapses in the leadership role and governance system in Cameroon:-

- Both leaders operated a governance system of 'exclusion' in various forms and degrees taking advantage of the existing political climate of the time;
- Biya is a true adherent of the Machiavellian ideology executed in a most scientific style. Coming from a well-structured cultural background, Ahidjo was guided by cultural traits in the exercise of his duties;
- The absence of a vibrant and purposeful civil society plays in favour of the two leaders. If the establishment of a monolithic party structure (Ahidjo's era) silenced the activeness of civil society, the return to political pluralism {Biya's era} should see the resurrection of a more purposeful vibrant civil society acting as the custodian of the peoples' rights and as instrument checking the activities and exigencies of the government. This has not happened. Why? There is political pluralism without genuine representative, participatory rights and respect of choices of the people. The 22 July 2007 elections testify this {See among others, Mbipgo 2007:1-2; The Post 27 July 2007:1; The Post 23 July 2007:2; The Herald 2007; Chefer 2007:1-2};
- Political leadership under the first and second republic established a governance system that generates insufficient material benefits to consolidate widespread support among citizens and aspiring elites. There was no opposition party during Ahidjo's reign. The emergence of opposition in Biya's era has failed to consolidate itself into a viable and alternative government. Opposition parties spend most of their fight fighting each other than confronting the ruling party. The ruling party makes things difficult for the opposition to function properly;
- Governance within the two republics fails in transmitting moral-spiritual ideological policies to convinced sceptics about the need to undergo sacrifice for the ultimate good. Of course, Cameroonians have sacrificed much during the past twenty-five years of Biya's reign, taking into account the 70 percent salary cut in 1994 and with no salary increase since 1982. The last salary increase in 1982 was a parting gift from the first president who resigned on 4th November 1982;
- On the other hand, transition from monolithic to political pluralism created a mobilising opposition, attracting greater legitimacy but unable to sustain that legitimacy for long. As such a situation exists where there the absence of a functional government and the non-existence of a credible and united opposition. Unfortunately, Cameroon finds itself in a situation where decisive elections producing stable and effective governments remain out of reach. Incumbents manipulate the electoral competition to favour re-election, raising issues of credibility and fairness of the electoral process, and leading opposition's parties to seek other means - legal and even illegal to overturn the results;
- During the Ahidjo era, clearly defined rules of succession could be identified, with a transparent, democratic procedure for choosing or appointing a new leader. This is not the case now. A situation that can easily throw the country in serious political instability and chaos; some may argue that the invisible Cameroon political magic may advert such a situation;

- The question arises; does the leadership create a situation for political regrets and of bequeathing a stable or chaotic nation to the next leader?

The question is how should political leadership manage crisis of governance which can easily become threats to democracy and governments before it becomes a crisis of regime change? Why is leadership important in ensuring the emergence of a developmental state? Why it is important to ensure a clean separation between political party activities and a professional, impartial bureaucratic public service? And why the opposition must reconcile towards one objective, the emergence of quality leadership and a functional government that *"puts people first"*. Current political leadership has not effectively and sufficiently balanced justice, short-term stability and long-term prospects for democracy to flourish in post-monolithic party environment. This remains one of the most troublesome political, governmental and moral questions of our time. Only Cameroonians can best find solutions to their problems of governance, democracy and development.

Still, it can be said that leadership has failed adequately to punish participants siphoning state wealth and instead has to a large extent, fostered particularly invidious cultures of impunity by allowing those who have participating in bleeding the state to death to hold high elected office or go scot-free through the justice next work. The international community has played significant roles in giving legitimacy to political leadership in the country, even where and were serous doubts have been raised concerning leadership style. It should be noted that external actors have neither the mandate nor the ability to forge the country's leadership style and sustain the person in office. Though the international community can help in pushing forward good leadership, it is ultimately up to the domestic groups to maintain stability and ensure democratic legitimacy.

Apparently the mobilising opposition groups face supposedly opposite values, populist, elitist, modern, collectivist and individualist. By organising a multi-class coalition and building from grassroots, networks, mobilising opposition parties can better establish powerful structural bases that democratically can dismantle poor leadership and failed governments. The first multi-party elections in 1992 provided such a democratic structural base for regime change. But due to greed, quest for power and immediate financial benefits, the mobilising opposition bodies feel on the wayside. They did not understand the cardinal epistemology of the theory of {a} authoritative; {b} intuitive, and {c} rational knowledge of politics, power and positions. Leaders of and members of the opposition parties failed to read into the "The Prince" [Machiavelli, 1961] concerning issues of the acquisition, detention and management of power that one *'must be as cunning as a fox and as fierce as a lion"*. No doubt, the lion has devoured the opposition. And the "lion" is the symbol of the incumbent Head of State. *"A truly free and fair democratic transition is the one thing that Biya should be proud to bequeath to the country and the people he would have rule for twenty-nine years when and if he retires in 2011"* [The Herald – Editorial Comment, 10-11 September, 2007]. In shaping and sharing the future of Cameroon, every citizen must work towards the creation of a comprehensive *"Cameroon People's Charter"* so that the people can better construct an alternative and sustainable present and future.

CONCLUSION

The present discourse focusing mainly on political leadership is far from helpful. A critical look at this discourse may be instructive, especially incorporating two broadly representative views concerning the question of "political leadership style and quality" in Africa, namely:{i} individual African political leaders causing crises in their respective countries: and {ii} that leadership is essentially based on a Fanonian perspective, where the ruling elite rather than individual leaders reflects the nature and interest of the class from which it comes. According to Fanon [1961], a sort of little greedy caste, avid and voracious, with minds of a huckster, only too glad to accept the dividends that former colonial powers handout. The get-rich quick middle class shows itself incapable of great ideas or of inventiveness". Not holding defence for this class, they have acted in partnership with forces in western democracies and have benefited enormously from the economic misfortune of their nations, with the intentions of sustaining the status quo as chaotic and depressive as may seem for the majority of African and liberal observers.

How valid is the argument and assertion that African political leaders as individuals are responsible for the African crises since they lack the necessary "leadership quality?" The solution that 'capacity building" as the answer is insufficient. The root causes have to be properly x-rayed and analysed in correct perspectives. Capacity building and training of leaders is needed everywhere – including the World Bank {WB} and the International Monetary Fund (IMF), World Trade Organisation (WTO) and other bodies. Therefore, capacity building though necessary is not a panacea for deep-rooted economic problems, political conflicts, social and cultural dislocation of the African people. Development in Africa and the resolution of the continent's crises requires serious structural transformation of both internal and external input factors [Bujra and Adejumobi 2002].

It should be noted that some people are born to be rulers, leading and organising people being an inherent part or gift from nature. Others aspire to be leaders. Some are forced to be leaders. These three or more categories of leadership would require different capacity-building inputs. Of course, their style of leadership will be different. Admittedly, education wise, Ahidjo never saw the fours of a university. History will not judge him as poor leader. His style of leadership was one committed to building and strengthening alliances within and across ethnic and national boundaries. The basis of these alliances, though brutal to begin with, was geared towards development, peace, mutual trust and non-exploitative and transparent relationships. In his own way, *putting people first* was paramount future in his leadership, which facilitated alternative social, economic and ecological relationship. Centralised authority could also be seen in the appointment of Ministers with most impunity and devastating impact. *"Ahmadou Ahidjo, his successor and political godfather, did it too. He would release his appointments until he was at the airport boarding the presidential Gulfstrean Grumann for his native Garoua. Strangely, as soon as he had arrived his attention would al be turned but to Yaoundé where for the next two or three days he would be receiving reports on the mixed reaction caused by the appoints"* [The Herald 2007:2]

The exercise of this prerogative of appointment must be central in Biya's feeling and being in charge. In his first ten years in office, the president reshuffled the government at the rate of one in six months. As a reward to the various constituencies and cronies the country has over 65 ministers which fail in putting the people and potential first and exploiting it to the best advantage of the society. Te talents of each Cameroon should contribute to the well being of the entire society. Leadership requires one who is a capable of standing up to the true values of an emerging and strong Cameroon society not an ethnic group. The first step in that direction is beginning a reconciliation process of healing the wounds and putting the interest of the nation first. Playing a true role of the royalists and foot soldiers and balancing acts of using power to suppress ethnic hegemony and promoting national unity. Such balancing acts require an independent, professional, efficient, effective and quality service delivery public sector. Cameroon is on a battle line to restore political pluralism and professional public service in its true context for serving the entire nation not a segment of it. A comprehensive programme for change is needed. How such a programme is forged is vital for the future as well as the present?

There was a commitment towards strengthening and regenerating local production and economies which acted as the basis of life support systems for the majority of people. There was a clear sense of direction of protecting and conserving natural resources through practices of sustainable use, promoting and strengthening the diversity of cultural and social practices. The practice of a five development plans contributed towards some form of balance and integrated development within the country, including grassroots involvement. Centralised administrative system was an impediment of his governance system. Little has changed today, in spite of the many structural reforms undertaken by the government or forced by international organs.

Forced by the changing geopolitical situation of the post-cold war era, Biya became committed in promoting democratic changes and promoting cooptation or inappropriate representation. All elections conducted during his reign points towards restricted or guided democracy and political changes, gripped by inertia in the implementation of the 1996 constitutional changes [see Tambeng 2007:3]. The joint declaration of the Embassies of the USA, UK and Holland categorically alluded to the call that *"an early and effective realisation of an independent election management body will b an important step because only a truly independent election body will give the citizens full confidence in the democratic process"*.

Cameroon is retrogressing instead of advancing the democratisation process. Ethnic animosity and cultural divide is high. Presently, there is rampant exploitation and exportation of human and natural resources at give away prices. There is an upsurge in human resources development: primary: secondary and tertiary education has expanded: freedom of expression in all forms is on a better course to say the least. Like his predecessor, long years {25} at the job as head of state, has taught Biya how to sustain and strengthen allegiance to him by using appointments to bring back despairing partisans almost from the grave. Even after ten years Biya has the knack of appointing people who otherwise had given up on the regime. The north West Provincial Chairperson of the main opposition party – Social Democratic Front {SDF} castigates the 7th September ministerial changes with the following statement. *"Biya is confused, he is suffering from indecision. He takes ex-convicts and makes them ministers. What has feymen got to do at the presidency? So you find that our government is going down the drain. That is what the world has to know, getting a criminal to become a minister tells Cameroonians all"* [Tabali 2007:6].

This brief comparative analysis of leadership style in Cameroon has attempted by organising critical interactions at the level of theory and practice, between social movements, activists and sensitive intellectuals and professionals to systematically search for new theories, philosophy, spirituality, strategies and alternative models, drawing from the enormous wisdom and practice of the past to understand future trends. In shaping the future of the country, integrating resisting, changing and building a sustainable tomorrow, an end must be to put to the existing bureaucratic-centralised-authoritarian administrative system. The state-centred-individualistic pattern of governance must give to open and inclusive governance hat the plight of the people must be seen articulated and addressed from a different but inclusive angle. Democratic governance is very demanding, because it gives lots of freedom to individual citizens, while simultaneously expecting the people to be responsible for their decisions and actions and on top of hat, think what is good of the whole society not just what profits the leaders and ruling elites and their close families or personally.

The strategy of *"putting people first"* should take priority stage. The struggle and building elements need to be seen as inseparable integrative aspects of a holistic political strategy. These constitute challenges of political leadership which the public service in Cameroon must address. The remarkable convergence of these two types of activities – leadership and quality service delivery or the struggle which also builds and building that engages in struggle – must be address in full consultation between the state-civil-society-private sector interface including the international community. Unfortunately, poor leaders create artificial separation between these vital inter-linkages for selfish ends and to make personal maximum gains of the conceptual dichotomy inherent in the *authoritarian-centralised-bureaucratic* state-centred strategy. It is equally vital that the kind of benchmark set for leaders must also be stipulated for all citizens – taking responsibilities for their decisions and actions. Dlamini [2007] citing Kouzes and Posner states*: "current thinking about leadership is that it is not necessarily a position but a process that involves skills and abilities. Leadership begins where management ends, where the system of rewards and punishments, control and scrutiny, give way to innovation, individual character and the courage of convictions"*. This is what the country needs to overcome pending predicaments.

Democracy, as a form of governance, respects individuals' rights and their own active and independent {i.e. autonomous} decision-making. Leaders / rulers are chosen by us and from among us, the citizens, through free and fair elections. We have the right to say whom we want to lead and represent us. The better we understand ethics and realise the role of moral judgement in democracy, the more equipped we are the more we are able to make good choice in terms of who should be the leader. And these choices are made based on the personal, characteristic, commitment, honesty, professionalism and expertise of the candidates and we cannot be easily fooled by nice words, campaign treats or empty promises. Those on bear the burden of leadership must restrain from self-interest, abuse of power and clinging to power without thinking of the good of the society. Laws should not be utilised for personal gain, letting criminals free and putting innocent people in prison.

Africa has produced great leaders from Fanon's 'greedy middle class'. But most of these leaders came from a poor or peasant background working themselves to an upper class, Azikiwe, Nkrumah, Nyerere, Nasser, Sekou Toure, Kenyatta, Tom Mboya, Mandela, Senghor, Tambo and hundreds of others. Their visionary ideas have been thwarted and disrupted. Visionary leaders can emerge from any social class. What is the response of the international community to their ideas? The drawback is the desire to remain in power too long without ensuring sustainable improvement in the quality of life of the vast majority of the population. African leadership potential must be constantly exposed to the duties, obligations and responsibilities in meeting the challenges of an increasingly inter-dependent world. Instituting a democratic governance system, ensuring inclusiveness and decentralisation, backed with human capacity build will aggravate ethnic, regional and class differences, restore confidence in leadership and the democratic process, promote economic development.

The plurality or variety of the people's views and ideas can help in improving the economy and the governance process, so that different groups of people are able to benefit from the economic and political development processes equally. Diversity and culture should be seen as assets not liabilities in the process of development. A critical aspect of organisational culture is the nurturing of diversity. Cameroon with is wide diversity of ethnic groups and cultural backgrounds remain crucial input factor to the transformation of service delivery. These cultural riches in diversity should be harnessed for the good of all, and not to create ethnic hegemonic domination and the imposition of one culture on others. The slogan *"power to the people with equal opportunities for all"* should contribute to the development of society is vital in constructing a sustainable state and in moving the state from its current status of a third to a first world. It cannot be gainsaid that leadership and public participation are fundamental tenets of good governance. Admittedly, public bureaucracies are frequent targets for positive and negative comments. Terms like harsh, aggressive, insensitive to people's plight, corrupt and oppression are the result of poor quality services delivery to society.

It can be argued that ineffective leadership and the absence of mass support represent behavioural conditions that can cause the disintegration of the bureaucratic-centralised-authoritarian administrative system. This has not happen in Cameroon partly because of the patronage clientele and reward system in place: and partly because the non-implementation of the vital clauses of the constitution limits the place and role of checks and balances within the system. Hence, corruption and poverty thrives, as the governance system remains vacillating, isolated and distant from the people and too dependent on foreign governments and the military for survival. We need common values in democracy in order to use our rights and responsibilities wisely. If there are no common values, then we end up disputing about our personal differences and interests. When there are common values, we can find our own ways to try to realise these values.

Good leadership is there to coordinate and harness these common values to enhance the sustainable transformation of society so that all can enjoy certain basic standards of living. Power and authority must be used in advancing the positive rights of all citizens – rights to education, health care, minimum income, pension, shelter, etc. If we do not have the basic living standards, enough education, health care, we hardly have the ability, time or inclination to worry about politics i.e. the public matters, since all our time is spent for looking means of our survival. The use of coercive force or arbitrary must be avoided at all cost. To often power and authority is used not for the common good but for destructive purposes to attend personal benefits. Corruption arises as part of the wrong use of positions, power and authority. The selfish randomness of leadership actions must not be tolerated in a democratic setting.

Coercive forces become arbitrary, inconsistent and sometimes contradictory. Public policies stemming from the leaders' impulsive whims and advice from ethnic groups and close associates rather than from broad based political-consultation and from diverse social groups either with the party in particular and society institutions at large. Leaders must be committed, refreshed and rejuvenated, ready to support and to learn from one another because people depend on one another and because they are different from one another. Diversity is vitality. It is through maintaining and promoting our diversities that we can more organically link with one another, laterally, converges in our efforts to resist subjugating forces, and building mutually enriching, plural relations for the common good.

Good leadership is the avenue of promoting a transparent and democratic form of administration and functioning among people's organisation. It should lead to the constructive bridge for refreshing, renewing and rejuvenating our journey for a people-oriented and sustainable development and our existence on planet earth. It is under the shade of quality leadership and inspiration and quality service delivery that the professional bureaucratic administration can fight the scourge of injustice, corruption, poverty and other ills plaguing the country. Without independent public service machinery, clouds of doubts, apathy and exclusion will continue to hang over the minds of the people and country thwarting its democratisation process. Uncertainty and fear are dangerous input factors that can derail the progress of a society. Good leadership can avert such destructive trends in society: as it can promote effective delivery of public services in the country.

For now and in the years ahead, Cameroon needs leaders committed to lead and democratically participate in the process of shaping and reshaping the country's visions of the possible, which is at the same time the process of learning from one another to articulate the country's problems and alternative anew, allowing the micro and the immediate to be reframed in national and global contexts. In their different ways and style of governance the two leaders have attempted in working for either development alternatives or alternatives to development. Either way, it implies significant paradigmatic change in the reconceptualising the state. A crucial aspect of democratisation processes is the need to reconceptualise the state within the context of and challenges of a rapid changing domination of a global based-knowledge economy and power centres.

Therefore, the choices of the "people" must be respected. *"Since the competition to provide representatives is limited to political parties in Cameroon, it is assumed that the reason for which political parties are formed is to take part in the competition, to ensure that the representatives freely chosen by the people, come from within the ranks of the party. Therefore, any grouping that claims t be a political party but fails to take part in this periodic competition can at best be said to be a single or multiple issue advocacy group"* [Asongangyi 2007:8].The political base must be broaden to encompass a wide selection of contestants and giving room for choices to be made by the electorate in the selection of their leaders and representatives. The entire issue centres on development, social justice, and equitable distribution of the wealth of the nation, and improved quality living standards for all. "Development' is a complicated issue.

While Ahidjo worked within the ideological orientation of planned and balanced economic development, Biya advocates advanced democracy, greater achievement and selective development or imbalanced development. Areas of the country that fail to support the party are neglected or a policy of victimisation is enacted. Each of the two leaders demonstrates peculiarities in public administration that reflect its own evolution. In the words of Dipoko [2007:5] "France and the Francophone leadership under Ahidjo were only interested in the land and the resources beneath and not the people and their culture" The situation has not changed. The country continues more that ever before *"with a system based on delays in correspondence, chasing files, man-know-man, bribery and siphoning money by a few, unemployment has soared, insecurity has become common-place, tribalism a religion, strikes, hither unknown, have become a way of bringing employers to their knees. People are even beginning to develop dislike, disrespect and hate for the government and those who govern them. This is not good for the country"* [Ambeno 2007:5. Tension on relationship between the leaders, state and civil society has risen to the point of near explosion. This calls for leadership in addressing the issues of the much awaited decentralisation programme, improving the quality of livelihood; ensuring equity and social justice within the context and *"concept of equality on merit in matters of state affairs rather than on issues of minority under repression or majority over representation"* [Awonfor 2007:5].

The correspondence between development and public administration is not so close so as to preclude other variables from having influence on administration. Development may not be so powerful a force that it controls the nature of administrative change in the country against counter-influences from cultural norms. During the era of the first republic, development and growth were experience under a heavy loaded autocratic administration without the requisite manpower. The administration was under an experimental face – call it the sic blind men and the elephant syndrome. In the second republic, manpower capacity exists with no significant impact on the quality of life for the vast majority of population. Rather the standard of living has decline, and civil servants go home with less salary pay. Without administrative reforms in the first republic, people enjoyed high standards of livelihood than today.

Each of the two leaders have shown tendency towards a clustering of development characteristics - accelerating the development process. Despite the similarities and peculiarities in administration exhibited by the two leaders, the following traits can be observed:-

- Among some of the more open minded elites, there is widely-shared commitment to development, given the long years of sufferings and decline in the economy. Others benefiting from the system are not so inclined to the ideals of system change. Their mindset is tied to the old-individualistic system;
- The economic sufferings of the past two decades puts a high reliance on the public sector for leadership, improved government to better redress the existing situation of wanton poverty and corruption;
- The Cameroon society is suffering from political instability and economic recession: the comments by the Embassies of the United States, Holland and the British High Commission concerning the conduct of the 22 July 2007 parliamentary and municipal elections are good example. The country has lost a golden opportunity for accelerating the democratisation and quality management processes for a better Cameroon;
- Popular disappoint provide support for still newer leaders who challenge those who steered the course for the demise of colonial rule. Cameroonians were fed-up with Ahidjo's longevity in office and centralised nature of the bureaucracy. They are having the same feelings following Biya's 25 years tenure in office with declined in the quality of living standards.

We must recognise that within this paradigm, the state has limited choices to respond to the range of democratic urges and assertions within society. Building and drawing from its human resources, moulding such resources through good leadership under inclusive politics, rule of law, social justices, respect of human dignity and equity, there is no reason why obstacles cannot be overcome collectively in the promotion of egalitarian and ecologically sane alternatives and right to development and in the national interest. An effective, efficient, a political public service is needed in conjunction with good leadership and in partnership with the people ensure the existence of a sustainable and progressive state.

It follows that the task of leadership for a democratic transformation, sustainable development, and in the ultimate interest of '*putting the people first*', must begin by drawing and incorporating the people at all stages of development to ensure sustainable national interest, without which, an erosion of he power of leader and credibility of the state to realise set objectives will remain a distant wish in attaining quality livelihood for millions of people trapped in poverty. Undoubtedly, quality and visionary leadership, a democratic state is more responsive and accountable than a dictatorial or militaristic state. The question remains, given the prevailing situation, what then should be the way needed to migrant think and act in the context of the present character and style of leaders and pressures on the country as well as of the regional and global alliances that are increasingly becoming part of?

Cameroon as Africa in miniature stands at the cross-roads and should offer the people and continent good leadership. However, given its bureaucratic-centralised and authoritarian system, is that what Africa needs at this transitional stage and after? Serious reforms are necessary within the public service to accelerate the process of economic growth and good governance. World Bank Report 2008 shows that Cameroon is a country that is difficult to do business. The report notes that though Africa has fallen from third to fifth place in the regional rankings on the place of reform implementation, three African countries, Egypt, Ghana and Kenya rank among the top ten reformers world-wide in 2006 and 2007 and made the most significant advance in the aggregate case of doing business ranking among countries in Africa. Kenya, Ghana and Mauritius were significant public services reforms undertaking are paying off. *"Whereas Egypt ranks first amongst the top ten reformers globally, Ghana and Kenya are third and eight respectively. The others are Croatia, Macedonia, Georgia, Columbia, Saudi Arabia, China and Bulgaria. Cameroon remains stagnant in its effort to reform business regulations and does not even feature among the 178 economies for the 2008 rankings on the ease of doing business. Cameroon is also one of the countries with the longest time to pay business taxes, a complex employment system and with many documents to import"* [Garriba 2007:10]. Following recent reports, [World Bank 2007] Ghana, Egypt, Kenya, Mauritius stand top on the list of foreign investors., reducing fees for registering property, easing the bureaucracy that builders face in obtaining permits, cutting time to import and export by seven and five days respectively. Mauritius with six reforms stands gigantic in Africa on the case of doing business, while Burkina Faso and Mozambique are reported to continue becoming more business-friendly. Sierra Leone recovering form many years of conflict is doing better in terms of attracting foreign investments in the country compared to Cameroon. In 2006, the Commonwealth Trade Council brought about 400 investors into Sierra Leone. How many foreign investors come to Cameroon?

With the state of stability, peace and tranquillity reigning in Cameroon, the country has yet to emerge as a pull of attraction for foreign investors as well as promote indigenous investments. More vigorous structural reforms within the public service are required to kick-start substantial development activities in the country. Leadership style and peoples' positive responses play important roles in the process. A change in mindset is required across the board for effective public services delivery in Cameroon. The state must play a mobilising role in spurring economic growth given that the private sector is too weak or non-existent and with the barriers to its expansion, such as poor infrastructure and lack of a developed financial system. The widespread market failures, along with huge financial resources involved in implementing the earlier stages of development, imply that the private sector cannot be expected to play the lead role. Government must make effective efforts in promoting state-private sector interface and to develop more legitimacy, competence and trust and transparency in related developmental activities.

Siphoning of state funds has attained an unprecedented level in the country. A World Bank report indicates that 40% of Cameroon's investment budget goes into private pockets, making it practically difficult for ongoing economic reforms to yield expected results. A European Union Report for the forest sector – a major contributor to state revenue after petrol and agriculture states that the state is loosing 50 billion Francs CFA yearly due to illegal timber exploitation. Cameroon is also losing out hundreds of billions of francs CFA of its customs earning and fiscal revenue collection due to ingrained corrupt practices. In addition the public service and the process of award of public contracts in the country is characterised by a chain of corrupt practices which deprives state treasury of billions of francs. According to Transparency International Corruption Perception Index for 2007, Cameroon is ranked 138 out of 180 countries improving slightly by two places from 141 in 2006. Even with these insignificant changes, the corruption stakes remain high and worrisome. Interestingly, government finds it difficult to acknowledge the viability of all these reports, though it acknowledges the seriousness of corruption trend in the country and the need to intensify its fight. Several measures to that effect have been put in place though without producing positive results [Ngalame 2007:2]

For now, the Cameroon bureaucratic-centralised-authoritarian administrative structure faces many challenges in its efforts to deliver quality services to the citizenry. It is overloaded with constraints, inefficient and ineffective; too ethnic hegemonic inclined and controlled requiring a leadership style that is innovative, and adopting cost-effective approach to service delivery. This calls for leadership that inspire and motivate managerial and front-line services ensuring people feel as integral part of the structure and functioning of the system to better build confidence and trust in government. Visionary leadership is required to determine and articulate the strategic approach to effectively management the concomitant institutional changes. Leadership must ensure that sound systems are in place, including checks and balances, transparency, accountability and regular consultation with the people, like the South African experience of *Imbizo* and the president's annual meet the people consultation - *National Imbizo Focus Weeks. This process of taking government to the people adds credibility, legitimacy and ensures confidence in the people about democratic governance.* It underscores the fact that development is about improving quality of life; social equity and justice, but it also requires mobilising and developing human potentials as the essential input factor of giving added value to natural resources; a growing economy in which redistribution is an essential and critical element. Practising the *"Imbizo"* in Cameroon implies the following policy actions:

- Bring the institution of central and local government closer to the people they serve by establishing outlets for state, regional, divisional local and rural administrative and public service agencies;
- Expand opportunities for rural / grassroots population participation in the formulation of policy and the implantation of programmes affecting them;

- Recruitment of more qualified personnel into the administrative sector, or intensify in house training for existing staff;
- Put and end to ethnic hegemonic forces over-lording things on other ethnic groups distant from the centre of political and economic power - avoid minority suppression and majority oppression by creating equal opportunities for all.

Good leadership is also about democracy and popular participation, and where inclusiveness constitutes the cornerstone. Good leadership must discard ethnic hegemonic forces and divisive tendencies that can satire towards state disintegration. Finally, *"a developmental state should be founded on the principles of democracy, justice and an abiding culture of human rights – conditions which afford people not only the right to benefit from the activities of the state, but also to take active part in improving their lives"* [Levin 2007, op it] We require to transform existing bureaucratic-centralised-authoritarian administrative service devoid of the peoples' interest and establish an *"in-ward-looking paper-chasing interest into a citizen-engaging innovation-brokering and growth-facilitating partners"* [Doh 2006:29] catering for the common good. Good leaders must be embedded with the 5Cs {content, context, commitment, capacity, clients/coalitions, communication} protocol and it's interlink ages to the synergise implementation process [see Brynard, 2007:20-42]. Transitional polities are in daring need of Leaders that establish and strengthens institutions for enhancing the productive capacity of the private sector for wealth creation and economic growth. The country needs leaders who are in synergy with the different stakeholders – political parties, ethnic groups, civil society, the private sector and the international community to improve the living standards of the population thus, making leadership *"a call to serve"*.

SOME PROACTIVE POLICY MEASURES

- There is urgent need for political leadership in the country to move away from the bureaucratic-centralised-authoritarian to a mobilisation and inclusive system and viewing politics and leadership role as a "call to serve";
- There is need for strategic interactions between incumbent power authorities, the ruling elites, opposition leaders and civil society to jointly affect transitions to a reconciliation and development regime for the best interest of the people.
- Put in place a governance system that upholds the rule of law, inclusiveness which enables the government to regulate interactions among social groups, guarantees individual rights, and restrains arbitrary bureaucratic state power;
- Ensure active political development and equitable redistribution of the wealth of the nation. The democratisation process must evolve with economic growth;
- The priority of putting people first must remain supreme and unchanged;
- Ensure that countervailing structures – competitive parties, interest groups, and the independent mass media – limit the central government's activities and promotes those cultural values needed for the efficient functioning of the state;
- Creating the enabling platform that ensures state, civil society, private sector interface, and where the golden principles of partnership, participation, responsibility and equitable benefit-sharing reigns supreme;

- Open the political space for competitive and plural politics, where a level playing play field exist for free, fair, competitive, transparent, accountable, credible elections exists and the defeated parties to accept defeat, as well as limiting the tyranny of the majority and minority;
- The separation of powers, legislative, judiciary and executive must be enhanced and respected with the people remaining the main custodian of power in society;
- Conduct free, fair, competitive, transparent, accountable and credible elections and enhance the decentralisation process to enable an administrative and political system of inclusiveness;
- Bear in mind that the prospects for immediately realising social progress through political system will vary from country to country and influenced by both internal and external input factors, and that all systems, whatever their type, reveal a contradiction between policy intensions and consequences
- Political development has scarcely brought paradise on earth. In every political system, people still await public policies that ensure greater individual rights, economic abundance growth and human development, which good leadership remains an input catalyst for its achievement;
- Political leaders in every office are responsible for establishing the atmosphere in which they lead; as well as understand that the 'spirit of the law' is greater that the letter. They must however, remain firm, resolute and just in their actions;
- Leaders must establish a high spirit of mutual trust as well as attach value to high standards of performances and have no tolerance for the uncommitted. They must encourage creativity, freedom of action and innovation among subordinates with the ultimate objective of the common good at heart;
- Leaders must never form selfish relationships and, there, take advantage of their subordinates, peers and superiors, but must hold a profound conviction of duty above all other ambitions;
- A responsible civil society is extremely necessary in supporting good political leadership to ensure success, development and equitable benefit-sharing.

REFERENCES

Adei Stephen [2004] T*he Promise of Leadership. Combert Impressions,* Accra, Ghana.

Ambeno Maurice [2007] *"Youths and Unemployment",* in Eden No. 215, 1st-3rd October 2007, Limbe, Cameroon. [www.edennewspaper.com]

Asonganyi Tazoacha [2007] *"Elections in Cameroon: Government Bankruptcy".* The Herald No, 1970, 20-21 August 2007, Yaoundé, Cameroon. [www.theheraldpaper.com]

Asonganyi Tazoacha [2007] *"Elections and Election Disputes in Cameroon",* The Guardian Post No. 0258, 16-22 July 2007, Obili -Yaoundé, Cameroon, p.8. [theguardianews papernet.TF]

Asonganyi Tazoacha [2007] *"Burning Issues: Celebrating 1st October'.* in Eden, No 215, 1st – 3rd October 2007, Limbe, Cameroon. www.edennewspaper.com

Arendt, H [1958] *The Human Condition.* Chicago University Press, Chicago, USA.

Aseka Eric Massinde [2006] "Globalisation, Leadership and Governance in Africa. A Theoretical Approach", *Paper presented at the Institute for Global Initiatives,* Kennesaw State University, 18th October 2006.

Aseka Eric Masinde [2005] Pitfalls of Ideology, Social Policy and Leadership in Africa: Instincts of Predatorial Leadership. *New EME Research Initiative and Publishers,* Nairobi, Kenya.

Atogho, Paul Enyih [1999] *Politics: A Call To Serve – Essay.* EDL'ACTION, Yaoundé.

Awonfor Paddy Prince [2007] *"Inoni's Mandate".* Eden, No. 215, 1st-3rd October. Limbe, Cameroon. www.edennewspaper.com

Bass, B. M. [1990] *From Transactional To Transformational Leadership. Learning to Share the Vision.* Organisational Dynamics, (Winter).

Bass, B. M. [1985] Leadership and Performance Beyond Expectation. Free Press, New York.

Bass, B. M. & Steidmeier, P. [1998] *Ethics, Character And Authentic Transformation Leadership.* See, http://cls.binghamton.edu/Basssteid.html

Bayart Jean-Françoise [1993] *The State in Africa: The Politics of the Belly.*

Bewaji [2003] "Leadership: A Philosophical Exploration of Perspectives in Africa, Caribbean and Diaspora Politics", *Journal of African Philosophy,* Issue No. 2.

Biya Paul [1987] Communal Liberalism. Macmillan Publishers, London.

Brynard A. Petrus [2007] "Implementation for Service Delivery in South Africa: Issues and Lessons of Experience" *African Journal of Publication Administration and Management,* Vol. XVIII, No. 1. January 2007, Kul Graphics Ltd, Nairobi, Kenya.

Bujra and Adejumobi [2002] Leadership, *Civil Service and democratisation in Africa.* MPMF. Addis Ababa. Ethiopia.

Burns, J. M. [1978] *Leadership.* Harper & Row, New York.

Chefer Lucas Teneng [2007] "Paul Biya, Governor Caught in Electoral Fraud" *The Reporter,* Vol. 1 No. 005, July 30 2007. Douala, Cameroon; E-mail: portdouala@iconet2000.com

Chia Ndi Charly [2007] "News Analysis – CRTV's Christmas Rice of Sorrow", *The Post,* No. 0892, 21st September, 2007, Buea Cameroon.

Chia Ndi Charly [2007] "Biya's Cabinet Reshuffle Razzmatazz" *The Post* No. 0889, 10 September, 2007, Buea, Cameroon. [www.postnewasline.com]

Dipoko Mongo Adolf [2007] "Lest I Forget: October 1st Is Here Again Today", in *Eden,* No. 215. 1st – 3rd October 2007. Limbe, Cameroon. [www.edennespaper.com]

Dlamini Musa [2007] "The African Leadership Crisis: Historical Perspectives And A Reflection on The Expectations of Independence", *Paper presented at the 29th AAPAM Annual Roundtable Conference,* 3rd – 7th September 2007, International Conference Centre, Mbabane, Swaziland.

Doh, Finlay [2006] "Wealth Creation and Governance in Cameroon", in A*frica Journal of Public Administration and Management,* Vol. XV11, No. 1. January 2006, pp 20-31. The Regal Press, Nairobi, Kenya.

Ekurhuleni Declaration [2007] *"On Fighting Corruption",* 2 March 2007, South Africa. See also Towards a Common Understanding of Corruption.

Fanon Franz [1967] *The Wretched of the Earth.* Penguin Books, London.

Forje W. John [2007] Enhancing Sustainable Governance and Development in Africa. A Reassessment of the Current Challenges and Future Prospects" in *African Journal of Public Administration and Management,* Vol. XV111, No. 1. January 2007, pp 43-54, The Regal Press, Nairobi, Kenya.

Forje W. John [2007] *Here The People Rule: Political Transition and Challenges for Democratic Consolidation in Africa* (Forthcoming).

Garriba Frank [2007] *"Cameroon Still Difficult Place to Do Business – World Bank Report"*, in Eden, No. 215. 1st – 3rd October 2007, Limbe, Cameroon. [www.edennewspaper.com]

Government of Cameroon [2005] *New Criminal Procedure Code of The Republic of Cameroon.* Law No. 2005/007 of 27 July 2005 on the Criminal Procedure Code. National Printing Press, Yaoundé, Cameroon. *(Note: The national Assembly deliberated and adopted, the President of the Republic here enacts the law set below).*

Government of Cameroon [1996] Constitution of the Republic of Cameroon. Government Printing Press, Yaoundé, Cameroon.

Hamilton Alexander [1961] *The Federalist Papers,* Mentor Books, New York; See papers No. 68, 72 and 84.

Israel, S. A. [2001] *"An Essay on the Perversion of Leadership Practices in Africa".* http://nigerdeltacongress.com/darticles/dishonourables.htm

Jackson Andrew [1829] *First Annual Message to Congress,* 8th December 1829.

Kale Ndiva-Kofele [1998] *Legislative Power in Cameroon's Second Republic:* Its Nature and Limits. Mokunda, Buea, Cameroon.

Kilpatrick P. Franklin, et al [1964] *The Image of The Federal Service,* Brookings Institution, Washington, D.C.

Kotter, P. John [1999] *What Leaders Really Do? Harvard Business School Press,* Cambridge.

Levin M. Richard [2007] *"Leadership and Service Delivery in The South African Context" Paper delivered at the 29th AAPAM Annual Roundtable Conference,* Mbabane, Swaziland, 3rd – 7th September 2007.

Little, I. M. D [2002] *Ethics, Economics and Politics. Principles of Public Policy.* Oxford University Press, Oxford.

Londesborough, Richard [2007] *The Cameroon Business Forecast Report. Business Monitor International,* London. [http://www.businessmonitor.com/bf/cameroon.html]

Mbeki Thabo [2003] *State of the Nation Address, 1*4 February 2003. South Africa.

Mbipgo Christian Ngah [2007] "As Voting Commission Meets: Elections Return Sheets Give SDF 74 seats. But Government Manoeuvres to Bring Down SDF Score to 14". *The Guardian Post,* No. 0260, 30 July -5th August 2007, Bamenda, Cameroon, pp 1-2. www.thegaurdianpostnewspapernet.TF

Mfoulou Jean [1981] "Ethnic Pluralism and National Unity in Africa", *Mimeograph,* University of Yaoundé, Yaoundé, Cameroon.

Muna A. Bernard [1993] *Cameroon And The Challenges of the 21st Century.* Tuma Books, Yaoundé, Cameroon.

Ndzana Mono [1992] *La Mutation Editions 1 Carrefour,* Yaoundé.

Ndien Eric [2007]"Western Embassies' Verdict: Elections Were Not Credible". *The Herald,* No. 1970, 20-21 August 2007, Yaoundé, Cameroon, pp 1-2.

Ngalame Ntungwe Elias [2007] "Ruining Cameroon's Economy: E U Uncovers FCFA 400 Billion Yearly Fraud", in Eden, No. 215, 1st to 3rd October 2007, Limb. Cameroon. www.edennewspaper.com

Ngwana Samba Albert [2001] *The Struggle for Political Pluralism and Democracy in Cameroon.* Africa Development Corporation Ltd: Jameson Broadman Press, Shomolu, Lagos, Nigeria.

Remy, R. C. [1980] *Handbook of Basic Citizenship Competencies.* National Institute of Education, Washington D.C.

Riggs W. Fred [1964] *Administration in Developing Countries: The Theory of Prismatic Society.* Houghton Mifflin, Boston, USA.

Staniland, M. [1985] *What is Political Economy? A Study of Social Theory and Underdevelopment.* Yale University Press, New Haven.

Tabali Bernard [2007] "Biya Makes Ex-convicts Ministers". *The Herald,* No. 1979, 10-11 September 2007, pp 6. Yaoundé, Cameroon. www.theheraldpaper.com

Tambeng Solomon [2007] "Joint Embassy State Regrets Conduct of Election: Cameroon Has Missed Opportunity – US, UK, Dutch Embassies Declare". *EDEN Newspaper,* No. 201. 20-22 August 2007, pp 3, Limbe, Cameroon. [www.edennewspaper.com]

The Herald [2007] Editorial Comment: Government reshuffle – Using Appointive Powers to Create Problems", *The Herald* No. 1979, 11 September 2007, pp. 3. Yaoundé, Cameroon, [www.theheraldpaper.com]

The Post [2007] "Twin Elections: Not So Free and fair", No. 0877. 23 July 2007, Buea, Cameroon, p.2. www.postnewsline.com

The Post [2007] "How MINATD, CPDM Elites Rigged Twin Elections" No. 0878, 27 July, 2007, Buea, Cameroon, p.1 www.postnewsline.com

Tumi Cardinal Christian Wiyghansai Shaagham [2006] *The Political regime of Ahmadou Ahidjo and Paul Biya, and Christian Tumi,* Priest. Printed by MACACOS S. A. Douala, Cameroon.

United Nations [1948] Universal declaration of Human Rights, New York; United Nations, Article 21(1); also available at http://www.unhchr.ch/udhr/lang/eng.htm

White, D. Leonard [1948] *The Federalist.* Macmillan. New York.

World Bank [2007] *Doing Business 2008.* Washington, D.C. USA.

Chapter 10

RETHINKING PUBLIC SERVICE REFORMS FOR A DEMOCRATIC DEVELOPMENTAL STATE IN AFRICA*

ABSTRACT

Reforming the public sector constitutes a long-standing issue on the political and socio-economic transformation agenda of transitional polities in Africa. Therefore, Africa needs Focused Structural Adjustment Policy Strategies [FSAPS] and "Servant Leaders" [SL} to pilot its transition from a third to a first world. Without an efficient, effective, productive, credible, professional and non-partisan, sustainable public service backed with comprehensive interface or constructive engagement between the private sector-civil society sustainable transition and development cannot be attained. The much needed aggressive, dynamic, confidence and vibrancy in both the public service and private sectors remain inadequate in many African countries which must constructively be beefed-up to accelerate its development process.

The public sector as the lead entity piloting policy-articulation, decision-making, implementation and development related activities is found wanting. A vibrant productive-private sector is lacking to back up the efforts of an effective, efficient and productive public administration in improving the quality of livelihood of the people. Reforming the public sector for the emergence of a developmental state in Africa requires, professionalism, servant leadership, detachment from the whims and caprices of political parties, and a democratic governance system among others. Without the emergence of a development state, Africa cannot be part of the globalised knowledge-base technological society of the 21st century.

The focus of the paper is an interface on capacity building [human and institutional], leadership and strategic policy priority choices within the broader objectives of effective governance and management as the modus operandi for navigating Africa from a developing to a developed society. The argument is that human resources development including in-house training is necessary in building the capacity for effective and efficient output services delivery under the canopy of "putting people first" in all developmental strategies. In this regard, the extended position is a call for a "servant leadership", "constructive state engagement", "good governance", "strong state institutions", a" productive and competitive private sector: and a "vibrant and responsive civil society,"

* Paper accepted for Presentation at the 30th AAPAM Roundtable Conference, Accra – Ghana on the sub-theme of Developmental state in Africa.

without of course, bypassing the role and impact of the international community. Africa is part of the global community and must engage with it.

It is a comparative analytical paper drawing examples from some newly industrialised countries in the South East Asian Regions - Singapore, Hong-Kong Malaysia among others. The paper equally addresses issues of building on the assets of potential partners - state-civil society-private sector - interface for quality service delivery [improving the living standards of the people].

The conceptual framework is construed within the premises of strength, weakness, opportunities and threats [SWOT]. How do we interpose SWOT within the experiences of some Newly Industrialised Countries? What lessons can be learned to put the continent on the right development path? How does Africa capitalise on its strength and exploit its opportunities? How does Africa convert weaknesses and threats into opportunities to better strengthen its developmental capacity?

It takes a historical perspective, retrospective as it charts prospective new ways forward for a new public service sector for the continent. Proactive strategic policy measures are advanced

Keywords: strategies, governance structure, leadership, constructive engagement, reforms

1. INTRODUCTION: FACING THE DEVELOPMENTAL CHALLENGES

Development has been stalled in African countries; the result of the lost terrain or missing vital compass directing the *input* and *output* functions of the state. While it can be argued that the *'input'* side aspect has been good to a large extent, the same is not the case with the *'output'* functions of state institutions. Navigating reforms within the public sector largely addresses the output functions of state institutions. Therefore, administrative reforms entail proper management, upkeep, constructive and meaningful changes in state institutions to function well in respect of enhancing efficiency and providing quality services delivery in meeting the needs of the entire society. Reforms are required in the private sector in some African countries

The system of governance must be constantly improved for the State [output functions] to fulfil its social contract and obligations with civil society and the private sector. Output functions of many state institutions in Africa remain weak, inefficient and overloaded with administrative red-tap due to the kind of governance structure and system in practice. The outcome is what now characterises many African countries as, *"failed states"*, *"collapsed states"*, *"and banana states"*. To a large extent, it is not generally the state that *"fails,"* it is the government or individual leaders. Society is entrenched with inertia, corruption and abject poverty. It cannot progress with such impediments.

The myriad and tremendous challenges facing the continent range from increasing abject poverty; poor infrastructure, global marginalisation, rapidly growing population with less increase or improvement in infrastructures to meet the social changes; climate changes and the growing dominance of narrow identity groups, bad governance under the phenomenon of sit-tight presidents? These challenges require a well trained professional public service sector and leaders who understand and are committed to the common good. Visionary leaders and a non-partisan bureaucracy are needed in reconstructing a new Africa capable of facing the challenges of the 21st century and improving the quality of livelihood of its population.

Failure of government or individuals requires constructive reforms of putting government back on the right developmental rails The paper attempts just to do that with a focus on {i}leadership; {ii}governance system; {iii] Empowerment; {iv} human capital development and [v] interface with the international community. The general consensus is that the goal of reform efforts *"should be the development of greater administrative and managerial capabilities, including effective use of science and technology, to achieve national objectives. This implies the achievement of efficiency, economy and responsiveness in the administration of the public service through rational, innovative, and constructive methods and systems of operations. The urgency and importance of such reforms is much greater in developing countries because of the more central role of government and in many cases, because of the start in economic and social development"* [Bentil 2004:40].

Africa is at across-roads: development or further decay. Re-colonisation or sustained self-reliance. Indeed, the legacy of colonialism, the Cold War, the structural adjustment policies of the eighties, despotic rule, poor socio-economic development choices are what the new – generation of African leaders will inherent. This *'inheritance'* will occur in the context of a rapidly globalising world in which Africa, particularly sub-Saharan Africa, is being increasingly marginalised [Gounden 2007:2].Africa should take advantage of the *"latecomer phenomenon"* to transform itself into a First World provided the *"political will and determination to develop"* exist to reconstruct the present and shape the future. The first issue in this long battle is for the people to have clear analysis and vision of the causes and consequences of the continent's current situation and challenges; where Africa is coming from and where it is headed. The public service and leadership role remain vital input factors in searching and directing a better future for the continent. Positive developments in quality public services delivery in some countries is visible as sign posts on which the continent can build on. This paper highlights the impact and consequences of failure of having a public sector that is unaccountable and unresponsive to the needs of the people. Therefore, emphasis needs to be placed on minimising the gap between the negative aspects of government and the added value to sustainable development activities.

.

2. CONCEPTUAL FRAMEWORK: METHODOLOGY AND DEFINITION OF TERMS

The conceptual framework draws from the *SWOT* analysis – *Strength, Weakness Opportunities and Threats.* While a literature review, secondary data, and the author's knowledge through *participatory observation* constitutes the background materials in navigating the reconstruction process for public services reform and constructing developmental states in Africa.

Many authors define leadership in a variety of ways. For example, Shelton [1997] adopts the terminology of "counterfeit leadership" as a factor affecting leadership in Africa today. Kong and Oakly [1994] adopt the phrase "enlightened leadership" as type of leadership that deals with real underlying problems rather than their symptoms. Thornton [2006] defines leadership as the process of helping individuals, teams and organisations to become more and achieve more than they ever thought possible. George [2003] looks at the moral aspects needed to demonstrate effective modern leadership. While Reddy [2007] looks at leadership emerging from a multidisciplinary and embodying theoretical concepts as well as strong experiential component.

However, a common silver-lining is that of giving a sense of direction, mobilising people [Blanchard, Hodges & Hybels 1999] ideals of *"teaching people by example"*, [Thornton 2006] the *"process of helping individuals or teams"* to do things that improves their conditions [Crossby, Barbara & Byrson [2005] *"for the common good".* To accomplish their goals, leaders display behaviours in one of the four types of frameworks, namely {i} Structural, {ii} Human Resource; {iii} Political, and {iv} Symbolic and they can either be effective or ineffective depending upon the chosen behaviour in certain situations [Bolman and Deal 1981]. To accomplish things for the common good involves interplay with others, for example, civil society and the private sector.

The argument advanced by Pass et al [2000] emphasising the public sector as that part of related activities concerned with transactions of government functions remains a crucial facet of state functions. The output functions of state institutions are fundamental in giving credibility to government. Hence, issues of efficiency, effectiveness, sustainability and quality services delivery constitute topical subjects of debate especially in developing countries{Africa in particular}were state bureaucracy is noted for delaying the output functions of government. Many reasons abound. Either state bureaucracy is not properly trained or extremely too partisan, and controlled by the whims and caprices of the governing party. The structure-functioning of the public service is heavily influenced by clienteles, patronage and ethnic hegemonic factors. It is vital for civil society knowledge gap to be addressed and for civil society to manifest its share of responsibility as custodians of state power in constructing a developmental state that carters for its citizens [see Diamond 1994, Fowler 1996; Forje 2007].

Development is about improving the quality of life; it is about equity and justice. Development entails a growing economy in which redistribution is a critical element. It includes the preservation and development of human resources in the form of skills-training, job-creation and the provision of education, health services, infrastructure, and an adequate social security system and so on. It is also about democracy and popular participation. A developmental state should be founded on the principles of democracy, justice and an abiding culture of human rights – conditions which afford people not only the right to benefit from the activities of the state, but also to take active part in improving their lives. [Levin 2007]

Leadership is an elusive and contestable concept with relatively new and emerging disciplinary, which are multidisciplinary and embodying theoretical concepts as well as a strong experiential component [Reddy 2007:3]. There is no agreed definition of leadership but two themes consistently emerge, namely {a} it influences the behaviour of others; and {b} this influence is intentional and directed towards some desired objectives [Reddy 2007; House et al 1999]. Perhaps the most encompassing definition of leadership capturing the essential features is given by Gardiner [1965:12].*Leaders has a significant role in creating the state of mind that is society. They can serve as symbols of the moral unity of the society. They can express the values that hold the society together. Most important, they can conceive and articulate goals that lift people out of their petty preoccupations carry them above the conflicts that tear a society apart, and unite them in the pursuit of objectives worthy of their best efforts".*

Democratic Governance to a large extent is simply how the government conducts itself. It involves the entire parameters in which the state operates, including vital areas like parliament, judiciary, bureaucracy, media and all the other organisations of society which remains in place when government changes. Furthermore, it entails the policies of government; and whether the government has the staff and organisational systems and capacity to design and implement policies in partnership with the population. Crucially important, whether the state fulfil the social contract with citizens in respect of providing he necessary social amenities and requisite security, ensuring accountability, credibility, transparency and enjoying the confidence of its electors. Democratic governance is an absolute fundamental input factor for the sustainable transformation of the state.

So far, African states have been slow to articulate, implement and sustain aggressive policy reforms capable of delivering rapid sustainable development similar to what nations in Southeast Asia have accomplished. Some may argue that it is not policy articulation which is the problem but lacking the will to implement such policies. What are the reasons for this? Society remains underdeveloped and exploited. The authority, credibility and legitimacy of the state are lost. Corruption takes over. Ethnic hegemonic domination, patronage and exclusion are the established rule of the game. Diversity as an asset for development is converted into a liability. In the end, the public service sector is polarised and flooded with quakes and misplaced priorities frustrating the ideals of good and inclusive governance.

Equality of opportunity for all only remains a fine piece of political rhetoric and political change wrongly managed. The promotion of good governance lies in turn at the heart of ensuring peace and stability in Africa because it gives voice to marginalised communities and constituencies, promotes a level playing field and fair access to resources and opportunities for development.

3. GETTING SYSTEMS RIGHT:
THE MISSING INGREDIENTS

As earlier indicated, navigating a new pathway for public service reform and a developmental state requires a combination of interrelated activities; democratic governance, leadership vision and sense of direction, empowerment, productive private sector, vibrant civil society, and mindset change among the key actors and an enabling environment. Critically, not all has gone well for post-colonial independent states in Africa in terms of democratic governance, credible and ethical leadership backed with independent functional bureaucratic machinery. Ethnic hegemonic forces and political party influences in different ways impact on the *input and output* functions of the public sector. Military dictatorships and authoritarian civil rule have influenced the structure of the system with the international community contributing a contradictory quota in the ball game of bad governance and poor services delivery. So what are the missing ingredients needed for public service reform, sustained growth and constructing a developmental state in Africa?

Apparently, it is evident that poor health due to the existence of endemic diseases reduces the productive capacity of the people. It is also true that poor policy articulation and implementation help to fuel poor outputs in various sectors. Equally, the extractive institutions inherited from former colonial masters have influenced the current weak institutions in Africa and have thus contributed to the unfavourable conditions of development.

This paper focuses on an often-neglected key factor in Africa's long-term development - navigating new pathways for public service reform, the growth of a developmental state and the need to - *"foster the creation of an independent and fair government apparatus, supported by a strong civil society, an effective private productive sector, and institutions that provide oversight of government actions"* [Bio-Tchane and Yehour 2007:44]. Effective solutions based on short, medium and long-term are required to kick-start the reconstruction of effective and efficient public service machinery.

The African Commission Report [2005] aptly streamlines the significance of leadership role in the developmental process. *"Africa needs leaders. Strong leaders committed to change are one of the key drivers to progress. Developing the capabilities of leaders at all levels and in all spheres – political, the public sector, business and civil society is critical to African led sustainable development."*

The corner stone of a developmental state is a sound constitution where the interests of the citizens are balanced with the separation of powers of the judiciary, and legislative from the executive. Many Africans call into question the legitimacy of the constitutions of their states in which the balance of power between the executive, parliament and the judiciary shifts towards a hegemonic executive. The existence of a dominant executive ignores the constitution prolonging an unconstitutionally permitted stay in power.

These are some of the fundamental issues that need to be addressed in navigating public service reform for a developmental state. More prosaically, for accountability to be effective, government policies, actions and system must be opened to scrutiny by the people. Openness, accountability, transparency and legitimacy have to be woven into the systems through which the state operates. The attitude and mindset of the society must be conditioned and tilted towards developmental state.

Some form of visionary leadership is imperative for the realisation of envisaged goals. Supporting such visionary leadership is truly independent judiciary capable of {a} aggrieved individuals would be sure of getting justice: {b} it would prevent people from taking laws into their hands; and {c} creditors and debtors would be able to settle their disputes amicably. The rule of law is the invisible hand that nurtures and strengthens democracy. Where it is not respected and judiciary is seen as partisan what would be achieved is a complete different brand of democracy. Obviously, only an impartial and fearless judicial system would help in building and creating the path towards constructing an unadulterated democracy in Africa. The continent is saddled with poor governance which makes the region a lackey of the western powers.

As earlier indicated, many reasons account for this state of affairs; an inferiority complex, poor leadership, economic dependency, the need for technical assistance, chronic indebtedness, and poor human capacity building among others. These factors have far-reaching ramifications for the socioeconomic transformation of the continent. It cannot be denied that deep-seated social and economic failures underlie some of the problems faced by African states, but it is equally accurate to state that these problems themselves are in key respects political ones requiring political solutions which must be sought through "servant and visionary leadership".

3.1. Leadership

Given current trends which places the African continent at the bottom of the socio-economic ladder of development there is dare need for leaders who can foster and galvanised a spirit of dialogue, reconciliation and mobilising society's forces by transforming the current state of divisive national relations and creating a new paradigm of cooperation, and understanding the values of diversity and difference as asset not liability to development. Africa's greatest dilemma is absence of visionary leadership capable of instilling a positive sense of direction in the mindset of the population. It was Harry Truman who stated; *"A leader is a man who has the ability to get other people to do what they don't want to do and like it."* In short, leadership is in service. There are numerous qualities making a good leader.

An outstanding factor is that a credible and trustworthy leader instils confidence, hope and confidence in people and complements the institutional framework of democratic governance to provide the necessary stability and climate for sustainable development, peace, stability, effective and efficient public service delivery in meeting the needs of the people. The leader upholds the social contract between the government and citizens and puts the interests of the people before than his/her own interest. This is what we may call *"Servant Leaders"* who serve and not wanting to be served. Unfortunately, the continent has been flooded with the category genre of leaders who want to be served. They transform themselves into what Meredith [1984] refers as *"the long distance men"* determined to cling to power for ever.

Most of the elected presidents convert themselves into a chieftaincy dynasty failing to understand that chieftaincy is hereditary and not elected. Elected servants must give account to the electorate at certain time intervals in order to renew confidence, trust and legitimacy. The democratic culture has yet to take effective hold on the political jigsaw of the continent. And for leaders to embrace the ideal of being "servant leaders", not authoritarian; to shove aside their agenda of self-aggrandisement and no longer about serving the people. A blend of traditional African values and contemporary African leadership within the context of global evolution must evolve on a platform of ensuring open government, legitimacy, consensus, dialogue and inclusion not imposition as the case is now. Open government equates into a functional public bureaucracy as the engine for development.

Conversely, absence of open and inclusive governance breeds ineffective, inefficient and none-productive public service sector with poor quality services delivery as a result. This is Africa's dilemma which must be immediately corrected for the continent to occupy its rightful place within the global system. African has to move from the deconstruction phase marshalled by "served-leaders" into a reconstruction phase which Zartman [1997] sees as necessary for Africa.

State reconstruction should be the prime objective of *"servant-leader"* after the deconstruction or destructive phase which many African countries have been subjected too since independence. The objective of such *"servant-leader"* is to transform the state into a real state even though it may be bogged down with numerous shortcomings, namely; state institutions, financial resources as a result of the misappropriations of resources over the years, and legitimacy.

Most African countries are no placed under supervisory authority of the Conglomerates of the Bretton Woods Financial Institutions - World Bank, International Monetary Fund and other Western Financial Institutions. The structural adjustment Programme {SAP} only added to the marginalisation and exploitation of the continent, leaving the greater part of the population worse off than before its inception. SAP imposed adjustment plans that ultimately weaken the state, increase unemployment, added social problems and poverty African states lost the leverage enjoyed hitherto. Of course; a few benefited and continue to benefit from the spoil process.

Leaders engulfed in the idea of being "served" are thwarting the developmental process of their nations. Figure 1 depicts the essentials of good leadership much needed in Africa

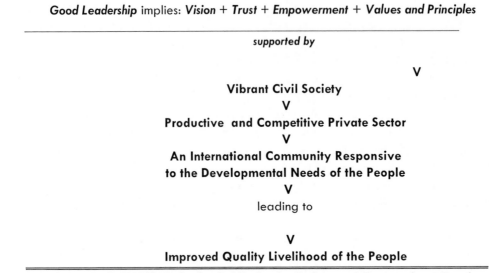

Good Leadership implies: *Vision* + *Trust* + *Empowerment* + *Values and Principles*

supported by

V

Vibrant Civil Society

V

Productive and Competitive Private Sector

V

**An International Community Responsive
to the Developmental Needs of the People**

V

leading to

V

Improved Quality Livelihood of the People

Source: John W. Forje [2008] Navigating Public Service Reform and Constructing a Developmental State in Africa.

Figure 1. The Kind of Leadership Required for Africa.

3.2. Governance System

Generally, Africa has tried both democracy and dictatorship. Civilian authoritarian or military rule has been the main governance form in the continent. Curiously these systems have failed to provide the necessary conditions for sustained economic growth and quality living standards. According to [Golder & Wantchekon, 2004] "Africa has been dominated by authoritarian governments; between 1946 and 2000, there were only 189 country-years of democracy in Africa compared with 1.823 years of dictatorship." The immediate post-independent year's elections were competitive on a pluralistic party basis and with voters exposed to a wide range of choices.

Due to the lack of a political culture or tradition competitive pluralistic party elections were replaced by monolithic party rule. Power rule is through the icons of big men with bad legacies, which often breeds conflicts, civil wars thwarting contemporary political changes and instituting guided democratisation process subjecting the country in a more confused and paralysed state-building configuration than before.

Transforming the public sector into a productive, efficient and accountable functional system with shared responsibilities between the state and key stakeholders will improve accountability, trust, confidence and efficient management of resources as well as attract foreign investments. Presently, there is a growing degree of stigmatisation where African states are regarded as collapsed or failure states, unintelligent, unproductive, discriminated and marginalised against on such grounds. There is need to seriously examine the governance system. It is a problem of politics and race leading to the exclusion from the corridors of power in global politics and in national politics by the marginalised population.

This group of marginalised population lack of access to means of production. In turn it affects their economic status, subjecting them to a constant state of dependency. We cannot deny the reality that's some African countries have and are making significant progress in the development of good governance. Much still remains to be done to create an enabling environment in restrain the degree of *"brain drain phenomenon"* plaguing the region. Though the brain drain issue can be converted to a brain gain in future, the immediate impact on the continent is disastrous for its economic and technological take-off.

An important element of good governance is embedded in democracy. Democracy is the active participation of the population in the political system. This is currently lacking in many African countries even with the return to political pluralism since the 1990s. The lack of active participation is a hindrance to democracy and good governance. It is the right and responsibility of the people to widen the definition of democracy and good governance.

In most Africa countries, democracy does not mean equal freedom. Democracy is a fight and a sacrifice – it is fight for inclusion in democratic process and good governance. Servant leadership should ensure the empowerment of the people in all facets, capacity building, healthcare and providing other basic necessities that improves the quality of life.

3.3. Empowerment

Empowerment is a vital ingredient in the development process. Power to the people with equal opportunities for all, creates the rigid foundation for improving on the state bureaucracy An improved functional public service constitute the first stage to providing the essential services to the population. Essential here is that of human capital development, the right of the people to choose and dismiss their leaders, the right to be actively involved in all facets of the political game ball. A particular group of people to be empowered are women and the youths. Without empowerment the conditions for development cannot be created.

The absence of empowerment of the people should be seen as the greatest tragedy of our times. Therefore, the right system of governance and capacity building, peace, security, inclusive development that champions investing in people and a serious call for partnership between all the key stakeholders. The female gender must be taken out of the ghetto of marginalisation, deprivation, discrimination and exclusion into the paradise of inclusive development as equal partners in the socioeconomic transformation of the society. Africa is not making use of its human potentials, especially the female gender that for time immemorial have been excluded from the development process. There is an urgent need to bridge the education divide between female and male gender. Existing disregard for women's advancement and empowerment remains a glaring obvious throughout the continent only helps to mortgage the future of the continent. The process should be geared towards more women in power to better release the nations strength in the developmental process. Development cannot come without the support of women.

3.4. Human Capital Development

The issue of achieving excellence in public administration requires human capacity development remains perennial. First, improving on human capital gives added value to the natural resources potential of the society. Second, the task faced by the public administration in the world today is becoming ever-complex. The public service is constantly challenged to solve problems ranging from technologically highly complex nature to such highly ideologically charged issues as promoting a society's economic well-being and addressing its problems of crime and delinquency. Third, the public service is faced with the challenges of propelling the country from a Third to a First world status. The challenges are enormous calling for professionalism, skills, and tact under visionary leadership reinforced with proper mobilisation and utilisation of resources.

Most African nations are confronted with two fundamentally interrelated crises: {a} the rate of growing inequality in the world {North-South divide} and within nations; and {b} the resultant inability to more effectively address issues of widespread abject poverty and the growing threat of insecurity and endemic diseases lowering the productivity of the people. Addressing these issues requires trained personnel, new and creative leadership on the part of government officials, public administrative, the private sector and civil society [see Rosenbaum & Kauzya 2006].

Given the state of incoherent bureaucratic institutions resulting from a highly politicised administration, it leaves the government incapable of resolving collective problems and transcending individual or group interests.

Therefore, human capital development is imperative if Africa is to rid itself of its current ghettoised status of abject poverty, marginalisation, exploitation and underdevelopment.

3.5. Interface with the International Community

African states are part of the global community. An interface with the global community is imperative. Unfortunately, there exist a hostile and rapidly changing international community that respond negatively to the needs of the African continent when it comes to elevating the regions status from a Third to a First world. Incidentally, there is a quick and positive response when it entails exploiting the human and natural resources of the continent for their own benefits. The international community is part of the existence the genre of Africa *"long distance runners"* who respond to the needs of foreign powers and not to the needs of their citizens.

To what extent will this double role or balancing act of foreign powers and ruling elites domination be sustained depends on the enlightenment and vibrancy of civil society taking its share of responsibility in the governance process. Civil society is gradually taking such responsibility as demonstrated by the current taxi and inter-city bus association engineered strike in Cameroon that paralysed the state from 25th to 29th February 2008. Thus a concerted civil society action has yielded some token reaction on the part of government following increase in civil servants pay rise on 7th March 2008, the first in 26 years and coming after a 70% salary cut in 1993 and a 50% devaluation of the currency in 1994. Or like in Zimbabwe where inflation is running at over 2000%. In Sudan and Somali where the people have known no peace, security and development but war and destruction for many decades. In Cameroon,

Chad, Nigeria and Gabon where the oil riches of these states are not translated into improving the well-being of the people but has only contributed to impoverishments and marginalisation.

Interface between state-civil society-private sector and the international community is essential. Africa needs the international community just as the international community needs Africa. The balancing act should evolve on the basis of respect for national sovereignty of each state as equal partners in development. A new global political and economic order of equality and respect should be effectively put in place. Given the importance of a functional harmonious relation between the key stakeholders mentioned, in the fight against corruption and poor governance, private sector development, civil society organisations {CSO}, and public fiscal institutions deserve particular attention, especially as aid to Africa is scaled up. It is the place duty and obligations of the state to provide social and economic security to the people, not the private sector. This is the only way to give the people voice and power in the development process.

Interface of state-civil society, private sector and the international community requires the input role of a *"free press"* facilitating the flow of information, educating the public, raising awareness and strengthening public institutions for honest, transparent and accountable governance system. The absence of a free media industry in Africa is hampering objective critic of the output functions of government. The media plays a strong role in empowering the people, enabling them know their rights and responsibilities in ensuring a functional governance system. An enlightened society is a productive and progressive one. At play here, of course, are the interactions between power and knowledge; between the desire to change and reconstruct Africa's future along a constructive path of inclusion and judiciously consciously deployment of resources.

The continuing problems of African societies can partly be traced to the intellectual crises concerning our understanding of the nexus between a number of dominant conceptual pillars constraining contemporary Africa – namely state-civil, society-private sector nexus or interface with the international community which are neither not coordinated, and harnessed nor enhanced to constitute the trinity in the development process. Once there is a dysfunctional structure within the state-civil society-private sector interface, the international community takes advantage in exploiting; the case of the Structural Adjustment Programme {SAP} that has contributed to the supervisory take-over of the state by conglomerates of the Bretton Woods Financial Institutions constraints the progress of the society, subjecting to the people to abject poverty should constitute serious lessons for Africa to craft a new developmental approach to the numerous problems plaguing the region. African states are forced to depend excessively on markets over which they have little or no control. These are policies advocated and imposed on the continent knowing that they are not consistent with European or American history [Chang 2005] but most be executed by African countries.

4. RETHINKING THE NEXUS

Quality services delivery in African can only improve when serious thoughts are given to the existing State-Civil Society-Private Sector interface. Our misconception of the triple-heritage posed by these three sectors as partners in development exposes the vulnerability of

Africa in global development. Of course, to put order requires a number of inter-related activities. First, the need to reconstruct the State. Second, to rethink the good governance agenda. Third, a holistic empowerment of the people in all facets is imperative. Fourth; integration, unity, cooperation and solidarity among African states acting as a single voice and commitment in facing the adversaries. Presently, the loyalties of most leaders are torn between the interests of their parties, ethnic groups and constituencies and themselves as against a general interest of the entire nation. In short, their personnel interest and not the common good remain paramount.

Since the state has always had a vital role in promoting growth, it is inconceivable that Africa will be the sole exception to this rule. Indeed, [Khan 2004:165] hits the nail on the head, noting that: *"Without strategies to enhance this role of the state, sustained progress on service delivery is also unlikely. Many of the consensus policies on reforming institutions to improve service delivery are based on partial reading of theory and evidence. They are at best unlikely to work, and at worst could further undermine the state's institutional and political capacity for ensuring a dynamic transformation."* The idea of quality life without the private sector and civil society evolvement is a fiction; so also the idea of service delivery state without social and political transformation is equally without foundation.

Therefore, an interface within the three solidifies quality services delivery and quality of life. This is the way to scale-up and navigate public service reform and quality services delivery for better quality livelihood in Africa. It means exploiting, understanding and utilising the SWOT analysis to restructure the continent. There is need to look at the strength, weaknesses, opportunities and threats across the board and to convert weakness and threats into opportunities and strengths.

A major strength for the continent apart from its rich natural resources potential is to build in the principles of regional cooperation, identification of common needs and pooling of available resources, in the spirit of NEPAD and its intention to build Africa capacity to deal with regional and national challenges. This should also include creating a framework for regional and national organisations, national management development institutions and international development partners to collaborate in a manner unprecedented on the continent; and finally, identify specific programmes of action for which African and international funding and other assistance can be sought, and the implementation of which can be monitored to ensure impact and sustainability.

5. THE ANALYSIS: A PROBLEMATIC NEXUS

The analysis based on the conceptual framework provides an opportunity for the continent to x-ray itself with regards to public services delivery reform and constructing a developmental state for that purpose. What should Africa read between these concepts? What lessons can be drawn from the past to help shape the future? To begin with, in Africa, a nexus was established by the forces of colonial rule latter to be taken over by Bretton Wood Financial Institutional Conglomerates {BWFIC} as the supervisory power. The BWFIC took over the reform of political and institutional changes and reshaping the market accordingly and not in the interest of African countries. Politically, the process destroyed the emergency of a servant leadership. The new leaders were to function according to the dictates of the new supervisory power. The first mission was to destroy a functional partisan bureaucratic public sector. Thus the absence of democracy and weak bureaucracies were to promote the deconstruction of the state and not to have a structurally functionally driven behaviour.

It was the support that entrenched the likes of dictatorial regimes in Africa, Mobutu (Zaire) Abacha (Nigeria) Apartheid (South Africa), Ian Smith (Rhodesia) and a host of *"leaders-served"* powers on the continent. The idea of downsizing the state was promoted as a way of restructuring to promote service delivery which failed. The *"leaders-served"* took advantage to enrich themselves through the process. Whereas the better approach was left out – that of promoting democracy, open and accountable governments, decentralisation and encouraging the rise of a vibrant civil society and a productive and competitive private sector – as ways of changing the structures of the state's ability to craft quality life for the people.

Downsizing the public service sector was a way of depriving the people from quality living standards. The drawbacks amounted to poor service delivery in respect of fundamental basic human needs, healthcare, social service amenities, poor human capital development all areas of fundamental importance to improving quality living standards. The is sluggishness on the part of BWFIC to see into the realities that plunged the continent into further decline, or collapse encouraging poverty, corruption and exploitation. Therefore, the SWOT analysis puts into concrete perspectives the kind of measures best needed in improving the efficiency, motivating civil servants, increasing the productivity and competitiveness of the private sector and ensuring that the rule of law and justice reigns supreme through an independent none-partisan or executive influenced judiciary upholding the constitution and laws of the state.

5.1. Strength

In spite of its precarious situation, the continent is endowed with abundant strengths that should be exploited to advance quality service delivery and promote the entrenchment of democratic governance. It is the least developed continent. It is also a continent endowed with vast potentials but the people are poor in the midst of plenty. China's [New Africa 2008:12-18] rush into Africa, and with the West wanting to maintain its hegemonic dominance shows how important Africa is to the world.

These are potential advantages that ought to be exploited by the new generations of *"visionary servant leaders"*. A new political ball game must come to play. African must negotiate from a position of strength in the evolving political dynamics of post-cold war era as well as capitalising on its resources in great demand by the developed countries. In short, Africa should exploit weaknesses prevalent within the developmental strategies of the west to strengthen its position, enhance and harness its strength and opportunities.

5.2. Weaknesses

What can be outlined as major weakness; include the absence of a democratic culture, the entrenchment of "served leaders", none-vibrant civil society and a weak private sector that is neither competitive nor productive. Education gaps, poor quality healthcare, unemployment, poverty, corruption, poor business development and the slow creation of wealth all add to threats faced by the continent. There is need to increase political participation and integration among African states, without which the advantages of globalisation cannot be maximised. A major weakness to address is that of building up the professional public service, void of political party, ethnic hegemonic, patronage mediocrity influences and ensures a holistic human capital development. Existing state of political and economic fragmentation must give way for total integration.

A holistic approach is required in solving the continent's existing plethora of problems. No single nation, no matter how endowed its natural resources are cannot alone address the tons of problems confronting the region.

5.3. Opportunities

The continent is endowed with vast opportunities yet to be exploited. The mere size of the continent which can take, [Europe, China, India, America, the Soviet Union, and Australia] offers vast opportunities of expansion, trade and development. There are many untapped resources of the continent waiting to be exploited. It has a fast growing youthful population. The continent should take advantage of the *"late-comer"* phenomenon to accelerate its developmental process.

In line with this, a new generation of leaders is called for with the advantage of learning from past mistakes and crafting a new construct for each nation and the continent in general. The threat of fear posed in the West with China's penetration in Africa should act as catalyst in creating and strengthening existing opportunities that the continent has. For example, China has created a fait-accompli, not storming Africa as would have been expected from a dragon but getting into it in a powerful but cautious way. Its money flow and development projects in Africa keep the West worried. *"Not only do Chinese strengths justify this uneasiness, but the fact that China has come up with an economic and political development model that seems to have produced tangible results in terms of poverty alleviation and national control of assets, makes the country more appealing to most African countries"* [New African 2008:14] A new form of play Eat against West as in the Cold war era provides the opportunities for the continent to advance its transformation process.

5.4. Threats

A major threat is the force of globalisation and neo-liberalism that puts the continent at a disadvantage given its low scientific and technological level of development. At least the following problems can be listed as threats of serious magnitude:-

- Invisibility in the global arena; the result of poor utilisation of its human and natural resources potential;
- Exclusion from global power, political and economic marginalisation;
- Stigmatisation, - stereotype, discrimination, lack of diversity; world perception of Africans as being unintelligent, unproductive and discriminated upon. A new image is required;

- Marginalisation, unequal provision of services; leading to a widening gap between the few rich and poor majority;
- Absence of solidarity, integration, cooperation and a united front against the common enemy of external exploitation, corruption, abject poverty and other ills slowing the progress of the continent;
- Failure in mobilising domestic resources for the development of continent subjects the region to dependency with all the consequences this entails;
- African leaders [served leaders] must stop inflicting the notion of poverty on the people by mortgaging the resources of the country at a give away price;
- Absence in deepening the state and process of democracy and democratic governance on the continent;
- Weak scientific and technological base and human capital development which fails to give added value to the natural resources potential of the continent;
- Hegemonic dominance of the state bureaucracy by partisan politics propagated by the ruling party;
- Ethnic diversity seen as liability rather as asset for development;
- The forces of globalisation are serious threats to a dysfunctional system with a weak democratic governance structure and underdeveloped technological base.

6. CONCLUSION: PROVIDING WAYS FORWARD

Navigating public services reform for a developmental democratic state in Africa calls for a new era of democratic governance on the continent. There is need for a new approach to making the public bureaucracy more functional and responding efficiently and effectively to the needs of the people. Over the years, there has been a decline in the performance of the civil service. That such phenomenon persists comes as no surprise.

First, the ruling party coverts public bureaucracy into extended services of the political party machinery thereby thwarting all forms of impartiality and rendering services on basis of patronage and ethnic affiliations.

The *Second* factor relates to the kind of supervisory nature imposed on states by Bretton Woods Financial Conglomerates through its structural adjustment programme of downsizing the public service and financial and social constraints brought as a result. States should endeavour to uphold their sovereignty.

Third, the gross absence of *"servant leaders"* to instil hope, confidence and vision for the re-railing of the system to be productive, efficient, effective and competitive in services delivery.

Fourth, the absence of a democratic culture constitutes serious drawbacks which impair civil service efficacy on the continent.

Fifth, the international community drives its agenda according to its needs and not those desires and aspirations of the people concern – Africa in this case. The continent's independence is controlled by the powerful nations;

Sixth, emerging new challenges for future leaders to learn from past mistakes, evolve on the platform of "servant leaders" with focus of prioritising the needs of their citizen's first, tailoring state bureaucracy to function in that direction.

Seventh, Africa must set its own priority strategic agenda, ensure its implementation within the framework of the prevailing international construct, resisting as much as possible any form of foreign hegemonic dictates; revitalise the continent's resolve to reconstruct itself from existing ailing state of underdevelopment and marginalisation.

These and other related factors have to be looked into objectively; endurable solutions sought to reinstate the continent on the right developmental path with the focus of improving the quality of life of the people. The people of Africa deserve more than this. Thus the challenge of the 21st century and the future beyond 2015 [meeting MDGs] would be for African governments to continue to anticipate needs that are likely to emerge from the continuing socio-political, economic, technological changes and challenges and administrative reforms. It has to be an ongoing process correcting past mistakes and taking new initiatives.

Attempts have been made to pinpoint some of the critical and salient factors inhibiting quality services delivery through the public service. It would be unrealistic for one to assume that the measures advanced here constitute the ideal solutions to all the problems of administrative reforms and other bottlenecks faced by African countries. To be realistic, this is a far-fetched hope given that administrative problems are situational being contingent upon changing political, social, cultural, economic, and technological circumstances. What African countries have in common is their colonial heritage with variance though.

Some African countries, especially Anglophone countries have made significant strides in reforming their public service sector. Reforms in Francophone Africa are still lacking. Both share the same dilemma – corrupt governance system, underdevelopment, marginalisation and exploitation. Such variance makes it impossible to advance common solutions and improve on the quality of life. The interferences of party politics into state bureaucracy, and the lack of professionalism in administration constitute a significant constraint in ensuring quality and efficient public service delivery.

Generally, all African countries are facing issues of a disciplined and technical sound approach to formulating and executing administrative reforms. Thanks to the penetration or infiltration of party politics and ethnic hegemonic tendencies into the *"input-output"* functions of public bureaucracy. Such interference inhibits quality services delivery, delays the development process and thwarts the continent's standing within the international community.

No doubt most of the administrative reform programmes fail partly as the result of ill-conceived, lacking clarity, political party influenced in the definition of objectives. One cannot dismiss insufficient public support for reform. Partly due to ignorance, political party influenced or that informed public opinion is not sufficiently articulate to provoke general interest in administrative reforms. Lack of interest may also result from the basis of who will police the police; will the administrators currently benefiting from a spoil system truly want a change in the system that will limit existing enjoyed advantages?

Yet these reforms are vital lifelines for the recovery of the continent and should neither be ignored nor delayed. Any form of delay would only accelerate the state of corruption, self-interest [served leaders] and nepotism in the public service which is the engine for growth and social responsibility in society. The demise of the one-party system and in the era of political pluralism, open and inclusive government should pave a concerted path for a new public bureaucracy reform. No one can refute the reality that African public service requires urgent reorganisation, strengthening and rationalisation of the machinery of government and that governments must equally embark on a comprehensive process of power devolution.

Static governance is not what the countries want; government must evolve, dynamic and progressive and the policy of government must reflect the aspirations of the people; and thus in public space called upon to execute these policies, must appreciate the thoughts and feelings of the people. The public service must be innovative, offering citizens and the private sector a convenient medium to engage with government on service delivery issues and improving on the quality of life of the people.

7. SOME RECOMMENDED ACTIONS

Based on issues discussed, the following suggestion constitutes recommended actions to pilot the continent through the stormy weather for providing quality life to the people through a reorganised, functional, efficient and effective public bureaucracy.

1. It is imperative and urgent to foster an environment favourable to reforming state bureaucracy through the right political, social and administrative climate;
2. In an age of political pluralism, the aprons of the monolithic party system should no longer prevail as a dark cloud over the public service sector;
3. A new democratic governance and administrative climate is needed to respond and provide the essential needs of the population; This is what cements the social contract between the government and people;
4. The governance system should create an enabling environment for gender empowerment and recruitment of more women into the top-decision making echelon of the administrative bureaucracy;
5. Public administration must be broadly representative of the country's people, with employment, promotion and personnel management practices based on ability, objectivity, fairness, and the need to redress the imbalances of the past to achieve broad representation for the common good;
6. Political party and ethnic interferences should be kept away from state bureaucracy; professionalism, meritocracy and objectivity should be the golden rule with *AAPAM's** motto and the South Africa's *"Batho Pele Principles"*** *as* the guiding compass;

***AAPAM Motto:**	*To none will we deny service,*
	To none will we delay service,
	To none will we pervert service.
=====➔	
** Batho Pele Principles:	*We Belong;*
	We Care;
	We serve.

7. Navigating a new pathway for administrative reforms should be an integral part of the national development strategy agenda;

8. Administrative reform must encompass suitable staff development – professionalism and motivation should be catch words;

9. A critical aspect of the public bureaucracy is to develop a culture of nurturing of diversity and making diversity an asset for development not a liability;

10. The idea and need for *'servant leaders"* cannot be overemphasised. Africa is in dare need of *"visionary servant leaders"* to instil hope and confidence in the reconstruction of a better, brighter, effective, efficient and productive bureaucracy geared towards providing quality life to the people by upholding the AAPAM and Batho Pele Principles ethos in the public service.

REFERENCES

African Commission Report [2005] Our Common Interest. *Report of the Commission for Africa.*

Bentil A. Michael [2004] 50 Years of Civil Service Reform Experience in Anglophone Africa. *Reflections On the Past To Guide Future Efficiency In Governance.* Design Solutions, Accra, Ghana.

Bas Bernard [1990] From Transactional to transformation Leadership: Learning to Share the Vision. *Organisational Dynamics*, Vol. 18, Issue 3.

Bio-Tchane Abdpoulaye & Yehoue B. Etienne [2007] *"Africa's Missing Ingredients,"* in *Finance and Development,* December 2007, Vol. 44, No. 4. Washington, USA. www.imf.org/fandd.

Blanchard Ken, Hybels & Hodges [1999] *Leadership by the Book: Tools to Transform Your Work Place.* William Morrow Company.

Bolman L and Deal T. [1981] *Reframing Organisation.* Jussey-Bass, San Francisco.

Chang Ha-Joon [2005] *Kicking Away the Ladder: Development Strategy in Historical Perspectives,* Anthem Press, London.

Chesterman Simon et al [2004] *Making States Work: From State Failure to State-Building.* International Peace Academy {New York] and the United Nations University, Tokyo – Japan. [www.ipacademy.org]

Crossby, Barbara C, John M. Byrson [2005] *Leadership for the Common Good: Tackling Problems in the Shared World.* John Wiley Publishers.

Diamond Larry [1994] "Rethinking Civil Society: Towards Democratic Consolidation", *Journal of Democracy,* 5, 4-17.

Forje John W. [2007] Her*e The People Rule: Political Transition and Challenges for democratic Consolidation in Africa.* CARAD Publication Forthcoming.

Fowler Alan [1996] "Strengthening Civil Society in Transition. Economies from Concept to Strategy: Mapping an Exit in a Maze of Mirrors" in Andrew Clayton {ed.} *NGO's, Civil Society and The State Building Democracy in Transitional Societies,* Oxford.

Gardiner John [1965]"The Antileadership Vaccine" in *The Annual Report of the Carnegie Corporation,* Carnegie Corporation, New York.

George Bill [2003] *Authentic Leadership*. Sage Publications.

Golder, Matt & Leonard Wantchekon [2004] "Africa: Dictatorial and democratic Electoral Systems Since 1946," in Joseph Colomer et al {ed.} *Handbook of Electoral System Choice*. Palgrave, London.

Gounden Vasu [2007] Editorial: *ACCORD - Conflict Trends – Leadership in Africa, issue 2, 2007*, South Africa.

Gerschenkron, Alexander [1962] *Economic Backwardness in Historical Perspective.* Cambridge, MA. The Belkkanp Press of Harvard University Press.

House, R. H., Wright, N. S. and Aditya, R. N. [1999] "Cross-Cultural Leadership-Organisational. Leadership: A Critical Analysis and Proposed Theory" in Earley, P.C. & Erez, M. {eds.} *New Perspectives in International Industrial Organisational Psychology.* New Lexington, pp 535-625.

Khan Mushtaq [2004] "State Failure in Developing Countries and Institutional Reform Strategies", *Annual World Bank Conference on Development Economics-Europe 2003*, Paris, World Bank pp 165 -96

Kong Doug & Oakly Ed [1994] *Enlightened Leadership.* Sage Publication.

Levin M. Richard [2007] "Leadership And Service Delivery in the South African Context", *Paper presented at the 29th AAPAM Annual Roundtable Conference, 3rd to 7th September 2007*, Mbabane, Swaziland.

Meredith Martin [1984] *The First Decade of Freedom. Black Africa in the Post-War Era.* Abacus, London.

New Africa [2008*] China-Africa: Why The West Is Worried"*, New Africa, March 2008, No. 471. pp 12-18, London.

Pass, C. Davis I, & Lowes B. [2000] *Economics Dictionary,* 3rd Edition, Harper Collins Publishers, Glasgow.

Reddy Jairam [2007] "A Conceptual Framework for African Leadership Development" in Conflict Trends, *Accord,* Issue 2, 2007, South Africa.

Rosenbaum Allan & John-Mary Kauzya (eds.) 2006. Excellence and Leadership in the Public Sector: The Role of Education and Training. *United Nations and The International Association of Schools and Institutes of Administration* {IASIA}

Shelton Ken [1997] *Beyond Counterfeit Leadership.* Sage Publications.

Zartman, I. W. [1997] *Collapsed States. The Disintegration and Reconstruction of Legitimate Authority.* Note: See Paper prepared for the Kampala 2008 IASIA Conference.

Chapter 11

Constructing a Developmental Nation: The Challenges of Political and Managerial Leadership for Change and Development in Africa

Abstract

The process of nation-building in post-colonial Africa has taken different dimensions – moving from "exclusion" to embracing quasi "inclusion". This calls for qualitative leadership and managerial skills. The paper provides an overview of the challenges facing African countries since the granting of independence and especially from the 1990s. It is set against a brief overview of the key aspects of post-cold war Africa and in the light of the continent's lost decade of the 1980s, and the challenges of meeting United Nations Millennium Development Goals [MDGs]. The first issue outlined is the massive democratic shift in the structure of African governments from monolithic to political party pluralism. The second underpins the development challenges in particular and interaction between the key stakeholders. The third question concerns the non-progress made after 15 years of the return to political pluralism in arresting poverty, corruption and poor quality service delivery? The fourth issue relates to establishing free, independent, professional bureaucratic machinery void of political party interferences, dictates and influence, but one ready to serve whichever political party legitimately elected into office. The fifth focuses on ways forward for an underdeveloped continent facing the forces of globalisation.

These developments underpin fundamental issues of political and managerial leadership for change and development in Africa. The paper looks at the absence of quality and visionary political and managerial leadership in the body politic of the state as serious threats to the progress of a nation. To what extent political and managerial leadership and democratic systems promotes or inhibits the level and nature of developments and change within a country? It argues for effective political leadership and strong government from the perspective of opening the political space as institutional imperatives necessary for rolling out and ensuring sustainable development. It demonstrates how effective leadership nurtures transitional politics to place these countries within the limelight of a developed polity.

My argument is that strong, visionary, effective and functional political leadership and managerial skills leads to "inclusive" politics as basis for constructing a developmental and sustainable nation-state focused on improving the quality of livelihood of the citizens. These implies meeting the development challenges of eradication extreme poverty and hunger, drastic reduction in child mortality, promoting gender equity and empowerment, control and eradicating killer diseases like HIV/AIDS, malaria, tuberculoses etc; putting in place radical measures halting the destruction and depletion of the environment, arresting corruption and wanton poverty among others. In short, poor leadership, poor managerial skills, bad governance and poverty constitute a threat to the development of the continent. The conclusion is, countries that have effectively demonstrated a unique combination of visionary, concerted, just and competent political leadership, managerial skills and backed by professional and impartial led public service, stand a better chance of achieving progress within a relatively short time frame in comparison to those lacking these attributes. Proactive policy measures are advanced.

Keywords: Governance, human development and security, leadership and managerial skills, bureaucracy, corruption, exclusion constructive engagement, globalisation

NUGGETS IN A NUTSHELL: IN SEARCH OF LEADERS AND MANAGERS

"The Africa of today is not the Africa of yesterday. Certainly, we have come of age. Democracy is on the march, the economies are getting stronger and stronger, and there is greater realisation of the need to work together towards the attainment of the lofty goal of African unity". *[President Jakaya Mrisho Kilwete of Tanzania, 2007:16]*

"We cannot solve problems by using the same kind of thinking we need when we created them". *[Albert Einstein]*

"It is not generally the state that 'fails'; it is the government or individual leaders" *[Simon Chesterman et al. {2004:2}]*

"Each of us is a knowledge worker and a learning champion in the knowledge economy. We all have a role to play in turning the Public Service into a 'Learning Public Service for Quality Service Delivery'. Let us pursue this ideal by using the Service Delivery Review as a facility for sharing our experiences, successes, mistakes and methodologies and for growing our own intellectual capital". *[Editorial: Service Delivery Review. Department of Public Service and Administration, Government of South Africa]*

"After more than half-a-century of independence, the people of Africa require more liberalisation, democratisation and progress in the economy to make life better for every citizen. The baffling question is whether Africa is bedevilled with poor leadership or what? Why has development bypassed the continent? What can be done to ensure that the train of effective political leadership and responsive citizenry for achieving economic progress, democratic governance and quality life for all is articulated, aggregated and retained within the contours of the continent?". *[John W. Forje. 1st June 2007, Buea-Cameroon].*

"Some people will blame our colonial oppressors. Well in some cases part of it is true but a whole lot of the blame should be put squarely on our soldiers. Independence was thought to be the beginning of the golden era where political freedom and expression, freedom of association, free enterprise, economic prosperity, less ethnocentrisms, responsibility and accountability of each and every one prevailed. These lofty ideals never happened because we replaced white imperialism with the black one". *[Ghana Drum, March 1992]*

"Let there be competent leaders, as many as are needed, and Africa would leap from recession to recovery, from limitation to liberation, from collective doom to continuous boom.

The vibrant dynamic and servant leadership of colonial and early independence years is hardly seen these days". *[William F. Kumuyi. 2006:20]*

INTRODUCTION: THE JOURNEY TOWARDS THE THRESHOLD OF MODERNITY

The focus of this paper is to provide the historical context in which to situate a number of contemporary issues impeding the rise of developmental states in Africa. The assumption is that the past influences the present in a variety o ways that explain the roots of contemporary problems, the continuity and resilience of various aspects of indigenous institutions, some limitations to initiating new changes, and the rhetoric of where Africa stands in world politics and how its people define themselves. Africa's portrait of the 21st century is disquieting, notes Kumuyi [2006:20]. "While Europe is taming the moon and befriending Mars, Africa trudges on in corruption, wanton poverty, disease and illiteracy. President Nyerere aptly noted: "while others are struggling to get to the moon, I have yet to reach my people in the village". This statement outlines the degree of diversity between the rich and poor, and the amount of work needed in transitional polities to move from third to first world

African people have been concerned with understanding and controlling the changing nature of their development since the so-called shackles of colonial rule was broken. However, this understanding ha snot led to appreciable strides, in improving the quality of life of the vast majority of the population. Africa remains poor in the midst of plenty [potential natural resources endowments]. What has gone wrong with the rising expectations generated by the euphoria for independence? Why has rising expectations converged into increasing destructive frustration? Why are things falling apart and the centre unable to hold together? Why has development bypassed the continent? Why this or that? These and many related questions are indicative of something wrong with the governance system and leadership style, and passiveness of civil society in charting the right path for sustainable development, so that the continent can move from its present classification as a third world to a 'first world'. Since the end of the Cold War, there has been a systematic trumpeting of the message of sanitised governance, with respect for human rights and mass participation in decision-making as the index of development.

The Highly Indebted Poor Countries {HIPC} initiative was designed to assist very poor countries out of the doldrums of abject poverty. The United States inspired Millennium Challenge Account {MCA} has nothing to do with debt cancellations, but offered based on a country's level of democratisation and entrenchment of human rights. It is an initiative of the United States under President George Bush as a strategy to project the image of the United States as the champion of democracy world wide. Given United State's leading role in the HIPC initiative, countries that fail to accept the fundamental principles of democratic governance may be denied the offer. The two - HIPC and MCA - subjects African countries to initiate changes in their governance system and to attend to the plight of their people. How to go about meeting these challenging needs remain the question?

Who actually calls the shots in the democratisation restructuring process? Government institutions and political parties require structural changes to meet the challenges. Some countries required a complete overhaul. These countries will require re-orientation and a total attitudinal and mentality change, for example, that the days of monolithic one party system and dictatorial governance regime form is over. In addition, the processes of policy development must not be disjointed; they must be operated in a symbolic relationship and within the confines of the state-civil society- private sector interface. Leadership style and skills are needed to successfully pilot such major changes in society.

Look at the socio-political arena of Africa and check on some of the people calling the shots at various leadership levels. Do they have the sincerity, vision, savvy and charisma of Nkrumah, the modesty, selfishness and integrity of Nyerere, the courage and tenacity of Mandela, the Spartan temperance and bravely of Awolowo, Jomo Kenyatta and the charm and brilliance of Azikiwe; fighting zeal of Patrice Lumumba, Tom Mboya; the courage of Nasser, and many fallen heroes of the continent? Post-colonial Africa is awash with leaders who misruled their nations, misled their people and misused their resources. Leadership is influencing others to accomplish an objective or objectives in the process; the leader keeps the various components of the organisation steady and running so that the set objectives can be achieved. Here, stated in simple explanation of leadership, is the basic thing that leaders are need to do; To birth visions, take the organisation to new heights and ensure it stays alive and runs well [Kumuyi 2006:20]. This is Africa's dilemma. A dilemma best addressed by the people for their ultimate benefit.

A crystal ball is not needed to see that things are currently not going well in the African reconstruction, reinstitution and construction processes. Institutions and member countries are at war with poor economic management and non-progress in the political democratisation processes. There is an ongoing trans-African /transatlantic relation failing to address the needs of the people. The inability to resolve the problems created by the wave of political dispensation and the polarisation of the democratisation process between the 'old Africa' {undemocratic governance system) as exhibited by military regimes and monolithic party structure; and the 'New Africa' (opening up the political process, political pluralism and democracy) creates uncertainty on whether Africa is back on the right track, are just a few challenges to name. With the fall of the Soviet Union, leading to the collapse of the monolithic dominant one party system that stirred the affairs of the continent, the development of civil societies in Africa now injects emphasis for the necessity of examining the problematic of state, leadership and democracy in the continent within a new perspective, namely that of the irresistible rise of forces hoping to be less subjected by the dictates of state, authoritarian leaders and with liberated energies within society.

As for Africa's competitiveness in the global knowledge-base economy of the 21st century, the picture remains rather gloomy; the continent has yet to reach the productive and competitive edges in all sectors. Africa's population is increasing in spite of the HIV/AIDS pandemic; the labour force remains largely illiterate with no employment opportunities for the most active and productive population group – the youths. This questions the over population nature of the African continent. In reality, Africa is under-populated compared to its size. This is a continent that can take China, India, Europe, and Brazil to name a few countries. Compare the total population of these countries to that of Africa. The population of China and India to say the least, over shadows that of Africa many folds. The Democratic Republic of Congo (DRC) is bigger than Europe. The DRC is smaller in size compared to Sudan. Africa's problem is not over-population, but rather under-population. Therefore, the issue of underdevelopment should be located elsewhere. The obvious is that the continent is at the cross-road. Looking at the dimensions of Africa's crisis, political, social, economic, and cultural, deliberate or deceitful policy developmental initiatives have only produced limited successes if any at all compared with parts of the world.

To begin with, Africa is the only continent and region in modern time where life expectancy has dropped by over five percent since 1990. Since the lost decade of the 19980s, the economic vulnerability of the region has been brought to the fore. The majority of the population live on less that 1$USA dollar per day; The regional GNP per capital of Sub-Saharan Africa was 17.6% of the worlds GNP per capital in 1975 and by 1999 it had fallen to 10.5%. Generally, the continent goes on record as the only region in the world where per head of more than fifty percent of its population has fallen lesser than what it was at the time of independence. It is not surprising that the greater part of the population is suffering from abject misery and wanton poverty. Health care, shelter and other social amenities have not improved. The region is hard hit with the HIV/AIDS pandemic and other endemic diseases. Child mortality is on the increase with over 100 per 1000 live births. Over 35-40 percent of the population is malnourished. Conflicts of one kind or the other abound. Work ethics and moral continues to fall. How may people put eight hours of work daily? Wrong cultural values and belief systems are copied.

Majority of the people are unable to cultivate and promote ethical, moral values and habits that promote progress. But leaders talk of "greater achievement" programmes for whom when attitude to corruption, incompetence, clientelism and poverty reigns high and is even institutionalised. The continent is facing leadership crises. Aryittey [2002] notes that from 1957 Africa has had over 150 Heads of State and only five have relinquished power voluntarily {Senegal, Cameroon, Tanzania, Botswana and South Africa}. Few African countries permit limited criticism of government policies. The existence of despotic messianic civilian administration where the vanguards of independence became regal or feudal lords and preside over the worst forms of political abuses backed by the total absence of integrity, accountability, transparency and widespread bad governance makes the continent more vulnerable to external exploitation. Some countries like Egypt, Morocco, Sudan and Somalia illustrate the difficulties of expression of the little wish for autonomy vis-à-vis the state and ideological and religious dogma within a traditional political system. The wind of political liberalism following has not allowed the emergence of a vibrant civil society in some countries.

On the other hand, Lamour [2007:30] assertion is that: "in modern economic relations, mechanisms of protection and development of northern markets and industries, and of exploitation and marginalisation of developing countries are still present in North-South exchange strategies. The unjust distribution of income from developing countries' produce is clearly illustrated in the example of banana. While European consumers pay 1.99 to 2.99 euros for a kilo of apples from neighbouring Italy, France and Germany, next on the supermarket counter, a kilo of banana from far away as Costa Rica, Ecuador, Cameroon and Cote d'Ivoire cost just 0.99 to 1.90 euros. And from this reduced amount, only 10 to 15% goes to the producing countries while roughly 85-90% stays in Western hands –with 25% for shipping; 35-37% for the import-export companies; 6.5% for transportation in Europe; and about 14% for the shop owner. While European governments get 12-14% of the selling price through taxes, governments in the producing countries earn less than 1% in tax". Consequently, the continent remains perpetually poor. Poverty breeds many other disastrous effects, consequently jeopardising genuine economic take-off. There is no level playing field for African countries in the structure and functioning of the global economy. It can be argued that Africa's imbalance within the global economic and political system gives birth to "weak and failed states" on the continent.

The gravity of the situation is best represented by the following states: "In 1960, whatever parameters you look at, whether social or economic indicators, Africa has declined compared to the rest of the world, particularly when, measured against those parts of the world that were comparable to us at that time such as Asia. Why are we Sub-Saharan Africa failing while the rest of the world is succeeding, Africa is not less endowed as other parts of the world? I believe one word answers that question...Leadership" [Obasanjo 2000]. Adding his voice, former United Nations Secretary General, Kofi Annan made the following pronouncement in 1998. "It is time for Africans to hold their political leaders and not colonialism responsible for the civil wars and economic failures that ravage their lives". In the same vein, Amoako [2004] Executive Secretary of the Economic Commission for Africa underscore the importance the importance of good leadership at the highest level if the Africa is to attain sustainable growth and ensure serious poverty reduction. The search for solutions to Africa's problems is therefore a search for alternatives, which mobilise and develop African resources – human and natural resources. Developing countries, Africa in particular, practically produce at null tariff to meet needs of Western societies and to support Western economic development. As earlier indicated, comprehensive alternative priority policy strategies are needed: Alternative human and natural resources management strategies; alternatives to imported primary commodities – e.g. food, medicine, habits and attitudes; alternatives to externally controlled markets, and other policy issues.

Poor policy articulation and implementation should be held responsible for the current plight of the continent. Poor policy articulation and the lack of political will to develop creates a non-enabling environment which now triggers waves of economic immigrants who often risk pr loose their lives in search of greener pastures in the West. How then can we expect the agenda for "growth, employment and democratisation {GED} to be effectively implemented when the borderline between public bureaucracy and political part machinery remains blurred or the former receiving serious interferences and control from the latter and the population excluded from the political and decision-making processes? Political party interferences in public bureaucracy impede effective and efficient service delivery.

Last but not the least; Africa is facing a key challenge of ensuring strategic leadership and direction at the national, regional and continental levels. Importantly, African countries have to recognise the need for alliances that should work for the good of the people, nation, region and continent. While there are few positive signs for such collaborative and focused leadership providing strategic directions the absence of political pluralism and democracy reflecting in the progressive well-being of the people puts into question serious doubts about political leadership. Therefore, to accomplish this goal, Africa needs leaders with courage, integrity, character, love, sound judgement, technical competence and much more Africa needs developmentalist leaders in the post-cold war more than ever for reconstruction process. Nations that have experienced the most sustained transformation development have in different ways been developmentalist states, for example, countries known as Asian Tigers. And some of these countries have not been democratic. Some were far behind African countries in the earlier sixties. Where are these countries today? They have within a generation radically transformed their societies. It is now the envy even of the developed world. Where is Africa?

That is why during the 2007 celebrations marking Ghana's 50th birthday, as the first Black African country to gain political independence, three main objectives for the jubilee celebrations were, namely:-

- Celebrate and commemorate Ghana's landmark achievement as the first country in Black Africa to attain independence from colonial rule;
- Reflect on the evolution, development, achievements and draw backs of the country over the past fifty years; and
- To look forward to the future, to our vision of excellence in all fields of endeavour in the past fifty years toward the country's centenary birthday as a nation.

This statement on the occasion of Ghana's fifty years of independence is a clarion call to the rest of the continent to wake up from slumber and face the realities of political independence by taking appropriate priority strategic policy measures in shaping the future of the continent. Broadly stated, it is a statement that goes down into the annals of the continent's history as "Africa's Strategic Visionary Plan for Development Beyond the 21st Century". In my opinion, it is a milestone visionary 21st paradigm for development and progress; the attempt in the right path to make mal-development, marginalisation and poverty history; a call to Africa for complete mobilisation in the 21st century against forces that generates widespread poverty, corruption and inequality by the side of localised wealth and prosperity; to galvanise forces that destroys the environment and undermines human values and the rich cultural diversity of the people. Ghana on 6th March 2007, invited African countries to join in a new process engendered by dynamic, constructive and interactive action plans within and among all the African countries to better address the issues and realities affecting the continent. To a large extent, Ghana is setting a new leadership paradigm for Africa; call it the – Reconstituting and Reconstructing a New Developmental Africa - rekindling the hopes set by South Africa after the collapse of apartheid in 1994. This is the premises on which to envision the challenges of political and managerial leadership for change and development in Africa.

Envisaging the type of leadership the continent requires for its developmental take-off is what one may term 'transformational leadership'. This is so when one digs deep into Salim Ahmed Salim [Former Secretary General, OAU] statement that "Africa is littered with failed institutions, mostly due to bad leadership and that bad leadership factor is the centre of African development proposal". Adding his voice Thulani Gcabashe, Chief Executive, Eskom Holdings Ltd, states: "Africa needs a new generation of leaders to define and pursue a dynamic political and economic agenda for Africa". No doubt, quality leadership remains central in the socio-economic and political development agenda of the continent. Looking back at the time of independence of African countries, the income of in sub-Saharan Africa was twice that of both South and East Asia. In 2002, the reverse is the case as Sub-Saharan Africa has an average income below half that of East Asia, Latin America and the Middle East [NEPAD Report 2002]. Africa is the only continent in the world that has made no progress. Rather, it is declining and stagnating despite its rich natural resources which gave so much hope for a preposterous future in Africa at the dawn of independence in 1960s [NEAPAD Report 2003. What message does this convey?

The message is simply:{a} the continent is faced with daunting political, economic, social and cultural challenges; {b] no one ever envisaged at the time of independence five decades ago, the degree of backwardness that presently exists in the continent given the euphoria that existed at the time of shaking away colonial chains and now we are embraced with empty promises dished out by political leaders;{c}the continent's rich and abundant potentialities in terms of human resources and natural endowment: and{d}moderate or limited successes recorded in some African countries. These factors earned the pitched name for Africa as the "Dark and Forgotten Continent". The various underlying causes to the predicament of the continent points towards a single direction, the role of poor leadership – as the roadmap for Africa's underdevelopment quagmire [Dada 2007; Adei 2003; Bewaji 2003 Mkapa 2007, Annan 1989].Or as Nelson Mandela notes; "Africa is beyond bemoaning the past for its problems. The task of undoing the past is on the shoulders of African leaders themselves, with support of those willing to join in the continental renewal". In Africa, "Leadership is a cause; and everything else is effect". Therefore, Adei [2003] asserts within the parlance of nation-building as: "Systematic improvement in the Political Economic, Social and Cultural well-being of a people within a geographical entities or countries". Adding that leadership has failed in Africa in four broad dimensions, namely:

- Stable and acceptable political order;
- Improvement in the material welfare of the citizenry;
- Social cohesion, conflict prevention and peaceful resolution of conflicts; and
- Cultural development via positive time orientation and attitude to work, savings, consumption and investment habits, meritocracy etc.

Alluding to the importance of quality leadership role in nation-building, Munroe [1993] states: "when ever a nation lacks quality, legitimate and just leaders, national deterioration occurs. Quality leadership is a key to prosperous and peaceful life and nation". Are the leaders looking towards that direction? We all wonder? Why have African leaders and the governing elites developed inertia and a nonchalant towards given a human touch to the continent? Why are the leaders so insensitive to the plight of their people? Why the leaders must trod the world-over with a begging cap in hand? Why should the viruses of conflicts, hatred, ethnic divide, poverty and corruption overtake the virtues of democratic governance system? Though no individual alone leads a nation, it is important to stress the effective exercise of leadership function in the form of setting a vision, developing an agenda and mobilising human and natural resources in the realisation of the vision. An important determinant factor in the rise and fall of a nation is the quality of its leadership. These underscore the difference in the Newly Industrialised Countries of Asian and African regions. The sordid development history of Africa south of the Sahara and north of the Limpopo should be sought in the gargantuan development leadership failure. The emergence of a democratic developmental state on the continent should be able to satisfy three overlapping circles of conditions, namely:

- Publicly adopting a strategic developmentalist ideology and mobilising forces towards its realisation;

- Adopting a developmental rhetoric approach without taking concrete measures for achieving developmental goals would be a serious flaw and betrayal of people's trust; Africa is not ready for another disappointment of rising expectations of the independence years;

- African countries must establish functional structures, ensure relative autonomy as well as promote social and economic actors without which the developmental state will degenerate into a soft/failed / weak and predatory state;

- The state must be people-oriented and societal embedded: without social embeddedness, the state becomes predatory as it is now.

It should be noted that the failures of leadership, development and democratic governance to the deterioration of quality livelihood breeds insecurity and religious fanatics, making the continent a fertile soil for crime. Unfortunately, the ruling political regimes and leaders prioritise their own well-being over the goals of the general well-being of the people. They equally fail in adopting a development strategy based on inclusiveness - partnership, participation and benefit-sharing between the various stakeholders - state, civil society and the private sector, including the donor communities. While the state remains the main authority, we equally witness situations were the state is authoritative without being authoritarian; relatively autonomous without being fully autonomous, and sometimes taking some unpopular decisions without being subjected to the shocks of political alterations of power. Africa is embracing economic liberalism without economic reforms; democratisation without political reforms towards opening the political space more democracy.

Many inter-related issues are contributing factors to the current state of underdevelopment in Africa. Nyamunga [2007] catalogues some of the contributing factors, as:-

- Firstly, both governance systems and physical infrastructure inherited by African governments from the colonial governments at independence were not suitable for the new governments;

- Secondly, most of the African leaders in the 1970s were despots who were more interested in looting the wealth of their countries than in developing them;

- Thirdly, Africans failed to diversify the economic base from a wholly primary commodity producer to a manufacturing one;

- Fourthly, the perpetual armed conflicts on the continent have generally scared away investors who view Africa as not a very safe place for investment;

- Fifthly, Africa has suffered heavy brain drain due to lack of attractive opportunities at home.

ORGANISATION

The paper is organised around the following major sub-themes. "Theoretical framework", which sets out the theoretical framework based on 'transformational leadership theory; 'trait theory' and 'system theory'; Leadership seen within the context of "The Age of Rising Expectation": "The Age of Delusion": "The New Agenda": "The Age of Renascent of Africa": "Conclusion and Proactive Strategic Policy Measures". The first part takes a historical run-down of independence and the immediate years of self-rule. The second looks at the state of disenchantment. The third addresses the emerging agenda. The fourth looks at emerging issues of Pan-Africanism under the umbrella of a Renascent Africa. The last explores the urgent need of developing a new brave Africa with leadership play a vital role in uniting and giving a sense of direction to the populace and calling on the people to positively respond to the new clarion call for mindset, change and development.

THEORETICAL FOUNDATION

The most acceptable theoretical premises of departure is that of "Transformational Leadership Theory", which maintains that people can choose to become leaders, by learning about the art and science of leadership through formal and informal means. To this can be added the "Trait Theory" which is similar to one known as the "Great Events Theory" which builds on the existence of innate leadership qualities, and attributes the emergence of a person as leader to some great events, which help unlock his/her potentials and puts them into action [Kumuyi 2006:11]. These theories can be analysed from the perspective of the struggle for independence, attaining independence, and post-colonial development activities showing that these countries had to some extent come of age or attained maturity from colonial slavery and to face the challenges that awaited each country. The conceptual framework further builds on the fluidity of two theories that directly or indirectly derailed the continent. The first is the concept of modernisation, tied on the principle of economic development as the central issue. One can also add the "system theory framework", where the environment, inputs, conversion process, outputs and feedback related to and interact with one another in [see Figure 1: The Administrative System]. An entire set of these elements and their interactions is called "an administrative system".

Sharkansky [1972] notes: a system is not simply the administrative unit that is contained in the conversion process. An administrative system is the combination of the administrative unit and all of the elements and process which interact with the unit: that is, the {a} environment within which the administrative unit operates and which influences and is influenced by the unit: and the {b} inputs to and {c} outputs from the unit which are connected to each other by the {d} conversion process and by {e} feedback mechanisms. AA system such as this is a useful framework for treating individual items it focuses attention not merely on a simple description of discrete parts, but on the importance and relationship of these parts to one another.

By thinking about political and managerial leadership within public administration in a systems framework we are bound to ask about the relevance of the individual components. What implications for inputs-outputs are to be found in the various features of the conversion process? How does the character of the conversion process respond to inputs from the environment? What kind of constraints over outputs is exercised by the amount of resources that come into the conversion process from the environment? This kind of questioning establishes the relevance of public administration to politics, leadership, managerial skills, and economics and to other features of its environment that interest us as political scientist and as citizens [see Easton 1965]. The input-output system analysis creates in-depth comparative analytical studies showing how leaders respond to different kinds of inputs and how outputs vary with the nature of administrative and leadership activities.

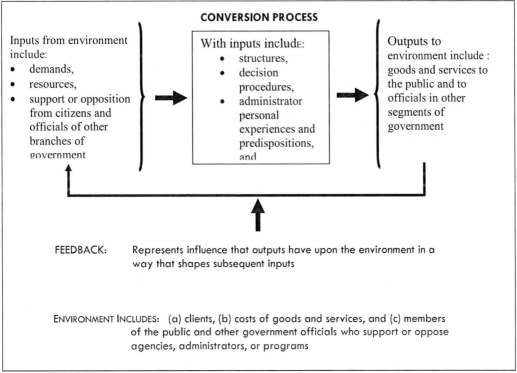

Figure 1. The administrative System.

To begin with, the struggle for independence was at the same time a struggle for economic development, democratisation and quality livelihood. Western economist had a field day in using Africa as the laboratory for testing their theories and models of development [Falola 1955; Voss 1973:10]. In the process of testing they equally exploited as well as solidified their economic and political hegemony over these countries. The second was the notion that Africa's development depended on the importation of western human power to transform its administrative structures. These beg an important question: why did they not develop the necessary Africa human capacity and administrative restructuring during their rule.

A major irony before independence was the belief that with international division of labour and comparative advantage, Africa would witness growth in the sales of its raw materials in exchange for imports. With the transition to an independent status, it was quickly realised that the theory did not hold. The argument of the modernisation theorist was for Africa to reform its institutions to aspire to become like the West, through a process of modernisation whereby indigenous ways of life would be replaced with Western models. Modernisation theories failed to deliver the goods. Many Africa leaders bought the ideological orientation of the modernisation theory. Africa failed to develop. Leadership derailed or influenced by the contending forces of the period. The rivalry among superpowers spilled over into Africa generating tensions and conflicts. Some countries were able to walk the tightrope, and some could not. Leadership was absent. Africa was unable to interact within the international community dominated by western influence on its own terms. The international actors remained stronger and Africa's ability to exert influence on international politics is weak.

This failure was severely attacked in the 1960s and 1970s by the Marxist arguing that improper international trade: dependency and capitalism were the primary constraints to development in Africa. Marxism held great promise for these transitional polities: but was soon scorned in the 1990s due to it's over gripped and heavily centralised nature of the governance system. African states adopting the centralised governance system that failed in fulfilling the rising expectations of their populace in respect of employment, education, health care and other social services. The virtues of the system were not promoted to address the needs of the people. Rather, the vices were exploited to bring greater benefits to those who controlled the spectra of power. The conversion between 'input and output" in the leadership and administrative system failed to work for the benefit of the people. The vanguards of independence that were good at securing political independence from the colonial powers did not succeed in delivering development creating room for military dictators and corrupt civilian leaders lacking the character, capacity and commitment to deliver national development but geared towards self-accumulation. These together with other factors contributed in derailing the emergence of a developmentalist state.

Leadership is the summary of all the issues discussed in this paper. The effective leader of an administrative unit or society uses his/her authority, communication, and incentives to guide and control subordinates. S {he} puts all together. It is already evident; however, that good leadership is not a simple process. There are various bases of authority, plus different kinds of incentives and communications. Authority may be questioned, communication can go astray; and the available incentives may not satisfy the desires of subordinates. There is no assurance that the holder of a formal position will be an effective leader. Africa is dire need of transformational leadership, how the leaders affect followers in respect of:-

- Increasing their awareness of task importance and value;
- Getting them to focus first on team or organisational vision, rather than their own interest;
- Activating their high-order needs. and to bring out the best in people;
- Democratic leadership that respects people and encourages self-management, autonomous teams and entrepreneurial units.

The absence of these together with other factors contributed in derailing the emergence of a developmentalist state. At least six things happened following the attainment of independence.
- First, domestic political scene could not be properly stabilized;
- Second, the centralised nature of the political system created room for a dysfunctional governance system, and party leaders went amok with power to the advantage of the West;
- Third, international affairs were neither conducted in a beneficial manner: which the western nations exploited to their benefits;

- Fourth, political and economic integration failed to materialise, leaving the continent disunited, disintegrated, and fragile to external exploitation;
- Fifth, poor leadership role paved the way for military regimes that ensued thus compromising both the liberty and freedom of the people and the genuine political emancipation of the continent;
- Sixth, the development of the continent was hijacked and compromised. National integration could not be realised. Ethnic hegemonic forces took control, with diversity seen as a liability rather than asset or instrument for development.

Africa has yet to overcome initial concerns; and to seek endurable solutions to the viruses plaguing democratisation, economic growth and quality living standards. It is therefore imperative that leadership development model be adopted to guide leadership development programmes at all levels - local, regional, national and continental; and to ensure the development of a crop of leaders across Africa who share common leadership orientation and seeing African leadership issues from a common and same perspective. Call such approach as shared leadership which may also imply "partnership-as-leadership; distributed leadership, and community leadership". According to Moxley [2000], the idea of leadership as partnership suggests the basic concept of two or more sharing power and joining forces to move forward accomplishment o shared goals. African leaders and manager should learn to share leadership role with other stakeholders. But shared leadership does not imply abdicating the formal leader's accountability. It does imply a shared responsibility for problem identification, solutions and action-taking and building a new culture of attitude, work ethics, morals, inclusion and skills to build a successful developmental state capable of competing in the fast emerging competitive global knowledge-based economy of our time.

THE AGE OF RISING EXPECTATIONS

This period saw the emergence of both a state of "hope and despair", and a state of "great confusion", - characterised by which development path for the continent? The new states were forced to grapple with issues concerning the continent's transition from a so-called 'backward' society into a 'modern' society. Some visionary and progress leaders advocated a strong and united Africa, under a centralised political command. Other leaders did not embrace the idea. Nkrumah's speech at the founding of the Organisation of African Unity {OAU} in Addis Ababa, Ethiopia, on 25th May 1953 [see also Akyaaba Addai-Sebo, 2007:10-11] espouses the kind of develop-mental leadership needed at the early stages of the continent's independence. Leaders with duties of taking the organisation somewhere and ensuring it got there. Leadership conceptualised in terms of change and progress. If no change is contemplated, no revolution is desired, and of course, leaders are not needed. But if dramatic or drastic turnaround and break from the normal ways of doing things, system change, for example, someone is needed to make things happen – a leader. Africa needs a push in the right direction, hence the call for leaders backed with managers and administrators to ensure that things are properly done

The period could also be classified as the 'age of euphoria'. African 'intellectualism' or 'professiarism' emerged up to the late 1970s [Tadesse 1999; Rashid 1994; Bujra 1994;

Mkanadawire]. Intellectuals sough to give scientific and object credence to political leadership through the affirmation of the nationalist ideal and rejection of imperial intellectual domination and neo-colonial machinations. Political leadership feel on the wayside. Managerial leadership skill not emerge either. The intellectual corps was split, disenchanted and persecuted by political leaders. It triggered a wave of the 'brain drain' phenomenon. By the 1980s an average of 23000 qualified academic staff were emigrating from Africa every year [Zeleza 1998]. That phenomenon has not abated. It is worse today as the continent exports both its natural resources and trained human power.

Unfortunately, 'political' orientation failed to marry with an equal 'economy' orientation {i.e. economic development and democratisation} that could possibly translate into improving the quality of living standards of the people. Managerial leadership skills were absent to usher the right path to industrialisation and proper house keeping economics. The Lagos Plan of Action was late in coming. It should have acted as a catalyst for a developmentalist African take-off. The Breton Woods Conglomerates {BWC} took the initiative to pressurised African leaders into accepting the Structural Adjustment Programme {SAP} which marked a defeat of the emergence of a "developmentalist state" - a defeat from which Africa has yet to recover. But Africa needed a comprehensive priority restructuralisation policy agenda {CPRPA} with a human-face. This was not forthcoming. The ECA Alternative to the SAP was not received by the architects of Bretton Woods SAP Agenda. So also The Popular Participation Agenda (Arusha Declaration} was not well received in the West. Africa's Lost Decade of the 1980s laid the foundation for the destruction of the socio-economic transformation of the region.

The imposition of SAP; failure of a United African Front (political and economic), absence of democratic governance system, and he exclusion of the people in the decision-making process portrayed the political weaknesses and poor leadership skills of African leaders. The immediate post-colonial period characterised by the power struggle among western countries created room for "opportunism, unflappable sycophancy, trenchant collaboration and have allowed tyranny to become entrenched. Leaders such as Doe, Mobutu, and other military dictators legitimised their regimes by buying off and co-opting African academics for a pittance" [Ayittey 1996:35]. The politics of survival played on the consciousness of these scholars. Of course, these leaders succeeded with the help of the West. The West was happy to see the collapse of the continent as they manufactured and sustained dictators of various shades on the continent. In Cameroon, accused of being an illiterate. Ahidjo went into the university, co-opted university lecturer into government. The system continues with very serious consequences for the country. Scholarly and critical objective discussions evade the country. The citadel of knowledge bowed to the whims and caprices of the political machinery of the country. Today, the intellectual class can hardly and objective proposes valid solutions to the plethora of problems plaguing the country. Every lecturer is waiting to be appointed. A kind of vicious circle emerges with the lecturers being their on enemies as well as thwarting the democratisation process. Critical thinking is evaded. The state is often misled by the desire of selfish interests. To say the least, the Cameroon intellectual class, are more politicians that the politicians for the very wrong reasons and though endowed with the requisite knowledge and skills, fail to put in place without bias, the necessary socio-political, economic and administrative needed for national development. Seeing these weaknesses the ruling political class inject ethnic hegemonic forces to further divide and exploit the elites.

The Mamdani's, Ake's, Mkandawire's, Mafeje's, Achebe's, Soyinka's, Ngugi wa Thiong'o's, Mazrui's, Zeleza's and thousands of other free thinking African intellectuals made impact towards injecting reason into the policy approach and strategies adopted by African leaders who failed to listen. Rather, malicious policy strategies were mounted against progressive African scholars who in the majority of cases embraced the "brain drain" phenomenon, dissatisfied, disappointed and disillusioned as they saw the noble course of the continent hijacked by diverse forces. Africa was moving from "state-building" to "state failure", and "state collapse". Africa is yet to recovery from the lost period. Without such recovery, it is difficult to see how the people will benefit from their God given resources to improve their quality of life.

THE AGE OF DELUSION

Resistance from African leaders to read reason into the views of African intellectuals created an era of disenchantment and disillusionment as intellectuals blamed the leaders for "betraying the nationalist struggle". As earlier noted, the alienation of African intellectuals deepened in the 1980s contributing to the continent's lost decade. Added to this was the fact that African leaders began eschewing the malicious agenda of the Bretton Woods Conglomerates that the continent did not need higher education for its transformation process. Universities were starved, making the citadel of excellence, free-thinking and scholarship and relevance non-relevant to the socio-economic transformation of the continent. Government policies could not be influenced by national priorities, but by the hidden obnoxious agenda of the west through the auspices of the World Bank Institutions.

The society was decaying rapidly and destructive frustration became the order of the day. To a large extent, "key elements of civil society relished the tribulations of African intellectuals" [Mkandawire 2005:32]. One saw a kind of un-ceremonial withdrawal o the intellectual body from the development debate. The men in uniform and civilian dictators had taken over the leadership role of the continent. The power of the bullet reigned supreme as against the power of the ballot box. Civil society was held captive with selective handouts dictating the pace of development. The politics of the belly [Bayart 1993] was in control, and political leaders used this to sustain their stay in power. The phenomenon of presidents for life was institutionalised.

State failure had attained the highest stage in Africa's political development. Failure in state governance was gradually sipping into managerial leadership failure. Most of the industrial settings were state owned. Established corrupt practices in government were transferred to this sector. State parastatals became the rewarding arena for those who toed incomprehensive government policies of bleeding the society to death. The fusion political party machinery and state bureaucracy made it difficult drawing the line between political party activities and public bureaucracy as the instrument for providing quality services delivery to society. Equal opportunities, shared-benefits and responsibilities were sidelined. Wealth was accumulated by a few. Billions of monies siphoned abroad only for the state to borrow what rightfully belonged to the people at exorbitant interest rates.

The borrowed sums were never ploughed into productive activities, but further stolen. The debt burden was to haunt and destroy the continent's future process of development.

Debt cancellations under the Highly Indebted Poor Countries {HIPC} are further siphoned in the case of Cameroon [see Ngalame 2007:2]. Seeing the failure of SAP which was not human-focused. The HIPC was an initiative designed to right the faults of SAP and to help very poor countries out of the doldrums of abject poverty. Beneficiary countries were to enjoy debt, relief and payments for such debts used for development. Unfortunately, government was slow in shaping the public sector to underpin the edifice of capitalism emerging as the global economic mainstay. The absence in the interface between state-civil society-private sectors contributes to the public sector being underdeveloped and private sector engraved with poor productivity and non-competitive in the local and global markets

Development within the international arena was not working in favour of failed Africa leadership. Towards the end of the 1980s, whistle blowing came from once herald system of governance which African countries had embraced as the answer to modernisation, capitalist exploitation and dependency. Countries behind the iron curtain suddenly turned their backs to the Marxist centralised governance system. A new lease of life was injected into Africa's civil society, which began demanding an all-inclusive role in the governance system. The issue of nation-building occupied centre-stage but dependency on "handouts" had eaten deep into the marrow of the body politic of African countries. The public sector popularly acclaimed as the engine of growth was not developed. Conditionalities basically dictated "African economic policy"; the debt noose was being drawn tighter for economies whose growth was not anaemic [Mkandawire 2005:45]

The West suddenly discovered that these conditionalities had to do with 'democratisation', which they had overlooked in the earlier stages. The struggle for political pluralism and democracy had taken grip on the continent. Africa could not be left out in this new bandwagon for system change. Advancement in science and technology accelerated the process as information and communication technologies {ICTs} added new impetus in advancing the process for system change and improving the quality of output of the system. The governance system could be modernising through the use of information technologies {IT}, though it did pose problems of lying off of some of the labour force. With good governance, some other opportunities were open, which included training facilities, a very liberal political environment and a democratic dispensation facilitating long-term planning market for skilled labour, backed by a vibrant private and financial sector offering opportunities to access loans for investment in human capital development and expanding the private sector.

With the emergence of ICTs, governments no longer had monopoly in the control of information. A new 'big brother' was now watching and influencing the pattern, speed, depth and trend in the democratisation process. The collapse of the Soviet Union and its satellite states was eminent. A new avalanche of development approach gripped Africa, calling for visionary political leadership and managerial skills responding to the changing and challenging features of the 21st century. The intellectual class could also be faulted. It had acquired special status and taste of western nostalgia, consumption pattern and life-style alien to the people, rather than embracing western organisation skills, productive techniques, work ethics, the cost and value time [Mazrui 1993:119] and educating their less fortunate country people on such issues as cardinal secrets and strength for development.

A new era of liberty was emerging. Society was caught between the trappings of holding on to the dominant one party system or embracing the new democratisation wave giving greater freedom, liberty and participation at all levels. To quote Judge Learned Hand

[1960:190], "liberty lies in the hearts of men and women; when it dies there, no constitution, no law, no court can save it; no constitution, no law can even do much to help it". Thus, building or rebuilding faith in the idea of the state requires a similar transformation in mentality as much as it does in politics, leadership and managerial skills. "For government to make well-informed decisions on matters of public policy, it needs to strengthen institutional mechanisms and improve strategies which are vital for sound policy development, implementation and evaluation programmes" [Buor Daniel 2007].Human capacity must be developed, fully and properly utilised

THE NEW AGENDA

Bringing down the "Berlin Wall" signalled a new dawn for Africa. The wind of democratisation and the resurrection of the lost development path could be seen twinkling at the end of the tunnel. The struggle for political pluralism and democracy bore fruits with the collapse of the apartheid system in South Africa. The excluded majority became part of the governing and decision-making process. Dictators after dictators crumbled in many arts of the continent. Political pluralism was gaining grounds. Civil society was becoming more vibrant. A new sense of leadership emerged embracing the politics of "inclusion, reconciliation, consensus, diversity as strength and asset for development". The emergence of the New South Africa rekindled the lost hope of the continent.

The challenge is to sustain this new wind of change [Forje 2004] by having a leadership style that stands to defend and protect the interest of the continent. For example, what priority strategic agenda exists for the 53 African states and members of the African Union in addressing the boycott machinery put in place by the West to thwart the sovereignty and rights of the people of Zimbabwe? Mugabe's policy might be blamed. But has Africa even considered that his actions are designed to liberate the continent and in the long-term interest of every black nation? Why must the West have to control African economies? Why must Africa be poor in the midst of plenty? Apparently, this is not an endorsement of Mugabe. We have to face the realities and challenges of our time if a new agenda is to be articulated and aggregated in the best interest of the continent. Leadership must work within the environment of bringing hope and a brighter future to the population.

Some form of committed trend towards greater focus on the problems of democratisation could be seen here and there. Yet issues of deepening economic crises had to be addressed to give credibility to an emerging governance system. A new form of political leadership was in the making. The intellectuals were back on the drawing board to rekindle the developmentalist ideals. The argument was clear: the problem with African economies was not 'market distortions', but 'state-society-private sector' relations or issues of 'governance'. There were crosscutting issues that could not be evaded in addressing the socioeconomic transformation of Africa [Ahmed 1990:1] and overcoming fear. Outstanding here were issues of leadership, national integration, unity, seeking common grounds, inclusive and open government with the obligations of extending benefits of its output functions and gains in productivity and growth to a larger number of people. But the proper stage and environment had to be created in linking theory with practice. To avoid features of democratic failure trough the politics of ethnic hegemonic tendencies, exclusion and marginalisation of the rule of law, the weakness of political parties and the absence of a vibrant civil society and productive private sector, the suppress of civil liberties, the imbalances between the bureaucracy and the executive or the domination of the bureaucracy by the executive and political party, some new grounds had to be found to ensure the retention of the right political and economic roadmap on the continent's transformation process.

Since the 1990s, political leadership was forced to address issues of 'development and democratisation' from a new perspective in the nation-building process. The continent is starved of right leadership. The dearth of leaders is the cause of Africa's misery. Africa now needs political leaders and managers to pilot the continent through the stormy clouds of globalisation and knowledge based global economy propelled by the unstoppable forces of ICTs. Leaders with the following characteristics and capacities to exhibit in full the "7Ds", namely: {dream, decision, direction, design, development, defence and discipline]. Taking just the first, 'dream' – the continent needs leaders to birth vision. Visions are dreams about a desired future – for example: Nkrumah's vision of a "United Africa" which was shared by Nnamdi Azikiwe [1936] of Nigeria in the concept of "renascent Africa", or the emerging "African Renaissance" agenda propagated by Mbeki [1998; and Mbeki 2004].

It takes a leader with courage and stamina to 'conceive, characterise and crystallise the change" so desired and "construct" the mechanism for its realisation. Africa's development is slow because it lacks enough leaders able to conduct diagnostic examinations of its moribund institutions, and surgical leaders to undertake the necessary strategic surgical developmental operations. The threat of poverty, corruption and bad governance is real and this thwarts the developmental process of the continent. Therefore, Africa needs solid defensive mechanisms to protect society from the crippling effects of internal and external sabotage, and an aggressive attacking forward to launch the necessary offensive and offer a new sense of direction and instil hope, faith, confidence and trust in the people for a brighter dawn.

Being at war with underdevelopment, poverty, corruption, and exploitation, a leader is needed to give a sense of direction and marshal the necessary forces for the defence of the society. Given the very nature of the African society, discipline remains vital to ensure compliance to work ethics, motivate and sustain productivity; it is discipline that builds society's reputation and output. Articulate leadership is required to hand out the juicy carrot, but also ready to wield the limber rod to ensure social justice and shared responsibility, if the continent is to claim the 21st century and be a part not apart. To claim the 21st century means both political and economic freed. This statement begs the lonely question. How free is Africa sixty years after the attainment of independence? How economically and culturally free is the continent? How free will the descendants of this generation. African societies will respond in diverse ways to penetrating European pressure and aggregation. Yet it requires a united front and common approaches to putting the continent on the right path to sustainable development; to make underdevelopment, corruption and poverty history.

Following the rise and collapse of the monolithic party structure and the return to political pluralism, the developed countries had benefit in the degree of manoeuvrability of African states, undermined their sovereign authority and lack of ability to develop the priority roadmap and direction of social development and context of socio-economic policy which had facilitated the institutionalisation of predatory oligarchy and a neo-patrimonial state where the rulers' subjective interests had erected the objective interests of the state and the people within their personal images and interests. Constructing a post-colonial, post-cold war and post-SAP state required critical and objective inputs from the citadel of knowledge if Africa is to develop and to do so democratically.

ENTER WHISTLE BLOWING

The return to critical scientific thinking, open discourses and cross-fertilisation of knowledge in mindset especially redressing existing 'top-down' to 'bottom-up' political and social engineering thinking could not be avoided. The resurrection of critical thinking initiated by the Dons of the University of Makerere in the 1960s and 1970s was imperative, particularly in responses to globalisation, which was the key factor in determining the trajectory of the state either towards, or farther away, from "democratic developmentalism'. Was the emerging political dispensation willing to contained a new relationship between political leaders and the academic community?

During the independence struggle, African intellectuals like Nkrumah, Azikiwe, Nyerere, Obote, Kaunda, Cabral and many others had a clearly-defined political agenda: that of assuming the reigns of government of African states. In pursuit of this noble ideal, they secured the support or connivance of the traditional elite and masses. Dlamini [2007] argues: "African intellectuals through putting an end to colonialism and all the evils associated with it, unfortunately, beyond these ideals, it has been observed that the intellectuals had little conception of the kind of society they wanted to build in the immediate post-independence era. They had internalised notions or concepts of Europeanisation or modernisation but had neither clear-cut goals nor a blueprint for people-oriented development. Although African intellectuals made reference to socio-economic development and / or national progress, they did not specify how such a vision for the future would be brought about". [See also Leys 1982].

Had the intellectual community put on the true thinking cap of being a citadel of knowledge free from political biases? Yes and No as the situation varied differently from one country to another. In Nigeria for example, in spite of the strings of military governance and economic setbacks, the university dons and the intellectual community stood its grounds not be derailed by political leaders. In Cameroon, university dons were an inherent part of the ruling party to an extent that they endorsed they endorsed the candidature in person of Paul Biya {CPDM} calling on society to vote massively in support of the incumbent president in the 2004 presidential elections. Why did Cameroon intellectuals take such a stand? How has this affected the democratisation process of the country?

Why is there always a strain relationship between the academic community, political leadership and the bureaucracy? The unfortunate relationship thwarts progress towards the attainment and consolidation of a developmental state that ensures efficient, effective management and quality service delivery for the ultimate objective on the focused goal of improving the livelihood of the people. The underlying factor constraining the relation is clearly articulated in the phenomenon advanced by Bayart [1993] – 'the politics of the belly' – what could be described as the 'politics for survival' in the case of Cameroon, given the declined state of the economy since 1985. Economic deterioration has not affected only Cameroon. All African countries have gone through worse scenarios without succumbing to embracing one party over the other. How free is their value judgement in parting critical and objective knowledge to students? A proper understanding between political leadership, the administrative machinery and university dons ensures creates a healthy atmosphere. Whistle blowing on the part of university dons should be seen as a system of "check and balances" awakening society on the failures of government as well as calling on civil society to take its share of responsibilities.

Leys observation is that some African political elites saw politics, or its involvement in it, not as an opportunity to advance the public interest, but more as an opportunity that guaranteed fame, adventure and the promotion of their narrow self-interests" [1982:26]. And Dlamini [2007] concludes that "unable to craft its own socio-political, economic and administrative apparatus for development in the immediate post-independence era, the political elite continued to use the machinery of government inherited from colonialism, hence the so-called colonial legacy persisted several decades after independence". Attempts to restructure capitalist ideology into socialist-orientated ideology like "Ujamaa" and egalitarian-based rural development in Tanzania did not go down in certain intellectual circles as some of these intellectuals place heavy emphasis on the acquisition and retention of political power, making it impossible to achieve most of the goals of development in post-independence era.

It is not surprising that many people in and out of government turned their direction towards the armed forces for a more logical and internal as well as efficient alternative to the political elite. In some case, the armed forces allied with the ruling elites in maintaining the status quo – Cameroon being a typical example. To a large extent, this explains the piecemeal approach and attitude towards the advent of the democratisation bandwagon. And why 'a significant portion of the energies of the state, politician, government officials and public institutions were and are often devoted to the struggle for power and towards keeping particular regimes in power and / or office. As a result, inadequate time or energy is left for the challenges and demands of development" [Dlamini 2007]. Ruling elite –civil society relationship is not of the best. This does not argue well for the entrenchment of democratic values and management principles in society.

The ruling elites fail to understand the realities that the development process in Africa requires foot soldiers and generals working hand-in-gloves and without such cooperation the fundamental issues plaguing the continent cannot be solved. "African leaders did not foresee, understandably, the invincible forces that have given impetus to the present socio-political and economic crises, including the crisis of leadership. African societies and nations are facing a leadership crisis, which arises mainly from the abandonment, by leaders, of the basic mission of leadership, in preference for themselves being served. The basic mission of leadership as being to serve, but instead we see leaders seeking services from those they are supposed to serve We also see pervasive styles and forms of leadership that demand obedience and subservience from the led" [Dlamini op.cit.].

It is vital that ruling elites should be more sensitive to the sufferings of the masses; to corruption; to poverty and mismanagement of the resources and wealth of the continent. It is only by reverting to the authentic mission of leadership – serving the people – that confidence, trust, legitimacy and credence can be restored in the governing class and democratic institutions. This the greatest challenge facing the rise of renaissance Africa. Whistle blowing is fundamental in this process. Generals and foot soldiers should draw closer and avoid the Actonian dictum that 'power corrupts and absolute power corrupts absolutely". There is growing optimism that Africa, can after all make it; the continent's socio-economic and political challenges cane be adequately addressed, via a democratic process and total mobilisation of the various stakeholders by embracing the fundamental principles of accountability, transparency, inclusion, social justice rule of law and good governance system: Africa can be better positioned to take its rightful place in the global community of independent nations. Apparently, the Community of Democracies {CoD} will be meeting in Africa, Mali November 2007 for the first time [Forje 2007]. This is also an opportunity for countries within the continent to open up to the democratic process. It is time for the continent to start strengthening political leadership and managerial capacity for development. "Africans should walk the talk" [Isimbabi 2004].Africa must take the total responsibilities for is destiny. "While the international community can provide much needed assistance, it is unrealistic to count on it to free African countries from bad leadership" [Isimbabi 2004]. Good leadership must generate from within the continent, having the support, legitimacy, trust and confidence of its constituency. Importantly, the international community must stop supporting bad leadership and sustaining dictatorial and authoritarian regimes or governments.

THE AGE OF RENASCENT AFRICA

Post-cold war Africa rekindles a new age of development. The insurrection of Pan-Africanism propounded by founding leaders like Nkrumah, Nyerere, Nasser, Keita. Kenyatta, Ben Bella, Luthuli, Azikiwe and thousand others. With varying degrees of commitment to the cause or even out of political expediency, as African nationalists, they could not be anything but Pan-Africanist [Shivji 2006:209]. For Nyerere, "African nationalism is meaningless, if anachronistic, and is dangerous, if it is not at the same time Pan-Africanism" [1963; 1967:104]; or Nkrumah's statement: "Ghana's independence is meaningless without the total liberation of Africa", portrays a vision and desire for a free and united continent that is being resurrected today under the banner of Renaissance Africa. Facing Mount Kenya, Mount Cameroon and others constitute challenges to fight fear, poverty, corruption and underdevelopment.

We need leaders for a Renaissance Africa that first converts the ideological orientation into the politics of quality life for the African people and giving primacy to inclusive politics, administration and democratic governance system. Second, Renaissance African leaders who see the process as a 'bottom-up' ideological orientation of putting pressure on states and monitoring state actions rather than a 'top-bottom' statist programme that fails to put people at the centre of development. Third, Renaissance African leaders who must gun for uncompromising approach as well as distance themselves from the position that development for the continent can only be achieved from western orientation: and that globalisation offers the best opportunities and must come from the west. Fourth, Renaissance African leaders must seek an organisational home in existing African movements and professional organisation to drive home the message of unity, development, cooperation and democratic governance. Fifth, leaders who see Renaissance Africa as a continental commitment: acting both regionally, continentally, anti-imperialist and [pro-people. Sixth, recall that the record of colonialism, in terms of the development of African colonies, was not impressive, hence the held perception that the demise of colonial rule would result in the elimination of poverty and underdevelopment – the euphoria for a rising expectation that never was, turned into destructive frustration. Corruption, abject poverty and other ills have proved difficult, if not impossible to eradicate, in that development process has benefit a select few at the expense of the vast majority of the population who continue to survive at the fringes of human existence. That the current situation is even worse in some countries than before independence accounts for the increasing, frustration, disenchantment, disillusion despair and apathy shown in the democratisation process by the population bypassed by the development process. "The general feeling is that the present socio-political and economic order is not what was expected from independence, thus raising the fundamental question to the underlying causes of the socio-political, economic and administrative paralysis that has engulfed the African continent"{Dlamini 2007].

These four broad transitional periods ['The Age of Rising Expectations: The Age of Delusion: The New Agenda; The Age of Renascent Africa"], of the continent is depicted by the following developments:

- Massive democratic shift in the structure of African governments from monolithic to political party pluralism to a gradual return to the one party system as reflected in many legislative assemblies, Cameroon for example;
- Non-progress in arresting poverty, corruption and poor quality services delivery;
- Concerns about establishing an impartial public bureaucracy – completely detached from the whims and caprices of political party hegemonic influences and dictates of an ethnic hegemonic leadership;
- Non-incorporation of both civil society and the private sector in the development process;
- Absence of visionary political leadership and managerial skills to push forward a developmental agenda;
- Articulating a concerted, constructed, comprehensive and inclusive policy strategy as road map for the future of the continent;
- Perception of the Opposition as Government in waiting; not as enemy to national cohesion and sustainable development.

CONCLUSION

It is clear that modern African state has exhibited many lapses and failings. The situation has to be corrected. First, government and leadership have failed to acquire legitimacy and credibility; and in most cases, the basis of power legitimacy lies in exclusion and violence. Strange enough, most of these governments started with huge support form the masses in the early years of independence – the [euphoria of rising expectations' soon degenerated into 'rising destructive frustration' because the promise of mass-based political parties soon degenerated to monolithic authoritarian states, and individual belly politics took precedence over the common well-being of the majority of the population.

Second, power has been deployed to steal from the state, thereby bleeding the nation to death. Political leadership is characterised by corruption, mismanagement, fanning ethnic hegemonic tendencies of divide and rule. Society or the state is constructed on clientelism;

political leaders rewarding their supporters with positions and money; mediocrity-taking precedence over meritocracy. Ethnic diversity construed as liability instead of being a valuable asset for development. Large-scale corruption compromises the management and development of the state, destroys morale, and wrecks the fabric of society. Since private and personal gains are to be made from state power are enormous, competition to control the state is fierce and often brutal. The politics of exclusion builds on the orientation of the end justifying the means; and winner takes all; and the policy strategy is to perpetuate oneself in power forever – hence the"President for Life" syndrome.

Third, there is no effective way of system change – of changing regimes. Elections are constantly rigged. The return to political pluralism has not contributed to free, fair, competitive, transparent and accountable elections since no level playing ground exists for contending parties. Political coercion and repression replace democracy. Political pluralism has not converged into plural political people's representation {PPPR}. A country like Cameroon is gradually slipping back into the era of monolithic party system. White imperialism is replaced by ethnic hegemonic tyrannical rule supported by Western countries. Africa needs a governance system construed within the principles of "Here the People Rule" [Forje 2007].

Fourth, political party leadership, especially the Head of State and the military are above reproach: Alternative opinion are discouraged or punished: advocates of different opinions are viewed as enemies or branded as anti-nationalistic, destructive elements thwarting the peace, coherence and stability of state institutions and society. This strategy is deployed to destroy critical thinking, emergence of a vibrant civil society mobilising and demanding reforms or acting as check on government. The voice of civil society must be heard. The politics of "inclusion" should take centre stage. Civil society must be mobilised to ensure that the leaders no longer betray the African course once again.

Fifth, there is no commitment to the rule of law. The judiciary is ignored or made a captive instrument of the executive. The same goes for the legislative assembly. The African state has failed to mover beyond the imperial doctrine of exploitation. The legacy of African leadership, to state the least, is one of brutalising and chaotic; putting their people last and themselves first. This is the time to make amends for failed leadership. African people deserve more than what they are getting from current leaders, representatives in the legislative assembly and public bureaucracy.

Of course, there are emerging hopes for positive leadership following recent changes in leadership in a number of African countries. The democratisation process is pay-off in some countries, as some of the emergent leaders are showing signs of being visionary and committed to the delivery of their respective national visions including a continental vision. But these positive changes in no way that leadership crisis has come to an end in Africa Leadership crisis and challenges continue to be serious issues to be addressed urgently if the continent is to claim its rightful position in the world development. The views expressed by Achebe on Nigeria {replace the word Nigeria with Africa) need to be seriously taken:

"The trouble with Nigeria is simply and squarely a failure of leadership. There is nothing basically wrong with the Nigerian character. There is nothing wrong with the Nigerian land or climate or water or air or anything else. The Nigerian problem is the unwillingness or inability of its leaders to rise to the responsibility, to the challenge of personal example which are the hallmarks of true leadership…We have lost the twentieth century; are we bent on seeing that our children also lose the twenty-first? God forbid"

These and other similar statements are indicative of the 'burning urge' or eminent rise of a new generation of transformational leaders ready to rekindle and relay the ideals envisaged during the independence struggles, which according to Simba Makoni [2006] former Executive Secretary of SADC addressing the Botswana Confederation of Commerce, Industry and Manpower (BOCCIM) in November 2006, aptly points out in these words: "African societies and nations are facing a leadership crisis, which arises mainly from the abandonment, by leaders, of the basic mission of leadership, in preference for themselves being served". These emerging new leadership and countries that have turned their back to authoritarian governance system must forge ahead a culture of restoring confidence, trust, hope and consolidated the virtues of democratic governance, whereby both political and functional leadership can be openly and unashamedly manifested. These new political and managerial leadership should self-consciously see themselves as operating with the confines of a priority strategic inclusive partnership for development.

ADDRESSING THE LINKAGES AND SYNERGY OF LEADERSHIP

The African developmental state fails due to many inter-related issues that must be adequately addressed:-

- There is disconnection from the structures of power, culturist, interest hierarchies, loyalties, and tradition that make up the diverse weave of socio-political life;
- In most African countries, the odds are stacked against democratic progress due to a number of unfavourable factors, reinforcing each other, for example, endemic corruption, poverty, bad governance and mismanagement drains away resources, energy and purpose of development;
- Approaches or embracing bad governance the more formidably difficult the challenge for improving effective good governance;
- Governance cannot improve and development cannot happen without the 'political will' for reform and backed by positive responses from the populace.

The linkage and synergy of leadership and managerial skills and political will remains crucially important to generate, deepen, and accelerate the developmental state. Therefore, 'mindset', 'political will' remain vital inputs in the process of change and development. Without robust commitment to fundamental reforms to control corruption, open up the economy, enhance the democratisation process, enforcing the rule of law, respect basic fundamental human and political rights, and allow independent centres of power within and outside the government, sustainable development cannot take-off nor the quality of life improved. Sustainable development takes off from three inter-related phases: form below, from within, and from outside {i.e. inputs from the Diaspora and international community}. In all phases, the role of leadership and managerial skills remains paramount. The vigour and depth of political will and leadership skills to undertake reform depends on how inclusive society is in the process of policy articulation, implementation and evaluation.

Therefore, policies must be open-minded articulated, taking place within a constitutional regime framework where decisions are taken by consensus and not done by decrees. In addition, the state machinery and the academic and professional community should be perceived as partners in development – the head and heart of the development process. Neither the state nor the academic community must distance themselves from one another. The academic community should work hands in gloves with the state without compromising excellence and scientific knowledge. Whistle blowing is necessary to correct any form of misdirection. The academic community must be committed to improving the services of the state in all its forms. This brings to mind Plato's conception of the academic community poised with a great respect for the institutions of government and a strong motivation to serve the interests of the public: the ideal ruling group being one of a class of men and women dedicated to the pursuit of wisdom and knowledge, with a taste for every type of knowledge. Such men and women endowed with unquenchable curiosity, possessing courage and self-respect, sought after justice and truth. Not being concerned with the pursuit of wealth, nor allied with property, they could achieve objectivity. For them, to govern is a matter of duty and obligation – a sacred calling. They possessed the capacity for temperance, self control, and a respect for authority. But above all they should be dedicated to the pursuit of wisdom and ultimate truth [Warner 1963].

We need in Africa an ideology of an ideal independent, professional public bureaucracy with strong emphasis on intelligence, intellectual values, professional ethics and culture, the notion of restraint, the drive for self-respect and the respect of others, the concept of duty consciousness and obligation. "These are striking reminiscent of the Platonic concept of the State. Even more significant is the emphasis in an independent professional executive ideology upon which the search for justice and the fair resolution of problems. Fairness to others, concern for the public welfare, honesty, and 'goodness' are characteristics held to be decisive" [Warner 1963:235-36].

EMERGING POSITIVE SIGNS

There are some positive noticeable exceptions coming out of the continent with quality leadership skills in post-cold war Africa. Countries like South Africa, Botswana, Mauritius and Rwanda. Recently, Ghana, Kenya, Nigeria, Mozambique are on the move. The transition from the Organisation of African Unity to African Union is indicative of the positive signs following the establishment of new structures like NEPAD, African Parliament. The Peer Review Mechanism under NEPAD is a historical development towards institutionalisation of democratic governance and creating a developmental state. Countries and leadership role are under scrutiny for performance management. The rise and strengthening the structures of regional economic integration bodies like ECOWAS, SADC, and CEMAC are pointers for a better tomorrow. Changes in the international community since the collapse of the Berlin Wall and the growing mode of a no zero-tolerance with military dictators, coup d'etats add to the effect of bringing evolutionary improvement in the quality of leadership and state performances in service delivery.

The institution of awards by AAPAM for initiatives improving services delivery is a welcome move; showing how serious the issue of leadership and quality service delivery is being taken on the continent. Countries in Eastern and Southern Africa are making serious improvements in public service reforms. Bodies like Transparency International through its Corruption Perception Index are pushing African leaders and governments to improve on leadership style and governance performance. The impact of ICTs as a watch dog cannot be ruled out. Governments no longer have monopoly over information. There is growing internal demand for good governance even though in some countries, civil society remains passive. Both the input and output sides need to be strengthen. Civil society must be educated to take its share of social responsibility; avoid political apathy and selling their consciousness for money during elections. Creating good leadership is a necessity. The role of the academia as whistle blowing factor is important. The issue of gender empowerment and the emergence of women in the frontline of political leadership on the continent are encouraging. Efforts should be strongly directed at accelerating the positive developments of leadership in Africa. The interface, state-civil society-private sector must be encouraged. It is also necessary that certain criteria be set for the election of members of parliament and the president.

Africa should draw experiences from other transitional polities in fashioning their new development agenda. Priority should be given to the deployment of ICTs in the development process. It is imperative that independent 'national think tank', civil society organisations, and other 'watch dog' on development agenda, good performances of institutions be established as checks and balances to state activities. The African leadership landscape has made some significant improvements during the past decade as evident in improved human conditions in countries like Botswana, South Africa, Mauritius, Mozambique and Ghana. Some of the war-turn or post-conflict countries like Sierra Leone, Rwanda and Angola are making significant progress. It may be too earlier to situate Liberia [Forje 2006]. The focus for these countries should be directed towards creating a culture of reconciliation, inclusion, and partnership among the various stakeholders. They should, at all cost, avoid ethnic hegemonic tendencies: an authoritarian imposition of the new administration on others: avoid either minority or majority tyranny and embrace the virtues of good leadership and democratic governance. The various stakeholders should be seen as potential and viable partners in development, and where benefit-sharing of the nation's wealth are equitably undertaken. The new leaders should embark on and priority strategic corrective measures to Africa's ruler ship maladies. "Africa knows all about failed and collapsing states, but the challenge is to create capable states".

In all, Africa must seriously face the 'leadership question'. These words remain fundamental in addressing and accessing leadership role in creating a developmental state in Africa: First "turning to the question of leadership in Africa, it is unfortunate that this is one subject that has often been addressed in the negative. A lots has been said about the complementary attributes of leadership, but very little effort has been made to develop a profile of positive leadership that is required in facing the continent's challenges" [Dada 2007; Salem 2004 in UNECA 2004]; Second, the United Nations Economic Commission for Africa [UNECA 2004] survey indicates that: "there is pressing need for the implementation of a bold and innovative programme to effectively develop and use Africa's governance capacity. There is the need to implement bold, cross-cutting and comprehensive Africa-led programme for capacity development, backed with substantial funding from development partners"; Thirdly, Ukaga and Afoaku [2005] posit that: "for Africa to overcome the many challenges to its sustainable development, two important ingredients of sustainable development – Servant leadership and Active citizenship – are imperative". Importantly, the urgent task of improving the quality of leadership in Africa, one that is self-denying and thoroughly understands the concept of the common good – of putting people first, must be the first priority of these emerging leaders.

The ongoing economic and political changes taking place in some African countries are integral part of the process of the shift towards a democratic developmental state. These developments should push towards a stronger visionary leadership and managerial style which the continent needs in transforming itself from a third to a first world. It is also imperative that whatever has been achieved in these countries should be consolidated as well as improved upon.

PROACTIVE STRATEGIC POLICY MEASURES

- African leaders must develop the art of serving their populace and not the other way round;
- Leaders must learn to convert dreams and visions into reality, with reality becoming blessing to society;
- Leaders and managers are needed who exhibit strong characteristics of: "love; empowerment; resilience; stress management; integrity; passion; attitude; heroism; and passion" which goes under the following: "seer, servant; strategist; shepherd; sustainers; steward and spokesperson". These functional qualities tells a lot about the nature and types of leader that Africa needs;
- Embark on the policy strategy of inclusion, not exclusion; partnership, participation and benefit sharing;
- Development is not an exclusive role of the state. Ensure interface between the state, civil society, private sector not bypassing the international community, which must respond positively towards the needs and aspirations of the people;
- Envisioned leadership and managerial skills with capacities to influence others positively to accomplish objectives in the process, capacity and integrity to keep the various components of the organisation steady and running so that the set of objectives can be best achieved;
- Making any progressive African leader the 'scarecrow' by the enemies of the continent without strong resistance from the people to defend their course, makes the continent the 'plantation' and experimental laboratory of the metropolitan powers, with conservative African presidents as their chief plantation overseers or caretakers;
- This then is the time that Africa needs more than ever before, more of the Mandela's, Kaunda's, Nyerere's, Nkrumah's and others to pilot the spaceship of United States of Africa throughout the rest of the 21st century and beyond.

REFERENCES

Achebe, Chinua [1958] *Things Fall Apart.* London.

Addai-sebo Akyaaba [2007] *"African Government Now", in New Africa,* No. 463, 41st Year, June 2007:06-21.

Adie Stephen [2003] Leadership and Nation Building. *10th William Ofori Atta Memorial Lectures,* 28-30 October 2003, Accra.

Ahmed, Z. [1990] "Introduction", in *The Longer-term Perspective Study of Sub Saharan Africa: Institutional and Socio-political Issues.* World Bank, Washington, D.C.

Almond Gabriel & G. Bingham Powell, Jr. [1966] Comparative Politics: A Developmental Approach. *Little Brown, Boston.*

Amoako, K.Y [2004] Governance and Development in Africa. The Critical Nexus. Paper Presented at *the Fifth Andrew Young Lecture of the Africa Society of the National Summit in Africa.* 18th February 2004, Washington, D.C.

Annan Kofi [2001] *Stop Blaming Colonialism: Text of Special Message Delivered at the Opening Session of the last Organisation of Africa Unity Summit.* 10 July 2001 Business Day, South Africa.

Aryittey, G [2002] *Africa's Shady Politicians Are the Root of the Continent's Destitution.* August 2000 Online article.

Aryittey G. [1996] *"No Tears for Africa's Intellectuals.* New Africa.

Azikiwe Nnamdi [1936] *Renascent Africa.* London.

Bayart, Jean-Francoise [1993]. *The State in Africa: The Politicos of the Belly.* Longman, New York.

Bewaji A. John [2003] Leadership – A Philosophical Exploration of Perspectives in Africa, Caribbean and Diaspora Polities. *Journal of African Philosophy: Issue 2.*

Buor Daniel [2007] Professor and Provost of the College of Arts Social Science, Kwame Nkrumah University of Science and Technology Kumasi, Ghana in an interview with Kofi Asante, *Africa Review on "Public Sector Shake-up for Ghana",* September 2007

Dada O. J. [2007] "Strengthening Africa Political Leadership Capacity for Development: Key Challenges". *Paper presented at the 29th AAPAM Annual Roundtable Conference, 3rd – 7th September 2007,* International Conference Centre, Mbabane, Swaziland.

Dlamini Musa [2007] "The African Leadership Crisis: Historical Perspectives And A Reflection on the Expectations of Independency" Paper presented at the 29th AAPAM Annual Roundtable Conference, 3rd – 7th September 2007, *International Conference Centre,* Mbabane, Swaziland.

Chesterman Simon, Michael Ingnatieff & Ramesh Thakur [2004] *Making States Work: From State failure to State-Building.* International Peace Academy, United Nations University, New York, NY.

Easton David [1965] *A System Analysis of Political Life.* Wiley, New York.

Easton David [1965] *A Framework For Political Analysis.* Prentice-Hall, Englewood Cliffs, N.J.

Falola Toyin [1995] *Development Planning And Decolonisation in Nigeria.* University of Florida Press, Gainesville, FL.

Forje W. John [2007] *Here The People Rule: Political Transition and Challenges for Democratic Consolidation in Africa* (Carad Publication – Forthcoming)

Forje W. John [2006] "Liberia: A New Beginning – From State Failure To State-Building". *Document Commissioned by UNDP for the Conference of Former African Heads of State and Government on Mobilising International Support for Post-Conflict Reconstruction in Liberia,* 28 October – 2 November 2006, Pretoria, South Africa.

Forje W. John [2004] "The Wind of Change: A Journey Through Africa's Political landscape And Search for an Alternative". *The Archie Mafeje Lecture - delivered 16 November 2004,* Africa Institute of South Africa, Pretoria, South Africa.

Hand Learned [1960] *The Spirit of Liberty,* 3rd Edition, University of Chicago Press.

Isimbabi M. J. [2004] leadership and Governance Capacity Building in African Countries. *Why and How Well – Off and Accomplished Africans, especially Brain Drain/Diaspora Africans Should Proactively Take Charge of Fostering African Progress.* [See Dada 2007, op cit.]

Kumuyi F. William [2006] "Wanted: Leaders", *New Africa,* 40th Year, No. 456. November 2006.

Kikwete Mrisho Jakaya [2007] "There is Hope for Africa", *New Africa,* No. 463, 41st Year, June 2007, London, pp 12-18.

Lamour M. Yves [2007] "The Diaspora And The Future of Africa" *New Africa,* 41st Year. No. 466, October 2007.

Ley C [1983] "African Economic Development in Theory and Practice", *Deadalus,* Vol. 111 (Spring) 1982.

Mazrui Ali [1993] "The Impact of Global Changes on Academic Freedom in Africa: A Preliminary Assessment", in M. Diouf and M. Mamdani (eds.) *Academic Freedom in Africa*

Mbeki Thabo [2004] *Speech at the Opening of the Pan-African Parliament.* 16 September 2004. [See Pretoria News, Friday, 17 September 2004:4 – "President Unveils PAP's New Home"

Mkandawire Thandika [2005] *African Intellectuals – Rethinking Politics,* Language, Gender and Development. Codesria Publications, Dakar, Senegal.

Moxley S, Russ [2000] *"Leadership and Spirit".* Jossey-Bass, San Francisco.

Munroe Myles [1993] *Becoming a Leader.* Pneuma Life Publishing

NEPAD (New Partnership for African Development) *NEPAD Report 2002,* South Africa.

Ngalame Ntungwe Elias [2007] "Ruining Cameroon's Economy: E U Uncovers FCFA 400 Billion Yearly Fraud", *Eden,* No. 215. 1st – 3rd October 2007, Limbe, Cameroon. www.edennewspaper.com

Nkrumah Kwame [1963] African Must Unite. Panaf Books, London.

Nyamunga A.O. Maurice [2007] "agenda For Improving Leadership Quality And Effectiveness: African Perspective". *Paper present at the 29th AAPAM Annual Roundtable Conference,* 3rd – 7th September 2007, International Conference Centre, Mbabane, Swaziland.

Nyerere J. K. [1967] *Freedom and Unity: A Selection from Writings and speeches.* Oxford University Press, Dar-es-salaam, Tanzania.

Obasanjo Olusegun [2000] *Blame Poor Leadership for Africa Decline.* Africa News Service, 6th March 2002.

Rashid S. [1994] *"Social Sciences and Policy-making in Africa; A Critical Review",* African Development.

Sharkansky Ira [1972] *Public Administration: Policy-making in Government Agencies. University of Wisconsin, Markham Publishing Company, Chicago*

Shivji G. Issa [2006] "Pan-africanism or Imperialism" Unity and Struggle Towards Anew Democratic Africa", *African Sociological Review,* 10(1). 2006, pp 208-220.

Tadesse Z. [1999] "Frome Euphoria to Gloom? Navigating the Murky Waters of African Academic Institutes", in W. Martin and M. West (eds.) *Out of One, Many Africa's: Reconstructing the study and Meaning of Africa.* University of Illinois Press, Urbana, II: USA.

Ukaga Ukechukwu & Osita Afoaku [2005] *Sustainable Development in Africa.* Africa World Press.

United Nations Economic Commission for Africa (UNECA) [2004] *Report of the Africa Governance Survey of 28 Countries To Measure and Monitor Progress Towards Good Governance.* ECA, Addis Ababa, Ethiopia.

Voss J. (ed.) 1973. *Development Policy in Africa.* Verlag: Nene Gesellschaft GMbH. Boon-Bad Godesberg.

Warner W. Lloyd et al [1963] *The American Federal Executive.* Yale University Press, New Haven, Conn.

Zeleza P. T. [1988] "African Labour and Intellectual Migration to the North: Building New Transatlantic Bridges", *Symposium on African and African-American Intellectuals,* Santiago, University of California, CA.

CONCLUSIONS AND PROSPECTS: WHAT FUTURE FOR AFRICA?

INTRODUCTION

"In the era of interdependence and globalisation, it's time for people to reach out and live together in harmony and peace as we all belong to one large human family" *[Haya Rashid Al Khalifa 2006, Ambassador of Bahrain to the UN and President of the 61st UN General Assembly]*

"A quick survey of the changes that the present day public administration have to contend with will show that many governments have to manage economies that have greater reliance on market forces, with a call for reduction in state intervention and operating with more openness to the external environment. One the African scene we have been witnessing, in most of our countries, immense pressure to reform the economic and political structures which necessitated governments to address administrative structures as well as to be responsive to the changes in political and economic spheres" *[Joseph Rugumyamheto: 2006, AAPAM Testimonial Lecture- Arusha]*

"It is at the family whereby the true reflection of the achievement of Millennium Development Goals achievement can be observed in individual basis instead of generalisation" *[Stella M. Manyanya, 2006, Member of the Tanzanian Parliament]*

"The Challenge now for Africa is to create conditions for democracy not apartheid. African countries must therefore gun for development not underdevelopment; brew science and technology for development not destruction; be proactive on war against poverty, corruption and underdevelopment, not being proactive for authoritarian regime forms, personnel wealth accumulation, and affluence at the expenses of the suffering poor. Africa should not condoned and sustain exploitative patterns of behaviour that promotes affluence for a select few" *[John W. Forje 1ˢᵗ June 2007]*

"Patriotism has an inherent flaw. By preferring one segment of humanity over the rest, the citizen transgresses the fundamental principles of morality, that of universality, without saying so openly, he acknowledges that men are not equal ...true morality, true justice, true virtue presuppose universality, and this equal rights" *[Todorov Tzvetan 1993:183]*

"We need more than just a fear of being caught. We need both a systemic and systematic understanding of the complexity of corruption. We therefore need systemic and systematic solutions designed to deal with the question of corruption" *[D. Busakwe 2006:17]*

There is great controversy about the nature, progress and effectiveness of the administrative, democratisation and developmental processes on the continent. On the one hand, we have optimistic views that the post-cold war period has ushered some degree of anticipated benefits to the continent in the areas of administration, democratic governance and development. During the past couple of years and especially since 2005 to-the present, we notice a number of elections taking place – signalling a gradual and conscious approach to advancing democratic governance on the continent. Only in the first half of 2007, elections have been held in Senegal, Mali, Mauritania, Nigeria, Algeria and Cameroon, though not absolutely free, competitive, fair, transparent as it should be but that a gradual return is made in the direction of ushering democratic governance, giving the people the opportunity to choose and sanction their representatives is a major first step in the right direction for the continent to improve the quality of life of its people. Of course, the controversy between 'power stay' and 'power shift' continues unabated, as the struggle penetrates all corners of society ahead of pending elections. There is the belief that 'power shift' or 'system change' will offer much protection for the proportion of society that have been at the receiving end of decades of mal-governance and power struggles between the contending forces. Opening the political space, will limit clashes between the advocates of 'power stay' and 'power shift'. But 'power shift' or 'system change' is what is required to build a new society.

Africa suffers from many ills and misfortunes. They range from the vagaries of poverty, corruption and underdevelopment to the tragedies arising from natural and human created disasters. Potentially, one of the richest continents in the world, yet millions of its population lives in conditions of squalor and abject poverty. The situation has been compounded by the various conflicts that have torn many of the societies and are seriously undermining efforts at socio-economic development. The litany of the continents problem is many and varied. Do the people and leaders recognise the nature and context of its problems? And if they do recognise that added to real ills that Africa is confronted with, we have also to confront the kind of stereotypical image of our continent, which is being projected in most abysmal terms. To the Afro-pessimists, Africa is nothing but a continent of problems – famine, hunger, conflicts, refugees, displaced persons, environmental degradation, corruption and mismanagement. They have reasons to be pessimistic because a condition of bad governance has been created and therefore, they are obsessed by their own negative portrayal of events in the continent that they fail to see the dynamic changes that are daily since the end of the Cold War Conflict and unfolding especially following the struggle for political pluralism and democracy.

Indeed, Africa is changing and doing so essentially because the African people expect and clearly want changes. It is a continent in transition both in the political and economic domain. The technological side is yet to catch up and stimulate as well as accelerate economic progress. Economic reforms are increasingly becoming a rule rather an exception after the long period of Africa's Lost Decade pf the 1980s. The process of democratisation is firmly on course and despite setbacks here and there, the process is irreversible. The people of Africa who fought against colonialism and racism are more and more determined to exercise their fundamental rights and sovereignty and to arrive at their destiny. Africans are determined more than ever before to say a strong input in the way they are governed, by whom and for what period. Having suffered the indignities of slavery and colonialism, they are equally determined to ensure that the issues of human rights and good governance are not treated as mere slogans in the continent and the world in general. Indeed change is unmistakeable. It is against the background of dashed hopes that Africa must now be striving to seize the initiative again and engage itself, with new resolve, vigour and determination, on the path towards economic and social determination, progress and peace and improving the quality of life of its citizens. Africa expects positive responses from the international community especially the former colonial powers towards envisaged goals for sustainable development.

Without any hindsight, we can consciously conclude that {a} democracy is spreading rapidly in Africa: the continent is slowing moving away from the shadows of dictatorship that clouded the continent to embracing the principles of *"Here The People Rule"* [Forje, forthcoming]. To a large extent, these are significant ways of a gradual move to establishing liberal democratic governance rule. {b} Of course, the spread of democratic governance and good principles of public administration has been far from uniform across the continent. It has not been possible to radically eradicate the aprons of dictatorship civilian or military that gripped the continent soon after independence. The disappearance of military regimes is clear; but pockets of such outdated governance system (civil or military) still exist on the continent. Many parts of the continent especially within the Francophone zones are yet to be truly baptised or converted by the genuine principles and love of democratic virtues. Sudan and Somali remain a disgrace on the consciousness of democratic governance in the continent The wind of democratic governance is yet to blow through those countries lacking behind on system of governance change. {c} Though some of the regimes are taking measures in reforming or transforming authoritarian rule to liberal democracy, the process is not moving fast as it should be and therefore, can be regarded as these countries 'falling short of democracy', see for example [Carothers 2002:5-21] {d} Africa needs governments and leaders to model the continent of responsible husbandry, using its natural resources for the benefit of the entire populace. As good examples is that of Norway and Gabon two oil producing countries but with varying levels of social justice and levels of development. Norway exhibits the judicious use of oil revenue while Gabon or Cameroon exhibits the exploitation of oil for the benefit of a few. Gabon started exporting long before Norway. The situation between North and South (i.e. Norway and Gabon/Cameroon) inescapably led to a comparison of the present conditions of these two parts of the world and the divergent paths they have followed. The difference boils down to leadership, focus and sense of purpose. In one case, putting the 'interest people first {Norway} takes priority and in other, 'exploiting the people {Gabon/Cameroon} tops the development agenda. Ongoing development trends indicate that Equatorial Guinea may follow the path of Norway using the oil wealth to improve the living stands of the people.

Africa is witnessing a changing world of the public service. Changes that should benefit the people of the continent by creating space for broader participation in nation building and consolidating the nation-state by providing adequate and quality services especially to the marginalized majority either during the intransigent colonial regime, apartheid era, or in post-colonial governance system. As the political space opens up in addressing the major constraints of poverty, corruption dependency, and underdevelopment, the focus should be 'putting the people first" and for leaders to serve the people not to be served. African leaders have an uphill task in bridging the disparity of development and underdevelopment among and within countries.

In many former colonies, the situation at independence was anything but favourable for achieving rapid growth, and for policies focusing on poverty reduction. Though progress has been made in countries with committed leadership skills, many others continue to lag even further behind owning to misdirected policies, corruption, economic mismanagement and weak government. Armed conflicts and natural disasters have aggravated the situation. Most

African countries are becoming even poorer owing to misdirected policies, an untenable debt situation, social and gender inequality and corruption.

Regimes that have enjoined the continent's political space exhibit growing problems to democratise are eroding their legitimacy among the public and undermining their ability of democracy as in Sudan, and Somali: the economic crises in many parts of the continent, the democratic trend is at the greater risk of reversal. Hope for a better democratic future for democratic countries like Mauritius, Botswana and of recent South Africa portray the continent's forward march from a third to a first world. Developments in Ghana, Benin, Angola and Libya are encouraging for the enhancement of democratic governance in Africa. More countries should join the bandwagon of institutionalising democratic governance in Africa.

On the other hand, one can question why has the politics of a discursive, representative democratic and inclusive character not succeeded in post-colonial Africa? In a country like Cameroon, which is undergoing transformation after may years of one-party rule and a dictatorial centralised governance system, most fundamental transformation impediments can be argued using the inelegant but useful phrase of "imperative-coordination" that ethnic hegemonic, patronage, personality cult worship and satanic religious organisations has hijacked the role and functions of the state and its institutions. Backed with weak leadership, it is able to control the state, its institutions, its laws, resources, its functionaries as well as the control of the ordinary people's imagination, which impedes social change and constructive transformation for the common good.

As such, Africa is rocked with a lack of justice and the exercise of fairness by its leaders given that position of power are used to access resources for selfish personal ends, for monopoly of key positions, for use to extract cash and labour from fellow citizens, for receiving bribes by pretends thereby constituting a widespread informal economy bedevilled with criminalities. Exploitation, oppression and marginalisation, which have been abandon by the fashionable discourses of the contemporary era, have left the majority of the citizens as fractured communities. Both internal and external forces creating a worrisome comucopia have devastated their geographic and miasma of social, cultural and political malfunctions of the state [Aseka 2006:4]

To a large extent the goals of the poverty-stricken population and that of the affluent class are not the same. The growing divergence between the two lass of people in the same society is a serious cause of concern. Indeed. Any expression of different interests or points of view can become intolerable, challenging the authority of leaders who see themselves as representing if not personifying the unity and identity of the nation. It is for these reasons that has led so many postcolonial elites to adapt forms of repression and exploitation characteristic of their former colonial enemies, stifling debate, censoring thought and deploying more or less extreme forms of violence, establishing what can be termed as "the state's right to violence and to silence"[Spence and Wollman 2003:150]. The people in these countries witness the suppression of the right to vote free, freedom of speech and association, as the different forms of authoritarian rule from military regime structures to the civilian dominant one-party regime form and military dictatorships have governed the continent.

The African experience does not augur well in this respect as noted by Olukoshi and Laakso [1996:110], the African situation is one bounded with tragedy with the 'state in most extreme cases more or less reduced to its coercive apparatuses'. Looking at what could be termed the catastrophic situations from Somali to Liberia, from Zaire {DRC} to Cameroon, and further North, Addi [1997:121] places the armed forces within the limelight of nationalism a congenial ideology: "military establishment typically see themselves as the guardian par excellence of nationalism. As officers work their way up the ladder of promotion, they draw nearer to the ideal type of nationalist individual, the soldier is convinced that he/she is the shield of the country and as such the rightful holder of their legitimacy from which all political and administrative authority most flow. Yet all this is merely an ideological cover for political inequality and impedes the emergence of citizenship".

The Post-Cold War era ushers a new way of organising social life through political pluralism and democracy making the society state-centred and expanding its jurisdictions over all aspect of social life. The idea that to be modern is to live in a state that is democratic, to organise society through its institutions of power that is representative, has not gone down well in the ethnic hegemonic, satanic religious cult and personality cult- worship that prevails and governs the state and society in many parts of the continent. The powers of these forces have not been dismantled to make state and society function in a democratic representative sense of *'power belonging to the people'* and not to an individual or a small select group. Africa must celebrate new opportunities – as these opportunities offered by a democratic governance system constitute the anvil for improving the quality of livelihood of the people. African countries should seek ways of returning to democratic principles and values. Deepening democracy in Africa is a must. The genuine return to the role of culture and consolidation of democratic values in Africa will the true representation of the people, their social reality, progress and development in a rapidly changing and hostile global environment. The situation calls for a highlighted need for unity and solidarity and reinforced efforts to address common problems and common struggles.

Being in a hostile environment implies that Africans of all strata are faced with at least four the common problems, even though in varied magnitude; namely:

- Invisibility: Both the rich and poor are faced with invisibility in the global environment. Even the few rich are discriminated in the global political and economic arena. Back home, the problem of invisibility is show by the gross neglect of the poor and a lack of an accurate census to show the army of those leaving under squalor and under the acceptable possible minimum level of existence. This also leads to exclusion from corridors of power, which leads to lack of access to means of production. Which then affects their economic and political status;
- Exclusion: exclusion from power, political and economic. An important element of development of democracy is the lack of participation in the political and economic system. It is hindrance to democracy. Education gaps, quality health-care, employment and economic security and the creation of wealth elude the vast majority of the population. There is an urgent need to intensify the drive to increase political participation and also solidarity between the various strata of society in building a sense of belonging. There is a responsibility to make sure people participate because that is the essence of democracy. All African governments must work harder and together to improve the condition of the people. The agenda of the African Parliament towards this initiative should not be compromised but to work seriously and collectively because the issues are similar in every African country;

- Stigmatisation: there is stigmatisation of Africans for various reasons, their underdeveloped status, as former colonies, and often perceived as unintelligent, unproductive and discriminated against based on such grounds impedes their process of development. It is the place of those whom the people have entrusted power into their hands to widen the horizon of the people by serving them in a democratic, transparent, and participatory process of inclusion. In most African states, democracy does not equal freedom. Democracy is a fight and a sacrifice – it is fight for inclusion in democracy in all aspects of life. An important element of democracy is the lack of participation of the vast majority of the people in the political system;
- Marginalisation: unequal provision of services. Shared-prosperity is grossly absent within the political vocabulary of the political dispensation of the continent. This goes against the true African culture of sharing. Political leaders have gone so-called modern by adopting a strategic agenda of "greed" and "self-accumulation". Articulate self-interest takes pride of place in society. The idea of "articulate national interest" is lost and features no way in the policy agenda of the various political parties. The marginalisation of the poor and vulnerable groups continues unabated. Without any representation at all levels of the political process and decision-making in the state, there is an unequal provision of services. Promoting a sense of belonging and identity will serve as unifying factor solidarity and shared prosperity need for the development of the society.

It should be noted that the key challenges are those that involve {i} basic human rights in its entirety. Once people are made the focus of the development process, then their basic right human rights are respected; {ii} creating equal opportunities for all – an enabling environment; and {ii} fostering national unity and regional integration. The problem of the continent is not poverty. It is the structures that have existed since the colonial period and exacerbated since independence. Therefore the responses need to be structural and a social movement of consolidated efforts - call it positive affirmative action – taking centre stage and being beneficial in solidifying their identity and their fight for self-determination through the continent. This social movement should include various types of social organisation ranging from youths, women, and children to support the political agenda of the total emancipation of the marginalised, disadvantaged and excluded in society.

The role of civil society needs to be actively engaged significantly play a constructive role in the development process. Many a civil society organisations role is ambiguous as they fall prey to the whims and caprices of political parties, serving to represent articulate self-interest and not national interests. The African Parliament should adopt a proactive – pro-people oriented approach in their deliberations. They should use their political position to truly engage civil society in order to ensure that the voices of the voiceless are heard and that parliament is working in the interests of all peoples. Africa needs a vibrant civil society that promotes positive affirmative policy measures and actions in the interest of the country.

In addition the cultural-diversity heritage of the people must not be trampled upon. The cultural diversity of the people is asset for development not a liability in the development process as political leaders make it to be. The importance of culture is that it can be used as a unifying factor. The use of cultural symbolism – the assimilation process has weakened African sense of community solidarity beyond the divide. The continent's cultural diversity is still a uniting factor for the overall expression of Africanise. Thus the strategy of social inclusion to strengthen African culture and unity must not be misinterpreted by politicians and zealous officials as ensuring "regional balance" to suit their personal hidden but destructive and divisive agenda. The joining of values – makes people more visible, it celebrates diversity rather than assimilation open to endless exploitation by foreign forces. There is need to fund to promote cultural expression and its sustainability. Africa needs to figure its own mechanism to strengthen its cultural diversity as uniting instrument – Renaissance Africa –to uphold the right to be different but united.

Finally, we need public policies, laws and on other safeguards on affirmative action. Affirmative actions include basic human rights. Positive affirmative action is needed to pilot the development process. Positive affirmative action and policies cannot be the only stronghold need to defeat existing marginalisation, decriminations and racial prejudices against the black community the world over. There needs to be proactive measures by all black people and social movements to address issues of internal and external marginalisation/racial/freedom, personal freedom and the defective idea of ethnic diversity that thwarts any positive movements towards national cohesion and unity. The present state of centralised hegemonic authoritarian rule is important to discuss, not just past and present prejudices that clouds the structural-functioning of the state system in Africa.

Ethnic diversity exists even in Europe or the America's; in short in all human society. But that of Africa is blown out of proportion and used by political leaders and their adherents to foster disunity, the demise and destruction of the continent; but who is responsible or who is obligated – it could possibly be the nation-states. More often than not, ethnic diversity is included in the analysis of political and economic issue Therefore, positive affirmative action is like beginning or a halfway point, it is needed to motivate change, revise issues, and rewrite it to match the current context of a growing and merging young democratic society. It raises questions but it also promotes inclusiveness, solidarity and creativity. In this ideological fight, positive affirmative action is a permanent victory; it is just a minor triumph. The people of Africa should gun for positive and not destructive affirmative action

Returning to political pluralism and democracy challenges the authoritative allocation of social roles abrogated by illegal centralised state system. Moving into equitable allocation of social roles, rewards and life trajections governed by the forces of people's power through a competitive, free, transparent, and fairly elected representation does not exist. A clash of cultures or values – authoritarian rule and representative democratic governance retards progress for societal and system changes. Political power resides within the realms of the authoritarian governance system. That system has to be overthrown either by a democratic means {ballot box} or revolt {military action or an orange revolution}.

Democratic participation has increased ordinary people's expectation about conditions and quality of life. But quality of life must be paid for. In a society which does not generate enough wealth to enable interest groups in society pursue their institutional aims with their own resources, all demands of amelioration for – hospital, schools, roads, water supply, shelter etc. – are directed at the state, which is the only possible sources for the creation of collective goods. Thus the rise of democracy has reinforced the tendency towards a constant extension of the bureaucratic state which zealous individuals take advantage to enrich themselves. Both administrative inertia and low productivity remains the major characteristics of African societies.

Drawing from Chilton's definition of development as: a shift of a culture from one way of relating to another that addresses and overcomes the structural ambiguities of its initial stage, political development can thus be understood as changes in the political culture that are adopted or acquired to accommodate arising complexities as a result of time and system evolution. The actual African states are relatively young, as the modern state based on territorial sovereignty and legitimate recognition in the international society were only adopted at the time of independence in the 1960s. Notwithstanding the dexterity and charisma of African traditional rulers, the political abilities for running a modern state remain relatively under-developed. There is need for a revamped awareness about continued learning to keep pace with changes and benefit from new thinking, especially with regard to political and leadership development [Chilton Stephen, 1991.6]. What is clear is that there is universal democracy – a democracy is linked to cultural experiences of peoples. The refusal by the West to acknowledge cultural experiences is leading to problems and serious political crisis throughout the continent. Because there is no universal democracy that neither gives the right nor should it be used as excuse by leaders not to adhere to the basic principles and tenets of democracy and its values. Democracy remains the standard for evaluating political life which leaders must adhere to. Democracy asks how *"good"* or *"bad"* government policies are in terms our own self-interest: do they help the individual or hurt him/her? It goes further to ask where government policies are fair or unfair compared to our own moral beliefs about equality, liberty, freedom, community, or justice. Still democracy will focus on whether government policies help or hurt the environment, economic growth, world peace or national interests. It remains an arena for continuing debate to enhancing and consolidating and protecting human rights which usually take the following form: {a} everyone has the right to the relevant good: and {b} the state must take reasonable legislative and other measures, within its available resources, to achieve the progressive realisation of this right for all.

African leaders must bear in mind that democracy is a distinct and limited ideal. It should not be confused with other social aspirations. But by ensuring reason-giving, by increasing exposure to diverse views, and by prohibiting second –class citizenship, a democratic constitution goes a long way toward promoting a wide range of social goals, emphatically including justice itself [Sunstein 2001:243]. The ideal of good governance must equally be seen within these perspectives. It should also be noted that the democratic constitution by itself does not guarantee good lives for citizens. Nor does it guarantee justice. But a democratic constitution nonetheless does a great deal. What ever is guaranteed is through the positive policy actions of those on whom the trust of the leadership. Therefore a combination of many inter-related input factors are necessary for rethinking government and reorganising the state.

Whatever the case, the *"struggle for democracy"* must continue on relented and unperturbed and in the overall interests of the people. It is for these reasons as noted by President Abraham Lincoln, on his First Inaugural Address "that there is a patient confidence in the ultimate justice of the people. Is there any better, or equal, hope in the world?" What is clear is that we live in an age of democratic upsurge. People the world over, and Africa in particular, often at great risk to themselves, have been demanding the right to govern themselves, free from the grinding hands of kings, religious autocrats, civilian and military dictators, or party bosses. But who among us has not been moved and inspired by the recent struggles for democracy in South Africa, Eastern Europe, and the former Soviet Union and in Latin America?

The return to political pluralism and democracy in Africa within the last couple of years is denigrating into liberal imperialism, and generating peculiar dynamics of destruction though the intensity of 'ganging up' between ruling elites on the continent and the forces of western capitalism, under the auspices and cover of globalisation and liberal economy. To a large extent, it can be argued that the return to political pluralism and democracy has only produced a new form of apartheid or caste system in some African countries. Though there is gradual, incremental development in respect of the suffrage in most states, democracy has yet to accelerate the process of total political inclusion. For example, in Cameroon the government and ruling party are restricting representative governance system, as the new entrants into the arena of politics are harassed in contesting the claim to representation, refusal of registration, voting cards or names not appearing on the voter's registrar. The entire arena of institutional politics is strictly in the hands of the old authoritarian guards. Change is required

To a large extent, it could be argued that, paradoxically, the institutions of democratic government the Cameroon way seem to function with impeccably formal propriety precisely because levels of participation remain low and popular expectations from democratic government remain limited. The existence of major problems of electoral politics – resources allocation on the basis of electoral pressure –, which makes rational long-term decisions particularly difficult, continues to haunt and retard democratic governance in the country. It is important o recognise the fact the universe of political discourse and system change is ringing with unceasing demands for recognition of the people's rights to govern – "Here the People Rule" [Forje 2007 forthcoming] cannot be discarded. Africa can draw experiences from India – the world's biggest democracy – that has been the relative success story of democracy in its own way. This does not imply that poverty is erased from the political space of India. But to large extent, the people are given the opportunity to have a voice, to choose by electing or dismissing their leaders. These opportunities are denied in many Africa countries to freely, fairly and on a competitive basis decide whom their leaders and representatives should be.

Many African countries are now implementing reforms and drafting strategies to combat poverty, curb corruption and ensure proper housekeeping. The establishment of the New Partnership for Africa's development [NEPAD], which is based on the idea that African countries themselves must take responsibility for their own development and for ensuring balanced development, is a good step in the right direction. The activities of NEPAD should not bogged down with the usual red-tap administrative procedures, but should be opened and services delivery administrative institution focused on improving the quality of livelihood of the people. Democracy in the formal sense has made progress, but much remains to be done when it comes to deepening democracy and ensuring its sustainability as well as ensuring the provision of basic necessities to the vast majority of the people.

For now, the most important liberal democracy in the continent is South Africa, which has sustained high levels of freedom despite years of political turbulences, economic hardship for the majority of the black population under the weight of the apartheid system. The African National Congress as the dominant party is making some significant progress to address the many years of wrong-doing by the white minority regime to establishing a non-racial society where freedom, liberty, and equality reign. By contrast Africa's other big states are all struggling economically and politically to reach the completion point of democratic governance. For example, the 2007 elections in Nigeria are heavily contested, which cripples the legitimacy and credibility of the new civilian led government. When the basis of legitimacy is eroded, the tendency of reversing to military rule is high. Nigeria runs the risk replaying such a development scenario path. However, no one hopes for such developments taking place. As one of the continents giants she should be at the forefront for the institutionalisation of political pluralism and democracy and functioning of democratic governance system.

On the other hand, there is growing tendency among opposition parties to reject the decision of the ballot box. Opposition parties harbour these feelings and attitude due the "the bad faith and manipulation tactics" adopted by the ruling regime. The absence of a level playing field jeopardises the democratic process. This attitude puts liberal democracy on threat and non-acceptance path. The results of observing teams at elections have to be adequately looked into. Just as countries must learn to conduct free, competitive, transparent and fair elections on a level playing field so that the people are given the opportunities to select their representatives without any form of duress. The best observers are not foreigners implanted at the last minute and expected to undertake a national coverage but the people and the good conduct of elections by whichever body authorised to be in charged of the exercise

This takes us to democratic transition and the international context input. Regime change or transition often focuses essentially on domestic political systems. An essential aspect is the role and contribution of the international system in the process. Given the nature of inter-relationship between the state and the international community external impact can equally play a significant role. Generally speaking, democratic transition runs from the point at which the previous authoritarian system begins to be dismantled, through the constituent phase of the new democracy to its inauguration and early operation. The external factors of environment may be either progressively unfavourable to the vulnerable authoritarian system in terms of prevalent values (such as in a given region like Western Europe) or promotive of democratisation through cross-national socio-economic change of a modernising kind. Democratic transition ends not merely once the constitution is in place but also when the new democracy begins to function with a popularly democratically elected government. People start to work the system and to adjust accordingly.

Here, Whitehead [1986:19] notes that the boundary between exercising legitimate external influence and improper intervention is far more blurred than most governments are willing to admit. However, there are three components of the international promotion of democracy: {a} pressure on undemocratic governments to democratise themselves: {b} support for fledgling democracies that are attempting to consolidate: and {c} the maintenance of a firm stance against anti-democratic forces that threaten or overthrow established democracies. South Africa during the apartheid era present good examples in respect of point {a} where external pressure pressurised the demise of the inhumane governance system and {b} support for the new black majority governance system that emerged in 1994. The African Union {AU} stands during the transfer or power from father to son in Togo in 2005. Of course distinction should be drawn between types of external actors – different foreign governments, international or integrative organisations – and also between governmental and non-governmental agencies, such as international parties or interest groups and the churches. In this sense, the question of models of democracy, in the socio-economic as well as political meaning of the term, becomes highlighted, given that systemic and ideological variants invariably determine the extent of its promotion from outside.

Furthermore, Whitehead [1988:6-7] points out: after any transition from authoritarian rule to emergent democracy will be a regime in which not all significant political actors have impeccable democratic credentials, and where democratic rules of procedure have yet to be 'internalised' by the society at large. Many established institutions have to be reconstructed, some demoted, some virtually created anew, to make them conform to democratic rather than authoritarian modes of governance. New and inexperienced political actors enter the stage, while long-established parties and interests find themselves required to compete on a quite different basis than before.

The rules for competition are up for negotiation, the outcomes are uncertain and often quite unexpected; no one is quite sure which elements of continuity remain in place. In short, the transition phase is often one acute uncertainty and high anxiety for many social actors. Such uncertainty may be exciting and creative, but if it becomes too generally threatening, or if it lasts too long without any fruitful outcome, then the chances of an authoritarian relapse become very great. This is why it is imperative that appropriate and comprehensive measures be taken to establish a level playing ground for all competing parties to better establish a functional, legitimate and credible governance system. Giving the people the opportunity to make their choices is crucial at the early stages of regime change to restore confidence, legality and sustainability and for the system to adjust accordingly.

Free, fair, transparent and competitive elections starts from the registration process up to the final pronouncement of results. Is not coming at the polling stations that one decide whether the elections are free and fair? The state must encourage a vibrant civil society as the watchdog and best choice to sanction elections in a country. Political parties must learn to accept the verdict of the ballot box. Though we need African solutions for challenging African problems, the third eye and ear, cannot be discarded to give greater credence to the democratic governance and administrative transitional stages of the continent. In this process attempts must be made to eradicate corruption. Attempts have been made in the past couple of years to come to terms and grapple with the question of corruption. Many countries have tried to establish anti-corruption units in ministries. The absence of moral and ethics constitutes major draw back in the fight against corruption. "The notion of 'to fear to be caught' is not a sufficient way of dealing with the question of corruption. We need more than just a fear of being caught. We need both a systemic and systematic understanding of the complexity of corruption. We need organisational integrity. To unlearn before we can even learn. For me what is important is a well-motivated public service, which should be preferred to one that operates in fear of being apprehended. It is not enough for you to fear being caught. You need to move to the next level, a paradigmatic shift in the notion of clean government" [Busakwe 2006:18].

Yet all these activities are best undertaken through an independent, non-partisan bureaucracy, which a public bureaucracy is supposed to incarnate. An it incarnates the policy of "to serve and preserve" [Rugumyamheto 2000] and further elaborated in a book "To Serve and Preserve: Improving Public Administration in a Competitive World" [Schiaro-Campo and Sundaram, 2001]. To be successful in the task requires a number of inter-related factors and coordinated actions: Leadership and the ability to influence changes and developments in the right pattern: Vision and Mission; Personal discipline, Personal integrity; Communication skills and ability to listen and learning from others including the role of the legislative assembly as the rule-making organ. Incidentally African parliaments are not active in promoting state-civil society- private sector interface. "The growth in numbers and successes of democratisation processes in Africa, coupled with the changing nature of conflict itself in the post-Cold War geopolitical environment, has significantly affected the role that parliamentarians can play, and has opened the door to a new recognition of their possibilities and responsibilities in conflict-affected countries" [Balch, 2006:21] as well as promoting economic growth.

But economic growth is not enough. Quality service delivery becomes an inevitable asset. Service delivery is viewed as an ethical imperative because its failure will not improve the lives of the ordinary citizen. Service delivery is also viewed as a legal imperative because it is at the core of our mandates. So it is both ethical and legal. Above all, service delivery, or lack thereof, either harms or improves the reputation of government. Therefore organisation integrity gives public organisation a comparative advantage. Nothing undermines the delivery of service more than lack of integrity [Busakwe 2006:19]. The role of leadership is vital in building organisational integrity. For now leadership constitute a serious problem in Africa?

Through its own leadership, Africans should solve its own problems and take its destiny in its own hands. Both the AU and NEPAD as the continental organisation should be at the forefront in the crusade in setting a new beginning and the reconstruction from state failure to state building. The move taken by members of parliament from central and East Africa to draw up guidelines for Parliamentary Action on curbing corruption and creating a more conducive environment for business, entrepreneurship invest and trade is a good beginning. On 8-9 September 2006, over 50 Parliamentarians from the Great Lakes Region, Central Africa and European MPs from Ireland, Sweden and Germany, participated in a seminar with the theme *"Parliamentary and Private Sector Cooperation for sustainable Development and Poverty Reduction in the Great Lakes Region"*. Organised jointly by the Association of European Parliamentarians for Africa {AWEPA}, The East African Legislative Assembly {EALA}, and the United Nations Environment Programme {UNEP}, the idea was to build parliamentarians' knowledge about the private sector development and strengthen links between parliamentarians and the business community.

This important encounter ended with the adoption of a set of Draft Guidelines for Parliamentary Action on Creating a Conducive Environment for Business Entrepreneurship Investment and Trade"[see Balch 2006:21, UNDP 2006]. A content analysis of the document shows strong emphasis on the importance of a thriving private sector as the engine of growth much needed to meet the Millennium Development Goals {7 percent by 2010 from current levels of 3 percent}. In short as guardians of democracy and champions of the people's rights, parliamentarians bear a heavy responsibility to deliver on the basics: peace, stability, health, prosperity, social justice and inclusiveness to ensure national integration, and unity in diversity. The diversity of Africa is paradise, which the entire world should enjoy and treasure as the continents contribution to the progress of humanity. Our diversity should be asset.

It is argued that the state of equality in the society requires an ever-increasing ability to integrate and unite rather than to separate and individualise. In a rapidly changing world, where all nations find themselves unbearably strained under the pressure of shifting environmental, economic and political upheavals, the ability to maintain the integrity, nobility of the human being and to prepare all citizens for national unity in a complex and shrinking world takes on paramount importance. It is imperative for the state, to be at the forefront to guide and pilot the pathways for people to understand their responsibilities in the nation beyond economic well-being to include setting an example of healthy human intercourse, mutual understanding through the auspices of peaceful co-existence among peoples and nations. Not every national group will possess the same objective or subjective characteristics. What is important is for *'unity in diversity'* to reign marked by a degree of indeterminacy. Miller [1995:27] notes: *"Instead of believing that for any given nation there is a set of necessary and sufficient conditions for belonging to that nation, we should think in terms of Wittgenstein's metaphor of a thread whose strength 'does not reside in the fact that some one fibre runs through its whole length, but in the over-lapping of many fibre".* People should endeavour to submerge individualistic interest for the collective interest. Your security depends on my security or vice versa, therefore we should collectively work for our common security and future without compromising the rights of the other to live in peace and harmony.

The individual and all people in society or the community environment are ultimately under the protection of the state; it is at this level that enlightened and responsible leadership is desperately required. Unfortunately, most governments, however, continue to abdicate their national obligations to society. Incidentally, they do not punish and prevent violence and exploitation of women, girls and the weak. Many governments lack the political will. Some fail to allocate adequate resources to implement the laws enacted for improving the living standards of the people. The era of developing legal frameworks must not be followed by an emphasis on implementation and prevention of crime against humanity. The foundation of such measures is a strategy rooted in the education and training of all people in society that enables them to develop intellectually as well as ethically and morally, cultivating in them a sense of dignity as well as a responsibility for the well-being of the people.

What is important is for African states to guard against bad governance. The failure to govern effectively ultimately takes toll on the legitimacy and stability of democracy. The democratic malaise is particularly visible in the trends in public opinion in countries like Cameroon, Nigeria, the Democratic Republic of Congo, Chad, Sudan, Somalia and others. Manipulation by the ruling CPDM in Cameroon prior to the 22 July 2007 parliamentary and municipal elections indicates how democracy and the democratic process, which the party claims to be "advanced democracy with great achievements", are constantly thwarted. However, this comes as no surprise.

A content analysis of Paul Biya's [1987:127] Communal Liberalism, which was healed as a breakthrough in ushering democratisation, rigour and moralisation states: "The present phase of the history of Cameroon does not permit the institution of a multiple party system. Our party is, therefore, responsible for the reduction of the existing ethno-cultural divisions in order to promote national integration which is the requisite for the institution of a pluralistic democracy". Can we talk of democracy when political pluralism does not exist? Can we talk of advanced democracy when the basics are denied the people and the non-existence of a levelling play field for all citizens to approve or sanction their elected representatives? The essence of democratic governance that creates room for social and system changes is the understanding that individuals have the right and moral and civic obligations to be active participants in the decision-making and development processes. Such obligations shape their understanding of the existence purpose, their responsibilities towards one another, the community, and nation.

Being partners in the process of structured system changes requires constructive changes in the legal, political and economic architecture taking the right shape and responding the needs and aspirations of the people. Asma Jahangir [2006], UN Special Rapporteur on Freedom of Religion or Belief on the occasion of the 25th anniversary of the United Nations Declaration on the Elimination of All Forms of Intolerance and the Discrimination Based on Religion or Belief, Prague, 25 November 2006, touches on an important issue. "We need to eliminate the root causes of intolerance and discrimination. To remain vigilant with regard to the state of peaceful co-existence and development and to ensure a sustainable world system as the platform for constructing and accommodating divergent views".

We cannot dismiss the fact that democracy provides the people with an indispensable instrument of electoral accountability to dismiss leaders who do not perform well and to restore confidence in those that offer services to society. The slogan "to serve is to take action: to preserve is to be reflective" constitutes the road map for a functional state system. The recent primaries leading to the 22 July 2007 elections in Cameroon is clear indication as many of the old parliamentarians within the Social Democratic Front [SDF] party and other parties are rejected by their constituencies for poor performances. The people must have their rights to making choices.

Cases where the ruling political parties blocks the process or denies this opportunity - the inclusiveness of the incumbenants – to restrain fair, competitive, transparent and neutrally conducted elections – the incentive of incumbents to restrain themselves and serve the public good withers. In most African countries, leaders and representatives become not only venal and distant from public concerns, but also increasingly abusive of human rights and totally insensitive to the plight of the people. It is imperative for national and international communities to create the social, material and structural conditions in which the people, especially the disadvantaged in society can develop their full potential. The creation of such conditions involves not only deliberate attempts to change the legal, political and economic structures of society, but, equally importantly, will require the transformation of individuals whose values, in different ways, sustain exploitative patterns of behaviour.

Democracy provides policies with freedom and institutional means, in between elections to scrutinise the conduct and policy decisions of public officials and hold them accountable. Of course, leaders in a democracy are under pressure and incentives to explain and justify their decisions, and to consult a broad range of constituencies before passing laws and making decisions. Again wider public dialogue and participation in a policymaking process produces decisions that are more legitimate and sustainable. It goes without saying that a competitive, free, transparent and fair elections are the *sin qua non* of democracy and this transplants itself in the public bureaucracy to render services to society. Africa must confront its crisis of political development from a holistic and inclusive manner. The political path to modernity involves critical changes of identity, and that individuals identified as members of the political community should be organised in productive and administrative institutions according to a rational principle. Productive and administrative capacity depends upon the rational integration or organisation of humans that share a common identity.

Many countries are making efforts in reforming the state bureaucratic sector. The imposed World Bank/IMF. SAP led a number of countries to downsizing of the state bureaucracy. The idea was that the public service was oversized and non-productive. Therefore, civil servants were sent on voluntary retirement, employment stop, eradicating ghost workers, and radical cuts in the pay packets, sales of state properties among other measures.- In Cameroon the idea of 'zero state fleet and housing policy' was adopted. To a large extent, some of measures backfired as it rather increased the poor living status of the vast majority of the population. It even intensified fraud and other corrupt practices. Today, the flashes big cars are back on the streets. The policy strategy of "Zero-state fleet" has converged into "surplus luxurious fleet" which does argue well for a constructive restructuring process. The sales of government properties – vehicles, houses etc. at give away prices were designed to meeting the needs of a particular clientele or ethnic hegemonic, political party needs or as compensation to these groups. This explains why Cameroon is poor in the midst of plenty.

The efficient use of both human and natural resources remains imperative for the sustainable transformation of Africa from a third to a first world. Funke and Nsouli [2003] in [Kuye 2006:74] states that weak domestic policies have contributed to lacklustre performance, though factors that are beyond the control of African countries such as negative terms of trade shocks, have also affected performance. Therefore, regional economic groupings like ECOWAS, SADC, CEMAC and NEPAD should become centres of excellence in mobilising resources and assisting local authorities with the development of local and national, regional and continental strategies, synergies and action planes to build local institutional environments for successful implementations of well conceived and focused development related activities.

Structural reforms are required but should be targeted towards areas that will improve the quality of life of the population. As noted by Sambo [2005:55], reforming government institutions should focused on -

- Towards a more efficient and responsive public sector;
- Security and administration of justice;
- Tackling corruption, and promoting transparency and accountability of government expenditures;
- Reforming government and its institutions including restructuring, rationalising and strengthening institutions;
- Right-sizing the public sector;
- Capacity building –which should include training and re-training;
- Increased use of scientific methods of policy formulation;
- Discipline and strong work ethics;
- Good citizenship at individual and corporate levels;
- Re-professionalising the public service.

The sum total of views expressed above and in other sections of the publication boils down to the views expressed in the Report of the South Commission [1990:1]: "the primary bond that links the country and politics of the South is their desire to escape from poverty and underdevelopment and secure a better life for their citizens". This calls for the deepening of the democratic process, improving governance and promoting an effective and efficient public bureaucracy, strengthening the rule of law from below and as well as above. Civil society must be organised effectively to ensure state adherence to the social contract. In a society like Cameroon, we have a civil society that is spoon-fed like a baby. It remains passive not vibrant. The governance system has instilled FEAR in the people making them unable to stand for and defend their inherent rights. The struggle for political pluralism and democracy as the best system of governance, there has arise greater demand and pressure by the people on government for more and active participatory role in state affairs.

The eradication of poverty in society, the eradication of violence against the female gender are issues that need serious attention by the powers that be and society in general. Of course, by many measures, the status of women and girls has improved significantly over the past decades. They have achieved higher rates of literacy and education, increased their per capita income, and risen to prominent in professional and political spheres. Their situation could have better if chauvinistic ideas and other traditional taboos did not grip our heads, hearts and behaviour. Moreover, extensive local, national and global networks of women have succeeded in putting women's concerns on the national and global agenda and catalysed the creation of legal and institutional mechanisms to address these concerns. Notwithstanding such positive developments, a relentless epidemic of violence against women and girls – perpetuated by social norms, religious fanaticism, and exploitative economic and political conditions - continue to wreak havoc in every corner of society and the world at large. {See One Country 2006}.

How can the state machinery rise above existing injustices and prejudice? This question is pressing in African countries where the state has become little more than an instrument for personal aggrandisement and a means to enhance the interest of those individuals and groups loyal to the operators of state power. State power should be brought under x-ray. What, then, are the issues to address? The first is perhaps that of state power in relation to the freedom of citizens. The second is that of the power of the state. The state, in the classic liberal account, is a mechanism for reconciling conflict and potentially incommensurable interests, by means of a common political form into which these different interests can be translated and through which they can be compared. The job of the state, is to enable people with very different wants and expectations to coexist, without flattering out the different things they have to offer, without prejudging what it is they want to expect from the transaction [Runciman 2003: 33].

It cannot be gainsaid that Africa needs serious restructuring but with a human face. Restructuring that brings human dignity and nobility to the people. For now, Africa remains very far from the ideals of harmony, prosperity and peace inspired by cultivating and nurturing the values and virtues of democratic governance. A first step in that direction is for the continent, to actively work towards attaining the MDGs that provides an impetus of reverse deterioration in human development. The leaders should show their genuine political will towards implementing the various issues required under the attainment of MDGs by 2015. One cannot overstress the importance of the education of women in achieving the goals of reducing poverty, improving health, and promoting education in society, especially giving training to the right education and upbringing that on graduation they become job-creators and not job-seekers in the public administrative sector. "There is no way a society can remain peaceful [and] develop meaningfully unless the state maintains its objective position in society" {Ekanola, 2005:52}.

Apparently, a number of clusters of political problems confronting African states include: ambivalence and frustration related to modernisation, internal cleavages based on sub national loyalties, political instability, and prominence of the military in politics. Since Africa's lost decade backed by poor policy formulation and execution, aspiration for better life has been eroded by population growth to a basic struggle for mere survival, and as traditional beliefs and order-maintaining social structures are weakened, little imagination is needed to foresee mounting political problems and pressures. Quality services delivery is not forthcoming to ameliorate the plight of the people and still a sense of hope, vision and confidence within the people.

Thus *"the crisis of the 'developmental state'* in African countries poses a critical problem. The central of the state in public administration, development planning and economic management has had a strong resonance in Africa. It was seen as a principal means of managing the economy, directing it away from the interests of financing capital and markets towards meeting national needs and aspirations. The crisis of the developmental state that emanated from this central role of the state in the 1970s and early 1980s in Africa and even recently, in the 1990s, has resulted in locational and social differentiation in a considerable number of countries" [Kuye, 2006:70-71].

The outstanding drawback in Africa's development is that of leadership. "The emergence of quality developmental leaders in democracies is not a matter of chance" [Adei 2004: 51]. Munroe [1998] adds: "quality leadership is a key to a prosperous nation. And it is obvious that our nations are painfully in need of such leaders". And a survey of corporate leaders in the United States shows that credibility is the single most admired quality by the followers [Kouzes, Posner and Peters 1995]. "Leaders do not only deliver on vision, strategies, mobilisation, and change management, but they are also credible and trustworthy. It is credibility that enables them to engage their countries' attention for long haul of transforming their national economies. This is what I call 'legacy-building leadership" [Adei 2004]. The leadership of Nkrumah, Nyerere, Mandela, and others could be placed in this category of African leaders. Legacy-building leaders are marked by three Cs, namely; Character, Competence and Care. A successful integration of these characteristics is what makes a complete leader. The sequences may differ and not all of African leaders have been able to combined and exhibit the leadership skills in all these fields depending upon the kind of analytical approach and belief in the individual. One can use any of the characteristics to fault Nkrumah's, Nyerere's or Mandela's leadership skills and style.

Africa has had a fair share of leaders capable of mobilising and instilling hope in the people. Some of the leaders were bedevilled by constraining circumstances, for example, colonial resistance towards the independence of colonies and internal factors for not meeting the aspirations of the people, quickly contributed to fall of leaders like Kwame Nkrumah, Sekour Toure, Nnamdi Azikiwe, Nyerere, Mandela, among others. These leaders were committed towards raising the quality of the nation's human capital, level of technology and improving the living standards of the people but in different ways had their shortcomings in the accomplishments of social and basic needs of the people. Of course, one cannot rule out the stranglehold of western capitalist systems (governments, financial institutions and donors) on policy through whatever support extended to these countries. A leader who works for his people but disliked by the west is often brought down through various means, especially the manipulation of the media, the academia and intellectuals, the religious bodies and industry or corporate bodies in sabotaging activities and working for the interest of foreign bodies rather than working in the interest of the country.

Leadership is the privilege to have the responsibility to direct the actions of others in carrying out the purposes of the society or organisation, at varying levels of authority and with accountability for both successful and failed endeavours. It does not constitute a model or system. No model or system of leadership behaviour can anticipate the circumstances, conditions and situations in which the leader must influence the actions of others. An evaluation of leadership principles is an effective base upon which to build other skills that may be important to success in specialised fields. What is most important for African leaders is to exhibit a sense of trustworthiness, integrity, justice and principle-centeredness as far as *character* is concern No one is asking for 'angelic leaders' for there are no 'angelic human beings', but leaders the people can believe in and trust: leaders who will enjoy the trappings of high office but not abuse them: leaders who will not steal and lie as a norm; leaders who care for their fellow compatriots.

In respect of *"Care"*, a leader must perform three "M" functions at the same time, namely, a *model, a mentor and a minister.* "Weak leadership shows itself in seeing a small group of people, often a sycophantic group, as the only ones to care for, to the neglect of most others and a significant opposition. The ability to neutralise a small destructive element may be part of effective leadership, but lack of a generous spirit and inclusiveness, which has dogged much of our national history, is a mark of weak leadership. In other countries, that has even led to civil wars and erosion of irreplaceable social capital." [Adei 2004:33]. Africa should be developing and utilising its human capital not for development, not destroying its most valuable resources.

Turning to *"competence"*, leadership is a function to prosecute, and to do so competently. Leadership competence requires the ability to think long-term and strategically too; to cast and communicate a national vision; and to manage the single biggest institutional apparatus in most countries – government [Adei 2004:32] In short, leadership is a value-based vocation or else it becomes dysfunctional as portrayed by people like Hitler, Mussolini, Mobuto, Sanni Abacha, Idi Amin and others. Legacy-building leadership requires a combination of characteristics that could be seen as opposites: a high sense of self-confidence, an assurance of one's vision on the one hand and humility on the other; a decision-making and problem-solving capacity on the one hand and team building on the other; the ability to motivate, inspire and encourage followers on the one hand and the capacity to endure loneliness, even treachery and sabotage on the other; overseeing huge resources on the one hand and not being corrupt on the other. The link between these otherwise opposite phenomena is what managing character is all about [Adei 2004:30].

Africa needs leaders with an independent mind and with the interest of the people at heart as the first priority in governance. When African leaders begin to place the interest of their people first, have independent but fatherly mind, firm in their decision without any biases, do not compromise on their own character and demand integrity from their key officials, Africa would have taken the first and rightful step in the direction of moving from a third to a first world. The first step in that direction is addressing corruption and nepotism while ensuring that democratic governance reigns supreme. The Prime Minister and Head of Government in Cameroon in a television broadcast in 1999 noted *"the government is corrupt from top to bottom"* [Ngwana 2001:146]. Under a democratic and responsible governance system, the best thing to do was to resign or be sacked by the President. Nothing of that happened. Indeed, Cameroon is Cameroon. Cameroon is not an exception here. What is evident is that when system of administration is essentially weak in them, and coupled with poor leadership skills or styles, they create vulnerabilities for the meat eaters. Gaps are opened for the meat eaters, the grass eaters and chancers. Leaders and values are needed. Leaders are the ethical teachers of the state. Their behaviour sends signals. Values define what we stand for; values are beliefs about how we see ourselves and what we want others to see in us. Importantly, values connect us to our vision. They also drive our strategy.

The values leaders place on people, not on systems or the bottom line of profit in the short run, determines the kind of progress the country makes in its transitional efforts to modernity. When leaders value people, they bring the best out of them. As noted by Adei [2004:33], If one wants leadership for power, wealth, or even to prove a point, one is likely to see people as instruments, or tools to achieve an end. In Africa, often, self-styled leaders cause so much mayhem and even loss of lives to attain power, and that makes one wonder whether they are real leaders of their people or merely butchers. This is where one class of leaders makes all the difference – servant leaders. Servant leaders are motivated by the desire to serve their people and not the other way round. Leaders with the vision and attitude of 'shared responsibility with the rest of society to advance the process of development. If you become a true leader who chooses to be a leader, you unleash pro-activity, accountability, responsibility and moral authority in people. One of the major problems of corruption and state failure is the gross absence of moral authority. Africa needs leaders and public servants with ethical and moral authority. The absence of good leadership and moral authority contributes to the kind of development reigning within the continent.

For now, the primary goal of legacy-building leaders must be focused on a new policy strategy contributing to equitable and sustainable national development. Development can never be externally created or imposed on people. Development is created by people in their own society. Therefore, the continent needs leaders who better at listening, but also at making demands for sustainable development through a policy based to a greater extent on the lives, experiences and capacity and priorities of poor and marginalised people. It is within this context that the leaders and people can draw their own experiences of reducing poverty, curbing corruption, in which peace, democracy, good governance, investment in human capacity building, economic growth, equitable distribution of income and resources and gender equality are vital elements.

In order to contribute to the achievement of the goal of equitable and sustainable development, all the components of the country's policy must be consistent with one another. It is crucial for legacy-building leader to focus on those who have not benefited from the prosperity generated by national development. Here, poor people especially the poorest among them, must be empowered and have a greater opportunity for benefiting from the advantages that increased global trade has yielded. Progress must not be excluded but inclusive. Benefits shared and not distribute to ethnic groups clienteles and party or financial tycoons. The 'have-nots' must be placed first and not the 'haves' given priority positions in society. This underlines the issues of equality, liberty and freedom with neither the tyranny of minority nor majority taking precedence.

The key issues and challenges of our time concern all people. They must accordingly be addressed at all levels, i.e. at local, provincial, national continental and global levels. The UN Millennium Development Goals represent concrete step-by-step objectives and targets in specific areas that should force committed governments in meeting the social contract. The goals of MDGs are of central significance not only in the context of national, but international development cooperation and for the global monitoring and evaluation of the commitments made by each African country in halving poverty by 2015. Addressing commitments within MDGs should be a must for African countries. The realisation of the MDGs shows which countries in Africa are people-oriented. The pursuit of equitable and sustainable development must be based on a rights perspective on development. This implies that poor people should not be regarded as recipients of aid, but as individuals and actors with the power, capacity and the will to create development and benefit from the process of development.

As earlier noted, development can never be externally created or imposed on people. It is a dynamic process. The perspectives of the key stakeholders and especially that of the poor and excluded should therefore complement the rights perspective. The poor and marginalised must shape their development. Of course, integrating the perspectives of the excluded poor and marginalised groups will involve shifting the balance of power from the rich and powerful to the poor, weak and excluded [Forje 2007, forthcoming], and from governments to individuals or groups. To a large extent, the power base of the state is eroded and challenged. If poverty and corruption are too combated vigorously, it is necessary to enable the poor and excluded themselves and their legitimate representatives to take active part in decision-making. The important issue is to ensure that the perspectives, interests, resources and capacities of the poor and excluded {women, men, children etc.} are represented in the national strategies and in the policy that is pursued.

With the gradual return to the democratic process, the people have mandated themselves with a responsibility and an opportunity to change the course of the African continent from a third to a first world. It is equally important within this context that efforts be made to develop central political principles and procedures for issues such as accountability, participation, transparency and the distribution of power and wealth. Forms and mechanisms for the prevention and peaceful resolution of social and political conflicts should be supported and further developed and consolidated within the system. Good governance and good public administration are important aspects of democracy.

These concern the management and distribution of public resources, equality before the law and procedures to combat the abuse of power. Corruption, nepotism and kleptocracy undermine citizens' legal security and favour established elites at the expense of the suffering masses. This weakens democracy. Africa cannot afford a weaken form of democratic governance at this stage. Efforts must be directed towards the return to political pluralism and democracy on the continent [see Ngwana 2001] as the way forward for the continent. By encouraging political pluralism and democracy, the continent will be crafting for itself a new dawn in the geopolitics of this century and beyond. The continent's law-making body fail to realise their potential influence and impact in crafting a new society, the responsibility and an opportunity to change the course of history. Individually and collectively, their actions can make a world of difference at the national, regional, continental and global levels to ensure that democratic governance and prosperity reigns.

The quest for democratisation and the wave of democratic elections in Africa {though not yet competitive, transparent, fair and free} in post –Cold War era, is generating a new breed of African leaders and creating excellent windows of opportunities for deepening and strengthening democratic relationships between the state-civil society and private sector to enhance the socio-economic, political and technological transformation of the African continent. It is important that parliamentarians do not miss these windows of opportunities by neglecting their obligations to their constituencies. Neither should they succumb to fledging executive powers, especially strong executives or dictators with skeletons in their closets to hide. For our law making bodies to be invested in, in order for them to be effective and efficient in exercising their duties in the fight against undemocratic and tyrannical, governance system.

Importantly, the struggle for political pluralism and democracy must continue unabated on the African continent. The people must proclaim a political ideology with a system of political objectives of the forcible over throw of all existing dictatorship, clan/ethnic politics, social injustice and exclusion, while exhausting all avenues to ensure free individuals, without exploitation, oppression, or alienation, and ensuring that the basic tenets of democratic values and virtues are observed and practiced to the letter. Since independence, the continent has witnessed a barrage of military coups, institutionalised life presidents presiding over shrinking economies with the worst human rights abuses in the history of the continent. As we embrace the 21st century, the goal should be constructing a region of strong, stable not weak and unstable or unorganised, inefficient, hesitant and ill-prepared states to be suffocated and chucked out by the cold-blooded rules of globalisation, neo-colonialism, neo-liberalism and capitalism.

Obviously, if Africa is to meet the challenges of third millennium, it must vigorously embraced a democratisation and decentralisation of political power, backed with marketisation of the economy, backed with a transformation process with a human-face. No doubt, democracy provides the best prospects of popular participation in the selection of the peoples' representatives and selection of leaders, and by implication, the choice of development priorities and strategies. Implicit n such a prospect is the opportunity for regular assessment of the performance of leaders as well as change of leadership through competitive, free, accountable, transparent, and fair elections

It goes without saying that democracy promotes and encourages accountability, responsiveness, efficient and human governance, while authoritarianism perpetuates tyranny, corruption and inefficiency, as clearly demonstrated in the majority of African states since independence. Happily, there is a silver lining in the Africa horizon [Ngwana 2001:4]. The collapse of communism, the demise of apartheid and the emergence or gradual return to political pluralism being demonstrated across the continent augurs well for a better and brighter Africa of tomorrow. Of course, the seeds for system change must be planted today and properly nurtured. The first step was the struggle for self-determination, pressure on non-conforming African countries to embrace the democratic principles and its virtues; the collapse of apartheid in South Africa, the reluctant abolition of the monolithic party state, and the acceptance of political pluralism by All African States, the gradual disappearance of life presidents, and the decrease of military coups, are clear signs that the democratic process is on course in Africa.

The momentum for change must be deepened and sustained for the region to arrive at the completion point – functional pluralistic democratic governance system. It is the ardent duty of every one to encourage and secure democracy and democratic consolidation on the continent. There has to be bridge-building within and between peoples and nations to ensure the smooth functioning and dimensions of the democratic political system. One effective way of confronting obstacles derailing the political process is too eschew grand-scale models for 'linkage politics' and to focus on placing people first in all policies endeavours. These countries should move away from authoritarian to democratic governance so as to harvest the advantages that go with a more open and inclusive type of governance system. With the end of the Cold War and the demise of monolithic party structure and centralised governments, every citizen should now play an active role in the governance system.

We all must be the active 'police officer' of the nation-state in particular and the continent in general. With every one playing this role, election rigging, corruption and other malpractices that have been the cause of political strive; violence and even civil wars leading to genocide in many African countries will gradually subside. Ngwana [2001:7] notes: the tendency for those in control of state power to exploit their positions to manipulate elections in their favour, irrespective of the will of the people, has been a major obstacle to the institutionalisation of liberal democracy on the African continent. Building national interest, goals and common objectives should be paramount. Nationalism should be seen in a positive light in relation to democracy. In his 'Considerations on Representative Government', John

Stuart Mill extended the idea of self-determination by arguing that "where the sentiment of nationality exists in any force, there is a prima facie case for uniting all the members of the same nationality under the same government, and a government to themselves apart. This is merely saying that the question of government ought to be decided by the governed' [1996:41]. The democratic process should be piloted and sustained by a governance system of "Here The People Rule" [Forje, 2007].

But democracy is not the panacea for development. It is just a means to an end. We must make it function properly to provide bread on the table, to ensure that freedom and liberty with responsibility reigns. The emergence of pluralist democracy as the best possible system of governance opens many avenues and windows of opportunities for active participation by the people in government, as well as it puts demands and checks on the government in fulfilling its social contract with the people. It creates room for power sharing and decision-making at various levels of governance. Africans must win genuine independence and not the shadow of self-rule. Above all, they must learn to run faster and faster with a strategic sense of priorities and purpose or else will remain where they are. They have to realise that neo-colonialism and dictatorship remains an impediment to the progress of the continent, with appropriate stand taken against existing dependency system. A new approach must be crafted about the democratic transition of the continent so that the process it is not hijacked by foreign interests.

ENVISAGING A SHOPPING CATALOGUE

Africa has to overcome the politics and policies of ethnic hegemony tribal and racial hatred. The challenge in Africa today is to protect the rights of the excluded majority pontificated or hijacked by a tiny minority. The tiny minority have abrogated for themselves the wealth of the nation. The politics of equation must take-over and restore confidence and trust in the political system. Reaching out to grass roots is essential for democracy to thrive as a system that provides the needs for all not a select few. Grassroots economic and political empowerment {GREPE} offers the right perspectives for equity and sustaining the democratic governance process. The politics of equity, economic and political empowerment {PEEPE} will bring out the best of both worlds for the people of the continent in a rapidly changing global climate dictated by the accelerating pace of a knowledge-based global economy.

There is something rotten within the core of many political parties – issues of cronyism, corruption, victimisation, longevity in office, dictatorial rule of one kind or the other that thwarts the political transformation of the region from a third to a first world. Africa needs to go beyond the politics of protecting leaders of the liberation movement who today have become tyrants and oppressors of the people they once fought on their behave. The other is to avoid populism without a sense of direction taking total control of the leadership of the dominant political party especially when such leadership is weak and prone to the dictates of cronyism and not focused

As a final component of this section, we need to consider creating an institutional voice and out ways for sub-state national groups to be participants in the process of reconstruction and development. We may consider a number of scenarios where there is a total breakdown in trust between the state and sub-national groups and the government. The situation in Zimbabwe points towards such a break. The silence of African leaders towards the plight of the people has much to do with leaders protecting founding fathers or leaders of liberation era as well as a kind of attempt to keep low the same issues existing their backyards. No one supports the bridge of agreement by western powers, which to a large extent has forced the Zimbabwean authorities to taking desperate actions for political survival. The same can be aid of Sudan. Things are falling apart and rapidly too. The situation has to be arrested before total disintegration between the state and society takes place. The worst fear is anarchy and genocide. Come to think of Rwanda or break away Biafra in Nigeria in the sixties. Why must these awful incidents continue repeating themselves on the continent? The situation in Sudan, Somali and Zimbabwe must penetrate into the consciences of Africa and the global community.

The other scenario is to distinguish the geopolitical situation and geographical groups and to rally these groups into a united piece though with diverse interests under a common canopy of national unity, peace, humanity and sustainable development that benefits all. The state and people must be an integral part of the solution to existing problems. The intercourse between state and people should be in the wider interest of the people in the society in particular, and humanity in general and within and between nations. What a future it would be for Africa not marked by corruption, exclusion and destruction, sad images that have gripped the world about the continent?

In a situation where there is an absence of trust, overt hostility, violence and bloodshed will prevail. Africa must search for benchmarks that foster unity, reconciliation and genuine signs for progress and sustained development for the benefit of all. In the face of an extreme lack of trust structure, guarantees are needed that can bring the people back to a negotiating table for dialogue and reconciliation. Such a guarantee is for the people having a voice, strong inputs and opinions for constructive system change in policy making and implementation. A voice or input by the people is essential to a successful institutionalisation where there is an extreme lack of trust. What is important is for all parties to act in good faith.

When trust is the issue, it is particularly important to emphasis that peoples representation is not necessary an alternative to forms of autonomous self-rule, but as a voice which is a necessarily implement to self-rule or 'here the people". Therefore, the processes of enfranchisement and legislative representation must remain paramount in promoting the well being of the people. Deep diversity may or does exist, but this could be narrowed as long as the politics and political will exist to address outstanding issues. Africa does not need a crystal-ball to see the significance of addressing deep diversity and disparity by allowing the people to rule as one of the central political pillars upon which to address current problems and seeking endurable solutions.

Putting people first provides the right path to endurable solutions to the plethora of problems plaguing the continent. The people must equally make sacrifices by taking their share of responsibilities to ensure that shared values and responsibilities constitute elements of building a sustainable society. The people having a say or voice in policy articulation and decision implementations processes provide a range of options. Government power and functions will operate proper when proportional representation and elected governance exist to give the voiceless a place in policy formulation, decision-making implementation and evaluation as well as usher greater satisfaction of unity for all is involved and practiced.

Quality service delivery, social justice, the rule of law and other forms of implementation remain the most existing arenas for ensuring social justice and integration, national unity and involvement. Therefore partnership between state and the people, between minority and majority provides the best way forward for Africa. The situation facing Africa has different elements and dimensions of the issues presented. In tandem with the rights and insights as well as good will of the parties involved, institutional change can be effectuated within the premises of transferability of structural reforms across different strata of society.

It is question of equity in development and restraining ruling elites from blocking institutional reforms needed to achieve greater equity, when system changes are against their interests. Fostering greater equity must be the goal. For when economic, political and socio-cultural inequalities reinforce one another, individuals belonging to excluded groups may be caught in 'inequality traps''. Greater equality of opportunity is good for development. Therefore, public action should seek to expand the opportunity sets of those who have the least resources, voice and capabilities. Achieving this may, however, involve reducing the privileges of those who reap special benefits from existing institutions and policies. Such a focus would aim to level the playing field in the crucial areas of human capacities, justice and the rule of law: access to land and infrastructure: and in the broad functioning of markets and the macro economy. Equity creates a safety net of sort for all in society. Presently the poor and excluded suffer not only from *economic* inequity but also political inequality. Solutions of '*anti-poor*' and *anti-growth*' policies must be found to create an egalitarian society so that '*Redistribution with Growth*' can be incorporated in development policies.

SYNTHESIS AND PROGNOSIS: WHERE DO WE GO FROM HERE?

The foregoing analysis shows that, most, if not all, African states are yet to embark on a genuine path for developmentalist state on the continent. What is the transformative image of the state in the wake of the challenges posed by the growing demands of society? Is the state a fiction or an abstraction that is given concrete form through rectification and personification? Whether the state is a fiction or not, it has been attributed purposes and intentions around which many things flow and evolve. Should system change be less revolutionary or what? "*Plus ca change plus c'est la même chose*". Changes are taking place on the continent; but continuity represents continuous change that enhances quality livelihood and not change for change sake. Africa needs change and shared responsibility and partnership where more people's power should be to establish a new equilibrium [Forje 2007]. An equilibrium that extracts from our body politic as a dentist extracts a stinking tooth all the decadent stooges versed with extorting the wealth, riches and freedom of the people in building an inclusive and sustainable society {see Achebe 1966]. A fair share of the national cake must trickle down to the people.

The development process flawed in the treatment of space in relation between different political and geographical scales of analysis and actions have frequently been inadequately articulated and aggregated. Therefore, we need to reconstruct a new society based on some of the views expressed in the foregoing sections. We may look at these as partly conclusions or as key consideration that should shape development policy in all it various forms – democratisation, economic growth, building a sustainable scientific and technological base among others. Seen within this context, the conceptualisation of such conclusion or consideration includes:

- Africa needs well articulated and comprehensive structural adjustment with a human face;
- The best path for a country is intensified efforts in building a solid democratic culture with respect to adherence to all the basic tenets that entails;
- Tackling poverty, corruption and inequality demands more than handout measures. It requires empowerment of civil society, the poor and marginalised to access to the bases for accumulating social, economic and political power;
- Sustainable financial inputs constitute a major backbone in altering the course of African development;
- The development space or system change cannot be treated in isolation from other facets of economy, society and polity;
- Many of the essays in the book highlight necessary components for building strong policies, setting priorities and strategies, at all levels local, national, regional, continental and functional for improving the quality of life of the people: important among them are:
  - Increased prosperity without sacrificing sustainability;
  - Integration between the state, civil society and private sector to enhance the effectiveness of state activities;
  - Availability of appropriate resources, training and powers;
  - Substantial grassroots participation and control over decision-making throughout the system of governance;
  - Respect for the rule o law.
- There is cause for optimism amid the gloom and crisis;
- Africa should build an inclusive society, by "putting people first" in all developmental challenges and changes;
- The present and future extent of the government's commitment to national development will be primary determinant of how the process of building an inclusive people-oriented society evolves on the principles of democratic governance. We need continued economic buoyancy and political stability and total participation by the society and other key stakeholders;
- Broad and direct involvement of citizens in public affairs, in the decision-making and problem solving processes on various development related activities, through capacity building, establishing and developing cooperation across the board should be embarked upon;
- Building on the degree of growing awareness among African countries of the continent's future intransigently linked to the adoption, nurturing of democratic, participatory, ethically sound, inclusive and accountable governance system with an enabling and level playing field for all the stakeholders to be partners in the development process;
- The Chinese proverb of "a thousand mile journey starts with the first step' backed with visionary leadership and responsive civil society, should create the right basis for Africa to move from a third to a first world within a generation. It only needs the

committed political will and the stamina to rise and start working towards the envisaged goal.

- All societies need rules and regulations that foster responsibility and a willingness to compromise among various interest groups.

- Growing expenditure in the weapons of human destruction {military hardware} is unnecessary. Rather, expenditure on weapons on human destruction should be converted into expenditure on human development.

- Our Parliaments as representatives of the people must play an even greater role to ensure that the democratisation process, peace, stability, and prosperity reigns throughout the African continent.

- Unfortunately, African parliaments have traditionally not played a role of any significance in oversight of the private sector and have frequently been totally marginalised or excluded from decision-making in this areas, part of the reason being that they are under-resourced, or often bought over by private sector interests and party hegemonic instructions

- The need for a vibrant civil society and an imaginative and productive private sector is imperative for the economic transformation of the continent from a third to a first world.

- The dynamics of African politic system are complex, complicated, diverse and deeply inter-linked, but its diversity constitutes an asset that should be explored and harnessed for the good of the region;

- Promoting policies to encourage entrepreneurs and small and medium enterprises among women and the disadvantaged groups constitute a sure way of alleviating poverty and improving the life of the people;

- Encouraging the media to report more positively and objectively and accurately on development related issues;

- There is need to espouse the positive linkage between male and female gender, localised environmental issues and the broader national developmental issues and how to harness the potential of the salient features of the female gender in the development process;

- Therefore, redefining gender roles, redrawing the rules that underpin poverty, and property rights, and propelling women into leadership positions across society, remains an issue of vital importance for Africa to transcend the boundaries of underdevelopment and exploitation and catapulting it from an underdeveloped economic to knowledge-based economy;

- Africa is at war with undemocratic governance system, poverty and corruption and the right weapons in combating these dangerous wars must be put at the services of the forces fighting the war against destruction and the war for development, human empowerment;

- The development crises of identity, penetration, distribution, legitimacy, participation prescribed in the long struggle between ideas of development and instrumental rationality, supporting political and, the cultural critique based on demands for democratic containment and control economic power, posses profound challenges and changes in state-building which must be seriously looked into. These changes and challenges in addressing the sequences of these crises is part of the evolving factors inscribed in the transformation process;

- The broad focus of encouraging and deepening political pluralism and democratic governance must be a long-term agenda while not by passing both short and medium strategic process and priorities that should adequately contribute to creating greater awareness of the benefits of a sustained democratic governance system to the people and society;

- Change we must, but how, when, for what and by whom? These are crucial questions the continent must address. A holistic and realistic approach to existing problems is necessary.

Two outstanding phrases by two of Africa's most illustrious sons, {Mandela and Nkrumah; "It is a long walk to freedom" [Nelson Mandela]: But "Africa is marching forward to freedom and no power on earth can halt her" {Nkrumah 1959], respectively paint a picture of hope, courage and determination for the continent to achieve political and economic independence and to advance on the pathway of total continental unity being sabotaged by neo-colonialist manoeuvres must be resisted with all the strength the continent can muster. This is an obligation owed to future generations by present generations. It is only through building and consolidating a continental nation state, that is young, strong and resilient, backed by the combined strength of the people's will to overcome all obstacles and ingrained in the spirit to *"win"* that a great and brave continent and people can be constructed. Without such virtues ingrained in the people, the region will forever remain weak and exploited.

What is important is to articulate strategic policy measures and concerted action plans geared towards fixing failed states. Africa needs to change direction by fixing existing failed states. Fixing failed states means {i} good leadership that is visionary; people-oriented and above all focused on serving the people and not the other way round: {ii} it means getting the electoral system right and respecting the wishes of the people at the ballot box and is representative, competitive, fair and free embedded with the ideal of one person one vote; giving the people their inherent right to make their choices and respecting choices made by the electorate; {iii} ensuring an inherent respect for the separation of powers between the three arms of government – executive, legislative and judiciary; {iv} a free media industry that operates objectively, judiciously, scholarly and scientifically with the cardinal virtues of informing and educating society.

Africa needs serious constructive change with a focus of deconstructing and dismantling existing weakness and threats that destroys the social fabric of society; dismantling existing dichotomies of ethnic divide and of the hierarchies of rich, ethnic hegemonic, centralised authoritarian governance system that makes people cling to power for ever. Constructive change is needed to claim power from the few powerful in society and passing power to where it belongs – the people. For power to belong effectively to the people requires respect of the verdict of the ballot box which is not contaminated. On that generates legitimacy; embedded with the inherent capacity of choosing representatives; providing political choice; and respecting voter's rights.

Current African leadership have accelerated failed states on the continent; just greed is the accelerator of capitalist economy. But greed must be replaced with sharing. Africa needs *"shared-government, shared-responsibilities, shared-opportunities and shared-prosperity"*. These are some of the virtues for fixing failed states. Virtues which must be tied with consolidating the democratic process, ensuing accountability, transparency, rule of law and social justice. The task at hand is to develop novel strategies informed by the realities of our national constrict and conditioned by the globalised world. Most importantly, national and international institutions should articulate and foster mutually reinforcing bonds between states, civil society, private sector and markets, which remains the key to stability and progress in the era of globalisation and national development

A United Africa remains the only hope to forge and sustain the freedom, liberty, peace and quality livelihood for the vast majority of the population. Only by being free and proactive that Africa would be respected. The idea of building and nurturing the spirit of *"optimism"* is essential for African countries and requires constructive change in existing mindset, attitude and behaviour. Constructive change constitutes the basis for "optimism" and the will to overcome existing difficulties and deficiencies in the governance system. For now the continent is suffering from *"leadership"* crisis. The ideals of *"servant leaders"* social justice and social equity

Leadership demands honesty and services to the people. Honesty, fairness and transparency should be the rule, not the exception in political life and services to the people and nation. A government that cannot keep its promises is a government that will not have the moral authority to govern. If African leaders want voters, trust, they must show that they trust themselves by pledging to resign if they break any promise, and by pledging to pass law making that empower voters to challenge dishonesty by politicians and government officials. It is, in fact, impossible for voters to choose from amongst the parties as long as it is legal for party leaders to lie. No matter how much time a voter spent comparing the parties, elections platforms, a voter cannot make a choice when they know that some of the platform pledges are false. That is why dishonesty in politics is a fundamental voter rights issue and the top government accountability issue.

Another promises and false claims make our politics dirty just like pollution makes our air dirty, so just like we need laws and taxes to clean up our air, we need an honesty in politics law and politicians *Hot Air Tax* to clean up the continent's politics. The cynicism and habit of politicians and government officials misleading the public will only be stopped when their dishonesty can be easily challenged and punished, similar to how the public can challenge dishonest corporate executive. The Continent needs laws to penalise leaders, politicians and officials for broken promises and false claims.

[http://www.dwatcef.ca/camp/RelsSep1708.html]

Fixing failed States requires that a governance system that creates equal opportunities, liberties, freedoms and progress for all, through returning power to the people, ensuring proper human capacity development, human and natural resources development; institutional capacity building; deconcerntration or decentralisation of decision-making powers; putting in place and reform of institutions as well as build strong, independent and functional state institution; restoring state authority; raising the awareness of the population on the fight against corruption; intensify regional and international cooperation.

The enthusiasm for reconstructing or rebuilding failed states requires shared-responsibilities, constructive engagement and participation by all strata of society. Reconstruction necessitates linkages, building bridges across existing divide in society. It requires adopting constructive engagement policies and action-oriented approach for the survival and progress of the state and the advancement of the well-being of the people. Therefore, great sacrifices from all section of society must be made towards the cost of development, liberty, freedom and national sovereignty. The best chances of preventing failed states is to create and open functional and democratic governance inclusive system; for the people to be even more resolved and resolute in taking their destiny into their hands. The future has to be constructed and nurtured today. That is the challenge for this generation. A challenge which must be faced realistically, honestly and truthfully. Both risks and responsibility must be taken by all.

It is only from the perspectives of truth and reality that the road to reconstruction and reconciliation with our past in building a better present and a stronger future can take the right form. The implementation of effective democratic governance and management processes poses enormous sacrifices as well as economic challenges to all African states. Very few states are able to launch a process on the scale of reconstruction. Without the reconstruction train and the efforts of the people, progress cannot be made. Recent events on the continent shows that the people are willing to take the bull by the horn – peaceful settlements of crisis like the Bakassi Peninsular conflict between Cameroon and Nigeria; the 2007 Post-elections crisis in Kenya and the 2008 Post-elections debacle in Zimbabwe are indicative that with a little bit of *"will"* Africa can make it to the top of the world in all aspects of development. Africa needs the following actions: {i} solidarity and unity is needed to move forward; {ii} Deepen reflections and love for country/continent: {iii} create linkages and build bridges across existing divide; {iv} choose dialogue, reconciliation, consensus and expand scope of interaction; {v} consolidate the organisations of these interactions; and {vi} be open to new ideas that advance the process of building a strong, united and developed continent.

As can be seen, democracy, good governance is the evaluative threads running this publication. It questions the degree to which government institutions and public officials advance or retard the practice of democracy throughout the continent. We question whether popular sovereignty, political equality, and liberty are enhanced or diminished by the way centralised authoritarian all powerful executive, a captive legislative and judiciary, and state and local government operate. The overall conclusion is that democratic principles have gradually improved over the years and in some countries at the governmental level, but that significant barriers to he full realistic of democracy still exist. This not surprising given that the typical African state is an authoritarian and centralised state bereft of the rule of law. It was of a far-reaching scope besides. African society remains heavily dominated by the state. An institutional context of this sort hardly yields a favourable soil for the growth of the civic capacities required for a vital democracy [Hadenius 2001:105].

Because of its historical past African politics exhibits a remarkably high potential for conflict. One factor often adduced in explanation thereof is the heavy dependence on the state: the occupancy of state office has furnished the golden road to social and economic advancement, for which few prospects otherwise exist. In reality, the functioning of the state machinery has been little affected by the winds of change until of recent. All along, efforts have focused heavily on the spoils to be gained from the occupancy of state office. In Cameroon for example, the issue or phenomenon of *"appointments"* has destroyed all forms of good governance and quality management, effective and efficient delivery services. The output functions of government remains dismal. Hence fundamental difficulties pivot in the irregularity characterising the African political landscape. These developments highlight the need for rethinking government and reorganising the state to incorporate the functional aspects of *partnership, participation and benefit-sharing* among the different stakeholders.

For now, a lack of rule-governed practices in the administrative and political realm, which opens the floodgates for excessive patronage and embezzlement, in combination with a far-reaching centralisation of powers, which strongly restricts access to the fruits of power, tend generally to lay the ground for a strongly confrontational political culture. To a greater extent, these conditions explain the mentality of implacability and the consequent difficulty of introducing strategies of reciprocity, which signifies African politics [Hadenius op cit. p.109].

The absence of sustainable interface between the state, the people and the private sector constitutes a serious dilemma towards consolidating the democratic process on the continent. The governance sector is infested with corruption and other forms of public kleptomania furnishing poor incentives for economic progress with the process getting worse as this often orchestrated from the highest level of the political echelon. Such activities acquire wholly new proportions and dimensions virtually impossible to stop. As the say in my native languages goes, once the water is dirty from its source, so it has to be done stream. The situation is even compounded with the state leadership made free of constitutional restrictions and accountability which makes it possible to escape efforts to inspect and control its doings, contains few barriers to political and administrative degenerations. The results could be very costly for society. The prevailing situation in Cameroon tells it all. The billons of state funds Francs CFA stuck in the private accounts of certain officials deprive civil society of shared-prosperity and quality service delivery.

Political power has always implied access to unrestricted privileges. Unrestricted power opens the floodgates to unrestricted appropriation of privileges. Most African states are imbued with a state bureaucracy that leaves the executive with no countervailing powers which makes such leadership becoming a parasitic power in society. That many African countries are bankrupt is not surprising. This mode of governance yields excellent opportunities for advancing articulate self-interest of the governing elite. The governing elites have often responded with short-term quasi-reform of redistributive measures under the slogan of creating a so-called developmental state. Very often, one-party states have tended to undertake such efforts, as have certain 'populist' military and dictatorial regimes. Even with the demise of the monolithic party system, it has resurrected through flawed elections which leaves the legislative assembly in a country like Cameroon with a one-party controlled assembly under the slogan of *"crushing majority"*. That Cameroon is undergoing a state of increasing fiscal and administrative disorder is not surprising. No one seems to be in control. The issue of succession is more confused paving the way for serious conflict situation awaiting the country whenever the country would be bracing for the *"Third Republic"*.

Hadenius [2001:263] is clear on these kinds of development which I cannot resist quoting at length: "A difficulty arises here, however, in that the growth of the apparatus, and the fragmentation following therefrom, makes the system much harder to control. In the same way, it becomes progressively less feasible to maintain a firm grasp on the system of privileges. These conditions, together with the fact that the space for rent-seeking expands naturally in step with the growth of the state, have in many cases led to an increasing fiscal and administrative disorder. The great and resolute developmental Leviathan state turns into a crumbling hulk torn apart by a multitude of particularistic interests, and it becomes progressively less able to implement any coherent policies. Many 'technocratic' military dictatorships in Latin America have met such a fate, as have a range of 'mobilising' one-party states in Africa and elsewhere. The result is a spread of predatory practices, which at times can be halted in part through a despotic and tyrannical government. The basic problem is that the Leviathan model, embodying as it does the principle of top-down rule, possesses but a limited governance capacity. When it attempts to exceed its potential, it falls prey to self-destruction, with administrative incapacity, poor macroeconomic performance, and diminishing legitimacy the result".

Apparently, the strength of an interactive state lies in a developed governance capacity founded on cooperation and consent. But that consent comes from the people who remain the legitimate source of power for constructive socioeconomic, scientific, technological and political transformation. A constructive engagement between the stakeholders constitutes the interactive state is democratically founded. Africa needs democratically founded states, for here rests its strength for the transition from a *'third to a first world'*. The degree to which the state possesses its capacity depends on its ability to control certain strategic instruments of coordination, and exploit them. The Cameroon government has been most successful in this respect as it continues to hold at bay the opposition parties and civil society and getting its 'voice' heard in all parts of the realm.

The apparatus for such control of the governance system is through regulation, a sizable apparatus of repression and control including inducement with appointments and handouts. Of course, access to economic resources and the weapons of mass destruction circumscribes the actions of the state. The revenue of the state is the state, Edmund Burke remarked which the Cameroon is taking full advantage. The political system in Cameroon promotes political obedience and domination and this does not contribute to the consolidation of democratic governance. So far, the Cameroon governance system is not suitable and efficient in ensuring administrative reform, but perpetuating inefficiency, inertia, corruption and widening the divide between the rich and poor, the urban and rural areas and intensifying conflicts between various ethnic settings in society.

For the system of governance is to be well-suited to its task, the agents of the state should not just be induced to do things in he right way – which is the administrative perspective as well as impelled to do the right things, that is the those things the state leaders want them to do – which is of being a *"servant leader"* in the political chase game within the African context. There is breakdown between state, civil society and the private sector which has to be restored for progressive developments taking place in the overall benefit of the people. The armies of poverty stricken people must be brought into the mainstream of the development process. No doubt the improvement in the situation of the poor would weaken the standing of the few rich which is against the wishes of those controlling the realm of governance.

Africa's challenges, therefore, is to continue the democratisation, good governance and economic recovery programmes; promote greater and equitable growth, based on a strategic policy on poverty alleviation and empowerment. Power to the people with equal opportunities for all – *shared-government; shared-responsibility; shared-prosperity* – should be the catch word for *rethinking government and reorganising the state.*

References

Achebe Chinua [1966] A Man of the People. Heinemann Books, London, Ibadan and Nairobi
Addi, L. [1997] "The Failure of Third World Nationalism", *Journal of Democracy,* 8 (4).
Adei Stephen [2004] *The Promise of Leadership.* Combert Impressions, Accra, Ghana.

Aseka Masinde Eric [2006] "Globalisation, Leadership and Governance in Africa. A Theoretical Approach", *Paper presented at the Leadership Room,* Student Centre, Institute for Global Initiatives, Kennesaw State University, Georgia, USA, 18 October 2006.

Balch Jeff [2006] "Parliaments And Leadership in Africa: Breaking New Ground", in *Conflict Trends,* Issue 4: 2006, South Africa, pp 21-25.

Biya Paul [1987] *Communal Liberalism.* Macmillan Publishers, London.

Busakwe, D. "Building Integrity in Public Sector Organisations: The Case of the NPA", in Service Review: *A Learning Journal for Public Service Managers,* Vol. 5 No. 1. 2006, Department of Public Service and Administration, Government of South Africa, Pretoria, pp17-19.

Carothers Thomas [2002] "The End of Transition Paradigm" in *Journal of Democracy,* 13, January 2002: 5-21.

Chilton Stephen [1991] *Grounding Political Development.* Boulder, Colorado. Lynne Rienner Publishers Inc. USA.

Ekanola, B. Adebola [2005] *"Beyond Isolation: Towards Cooperative Relations and Resolution of Ethnic Conflicts in a Contemporary African Society"*, Africa Insight, Vol. 35. No. 3 September 2005, Africa Institute of South Africa, Pretoria, pp49-54.

Forje, W. John [2007] *Here The People Rule. Forthcoming,* Nova Publishers, USA.

Hadenius Axel [2001] *Institutions And Democratic Citizenship.* Oxford University Press.

Kouzes, J. M., B. Z. Posner and Tom Peters [1995] Credibility: *How Leaders Gain and Lose IT: Why People Demand It.* Simon & Schuster Books, New York.

Kuye O. Jerry [2006] "The NEPAD-AU-Equation: A Dialogue on Leadership And Governance Imperatives For Africa' in *African Journal of Public Administration and Management,* Vol. XV11, No. 2, July 2006, pp67-78.

Mandela Nelson [] *A Long Walk To Freedom.*

Mill, J. S. [1996] "On Nationality", in Woolf, S. (ed.) N*ationalism in Europe 1815 to The Present.* Routledge, London.

Miller, D. [1995] *On Nationality.* Clarendon Press, Oxford.

Munroe, Myles [1998] *Becoming A Leader: Everyone Can Do It.* Pneuma Publishing, Bakersfield.

Ngwana S. Albert [2001] *The Struggle for Political Pluralism and Democracy in Cameroon.* African Development Corporation Ltd, Douala, Cameroon and Jameson Broadman Pres, Lagos, Nigeria.

Nkrumah, Kwame [1959] *Speech in the National Assembly,* 16 December 1959, Accra – Ghana.

One Country [2006] "in One Country, Vol. 18. Issue 3. October-December 2007 The Eradication of Violence Against Women and Girls", and also the following document" *"Beyond Legal Reforms: Culture and Capacity in the Education of Violence Against Women and Girls",* http//statements.bhai/o6-0702.htm]

Olukoshi, Adebayo and Laakso [1996] "The Crisis in the Postcolonial State Project in Africa", in Olukoshi, A. and Laakso (eds.), *Challenges to the Nation State in Africa.* Nordiska Afrikaansinsitut, Uppsala, Sweden.

Rugumyamheto, Joseph [2006] To Serve and To Preserve Motto for the Effective Permanent Secretary in a Changing World of Public Service. *AAPAM Testimonial Lecture,* Delivered at the 28th AAPAM Annual Roundtable Conference, Arusha, Tanzania.

Runciman David [2003]"The Concept of the State: The Sovereignty o a Fiction." In Skinner Quentin & Strath Bo {eds.} 2003. *State and Citizens.* History, Theory And Prospects. Cambridge University Press, Cambridge, pp28-48.

Sambo I. Bala [2005] "Issues, Problems and Prospects of Government Reforms on MDIs In Nigeria", in A*frican Journal of Public Administration and Management,* Vol. XV1. No. 1, January 2005, pp53-59.

Schiaro-Campo, S and P. S. A. Sundaram. [2001] *To Serve And To Preserve: Improving Public Administration in a Competitive World.* Asian Development Bank.

Spencer Philip and Wollman Howard [2003] *Nationalism: A Critical Introduction.* Sage Publications.

South Commission [1990] The Challenge to South. *The Report of the South Commission.* Geneva.

Sunstein R. Cass [2001] *Designing Democracy. What Constitutions Do.?* Oxford University Press.

Todorov Tzvertan [1993] *On Human Diversity: Nationalism, Racism, and exoticism in French Thought.* Cambridge University Press, Cambridge MA.

UNDP [2006] *Guidelines for the International Community on Parliaments, Crisis Prevention and Recovery.* See http://www.parlcpr.undep.org/brusselconf.htm

Whitehead, L. [1986] "International Aspect of Democratisation", in G. O'Donnell, P. Schmitter and L. Whitehead {eds.}, *Transition From Authoritarian Rule,* John Hopkins University Press, Baltimore. Pt. 3, pp 3-46.

Whitehead, L. [1988] The Consolidation Of Fragile Democracies. *European Consortium for Political Research {ECPR} paper.*

INDEX

B

F

J

S

T